# APOLLO'S
# FIRE

# APOLLO'S FIRE

## IGNITING AMERICA'S

# CLEAN-ENERGY

## ECONOMY

**Jay Inslee**
**Bracken Hendricks**

Foreword by President Bill Clinton

ISLAND PRESS · Washington | Covelo | London

*Library of Congress Cataloging-in-Publication Data*

Inslee, Jay.
  Apollo's fire : igniting America's clean-energy economy / Jay Inslee,
Bracken Hendricks.
    p. cm.
  Includes bibliographical references and index.
  ISBN-13: 978-1-59726-175-3 (hardcover : alk. paper)
  1. Energy policy—United States. 2. Renewable energy sources—
United States. 3. Global warming. I. Hendricks, Bracken. II. Title.
  HD9502.U521536 2007
  333.790973—dc22

                                                              2007026185

The paperback edition carries the ISBN 978-1-59726-649-9 and the
ISBN 1-59726-649-3.

*British Cataloguing-in-Publication Data available*

Printed on recycled, acid-free paper ✿

Manufactured in the United States of America

09  08  07  06  05  04  03    10  9  8  7  6  5  4  3  2  1

*This book is dedicated to my mom and dad*
*—Jay Inslee*

*And*

*to my wife, Alice, and my children, Galen and Clea Rose*
*—Bracken Hendricks*

# CONTENTS

vii

# FOREWORD

As I sat down and read the preamble to Congressman Jay Inslee and Bracken Hendricks's new book, *Apollo's Fire: Igniting America's Clean-Energy Economy*, I immediately noticed something. The energy in their words is tangible as they recount President John F. Kennedy's 1961 announcement of his plan, by decade's end, to land an American man on the moon.

Just a sentence or two brought me right back to that day, when I was fifteen. Like the rest of America, I was mesmerized by President Kennedy's ambition and entranced by the novelty and urgency of the Space Race. Our potential was so great that it was nearly impossible to digest, and though times were uncertain, the threat of the Cold War was tempered by the promise and, yes, the energy of the American pioneer spirit, surging ever forward into uncharted territory, always innovating along the way. Our pragmatism and our optimism, our diligence and our sense of duty are the ideals that serve as the nation's cornerstone, beginning with the Puritan "errand into the wilderness" and enduring today, into the new millennium, as we face new and insistent challenges.

If there is just one thing we can glean from days gone by, it is that history is full of themes that repeat themselves, often in the most ironic of ways. Energy—in a variety of ways, ranging from its detrimental effects on the environment to the quest for clean alternative forms, and finally, to its role as the driving force behind innovation—is one of America's recurring themes, and also one of the most pressing.

If the great conflict of the later twentieth century was the Cold War, that of the early twenty-first is, ironically, the battle against warmth—specifically, global warming, its causes and its effects on the planet. In their book, Congressman Inslee and Bracken Hendricks eloquently assess climate change writ large, and the many underlying issues associated with it, as the greatest threat to our nation and our world's security and sustainability. Perhaps most interesting of all, both the root cause of and the solution to the problem boil down to one word: energy.

The studies, the headlines, the television reports, and the films are disturbing. Conventional energy sources, when burned, produce greenhouse gas emissions, thus raising temperatures, melting icecaps, creating severe weather patterns, and otherwise threatening to upset the delicate balance of the planet's equilibrium. Our patterns of consumption and disposable culture of convenience make the problem worse. We're increasingly dependent on foreign oil, which is not only a finite resource, but also one that is concentrated in a region embroiled in conflict and bloodshed. We've developed the technologies for alternative clean-energy sources and production and energy efficiency, but lag in output. Meanwhile, we have an economy with an ever declining manufacturing sector and a growing trade deficit. At face value, the future looks bleak, and to many, even apocalyptic.

Yet, while Inslee and Hendricks discuss the grim reality of what can—and will—happen to our planet if we choose to ignore the problem of climate change, *Apollo's Fire* is anything but a doomsday account. Rather, it is hopeful and exciting, engaging the reader as it recounts America's history of leadership and ingenuity. Though the climate crisis is daunting, it affords Americans yet another tremendous opportunity to show the rest of the world what we are made of. If we act now, it's not too late.

To anyone who says that Congress does not have a plan for combating climate change, Representative Jay Inslee has not only an answer, but a field guide for our future—and a comprehensive one at that.

Inslee and Hendricks identify the stakes, the goals, and the rewards of a clean-energy revolution. They name the diverse players, the cutting-edge technologies, and the stunning implications for America's economic growth, both domestically and in emerging markets abroad. Implementing new energy technologies will create a huge number of good jobs in America—in venture capital, in research and development, and in manufacturing and other skilled labor—as well as a means to reduce our international trade deficit. The only way we can raise incomes and living standards is to create good jobs for the economy of the future. We can't afford not to, and the beauty of it all is that we have unlimited resources in clean energy and improved efficiency ready for harvest.

Inslee and Hendricks's vision is true to America's competitive spirit, but it is capitalism with conscience. It is innovation for the improvement of humanity. It is science as stewardship. This is our errand into the wilderness, and it is our obligation to our children and to the global community. *Apollo's Fire* calls us to our destiny. As it was our destiny to land the first man on the moon, it is our destiny now to lead the world toward clean energy and to supply it with the new technologies to achieve that goal. We have a unique opportunity to unite America, urban and rural, coastal and midwestern, red and blue, under the banner of a truly unifying national effort. We can start right now.

*President Bill Clinton*

# Introduction to the Paperback Edition

Since this book was first written the world has changed. It has a tendency to do that, and most often in ways none of us can predict. But while we have been rocked by a financial crisis, we have also witnessed the beginnings of the clean-energy economy outlined in these pages. It is pleasing, of course, when one's predictions turn out to be accurate.

What we first reported as just the seeds of a new industrial base are now starting to spread leaves. This emerging industry is relatively small, of course, but it is infused with excitement and unlimited potential. So it is with concentrated solar power. When we first wrote about the Ausra energy company, it had about eight employees. Now it has opened the first concentrated-solar reflective panel manufacturing plant in Nevada, and orders are out for at least six new megawatt-scale plants across the nation. The same can be said of the algae-based biofuels industry. When we first referenced it, the idea of turning unicellular algae into the stuff that drives our cars seemed a bit odd. But now the Sapphire Energy company has started to develop the first multiple-acre ponds of saltwater in the deserts of the Southwest, within which they intend to brew up sweet gasoline, with no net $CO_2$ emissions.

What we described as merely enticing ideas became business plans, then became investments, and now are becoming products—just in time. We were optimistic; we were ambitious; you might even say we were dreamers. But we were also right. When we Americans put our minds to something, we can achieve things that no one thought possible.

But we were not right about everything. We were wrong about the pace of global warming. The speed and scope of this threat have turned out to be even worse than we portrayed and the scientific community imagined just a year ago. We used to be deeply concerned. Now the threat has become more urgent. To neglect this crisis would be both irresponsible and scientifically illiterate. Every month we have been slapped in the face with new evidence showing the quickened pace of fundamental changes. These shocks have come from every corner—from air, sea, and land—and they add up to the conclusion that we have less time to act than we thought just months ago.

Ocean acidification is a prime example. As we were writing our book, this problem was just starting to surface in the public consciousness. We knew that the oceans had become 30 percent more acidic because of the emissions streaming from our homes, our factories, and our cars' tailpipes. But this was seen as a long-term risk, not an immediate threat to biological systems.

Then in October 2008, a new white-hulled NOAA research ship docked in Seattle with a bombshell of information aboard. The ship had just returned from examining the acidity levels of relatively shallow waters off the Washington state coastline. What the scientists on board discovered stunned them. Their models had predicted that the increasing acidity of the oceans at these shallow depths would not reach dangerous levels for over a century, but their one voyage showed the awful truth—even in shallow water the Pacific Ocean had become so acidic that it could start to interfere with life forms in just a few decades.

Within the century, these waters could be so acidic that they would literally dissolve a clam shell. What is worse, about 40 percent of the plankton that forms the base of the oceanic food chain depends upon a calcium carbonate body structure to exist. If those structures can no longer be formed, this fundamental building block of the ocean's biosphere could be toppled.

We thought we had more time to really launch Apollo. We don't.

December brought further trouble. NASA released two incredibly sophisticated research project results evaluating the ice caps in Greenland. They found not only that the Greenland ice sheet is melting, but also that it is melting three times faster than it was just five years ago. According to the study, Greenland now loses 48 cubic miles of ice each year. Jay Zwally, glaciologist with the NASA Goddard Space Flight Center, commented, "I would say Greenland now is beginning to contribute significantly to sea level rise. There's been a significant change in a relatively short period of time."[1]

When it comes to global warming, there has been only one kind of news over the last year: bad news. Perhaps the worst is the conclusion reached by researcher Mark Serreze and his colleagues at the National Snow and Ice Data Center. Based on extensive study of the arctic ice sheet, they have determined that the Arctic has reached a tipping point—that is, a point at which we face a dramatic and irreversible slide to the ultimate disappearance of summer ice in the Arctic. This means much more than just the loss of a livable habitat for polar bears. It means the earth will be absorbing huge amounts of energy that were previously reflected into space by that ice, energy that is now absorbed by the Arctic Sea. This has ramifications for the world as a whole, because, as Serreze says, "The Arctic is the heat sink of the Northern Hemisphere: The circulation patterns of the oceans could change dramatically."

This additional absorption of heat has long been recognized as a problem—what might be called the "arctic acceleration" of global warming. But the new evidence shows that damage to the ice cap that was expected to occur twenty years from now has already happened. "The models are giving us the big picture of what is going on, but it's all happening much faster than expected," says Serreze.[2]

But amid this northern gloom, dark as the polar winter night, there is one glimmer of hope. It comes from Cecilia Bitz, a University of Washington researcher we'll meet in the book. She doesn't believe we have crossed the tipping point yet, at least not the point at which we have no chance of arresting and then reversing the decline in the Arctic ice cap. She believes that if we can hold global $CO_2$ levels at 2000 numbers, there is a chance that the decline can be slowed and then stopped. In short, if we can succeed in creating a new clean-energy economy, we have a chance of saving the Arctic ice cap upon which so much depends.[3]

Notice that Dr. Bitz does not guarantee success. She does not guarantee that if we invest in a clean-energy economy, the Arctic can be saved. But she has given us as much as we can ask for after so many years of neglect: a fighting chance. Given the stakes involved, it is a chance we can, should, and must take.

Will we win this battle for the Arctic? We must, for in the words of Winston Churchill when asked about the great struggle of his generation, "What is our aim? I can answer with one word: Victory—victory at all costs, victory in spite of all terror, victory however long and hard the road may be; for without victory there is no survival."[4]

---

Box I-1. A Revelation at Keyport

*Jay Inslee*

On a snowy day in December 2008, I stared at a wall-size war games monitor and tried to stifle a wave of frustration. The multi-million-dollar real-time display of torpedoes attacking one another at the naval base at Keyport, Washington, looked like a combination of the Big Board in *Dr. Strangelove* and the world's most advanced video game. It evoked both awe and dismay. But I choked both down. A congressman being briefed on the navy's new anti-torpedo system must suppress any emotion, by navy custom and by congressional tradition.

My irritation wasn't aimed at my constituents at the base. I had spent the morning admiring their brilliant work: how they'd deployed the only laser-guided casting tool in use in the navy, how they'd developed the world's most advanced refurbishing system for helicopter blades, and how they'd built an ingenuous gyrocompass that guides our F-18 fighters without the use of a moving part. There was ample reason to take pride in their achievements—both in advancing technology and in saving the taxpayer money.

But where were their counterparts who were using laser technology to hone wind turbine blades? Where were their colleagues who were using this whizbang metal-casting machine to fashion advanced pumps for geothermal systems? Where were the federal engineers who could use the electronics that guided the F-18 to guide the smart grid we need to manage the renewable energy sources of the future?

We had spent over $82 billion to fight a war over oil and only $3 billion to develop new energy sources so that we would not have to fight such wars. Billions went to the Pentagon, while energy R&D got chump change. For five years, I'd been pushing for legislation supporting clean energy. But while I had been tearing my hair out and redoubling my speechifying, my bills rotted in obscurity and the glaciers continued to melt.

I wanted to stand up and yell, "I'm fed up, and I won't take it anymore!" But that would have been seriously out of order, so I did the next best thing. When we returned to the captain's conference room, I asked the base's management team if the skills needed to maintain torpedo pumps were transferable to designing pumps for geothermal systems. Somewhat to my surprise, several of the managers lit up at the idea. One mentioned that just that work was his passion before he became involved in navy work.

Then, to my satisfaction, our talk turned to using the Pentagon budget to foster that and similar work. They understood the enormous power of the military-industrial complex, something that Eisenhower had warned us about, but which is, in fact, the most innovative industrial machine ever. Could it be used to build what the times now demand: a clean energy-industrial complex? My constituents around the table had plenty of ideas about how to use the DOD budget to advance that end.

Those Pentagon engineers got it. The thought struck me that we need a response even more like the military one in World War II than the scientific one in the Apollo Project. In response to the WWII threat, we went from making 3,000 airplanes in 1939 to making 35,000 in 1944. Why can't we do the same for energy? The need is that great, the revolutionary changes that systemic.

It's not just the globe's climate that is changing. Our country is changing, too.

Many months ago, when this book was first published, we took the opportunity to travel around the country to large groups and small, evangelizing on the need to shift priorities and to watch closely the warning signs and science data that come in daily. We have returned often to this evidence of melting sea ice as a sign of gathering threats to a warming planet. But we have found that it is hard to organize a people around a threat to ice. It's hard to mobilize a nation for a hazard that seems remote in time and space. And, in the midst of economic crisis, it is discordant to fight for the fate of polar bears. It's not the thing to bring up to someone facing foreclosure or another round of pink slips at the plant.

In our travels, we often returned to the story of Shishmaref, Alaska, which you will find in Chapter 1. It was only as we completed this volume and the final text was going to print, that we called back Luci Eningowuk in Shishmaref to ask her for a photo of her neighbor's home falling into the ocean. When she e-mailed us the image published here, it became clear in a very personal way: Global warming has a human face. This is not just about the loss of distant species or biodiversity, it is not only a matter of the fate of glaciers or the productivity of the soil. It is all of that, but the gathering threat of global warming is also about something far more intimate and profound. This is a crisis that will affect people in their homes. It is about families and friends and neighbors. And it is rooted deeply in community.

As we again and again told the stories of building a clean-energy economy, in union halls and bookstore cafes, in board rooms and church sanctuaries all around the country, it became increasingly clear to us how stark a choice we face. The path of inaction leads inevitably to climate crisis; the case for building something new only becomes more compelling. As this book makes clear, there is a tremendous opportunity at hand to build a better way forward—an opportunity that is also grounded in community.

To rebuild our economy on the foundation of clean energy will require skilled work; new businesses and business models; better transportation choices; more efficient homes; and investment in schools, offices, and factories. All this must happen at a speed, a scope, and a scale that we have not seen in generations. But just as we underestimated the dangers of the science, the greater danger is that we will fail to comprehend the vast potential of this opportunity.

When we began writing this book, we had little idea of the economic depths to which we were headed, with a brutal recession driving home foreclosures and job losses to levels not seen since the Great Depression. Indeed, with the collapse of global financial markets, nearly four and a half million people have lost their jobs—one million construction workers in the last year alone—and $2 trillion in family retirement savings have quietly vanished. Auto companies now require emergency bailouts, and banks have stopped lending, while regulators sort out how to save them—all of this driven by rampant speculation and spectacular regulatory failures over a generation, as we failed to invest in our deeper long-term priorities.

But underlying this moment is yet another opportunity. Just as global warming has forced the choice to build a green economy or face extinction, the financial crisis has forced the nation to decide to rebuild, to reinvest, and drive demand back to where it is needed most. America is ready to make this choice. This has been demonstrated in the most important choice of all for our nation: the selection of our new president.

*Apollo's Fire* is a book, first and foremost, about leadership. It is a call to action to forge a national sense of purpose and rally our citizens to the job at hand. We built this book around the visions of John F. Kennedy and Franklin Roosevelt and Thomas Jefferson for a reason. In a moment that has called for a politics of hope, this journey from climate crisis to a clean-energy revolution is poised to become an organizing principle for meeting a generational challenge. Just as we pulled together to face World War II and stare down fascism, we are again at a moment that calls on our best potential. And this brings us to today . . .

On a recent balmy Friday morning in Washington, D.C., Joe Biden boarded an Amtrak train headed for Philadelphia. For the vice president of the United States, security was relatively light. It was not an extraordinary trip for this former senator from Delaware to ride these rails. He had done that nearly every day of his tenure in Congress. But it was a remarkable day in the drive to build a green economy. Before the cabinet was even fully assembled, the freshly minted president of the United States, Barack Obama, had tapped his junior partner to head up a carefully chosen mission. He would lead a task force on restoring security to America's struggling middle class, and front and center in that effort would be a "green jobs" initiative.

That the White House chose green jobs as the framework for launching its middle-class task force is remarkable, and it shows the length of the journey we have traveled in just a few short years. We have moved from a fight with our leaders over *whether* to take action to save an imperiled planet, to the current moment when we are asked *how* we will respond to this threat. The tales in this book on grappling with the administration of President George W. Bush amply demonstrate just how hard the fight has been. But we have now moved swiftly from pleading for leadership to the jarring realization that when challenged by our leaders with a call to action, it is up to each of us to bring about the change we need.

Today, we have a president in the White House who is committed to a green economy as a source of renewal and opportunity. As a candidate, he ran on a pledge to create five million new *green-collar jobs*, a term that was scarcely in use when we first put pen to paper for this book. Van Jones, then an obscure community activist from Oakland whom we wrote about in these pages, is now a deputy in the White House Council on Environmental Quality, focusing on building green enterprises and green careers.

After Barack Obama arrived in the Senate in 2004, one of his first acts was to introduce the Health Care for Hybrids bill. He offered Detroit car manufacturers federal assistance with their legacy health care costs in exchange for their agreement to make high-mileage hybrid cars. The strategy was to join the nation's need for cleaner vehicles with Detroit's need for financial assistance. Two years later, the same automakers came back begging for a $25 billion bailout. It was only after facing bankruptcy that they would consider a change in business models.

When Obama barnstormed the industrial Midwest as a presidential candidate, he promised to make clean energy the bedrock of a restored manufacturing economy. When he spoke to neglected cities in the Northeast and on the Gulf Coast, he spoke of weatherizing homes for energy efficiency as one part of rebuilding urban America. And when he spoke to farmers in the nation's heartland and Native Americans on reservations, he talked about the hope (and paychecks) that clean renewable energy could bring to struggling rural communities.

As one of his first acts as president of the United States, Barack Obama introduced a proposal for economic recovery and reinvestment, the energy portion of which was the largest clean-energy package ever to move in the halls of Congress. It more than tripled the amount that would have been spent on our infrastructure for renewable energy, efficiency, and ending dependence on oil.

Now the country must get ready, and quickly, to embrace the bold, innovative spirit Obama represents. It took real boldness for a first-term black Senator to run for president. It will take real boldness to turn an economic crisis into a clean-energy opportunity.

We tend to cling to the status quo until the threat of imminent peril pushes us out of our comfort zones. People jump only when there is a perceived need to do so. This economic crisis provides a motivation to jump.

Obama decided to sail right into the economic gale by proposing a $150 billion clean-energy fund. He attacked unemployment by launching a green building program to put tens of thousands to work retrofitting our energy-sieve homes and buildings. He forcefully pushed a cap-and-trade proposal to defeat global warming as a centerpiece of his budget plan.

It is in our tradition to rise to challenges, particularly those that threaten to put us in a subordinate position to other nations. The moment that Americans learned of Russia's *Sputnik*, that little satellite ignited a national fever to best the communist challenge. Now we face a somewhat similar challenge to our competitiveness. As we move to electric cars, China is poised to dominate the newest strategic energy technology, the electric battery, which is likely to power our mobility for generations to come. The quintessentially American response would be to ignite a national effort to pour both human and capital resources into creating new American technologies and manufacturing plants to build those batteries and electric cars.

This is exactly what President Obama calls for us to do. It would help, of course, if the Chinese decided to name their first electric car model the "Sputnik," but even without this prod, all systems are go for the launch of this national effort. We should support the president's efforts not because of who he is, but because of who we are, a people who have historically seized any crisis by the throat and wrung every bit of opportunity out of it. From the Cold War we got the original Apollo Project, from World War II we got the most powerful economy on earth, and from this challenge we will get a whole new clean-energy economy.

We can achieve this partly because we were smart enough to elect a leader who understands the possibilities of crisis and has the moxie to realize those possibilities. And the Obama energy plan is basically right out of this book.

The details will change as new technologies are developed and fail, and fail again, before they finally succeed. But the principles will remain the same, and only by understanding those principles can we guide our economy into the new era. In this book we set out Ten Energy Enlightenments, which, while perhaps vaingloriously named, have served to organize the larger strategy of this endeavor. As you read this book, it is worth reflecting on those enlightenments and how they help us to think about the promise and pitfalls of the journey we are about to undertake. At the end, we challenge those enlightenments, to see how they have performed since this book was originally written.

It is to history that we all will ultimately have to answer if we fail. We are at a historically pivotal point unlike any that any of us has seen before, and the task has fallen to us to build a better way forward with the work of our own hands.

In the original Apollo Project, we saw what can happen when a young leader steps forward and inspires a nation to abandon old habits, to call on its best potential and launch a new technological adventure. And we have seen the power and ingenuity of the American people to innovate and give form to revolutionary ideas when challenged to come together in building a future worthy of our best traditions. We have done it before.

It is time to do it again.

# The First Apollo Project

> We choose to go to the moon in this decade and do the other things, not because they are easy, but because they are hard, because that goal will serve to organize and measure the best of our energies and skills. . . .
>
> —*President John F. Kennedy*

On the evening of May 25, 1961, a man walked into the United States House of Representatives bound to set his country on its longest journey ever. They swarmed about him like bees in a congressional hive as he made his way down the choked center aisle. They all wanted a piece of his glamour, his charm, and his youth. President John F. Kennedy had come to deliver a special address to Congress.

Presidents did not do this very often. An American commander in chief entering the chamber just after the sergeant at arms has announced, "Ladies and gentlemen, the President of the United States," always sends a thrill through the thousand people gathered for this uniquely American event, but this time it was an electric current several thousand watts more intense than usual. The congressmen and senators pushed toward him like teenyboppers at the Elvis concerts then sweeping the globe.

After years of national malaise, Kennedy had lit up the country with a charm and youthful spirit that brought Camelot to the shores of the Potomac. The country felt an optimism and sense of possibility it had not experienced since before World War II and the Great Depression. He embodied the nation's creative energy boiling just below the surface and waiting for a leader to bring it forth.

As the president wound his way toward the speaker's rostrum, he no doubt had put out of his mind his titanic failure just two months before, when he had given the go-ahead for the Bay of Pigs attack on Cuba, then watched as the attack collapsed. What he was about to do would permit no self-doubt.

As he handed copies of his address to Vice President Lyndon Johnson and Speaker of the House Sam Rayburn, he knew he had to give the country a sense of unwavering confidence in the possibilities of a grand journey. That requirement was made all the more urgent by the fact that the country had no idea what he was going to say. He knew it would be a bolt out of the blue.

Ten minutes into his speech, he gave the United States a mission of exploration unequaled since Thomas Jefferson sent the Corps of Discovery, led by Lewis and Clark, across the American continent: "I believe this nation should commit itself to achieving the goal, before the decade is out, of landing a man on the moon and returning him safely to earth."[1]

Thus, the Apollo Project began.

Those twenty-nine words changed America, the world of technology, and the moon. Only a few footprints were made on the moon, but they left a huge impression on America. Perhaps no other utterance in human history has resulted in such a stunning scientific advance in such a short period of time by such a large group of people. One can be impressed with other declarations, such as Archimedes's "Eureka!," but he was just one man in a bathtub. Kennedy rallied a whole nation to a singular cause whose completion could only be the product of the synchronized labors of literally millions of people.

At that moment Kennedy's boldness bordered on recklessness. As he stepped across the threshold of the race to the moon, America was in a distant second place to the Soviet Union. Yuri Gagarin had become the first man in space by making several full orbits in April 1961. America could respond only by rushing a small "spam in a can," a one-man shot for fifteen minutes, into the edges of the frontier. The Russian missiles were several times as powerful as NASA's. Kennedy knew the Soviets would soon achieve the feat of putting multiple men in one capsule orbiting the earth. America had not yet even invented Tang.

But Kennedy knew three fundamental things about the American people. First, he knew that Americans were the most prolific tinkerers, builders, and innovators the world had ever seen. The creators of the light bulb, the airplane, and the automobile shared a nationality. This was no accident. Americans are immigrants who have come from every corner of the earth, drawn by democracy and opportunity. We are bound together by a common culture of pragmatism and innovation, driven by determination and ingenuity, a commitment to results, and an innate optimism that we can achieve them, regardless of the odds. Kennedy knew that throwing a technical challenge to Americans is like throwing a dog a bone. Others may have been concerned that our rockets were weak, our life support systems unproven, and the missile engines needed to fire the second stages of the mission untested. But Kennedy knew that if he provided the first stage of the mission, the inspiration, the American people would supply the second stage, the technology.

Second, Kennedy knew that Americans are inherently competitive. George Patton was right: Americans love a winner. Now Kennedy was setting up the grandest race of all time, to the moon. The Russians served as the foil in this competition, pushing Americans to bend every ounce of creative technological force to the purpose of beating them. Kennedy knew that once such a national contest was begun, Americans would run like racehorses, chomping at the bit to get out of the gate.

Third, Kennedy knew that the American people would rally around the cause of national security, as just decades before they had rallied in response to World War II. With Russian satellites flying overhead, and now manned missions circling the globe, America was at risk of Russia dominating space. He did not want the emptiness of space to be filled with Russian weaponry. He knew that a race to the moon would immediately become a proxy for a race for military supremacy in space. Here, in the Sputnik moment, fear was the driver, not hope.

Those three stallions of motivation were put into harness and allowed Kennedy to rouse the nation's interest and innovation. Talk to an aircraft engineer who came of age in the early 1960s, and you will find that he was motivated to go into aeronautics by the blaze of excitement surrounding the moon project. Ask a congressman why he voted to give Kennedy virtually every dollar he requested for the space program, and he will tell you it was self-preservation. America adopted the *Mercury 7* astronauts and insisted on seeing them fly.

The pace of invention Kennedy inspired was breathtaking. In 1961 engineers had rudimentary, back-of-the-envelope sketches outlining five different ways to get to the moon, none of them involving rockets

President John F. Kennedy at Cape Canaveral, attending a Saturn briefing by Dr. Wernher Von Braun. (NASA/John F. Kennedy Presidential Library and Museum, Boston.)

then in America's arsenal. On July 16, 1969, they launched the *Saturn V* rocket, a three-stage titan only one foot shorter than St. Paul's Cathedral in London, that had been tested only five times. We strapped three fighter pilots to the top of it and lit the candle for the first lunar landing of *Apollo 11*. In 1961 no human had even approached trying to dock one satellite to another. But just eight years later we docked an American lunar orbiter with a capsule containing the first two humans on the moon. Only fourteen years before Kennedy's address, Chuck Yeager had used nitrogen to power his "Glamorous Glennis" to first break the sound barrier. Not long after, Neil Armstrong and his crew used hydrogen to run a fuel cell to power their *Apollo* spacecraft as she sailed to the moon.

Seven months after his address to Congress, in a speech at Rice University, Kennedy captured the significance of the challenge in this way: "The space effort itself, while still in its infancy, has already created a great number of new companies, and tens of thousands of new jobs. Space and related industries are generating new demands in investment and skilled personnel, and this city and this state, and this region, will share greatly in this growth."[2] The nation grew rich not just technologically or strategically but economically, with contracts let in every state. Large companies like Lockheed and Boeing led the way, and small fabrication shops and tiny software developers grew as well.

That was just the beginning, of course. Despite the glamour of the technological developments in the original *Apollo*, they were really just the seeds of fundamental advances made in a host of scientific and technological fields. The entire computing power of the *Apollo* spacecraft is now nested in your cell phone. Those computing advances surely accelerated that day allowing companies such as Microsoft and Google to revolutionize the world. Anyone who gets a new hip or knee now can be thankful for the materials handling and fabrication developments in the exotic composites used in reaching the moon. Someday, when we install a solar panel or a stationary fuel cell in our home, it will be because of strides made in providing the electricity for the space program. Our daily lives, from the Internet to medical care to our ability to call our teenagers on their mobile phones, are attributable to Kennedy's vision and Americans' response.

*Apollo* also proved the importance of backing vision with policy and investment. Meeting the challenge meant making a commitment to expanding the capabilities of the nation in both industrial might and intellectual prowess. Like the expansion of the railways before it, whose growth was accelerated by Lincoln's policies, *Apollo* could not get to the moon without vigorous governmental action.

So Kennedy gave his people the most important service a leader can provide. He gave them a goal. He provided trusted leadership in rallying to that goal. He recognized the innate but dormant qualities of his countrymen. He offered them a compelling vision for putting those qualities to work. He then mobilized the resources to see the job through.

Today America is ready for that same kind of leadership. We face challenges every bit as daunting as we did in the days of *Apollo*, including security concerns. This time the threat is from Middle Eastern oil instead of Russian ICBMs. This time we are in an economic race for the jobs of the next century. What's more, we now face the greatest challenge ever faced by all of humankind at the same time—global warming.

Success will not involve instant gratification. Our forthcoming clean-energy revolution, like the original Apollo Project, will not be easy. It will not be instantaneous or without risk. Kennedy knew how to face such major challenges—with action. "All this," he said, "will not be finished in the first hundred days. Nor will it be finished in the first thousand days, nor in the life of this administration, nor even perhaps in our lifetime on this planet. But let us begin."[3]

## CHAPTER 1

# A New Apollo Project for Energy

Where there is no vision, the people perish.

*—Proverbs 29:1*

No one ever climbed a mountain they believed could not be climbed. No one ever started a business they believed would fail. And no nation ever undertook a major initiative it believed was destined for dust. When Kennedy said America was going to the moon, he did not believe we would fall short. So too, America will not commit itself to tackle the challenge of global warming or break free from the clutches of Middle Eastern oil until we have confidence that we can build a clean-energy future that will be brighter than the world we are living in today.

Why has America not risen to the challenges of climate change and oil dependence to date?

The problem is not inadequate information or insufficient scientific talent. It is not even the relentless obstructionism of vested interests, though we can't underestimate the tenacity and cleverness of the oil and automotive industries and the politicians indebted to them. Rather, the problem is an overabundance of fear. Fear that we cannot solve the problem. Fear that we cannot change the course we are on.

People have a finely developed ability to ignore problems—like the inevitability of our own death—that we believe we can do nothing about. Yet today, we do not have the luxury of ignorance. Our shift to a deep and abiding hope must be grounded in our ability to guide the forces of change for human betterment, informed by the dangers we face but guided by a belief in our own innovative potential.

As we shall see in the pages of this book, the spirit of innovation is alive today. It is alive at the labs of the Nanosolar Company in California, where a new type of solar cell may bring the world cheap electricity from the sun. It is alive in the wheat fields of Idaho, where the first commercial cellulosic ethanol plant in the world could be built. It is alive at the home of Mike and Meg Town in Washington State, which generates more energy than it consumes. In all fifty states of this union, individual Americans and their companies and communities are ready for the liftoff of a second Apollo project. Now we just need to engage the full scope of our national resources to that end.

Kennedy's original Apollo Project invested $18 billion per year (in 2005 dollars).[1] The federal government's R&D budget for energy is now just over $3 billion. Kennedy got us to the moon. The current energy budget will not get us anywhere but to the next high-priced gas station. To put this miserly $3 billion budget into perspective, the federal government spent $6 billion last year building a truck to withstand improvised explosive device (IED) detonations in Iraq. This budget is eclipsed by that of just one company, the Microsoft Corporation, which invests twice that sum, or $7 billion a year, in research.[2] Just one new biological drug can cost a pharmaceutical company $1 billion to develop and bring to market. Even more astounding, according to the *Economist* magazine, the U.S. power-generating business, arguably the world's largest polluter, spent a smaller percentage of its revenue on research and development than the U.S. pet food industry did. Clearly, our priorities are in the wrong place.[3]

We don't need an incremental increase. We need the equivalent of a new space program. As with the original Apollo Project, much of the capital will flow from the private sector, but it will take federal investment and policy to move that capital toward new technologies that solve these problems.

It is not just money we need. Kennedy did much more than just write a budget. He wrote a new vision statement for the country. He created a national consensus that we were going to do whatever it took to reach that national goal. When young minds of a scientific bent asked "what they could do for their country," their answer was frequently to go into the space program. Our national leadership must now rekindle that sense of national purpose.

Fortunately, we have leaders today who can articulate the vision of a better future. We are about to meet some Americans who have already set out on that path. This book has been written as a map for the journey. It examines in turn each of the technologies in which we must invest to reach our goal, as well as pioneers of the new energy economy who are leading the way. While these inventors and activists can provide the engines of a new energy economy, it must ultimately be the people and our political leaders who set the course. If we choose wisely, when we reach our destination, we will have transformed the face of our nation. In so doing, we will have addressed the three legs of the new Apollo mission: attack global warming, reestablish our national security, and revitalize our manufacturing economy.

But while Kennedy had a decade to perform his feat, we may have far less time.

## Surviving the Bomb, Dying from the Heat

To see the consequences of failing to act, we can look to an island nation once the home of America's nuclear testing program and now home to 60,000 very worried people. In the middle of the Pacific Ocean, about halfway between Hawaii and Australia, lie the Marshall Islands. In 1948 they were a charming series of 250 coral atolls that had been home to a gentle and friendly group of Micronesian communities for a thousand years. Those people lived an idyllic existence among the palm trees and abundant coral reefs.

Then we tried to blow it up.

We gave it all we had. We exploded twenty-three nuclear bombs on the Bikini atoll between 1946 and 1958 alone, one of which was the largest hydrogen bomb ever detonated by the United States. We hammered that little island with weapons generating temperatures equal to those on the sun itself. Ours was a scorched-earth policy.

But it did not destroy the will of the Marshall Islanders. They moved away from the Bikini atoll to other islands in the group and resumed their long traditions of living close to the land and sea. Their culture remained intact. The Marshall Islands, as a whole, survived.

But they may now be doomed by the more powerful, more pervasive, more insidious threat of global warming. A nation that survived hydrogen bombs may now succumb to $H_2O$.

With their average height just seven feet above sea level, and the seas rising due to global warming, the Marshall Islands may be a nation that comes to know how the world, or at least their world, ended. As a nation that is literally built upon thousand-foot-tall coral reefs that also serve as critical bulwarks against the surge of the sea, it could drown. What is now an ocean paradise could become an underwater reef. The process has already begun, inch by inch.

The president of the Marshall Islands, a genial leader with a warm smile named Essay Note, knows what it is like to have one's nation nibbled away bit by bit by the power of the sea. "Our situation is already critical. We have seen the sea coming in and destroying our coastal areas. So much of our land is being washed away," he says in a tone that is remarkably calm given that his ship of state is sinking beneath him. "We live close to the ocean here. The sea is both our garden and our neighbor. It is so hard to now see it coming right into our homes. We have had to relocate people already. We have tried building sea walls, but that has limited success on an island that is two feet tall."[4]

When you talk to this president, he will emphasize that the damage to his people has been as much cultural as physical. "Our whole culture is tied to the sea. Our traditional way of preparing food, of teaching our kids, of living in every way is interwoven with the coral reefs that sustain us. But the whole ecosystem around those reefs is now being killed.

Our people have to go farther and farther out to get any fish. The reefs themselves are bleaching, and parts of them are dead. With them goes our culture."

His reefs are getting a one-two punch. First, water temperatures are rising as the ocean absorbs huge amounts of energy from the warming atmosphere. Second, the ocean is becoming more acidic as it absorbs $CO_2$ from the air, the carbon dioxide going into solution and changing the pH level of the seas. The combination of warm water and acidic conditions is a deadly cocktail for coral.

If trends continue, there may be no healthy corals anywhere in the world in the next century, because the calcium that builds coral cannot be precipitated out of such acidic conditions. The acidification of the oceans poses a broader threat to our food supply since a substantial number of the tiny creatures that form the foundation for many food chains will also have this problem.

"It's not just the water level that threatens us," President Note explains. "Global warming causes more frequent and powerful storms that wash over us and can destroy what little margin we have to keep our noses above water. This is just another reason so many of our people have moved to places like Oregon and Seattle. It's a real problem."

The people of the island nation of Tuvalu have already agreed to move to New Zealand when their home becomes uninhabitable. President Note sees the United States as a more likely destination for his island's climate refugees due to political ties. We put Katrina refugees in the Astrodome. Where will we put the Marshall Islanders?

But President Note's first instinct is to stay and fight. "The United States is responsible for 25 percent of all the $CO_2$ emissions in the world. How can it drown my nation and not do something about that? What gives it the right to do nothing as my nation goes under?"

## Global Warming beyond a Reasonable Doubt

The science of global warming is well understood. Certain gases, principally $CO_2$, absorb solar radiation that would otherwise be dissipated back into space. Like a down comforter on your winter bed, they then radiate that heat back to the earth. The more of these gases in the atmosphere, the more energy radiated back to earth. The higher the percentage of carbon dioxide ($CO_2$) in the atmosphere, the greater the amount of the sun's energy that is trapped on earth. The basic principles of global warming are as scientifically accepted as gravity.

These gases are called greenhouse gases for good reason. Their presence at the right concentrations is vital to life on earth. Without them, we would be a frozen planet. But we know with a high degree of certainty that over the last two centuries, human activities have increased the concentration of these gases to levels never before seen during human existence and probably not during the last 20 million years.[5] The levels of $CO_2$, for instance, have risen from 280 parts per million (ppm) in preindustrial times to 382 ppm today. And $CO_2$ stays in the atmosphere for a long time; the carbon we emit now will be part of our atmosphere for another fifty to two hundred years. The question is not whether we are causing global warming, but whether we can avoid almost doubling preindustrial levels of these gases in our atmosphere. Unless dramatic changes are made in our energy economy there will be between 500 and 600 ppm of $CO_2$ in the atmosphere by 2050, and 800 ppm by 2100. These are more than just numbers.

In other words, by the middle of the century, the gases that trap heat on our planet could be nearly twice as "thick" as they were before we started cutting down our forests and burning oil and coal—if we're lucky. Does it stretch the imagination to think such a titanic global change would have a dramatic impact on our lives? Much worse, should it not alarm us to realize that these projections may understate the problem, since world economic activity based on fossil fuels is accelerating, and these projections are based only on the rate of increase we are suffering today, about 2–2.5 ppm per year?

Among all but a few scientists, it is a given that we have already irreparably altered the course of life on earth. Mean temperatures have risen by 1.4°F and sea surface temperatures by .09–1.8°F over the twentieth century.[6] Sea levels have risen nearly .2 meter, and the extent of Arctic ice has decreased by 7–15 percent, depending on time of year.

According to both the National Academy of Sciences and the Intergovernmental Panel on Climate Change, the evidence that human activity is causing most of this change is unequivocal.

But this is only the beginning. It is virtually certain that continued buildup of greenhouse gases will cause increased warming, with the potential for sudden changes in major ocean currents, tundra meltoffs, and other unpredictable results presenting additional dangers.

We can expect further increases of between 3.24 and 7.2°F this century if $CO_2$ emissions continue on their present ominous path.[7] To put that in perspective, the difference between the last major ice age and our current climate is less than 10°F. Such temperature increases mean longer periods of severe storms as energy in the environment increases. As rising sea levels threaten our shorelines, increased storm surges and extreme wind events become matters of concern. Declining soil moisture will mean lost agricultural productivity and more frequent drought, pests, and forest fires.

All of these statements represent the consensus of an enormously diverse community of scientists from around the world. At a hearing of the U.S. House of Representatives Energy and Commerce Committee in July 2006, organized to challenge the science of global warming, even the witnesses called to question the science ended up agreeing to these basic findings. And of 928 peer-reviewed articles in scientific journals randomly selected from the thousands that have been published in the last decade, not one questioned these fundamental conclusions.[8]

Like the tobacco industry of the 1960s, which declared, "Doubt is our product," some in industry have nonetheless continued to stress uncertainty to promote inaction; but questioning the basic fact pattern is no longer acceptable in public debate, and many signs of change are emerging. As an example of how far the conversation has moved, even Shell Oil has come out in favor of managing $CO_2$ to reduce the threat of global warming, and Exxon has dropped some of its support for groups questioning global warming science.[9]

But the scientific news has not gotten better as the picture has become clearer. The damage predicted is more imminent than it was considered just three years ago when the world's largest scientific panel ever assembled—the Intergovernmental Panel on Climate Change (IPCC), established by the World Meteorological Organization (WMO) and the United Nations Environment Program (UNEP)— released its Fourth Assessment Report. "All the new information makes it more ominous. Ice caps are melting faster. Greenland is melting faster. Permafrost is melting faster. Beetles are killing millions of acres of forests—since 2000, we have lost an area the size of Illinois to forest fires—and this wasn't even contemplated. Extreme weather events are accelerating in frequency. Feedback mechanisms like methane escaping melting permafrost were not even considered by the IPCC. It's worse than we thought," says Joe Romm, whose book *Hell and High Water* ought to make the most sanguine concerned.[10]

For example, hardly anyone had heard of the problem of ocean acidification three years ago. Some even proposed pumping $CO_2$ into the ocean to store it. Now the evidence is conclusive that $CO_2$ from the atmosphere is entering the water and turning it more acidic. Little eco-system bombshells like this keep going off as our understanding of the climate grows.

When it comes to responsibility for global warming, not all men are created equal. We Americans are the leaders, unfortunately, in global warming. We are only 4 percent of the world's population, but we emit 23 percent of the world's $CO_2$.[11] On a per person basis, the average American is responsible for close to twenty tons of $CO_2$ each year, nearly ten times what an average Chinese citizen emits.[12] We must do better, and we must do so urgently. It is literally a matter of survival.

## Kissing the Arctic Good-bye

It's not just foreign nations that will suffer. To our north lies a threatened place that holds the key to the world's climate, the Arctic.

What is going to happen to the Arctic, home of the polar bear, the Inupiat people, and countless dreams of adventure? "I think it will all be gone in the next century," says one who is in a position to know,

Dr. Carol Bitz, professor of atmospheric science at the University of Washington. "It is melting rapidly now, and 80 percent of the summer ice will have disappeared by 2040 and the remaining remnants by 2080."[13]

After extensive research she knows why as well: "The Arctic is suffering two major blows right now. First, it is absorbing huge amounts of solar radiation because as the ice melts, the dark sea absorbs about five times as much energy as would the white ice. Second, we have now found that as the sea ice retreats, it draws warmer ocean water into the Arctic. Maybe the Arctic could survive one blow, but it cannot survive both."

Dr. Bitz has spent her professional life creating computer models to predict the consequences of the continued rise of $CO_2$ on the polar ice cap. To do that, she uses the most powerful computers in the world, including the ones also used by the U.S. Department of Defense to model nuclear explosions. Her team's report in December 2006, incorporating the latest information and predictions about the Arctic, rocked the world. "We found that the polar ice cap will be essentially gone during the month of September by the year 2040," she says. Forty years later, it will be completely gone.

The context of Dr. Bitz's research is even more frightening. Her research was triggered by findings in the Greenland ice core showing enormous changes in world temperatures taking place in extremely small time frames during times past. "We saw swings of 10°F in just a decade or so. This means there are mechanisms in the system that can change the whole world climatic system in the blink of an eye. Given that we are expecting 5° changes just in the next century, this is terrifying news. The whole climate could change overnight in a sense."

"It's not just the polar bears who are going to suffer," she says. "When the polar ice cap melts, so will a lot of people's expectations of what their lives were to be like." A World Bank map shows that just a one-meter rise in sea level would inundate half of Bangladesh's rice land. And rising sea levels could create millions of climate refugees in Asia.[14] Such events could make Hurricane Katrina's warmup act appear as child's play.

Dr. Bitz's concern has only grown in the last few years. "The new information keeps coming in with bad news," she says. These projections must be disturbing for the very reason that we know how plastic, how dynamic, the world's climate has been. About 25,000 years ago the upper half of the North American continent was covered with an ice sheet 9,000 to 12,000 feet thick. Dr. Bitz does not mince words. "The polar ice cap is a central factor in the world's climate. When it goes, the whole world is going to change."

The small world of one American community has already turned upside down. For thousands of years, Americans known as the Inupiat have lived by hunting seals on Shishmaref, a barren island five miles off the coast of Alaska's Seward Peninsula. Theirs is a survival on the edge of human existence, sustained through the polar night and unbelievable cold, their metabolisms powered by seal blubber. For eons their village has been protected from winter storms by thick buttresses of pack ice. But in the early 1990s the Inupiats began to notice that the ice was thinning, even becoming slushy. The Inupiat's transportation director, Tony Weyiouanna, describes this as "slush puppy" ice, and says its appearance caused great alarm among the Inupiat. The weakening of the ice cut them off from reaching their hunting grounds and stranded hunters on the seas as they pursued the ringed seal, threatening their very way of life. Describing his reaction when he saw it, Weyiouanna says, "Your hair starts sticking up. Your eyes are wide open. You can't even blink."[15] You can trust him to know his ice; his people have been tuned to ice like a maestro to his violin for centuries and have at least three words for it: *sikuliag*, young ice; *sari*, pack ice; and *tuvag*, landlocked ice.

More important to the survival of the village, the thinning of the buttress of ice began to expose the villagers' homes to the ravages of the surging Arctic sea. Storms began to breach the barriers in the mid 1990s. In 1997 a storm washed away 125 feet of the town, taking with it several homes.

With the protection of the ice wall gone, with the tundra melting beneath their feet and seals becoming impossible to reach, the villagers

The first American homes to be destroyed by global warming have already been lost to the sea in Shishmaref, Alaska. (Johnson P. Eningowuk.)

decided it was time to go. In 2002 they voted 161 to 20 to relocate to the mainland and try to find a way to live there. It was not easy. Many elders felt that away from the sea they would be cut off from a life force that had sustained them. As one elder explained, "It is so lonely." In December 2006 they chose a site, Tin Creek, thirteen miles south of their present location, for their new home. "We don't know exactly where the $180 million will come from to move," says Tony Weyiouanna, "but we don't have a choice." Luci Eningowuk, chairperson of the Shishmaref Erosion and Relocation Coalition, knows the transition will be hard for many but can say only: "Our children need a place to go. Our home is gone."

## The Grapes of Global Warming's Wrath

Americans far to the south are also feeling the ominous brush of global warming.

Cattle and sheep rancher Ogden Driskill is owner of the Camp Stool Ranch near the Devil's Tower in northeastern Wyoming and as plainspoken and tough minded as any dirt rancher in America. He says, "Something is way out of whack in our climate right now. I've got hundred-year-old oak trees that are dying, maybe because of the drought or maybe because the seasons are all fouled up. Some are in bud right now when it's in the mid-50s in December."[16]

Perhaps it seems strange that a cattle rancher would care at all about oak trees, but to Ogden their condition portends troublesome change: "It seems everything is changing, so we have to make management decisions based on that change. We've been in a prolonged drought that is a major problem. It can be worse than the statistics show, too, because even if we get the same amount of rain a year, it will just be coming down in buckets for a day and then nothing for months. That is not usable irrigation. And, sure, we now can have our cattle getting to the grass for two months more a year because it's so warm, but what is that doing to the soil moisture? My friends out in Nebraska are getting killed by these changes. Who needs another dust bowl?"

These are not the rantings of a farmer down at the coffee shop with too much time on his hands. They represent the dirt-level view of a scientific reality. "We are in the century's third-worst drought so far," says Brad Rippee, agricultural meteorologist for the U.S. Department of Agriculture (USDA). "Fifty-five percent of the counties were in drought conditions in 2006. The somewhat marginal soil moisture areas west of a line between Montana and West Texas are at risk."[17]

As Driskill points out, the changes in intensity of weather have had a real impact. "The increased incidence of severe weather events, intense precipitation, [and] high winds have made a real difference. Rain falling at huge rates just cannot be absorbed by the soil, so it doesn't help the farmer. A big variability seems to be imbedded into the climate now, so lots of adverse changes are taking place." Corey Moffet, rangeland specialist for the USDA, cannot say these changes are permanent. That is for another agency. But his conclusion is disturbing: "Maybe it's not permanent. Maybe it's a ripple. But I can tell you this, it's changing the whole face of agriculture."[18]

For Ogden Driskill it is not an abstract matter. "We're losing species.

Rancher Ogden Driskill sees the impacts of climate changes on his land in Wyoming. (Povy Kendal Atchison.)

We're losing soil moisture. We're losing way too much. Something needs to change."

## Addicted to Oil and Living in Fear

James Woolsey, former director of the CIA, is a worried man. He worries that the threat we face from our dependence on foreign oil could be as dangerous as the threats we faced in the 1960s during the Cold War. He knows that every year we send billions to the very region that sent us 9/11. He knows that the money that financed 9/11 came from oil proceeds. He knows that the amount of fissile material in the world is increasing. He knows that some of that may one day be for sale, or already is. He is entitled to be worried.

In his 2006 State of the Union address, President George W. Bush declared, "America is addicted to oil." This was news coming from a president who once declared, "There's no such thing as being too closely aligned to the oil business."[19] And his admission of our collective national oil addiction is a testament to the depth of the nation's unease and our current precarious relationship to energy. Americans of all stripes—liberals, conservatives, and Red Sox fans—are uneasy about our reliance on oil.

The United States uses nearly 21 million barrels of oil a day. That amounts to a staggering 25 percent of total global consumption. Of the oil we use, we import over 65 percent, or 13.5 million barrels, each and every day. That number has risen from 37 percent in the 1970s, at the time of the Arab oil embargo, and 58 percent in 2000. Disturbingly, the trend shows no sign of slowing.[20] In 2005 alone, the United States sent nearly $40 billion to the Persian Gulf region to purchase oil, even as we financed a war on terror.[21]

Woolsey is a defense hawk, and he has dedicated his career to tracking threats to American interests. Today he has become something of an evangelist for clean energy as well. As he puts it, "One of the most powerful things about the fight to break our dependence on oil is that it transcends ideology. Across the whole political spectrum, whatever you think about the war in Iraq and what's gone wrong there, or how hard to push Israel and the Palestinians, it is the height of foolishness to be dependent on this part of the world to keep our economy running." In his words, "Allowing 97 percent of our transportation reliance to be dependent on a substance centered in the Persian Gulf is about as irresponsible as a country can get."[22]

Even the mere threat of chaos in the Middle East boosts what we pay for energy. It has been estimated that volatility in the oil market has cost the U.S. economy $7 trillion over the past thirty years.[23] Oil dependence has direct costs to our military, as around the world U.S. forces are engaged in protecting pipelines and refineries from terrorist or insurgent attacks in Iraq, Colombia, Saudi Arabia, and the Republic of Georgia. The Department of Defense has stepped up its arms deliveries and training to forces in Angola and Nigeria. And the U.S. Navy is patrolling the tanker lanes of the Persian Gulf, the Strait of Hormuz, the South China Sea, and the Strait of Malacca.[24]

And if you don't think the Iraq war is mainly about oil, ask yourself this: if Saddam Hussein had been the bloodthirsty dictator of Swaziland instead of Iraq, would we have 140,000 American military personnel in that country? Had he not been sitting atop the second-largest pool of crude oil in the world,[25] the strategic assessment and decision to go to war would have been very different calculations for U.S. planners.

One thing that keeps Woolsey up at night is the possibility of terrorists flying an airplane into the unique sulfur-cleaning towers near Ras Tanura in northeastern Saudi Arabia. A single attack could take six to seven million barrels of oil a day off the market and require one to two years to fix, sending crude oil prices well above $100 a barrel for a year or more. The U.S. economy would come down with the towers.

Since democracies tend to befriend other democracies, we have a stake in creating the conditions in which other societies can develop new democratic traditions. But the dominance of oil has retarded the progress of democracy in the Middle East. Tom Friedman has called it the First Law of Petropolitics that "the price of oil and the pace of freedom always move in opposite directions."[26]

Woolsey puts it similarly: "Putting oil money in people's hands allows for very high economic rents and concentrates power in the central government. If you have a mature democracy, this can be balanced, but with authoritarian regimes, dictators, and tribal kingdoms this concentrated power is very dangerous." It is not a coincidence that of the ten nations with the largest proven oil reserves (the United States is eleventh), only one (Canada) is a true democracy.[27] Governments with an independent source of income like oil face little pressure to invest in the skills and social capital of their people. Oil truly breeds a vicious cycle.

But as bad as the threat is today, it is only growing. The United States has nearly five hundred passenger cars for every thousand people; in China there are ten and in India only seven.[28] When those countries demand cars, the new demand for oil will squeeze out any cushion left in the oil market. For example, recent labor unrest in Ecuador, a political incident that formerly would have caused little notice in oil markets, contributed to a jump in prices of $2 a barrel, causing real pain.[29]

The projected increase in world demand for crude oil will require an increase in world production capability of about 25 million barrels per day by 2025, a 30 percent increase.[30] That is almost the equivalent of three Saudi Arabias, a demand that will be hard to meet. If we do not act now to break our dependence, we are certainly in for more oil shocks.

## At What Cost to America and the World?

The problems of oil are not just questions of climate and security. They go to the heart of our economic welfare as well. In 2005 the United States spent the staggering sum of over $200,000 a minute on foreign oil.[31] That represents real resources flowing out of the economy. Think what could be done with $200,000 a minute in domestic investment in American communities. In fact, oil imports represent the largest single contributor to our spiraling national trade deficit, which set a record in 2005 of over $791 billion and was expected to climb to well over $850 billion in 2006.[32] Over the two-year period from August 2004 to July 2006, the petroleum-related trade deficit accounted for 80 percent of the deepening overall deficit as oil prices climbed.[33] That is not a recipe for a strong economy, and it costs American jobs, while globally, high oil prices have increased poverty in developing countries, wiping out hard-won gains from debt relief.

Ironically, while oil costs our economy so much in both jobs and treasure, the argument against doing something to curb our addiction to oil or fight climate change is that it would be too costly. Changing the course of our energy use is too often presented as an expensive burden on our economy, rather than an opportunity for innovation. The conventional charge when confronted with curbing oil use or moving to carbon-free renewable energy is that workers and the economy would suffer. In effect, we are being asked to choose between putting food on the table for our children today and protecting the welfare of our children tomorrow.

The road to hell is paved not only with good intentions but also with false choices, and this may be one of the falsest choices ever. In the words of United Steel Workers president Leo Gerard, we cannot choose between jobs and the environment: "We must have both, or we will have neither."[34]

The job concerns of Americans are real. America is not only embroiled in a climate crisis and an oil crisis, but we have been hard hit with a jobs crisis as well. This country has lost over three million manufacturing jobs since the year 2000.[35] There is a steady exodus of high-value-added production employment, often in areas where our government has put R&D money into the very technologies that are being moved offshore. At the same time, even in the face of an economic recovery, the benefits are not being shared with working Americans. Inflation-adjusted wages are only just getting back to where they were at the start of the economic recovery in 2001,[36] and median household incomes have fallen for five years in a row.[37] The spoils of a growing economy have not been reaching average people. Too often this economic insecurity is cynically played on to pit jobs against the environment.

## The Apollo Energy Project

A new Apollo Project for energy is really a mission to rebuild our economy. Smart energy policy is, in fact, good economic policy. The two are inextricably intertwined. Done right, solving our crises of climate change and oil dependence can create tremendous opportunity for America and the world, not only by avoiding the severe economic harm of climate disruption, but also by driving new investment into local and metropolitan economies, increasing social justice and reducing economic disparity by creating new career ladders and skilled domestic jobs across the economic spectrum.

What energy strategy, then, can build a clean environment, greater national security, and a transformed and growing economy? We have leaders with answers. These men and women can be considered to be in the vanguard of a national movement that will build the new Apollo energy project, even though it as yet has no formal structure, address, or registration. One is Leo W. Gerard, an untiring advocate for a clean-energy reindustrialization of America, who began his career as an eighteen-year-old worker in a nickel smelter and is now president of the United Steel Workers. Gerard represents people who make not only nickel and steel but also a host of manufactured goods that go into new energy technologies, from utility workers who power our cities to the makers of glass for energy-saving windows and rubber for the tires of our cars, to the producers of fuel cells, wind turbines, and the concrete for modern buildings. Today Gerard is organizing aggressively around clean-energy job growth for good reason.

Gerard placed his bets early on clean energy, and it's paying off. He worked closely with Pennsylvania governor Ed Rendell to pass the Alternative Energy Portfolio Standard, which created a large market for wind energy and brought the wind energy company Gamesa to Pennsylvania. Today Gamesa is working on building its fourth facility to manufacture components for massive wind turbines in the United States. The first plant is already making windmill blades the size of the wings of a 727. To complete the poetic justice of the enterprise, three Gamesa facilities occupy the sprawling site of a closed Bethlehem Steel plant.

What started as a clean-energy policy for Pennsylvania now means seven hundred new high-skill union manufacturing jobs with family-supporting wages and benefits for workers at Gamesa. For Dave Moore, a union steel worker at the new Fairless Hills plant, it means one very important job—his own—manufacturing wind turbines in the same plant where his father once rolled steel. For Gerard, this is just the beginning. To come are new industrial dynamos and literally millions of jobs in building solar thermal plants to produce electricity, manufacturing hybrid drive trains for a new generation of cars, and developing a whole new "smart" grid system to save energy and enable renewable energy production. This is not about sacrifice; it is about economic growth, productivity, and investment.

The connection between clean-energy systems and a growing economy is a direct one. We can take money that would otherwise flow to foreign emirates and invest those same dollars in local jobs. We can reduce harms to public health and the global commons by investing in skills, technology, and productive infrastructure.

A clean-energy revolution represents the jobs of the future.

What some in Washington have fought as they beat back efforts to solve the climate crisis or wean ourselves from oil, the investment community has begun to recognize as valuable. In the past three years, renewable energy investments have nearly doubled, and between 1995 and 2005 they increased their value six times, from $6.4 billion to $39 billion. Over that ten-year period cumulative investment was nearly $180 billion.[38] In 2006 alone, more than $7 billion was invested in wind energy and biofuels.[39]

But this growth is a drop in the bucket compared to our potential, and to our need. U.S. consumers spend over $500 billion a year on energy, and the figure has been rising each year for decades.[40]

We need a crash national program. Princeton scientists Stephen Pacala and Robert Socolow estimate that to realize the potential of renewables to address our climate challenge, wind energy generation will have to increase to fifty times current levels, and solar installations must rise to sixty times the current rate of deployment. When a project to retool our society to rely on clean and renewable energy is finally developed, the capital flows will be both massive and transformative of our economy and our communities.

The Apollo Alliance, a national coalition of business, environmental, labor, and community groups dedicated to promoting clean-energy jobs, conducted a detailed economic analysis of the potential benefits of a crash program of investment in alternative energy. They found that investing $30 billion per year for ten years would add more than 3.3 million jobs to the economy, stimulate $1.4 trillion in new gross domestic product, and add $953 billion in personal income and $323.9 billion in retail sales, all while generating $284 billion in net energy cost savings.[41]

Separate studies by the RAND Corporation and the University of Tennessee found that producing 25 percent of all American energy—fuel and electricity—from renewables by the year 2025, the goal of the "25x'25" coalition of farm-based clean-energy advocates, would produce $700 billion of new economic activity and five million new jobs, all while reducing carbon emissions by one billion tons.[42] In 2005, the U.S. ethanol industry alone created nearly 154,000 jobs throughout the U.S. economy and generated $5.7 billion in new household income.[43]

The jobs that come from the shift to clean and renewable energy are concentrated in manufacturing, construction, and skilled facilities operations. These are jobs for electricians, carpenters, pipe fitters, laborers, designers, engineers, and refinery and utility workers. They are grounded in communities and hard to outsource. They are good jobs that rely on highly skilled workers and offer family-supporting wages and benefits.

According to a study by the California Public Interest Research Group, renewable energy generates four times the number of jobs per megawatt of installed capacity as natural gas does. This makes sense, because the cost of obtaining electricity from natural gas is largely driven by the cost of fuel, while the cost of renewable energy is driven by the costs of capital investment and skilled labor. The Renewable Energy Policy Project finds similarly that renewables create 40 percent more jobs per dollar of investment compared with coal-fired plants. Energy efficiency likewise redirects capital flows away from energy imports and waste and into high-quality local construction and operations, creating good jobs in the process.

Increasingly, across the country, from Oakland, California, to the South Bronx, community activists are finding that these "green-collar jobs" can have a role in redistributing wealth and opportunity to those who have been passed by in previous economic booms. These efforts are putting in place policies that encourage community hiring and the right to organize, invest in local manufacturing, and encourage new career ladders through links to apprenticeship programs and training for clean-energy jobs like energy-efficiency and weatherization retrofits and solar panel installation. At the same time, major public pension funds like that of the California Public Employees' Retirement System, with $190 billion in assets in 2005, and other socially responsible investors are putting money into clean technology and finding that the new energy economy meets their social and environmental goals even as it makes a profit for their bottom line.

Even if an overhaul of our energy economy didn't throw off these vast economic benefits, it would be worth doing, if only because it can help us avoid the shock to our economic system that climate change will bring.

In the fall of 2006 the head of the UK's Government Economics Service, Sir Nicholas Stern, released a seminal report that put hard numbers to the question of how climate change will affect the economy. Unlike many past studies on the issue, it did not make the baseless assumption that inaction on climate change has no cost. While some have taken issue with the precise analytical methods and how costs were measured, this report finally compared the costs of preventing climate change to the likely negative economic and social impacts of a warming planet and chaotic environment. It did not minimize the difficulty of the path ahead, stating, "Climate change presents a unique challenge for economics. It is the greatest and widest-ranging market failure ever seen."[44]

The startling finding of the Stern report is that far from being a death knell for the economy, compared to the costs of inaction, dealing with climate change will provide substantial benefits to the economy. "Mitigation—taking strong action to reduce emissions—must be viewed as an investment, a cost incurred now and in the coming few decades to avoid the risks of very severe consequences in the future. If these investments are made wisely, the costs will be manageable, and there will be a wide range of opportunities for growth and development along the way," says the report.

The report concludes that a 5 to 20 percent loss of economic output globally could occur due to global warming. These findings are staggering. Yet for an investment of only 1 percent of GDP we can head off those costs. Put simply, we have the opportunity to make low-cost and economically productive investments now in new technology that yields substantial benefits, instead of accepting a much larger reduction

in our overall prosperity through such real costs as lost agricultural productivity and increased harm to human health. The stakes couldn't be
higher.

This basic finding has been echoed in recent reports by the Intergovernmental Panel on Climate Change that support the economic
value of investing in climate solutions. In the same time period as the
Stern report, the International Energy Agency (IEA) released findings
of its own that underscored the Stern report findings. The executive director of the IEA, Claude Mandil, states succinctly, "The energy future
we are facing today, based on projections of current trends, is dirty, insecure and expensive. But it also shows how new government policies can
create an alternative energy future which is clean, clever and competitive. . . ."[45] Enough said.

It won't be the first time we've changed the way we power our
economy. We once relied heavily on whale oil for light and wood and
coal for heat. We moved from gas light to electricity, and in modern
times we made the shift to reliance on oil for transportation. A young
Winston Churchill famously made the strategic shift from coal to crude
oil from Persia to fuel the Royal Navy, and in so doing positioned England to win the First World War by offering greater speed and flexibil-
ity. "Mastery itself was the prize of the venture,"[46] Churchill later said of
that idea. Now "Mastery of clean energy" should be our war cry. We can
enjoy a rebirth of high-tech manufacturing in clean energy, or we can
sit and watch steel mills rust. The choice is ours.

We are about to meet some Americans who opt for action. And one
who is still waiting.

## GLOBAL WARMING COMES TO THE WHITE HOUSE—OR DOESN'T

*Jay Inslee*

Walking through the Marine-guarded door of the West Wing of the White House is always a bit of a thrill, no matter how flawed the mortal occupying the presidency at the moment. So on October 15, 2001, as I walked into the quiet anteroom with my fellow representatives to wait to be called to meet the president, I had the same sense of history any congressman has when asked by the president for a vote. Knowing that I had something the president wanted, my vote to give him additional authority to negotiate trade agreements, made the prospects for the meeting more interesting than just a grip-and-grin session.

George W. Bush in person is a charming fellow. We shook hands and started talking about baseball in general and the Seattle Mariners in particular. The president may not read many op-ed pages, but he obviously follows baseball. His enthusiasm for the Mariners was well founded because they played together as a team as well as any in the majors.

Then I listened patiently as the president plied the thoughts of my colleagues, each in turn. He wanted their votes.

When it came to my turn for the treatment, I decided to take a somewhat different approach from the direct engagement of the issues my colleagues had employed.

I said, "Mr. President, you really like the Seattle Mariners, don't you?" He replied that he sure did. Continuing, I said, "The reason you like them is that they work really well as a team, rather than relying upon just a couple of big stars, right?" He agreed.

Here, I took a leap of faith that I would not be thrown out of the White House and replied, "Well, Mr. President, that's exactly the problem with giving you trade promotion authority. You don't show any teamwork whatsoever with the rest of the world. Here you want us to give you the authority to supposedly work with other nations on trade, but you adamantly refuse to cooperate with them on anything else. Why should we grant you more authority when you have repeatedly refused to work with the world now?"

At this point, the jovial look he had while talking baseball soured, but I plunged on. "Mr. President, you stiffed the rest of the world on the land mine treaty, you poked your finger in the rest of the world's eye on the International Criminal Court, and in the real capper, you have abjectly refused to do anything about global warming . . ."

Here he interrupted me, teeing off on the Kyoto Global Warming Treaty with a visceral passion. It would wreck the economy, he spouted. There was no way he would ever sign it. It was a disaster, he said. His gesticulations matched the disgust in his voice. He was on a roll.

But now it was my turn to interrupt, and I did so, respectfully, of course. "Hold it, Mr. President. Hold it a second. We understand you have problems with Kyoto, we know you sincerely believe it is flawed. We respect that. But Mr. President, as they say in Texas, what have you got? What are you offering as a solution? What are you going to do about the problem?"

His reaction was stunning for its sudden stillness. For a few long moments he just looked at me, as if he was actually thinking about a meaningful response. He shocked me by giving me one.

He finally broke the presidential silence by calmly saying, "You're right." That George W. Bush would say I was right about anything more significant than the time of day was amazing, and utterly unanticipated. He said, with seeming sincerity, "I know I have to do something about this. I know it's a problem that I have to face. And I want you to know that I have the finest minds in my administration working on a plan to handle this. I am not going to ignore this problem."

I did what anyone would do who had just heard the president of the United States essentially pledge to address the planet's most pressing problem. I said thank you.

As we walked out of the room, I honestly felt like I had witnessed an epiphany by the most powerful man in the world. The way he stopped talking, the way he paused for such a long period of time, his almost plaintive tone of voice asking for recognition for his fine work on the subject all made me feel I had seen the president take some huge step forward on the path to enlightenment.

So I was feeling like pretty hot stuff as I drifted out underneath the portico on the north side of the West Wing and sauntered toward the ornate iron gate separating the rulers from the ruled. After all, I had walked into a White House dominated by big oil and walked out with a presidential commitment to engage in the fight to stop global warming. That seemed like a decent day's work to me. I had, by the mere power of personal confrontation, dramatically changed the president's thinking on the subject.

Then the gate clanged shut behind me, and my reverie was interrupted by the crashing realization that I had just been conned. It may have been presidential, but it was still a con job. George W. Bush was about as likely to do something about global warming as Don Corleone to do something about crime.

History has, unfortunately, proven that belated realization true. Other than rhetorical flourishes in State of the Union speeches, the sum total of George W. Bush's plan to stop global warming is a "voluntary" program in which polluting industries are supposed to come forward out of the goodness of their hearts and sign up to make multibillion-dollar investments in retooling their plants. This president believes a global warming program can be run like a PTA bake sale.

In June 2007, when Bush made the news at the annual G8 meetings by promising to take the lead on global warming, he won widespread coverage in the United States for an apparent reversal on climate change. But that was just another con job. His real promise was to put off setting binding $CO_2$ reduction goals by 2008—the end of his term—as he sidestepped real commitments with European allies under the framework of the United Nations.

Until our leaders take the problem seriously, we can't solve it. We'll get only empty promises, not real action. We have to know the difference.

Although the president did not step up to the plate that day in 2001 (nor did he get my vote for fast-track trade authority, which could weaken both labor and environmental protections in trade negotiations), I know the American people are ready to tackle global warming.

Presidents come and go. American ingenuity endures.

# Ten Energy Enlightenments

The Bush White House may never become enlightened about clean energy, but the nation must be—and will be. Albert Einstein once wrote, "The significant problems we face cannot be solved at the same level of thinking we were at when we created them." Our energy problems are the result of an entrenched way of thinking that will be difficult to transform. One conversation in the White House won't get it done. No single effort will be sufficient. We will need sustained effort from many quarters to make this shift. We offer here some principles to keep us on track in this revolution.

Every grand endeavor designed to break the bonds of old conventions needs a set of core beliefs. American democracy is based on the Bill of Rights embodied in ten amendments to the Constitution. The Good Book is based on the Ten Commandments. The new Apollo energy project is more than a few rungs down the ladder of world importance from either of those efforts, but this project is vital enough to have its own set of core principles, which we will call the · Ten Energy Enlightenments. These ten insights will not only help to guide our thinking, they will also serve as an intellectual road map to the rest of this book.

## ONE
### *Opportunity Is Best Found in Crisis*

Is global warming a challenge or an opportunity? Is energy dependence a security risk or a chance for economic growth? These are, of course, trick questions, for the fundamental fact is that while global warming is a planetary emergency, it is also a huge economic opportunity for America. It is an opportunity to build new industries that can supply the world with clean-energy technology. Dependence on imported oil is both a challenge to our security and a chance to promote new domestic alternatives for keeping capital, and jobs, on our own shores.

Soon virtually every nation in the world will be crying for new technologies to battle the scourge of global warming. America can grab the chance to be the world's supplier of those technologies and clean-energy products, just as it was the world's supplier of steel and cars after World War II. We were the arsenal of democracy in WWII. We can be the arsenal against global warming now.

We have already seen how the coming crisis means change. America thrives on change. We are the world's best innovators, and innovation is most valuable in a time of change.

## Two
### *Boldness Is Required—Tinkering at the Edges Didn't Put a Man on the Moon*

Transformation of an energy economy on the scale demanded by a new Apollo Project requires structural—not ornamental or peripheral—change. The original moon shot was not accomplished by shifting a few boxes on an organizational chart. It required creation of a new NASA. It required a huge increase in national research and development. It needed the influx of a whole new generation of engineers into aerospace. It was the result of a national challenge by an American president, not just a passing press release from a government agency.

Half measures will not cut the mustard. Research needs to rise not by single-digit percentages but by several factors. Incentives have to jump. $CO_2$ limitations have to be adopted, not just debated, and new technology must be deployed.

It is truly a time to think big. We need to get to the moon of clean energy. Our current policies will not get us to Cleveland, or out of Detroit's predicament. To truly revitalize our domestic auto industry, we must radically transform it, not just improve it at the margins.

THREE

*We Must Reject the Tyranny of the Present*

There are many tyrannies in the world, but the worst are tyrannies of the mind, mental straightjackets that imprison imagination. When it comes to energy, the tyranny of the present is a box that confines us to considering only the technologies of today as we envision the future.

Some say we are helpless in the face of global warming. Those "nattering nabobs of negativism" will constantly point out irrelevant facts about how expensive alternatives are compared to fossil fuels, how inconvenient they are, and how undeveloped they are. Those unfortunate victims of the tyranny of the present cannot envision the inevitable growth in efficiency, declining costs, and ever increasing accessibility of clean and renewable energy.

We must understand the awesome power of the human intellect. That is the real renewable energy. That intellectual power is now on the cusp of perfecting the ultimate clean energy: solar power. If we see only what is possible today, we will miss the most transformative technologies and overlook clean energy's greatest potential.

FOUR

*There Are No Silver Bullets*

We humans are accustomed to seeking one savior for our host of problems: the silver bullet, the golden ring, the magic flute. Believing in such a panacea for our energy woes would be comforting, but it would also be foolhardy and dangerous. It would be foolhardy because there is simply no evidence that any such spectacularly powerful technology is anywhere on the horizon. It would be dangerous because the expectation of a silver bullet would expose every technological improvement to the criticism that it was not, indeed, the silver bullet.

We must recognize that no one thing will solve the problem. The climb to the top of this mountain will be step by step, inches at a time, and any objection to any of those steps not getting us to the top in one fell swoop should be ignored. Just as no one person could have authored Wikipedia, no one author, no one company, and no one technology will produce our energy solution. The new Apollo Project relies on open-source architecture. Anyone can contribute. In this context, we have a different word for this design. We call it democracy. We need to keep democracy from being perverted by the forces of large, centralized power, so that all new decentralized technologies can grow. The most democratic and decentralized energy solution of all is energy efficiency. The energy we learn not to squander is just as important as the new energy technologies we learn to build. The energy we do not waste can make the biggest difference.

**FIVE**

*Everybody Needs to Get on the Bus*

When Gandhi said, "You must become the change you seek in the world," he could have been talking to those of us who desire a new American energy economy. That economy will ultimately not be a product of a few decisions made by politicians in our nation's capital. The true source of change will be the billions of individual decisions we make in our own homes, schools, and offices.

Using energy-efficient lighting, driving a fuel-efficient car, using public transit, reasonably insulating our existing home, and buying a green home next time will not stop global warming singularly but will do so collectively. It is vital that we make these individual changes in our lives and homes, but a still deeper collective action is taking root in this clean-energy revolution, with entire communities coming together to work toward a common and renewed vision.

Cities, towns, and neighborhoods have the chance to rebuild

their local economies by creating new consortiums, new companies, and new centers for job growth using their own talents and unique resources. They are reorganizing their economies not only around clean energy, but also to capture new opportunities to include those who were left behind in the old economy, to make not only a more sustainable but also a more just and prosperous world.

By thinking globally, they are creating jobs, access, and a deeper prosperity locally, banding together and recognizing the importance of all of our talents, with the mandate that no one be left behind. In this clean-energy revolution it is essential that everyone gets on the bus.

## Six

### *If Government Sets the Road Signs, the Market Will Drive*

As we remake the American energy economy, government action is indispensable for setting the rules of the road, but its true power will be in harnessing and directing market-driven investment, market-driven innovation, and market-driven profit. The scale of transformation is too great, too grand and sweeping, for government initiatives alone to build a new economy. At their roots, solving climate change and creating a clean-energy revolution are about transforming the economy, setting the rules that focus the attention of industry and entrepreneurs on the task of solving intractable problems through innovation.

Government measures are essential to channel private investment, but they do not have the power to replace it. We are now seeing just how powerful new investment, in both cash and intellect, can be in creating a new economic dynamic as the veterans of the software revolution rush into the clean-energy revolution.

The story of biofuels shows clearly the interplay between government and economic drivers. We speak through our representatives to make choices about infrastructure, to set rules on the carbon content of fuels, and to assist in commercializing new technology. But it will be inventors and new companies with good ideas, farmers and scientists pursuing their crafts that get the work done. This interplay and partnership are key to breaking free of our current energy crises.

## SEVEN

### *Failure Is an Option*

In George C. Scott's penultimate portrayal of General Patton, his most memorable line was "America loves a winner. America can't stand a loser." When it comes to the energy revolution, however, there will be plenty of losers, boatloads of bankruptcies, masses of missed opportunities, and scads of sour endings.

The one and only guarantee that can be made about developing energy companies is that hundreds of them will fail. Such is the nature of innovation. In the original Apollo Project, missile after missile blew up on the launch pad. *Apollo 13* was lucky to get home at all. But Americans understood that those failures were a necessary part of exploration.

The wind energy industry is arguably the first mainstream commercial success in renewable energy. U.S. factories now create thousands of jobs turning out turbines, and around the world global wind energy production is exploding. But the pathway to today's robust wind industry was paved with false starts and failed efforts. We must embark on the clean-energy journey with a commitment to success but also with the understanding that there will be setbacks on the way to reaching our goal.

Success through failure. It is the way of innovation.

## EIGHT

### *Prejudices Are Best Left at the Door*

Take coal. In its present form, to some it is a dirty, neurologically disabling remnant of the Industrial Revolution; to others, it is the only reliable source of cheap power. Neither story is complete.

The current state of affairs gives us cheap energy and deep environmental harm. There is a different possibility—that coal could one day be burned and gasified, the $CO_2$ removed and safely injected into porous seams in the earth. If that vision is to be realized, two big changes will have to take place.

First, huge strides must be made in advanced coal technology and great uncertainties resolved about the ability to permanently sequester $CO_2$ in deep storage. Second, many people will have to surmount their current image of coal as the devil's favorite fuel, while others will have to let go of the increasingly futile hope that high levels of emissions can persist indefinitely without changing course.

Globally, coal fuels much of the world's growth, and demand for coal is skyrocketing. Climate's protectors cannot wish that fact away. Likewise, coal's proponents cannot ignore the costs of carbon, or treat renewable energy and clean alternatives as something more akin to Tinkertoys than to a real energy policy.

We must face these matters squarely.

## NINE
### *Clean Energy Will Be Powered by New Politics*

Politics may seem dirty, but without it, energy will never be clean. A new clean-energy economy will not appear miraculously as the result of drum circles, herbal remedies, and self-help books. The restructuring of the American economy that is needed to bring us industrial-strength clean energy first requires industrial-strength change in the politics of the country. We need a movement.

Clean energy requires clean policies. Clean policies require new politics. New politics requires new people in the process, new coalitions, and new political strategies. The wealth and power of the old energy industry still maintain a grip on democracy that, while it is weakening, can be broken only with new political forces. A new political environment must be established for the success of the clean-energy revolution to be assured.

The change ahead is massive, a transition on the scale of nothing we have seen in generations. We will need the power of people and the power of politics to build a movement for change.

## TEN

### *No More Free Lunches*

Oil survives, thrives, and dominates because it is the beneficiary of the biggest protection racket and the biggest subsidy in the solar system. Up to a quarter of the country's defense budget is dedicated to our massive capability to "intervene" to protect the sanctity of precious oil fields and shipping lanes.[1] When oil's century-old gravy train is eliminated, new clean-energy sources will thrive on a level playing field.

But this is chump change compared to the greatest subsidy the fossil-fuel energy system has enjoyed since its inception: treating the world's atmosphere as a dump for emissions free of charge. Every ton of coal and every gallon of gas we use sends $CO_2$ into our atmosphere, gratis, with absolutely no tribute, no cost, no payment of any kind. We can no longer afford this luxury. It will only be through smart policies that we rein in these "external" costs that have been passed on to us all. It is time for polluting industries to pay for using up the limited carbon-carrying capacity of our atmosphere. Capping the amount of $CO_2$ that polluters are allowed to emit will be pivotal to incorporating the true cost of our energy into every technology choice and leveling the playing field.

By the same token, we cannot have a solution to these problems without boldly investing in alternatives. We must make a commitment to deploy new technologies, to invest in the skills of workers, to ease the costs of transition as businesses retool, and to pay the price of research and innovation. We will not reach our goal if we try to do it on the cheap. This is, after all, a global challenge, requiring an unequivocal national commitment.

The principle of "no free lunch" applies to all of us as well. We are all $CO_2$ emitters, and we cannot live off of this "free lunch," believing that it is up to someone else to build a clean-energy future. We can all be personal architects of a new energy world—or we will all be victims of a worldwide collapse.

## THE SUM OF THE ENLIGHTENMENTS

The Ten Energy Enlightenments have the power to work in a harmonious whole because they embody basic principles of change. In the pages that follow, we will come to know some of the Americans who today are pushing the envelope of change by embodying these principles in their businesses, communities, and daily lives. We will meet Mike and Meg Town, who profit from the wonders of solar energy in a rainy climate and personify the principle that technology is not static. We will get to know one of the richest men in the world, Vinod Khosla, who knows how to use the power of private markets to bring to fruition a rich source of biofuels. We will hear the story of the day a new technology, wind power, could have decapitated the entire leadership of its industry and how that technology is now becoming a force to be reckoned with nonetheless.

From garage mechanics who have invented a new kind of car to community leaders who envision a whole new "green-collar" suite of jobs, we are about to see the handiwork of a unique group of American revolutionaries. These folks know that small steps are not enough and that we are all in this together.

Whatever their technology or location, the Americans we are about to meet recognize one central truth: To change the world, first we have to change our minds.

## CHAPTER 2

# Reinventing the Car

To see the future of the American automobile, take a spin down to Corte Madera, California, and introduce yourself to the CalCars boys.

This group of rebels met one sunny day in April 2004 in the garage of a typical condominium ten miles north of the Golden Gate, determined to roll out a car that could be "fueled" by plugging it into a wall at night with a standard extension cord and run on gas when needed. It was a Toyota Prius when they started and a symbol of an American revolution in automobiles when they finished.

The group was led by Felix Kramer, an entrepreneur who had an idea as big as his mustache. In 2003, after selling his Internet start-up, he cast about for his next adventure and landed on an audacious quest: to revolutionize the auto industry. He knew that gas-powered, internal-combustion cars were destroying the atmosphere and deepening our addiction to oil, and that things had to change. He stumbled on the work of Andy Frank at UC Davis and Bob Graham at the Electric Power Research Institute, brilliant inventors who had radically rethought how to power a car and created a blueprint for the first hybrid you could charge on the grid. Felix decided to build a mass market for this change.

"Our whole auto configuration was decided by just a very few people, a handful of big auto company execs and the government. They had fouled up. It was time to expand the number of Americans who had a hand in this future. So I decided to build a large group of folks who would demand the production of a clean, efficient car. To do that, I knew we had to first build such a car. So that's exactly what we did."[1]

A multitalented group of innovators answered Felix's Internet call. They met in Ron's garage. The team then put the Internet to work to generate "open source" ideas they could incorporate into the design. Two years and a thousand feet of wire later they had converted a 2004 Prius into a car capable of driving on nothing but electricity from the garage wall jack for its first twenty-five miles each day. Felix's plug-in may be the first car ever built "over the Internet."

It was not an easy project. They succeeded only after discovering a secret switch that had literally been hidden in the American version of the Prius hybrid, which allowed the car to run in an all-electric mode, never relying on the gasoline engine. That discovery triggered Felix's revelation that if he could boost the battery capacity, he could create a hybrid with monstrous mileage. So they went to work with a collection of tools, $700 worth of old nickel hydride batteries, and a growing collection of car enthusiasts who hovered around the garage at all hours.

When they finally drove their number out of the driveway and down the street, Felix felt justifiable pride. "All kinds of people want this kind of car: people like generals who care about security; environmentalists who care about the planet; and municipalities who care about cost. But it seems the last people in the world to 'get it' are the big car companies. Now that our CalCars cars are on the road, and these cars are being built in various places around the country, our vision is going to force changes. That is now happening."

It sure is. Felix now has been tooling around California for 15,000 happy miles in his second-generation plug-in. It uses lithium ion batteries, gets a hundred miles per gallon of gas, and costs one cent a mile to run—compare that to nine cents a mile to fuel a typical car with just gas. It is a miser of a car.

Felix owns the first plug-in hybrid ever commercially sold in America. Plug-in hybrids are not yet rolling off assembly lines, but custom

The auto industry may be slow to start their engines in the race for plug-in hybrid cars, but Felix Kramer and the do-it-yourself team at CalCars are busy proving that a car that gets over 100 miles to a gallon of gas is practical today. (CalCars.org.)

conversions like Felix's—built by EnergyCS, a small start-up in California that is beginning to make plug-in conversions available to the public—are being sought by an ever growing market. Many more will follow.

Felix takes joy in the car's simplicity. He plugs a nineteen-inch cord in the rear bumper into a standard extension cord in his garage at night. Tooling around town, he is in all-electric mode for the first twenty-five quiet miles, covering the majority of his commutes gasoline free. He delights when he goes into forums of energy experts and shows them the little cord he uses. "This is all the infrastructure we need to remake our car world," he is proud to say. "We don't have to build huge infrastructure for hydrogen. We can just ship clean electricity over the wires."

What's more, Felix can smile as he drives, because with every mile he is saving $CO_2$ emissions. He says, "When the car is in all-electric mode, it is putting out 60 percent less $CO_2$ than a normal gas car, even taking into consideration all the $CO_2$ coming out of the stacks of the plants that generate the electricity. Even if we never improve our electrical grid a bit, and even if people drive way more than the batteries can hold, some studies have shown this car can reduce $CO_2$ by 36 percent. This is the best thing on the global warming front going."

As an added bonus, Felix's wonder car has an attribute no mortal and few machines can claim—it gets better with age. "The electrical grid feeding my car is going to get cleaner over time," he explains. "Instead of burning coal that releases carbon, we will be relying more and more on wind power, solar power, and geothermal. So the fuel— electricity—driving my car is going to get cleaner every year. How many cars do you know that get better the longer they are on the road?"

When plug-in technology is combined with a flex-fuel engine that can burn gas or biofuels, it can actually get vastly higher mileage per gallon of gas—but that's getting ahead of our story. Even without using biofuels, it reduces our dependence on foreign fuel, because 97 percent of the electricity it comsumes is produced from domestic energy sources. Felix's car is virtually free of Saudi Arabian influence.

Excitement for hybrids is not confined to the road. Utilities salivate over the prospect of turning the storage capacity of plug-in batteries into an adjunct to the electrical grid. Power plants may soon be able to feed their juice into our car batteries at night when demand is lowest, using base electric load more efficiently and storing energy in our cars while they are parked for use during the day. In this way, our cars may one day serve to level out electrical supply and demand on the grid as we slumber.

Roger Duncan, vice president of Austin Energy, a Texas utility, is working to make plug-ins a regular feature of the grid. He has organized a massive national grassroots initiative called Plug-In Partners, which has demonstrated the demand for these cars with pledges from literally hundreds of cities, businesses, and nonprofits from Chicago to Phoenix, from California Edison to the U.S. PIRGs (Public Interest Research Groups). Chicago is retrofitting 850 plug-in hybrids, and New York State is converting the 600 hybrids in its fleet to plug-ins.[2] Several companies are already converting hybrids for commercial sale using the ideas of these pioneers.

A garage gave birth to Hewlett-Packard and the electronic age, not to mention rock and roll and the modern entertainment industry. A garage may also have given birth to the future of personal transportation and the age of the plug-in car.

Maybe. As we will see, there are other suitors in America's ongoing love affair with the automobile. The question is whether any of them will be headquartered in Detroit. Detroit cannot lead the way into the future by tinkering at the margins of its old business model. Nor can it get away with disingenuous promises of cleaner cars and ad campaigns that show gas-guzzling SUVs bringing us closer to nature. It will have to adopt the same spirit of innovation as Felix Kramer and his plug-in crew.

Will Detroit deliver the real deal?

We asked Tom and Ray Magliozzi, better known as Click and Clack, the Tappet Brothers, stars of the nationally syndicated radio talk show *Car Talk*. Their opinions are not exactly nuanced: "For thirty years now the companies have put everything they had into more power instead of more efficiency."[3] Ray, who has a degree from MIT—as does Tom—and now runs Ray's Garage in Cambridge, Massachusetts, elaborates: "The technology has been incredible, but it's all about power. If the companies had put into efficiency what they have put into power, we would be driving cars getting sixty miles per gallon now. They have done fuel injection and computer-controlled engines but have not put those gains into efficiency. Any high schooler could have done better if they had wanted to."

## The Twin Cities Assembly Plant

Ford Motor Company's Twin Cities Assembly Plant (TCAP) in St. Paul, Minnesota, is an anchor for the community. It is also slated for closing. The workers there have built Ford Rangers for the last twenty years. Their parents and grandparents built tanks there during World War II. Rich in history, it was also the shop that painted Minnesota senator Paul Wellstone's storied campaign bus green.

The plant itself is "green"—one of a few in the world that generate all their energy from clean, renewable sources on an industrial scale. In 1924, Henry Ford built the plant around hydroelectric energy on the Mississippi River. Because the plant has no smokestacks belching pollution, the surrounding region sustains remarkable biodiversity to this day. Residents nearby like to boast of the bald eagles that fly over the parking lot.

It is not just a zero-carbon plant, either. In its paint shop it produces only half of the amount of volatile organic compounds (VOCs) that Minnesota allows. This is a plant and a workforce that have taken the idea of clean manufacturing to heart. The workers themselves have contributed to greening the plant. By negotiating a four-day work week and ten-hour shifts, they took two thousand round-trip commutes off the road each week, cutting $CO_2$ emissions and freeing up an entire day's worth of clean, pollution-free, peak electric power each week to feed back onto the grid. For this progressive workforce, the three-day weekend was the cherry atop the environmental sundae.

Age has given the plant a rich history but has also threatened its existence because Ford has not invested in the modernized equipment necessary to keep it on the cutting edge. So when the company faced pressure to downsize, it was exactly this sort of older plant in need of new capital investment that was put on the chopping block. Yet like many others, the St. Paul workers rallied to save the plant by developing a plan. Their plan was to sell the green attributes of the facility as a benefit to the company.

Fortunately for the workers of the Twin Cities plant, they have a secret weapon in the person of Lynn Hinkle. Hinkle is a second-generation union man who has spent thirty years in the auto industry, starting out on the assembly line, where he worked for ten years as a shop steward fighting for air and water quality inside the plant and defending benefits for the workers. In his words, he "bleeds union." While committed to the auto industry, Hinkle is also terrified about what's happening to our climate, calling global warming a "climate crisis," not just climate change. "I know where the jobs of the future are. They are in green manufacturing and clean energy," he says.[4] So Hinkle led his team in making what they called their "green proposal" to convert the plant from one making trucks to one making flex-fuel or hybrid cars. The workers were optimistic, since their proposal was in line with Ford's stated intent to become a green car company. They made the argument all the way up the line to Bill Ford himself. Their proposal kept the plant open for several years.

In the end, Ford turned down the green plan. On April 13, 2006, TCAP workers were informed that the plant was slated for closure in the spring of 2008.

Today there is little chance that Ford will continue producing trucks at TCAP. After eighty-four years, that fate seems sealed. But the story is not over. The river will still flow, and the turbines will still churn out valuable power; the plant will still be primed to make high-quality industrial products for a changing economy in need of heavy industry, clean production, and a new generation of vehicles.

The team that put together the green proposal has not stopped moving. Today they are pursuing a green conversion proposal that focuses on other clean-energy product options for manufacturing in the facility. The State of Minnesota is eager to preserve its industrial base, too, and energy innovation is the obvious way forward. The legislature launched a study to convert the state's fleet to plug-in hybrids, with an eye toward manufacturing the retrofits at the Twin Cities Assembly Plant.

The Twin Cities themselves are partners. A joint green manufacturing initiative has been launched by Minneapolis mayor R. T. Rybeck and St. Paul mayor Chris Coleman committing to plug-in hybrids and other clean technology. They were joined by the likes of Steel Workers president Leo Gerard and the head of the Sierra Club, Carl Pope, as they announced the partnership right out of the UAW union hall.

Ford may be leaving this car town, but manufacturing will continue, and it will be driven by changes in energy. Whether the next employer at TCAP is the firm that makes railcars for transit systems or the high-end electric car manufacturer the conversion team is also talking to, or the company that builds taxis to run on compressed natural gas, cutting carbon emissions by 30 percent, remains to be seen. Or there is Hinkle's favorite, the manufacturer of wind turbines to supply the booming Minnesota wind energy market.

Each product line has demonstrated demand, and serious manufacturers with reasons to locate in the region are taking the opportunity to manufacture at TCAP seriously. The effort to retrofit the plant for a new generation of clean-energy jobs has the backing of the union, the Twin Cities, and the state. So even with Ford leaving the picture, the chance for good manufacturing jobs in transportation and energy remains strong. If Hinkle and his team succeed, it will truly mean a changing of the guard, as the car company with the worst fuel economy closes a chapter on its history and turns over the future of this green plant to a new generation of clean technology.

## Detroit's Automakers: Cheering for the Hometown Team

America has a new tradition regarding Detroit. On Thanksgiving Day we root for the Detroit Lions, as usual, and now during the week before Christmas we lament the latest news of laid-off Detroit autoworkers. In late November 2005, one news story read, "The Motor City is facing a fearful holiday season after three of the auto industry's biggest companies announced nearly 60,000 job cuts in the past week, with more to follow."[5] The Big Three have had more big layoffs than big advances in the last decade. In 2005 GM announced plans to stop production at twelve plants and cut 30,000 hourly jobs by the end of 2008. "We're all worried. Everybody is worried," Robert Paulk, an hourly worker at the GM Warren Tech Center, said that November. "You can't help but think about it."[6]

The cause of this decline is no secret. Foreign competitors have eaten Detroit alive. Poor design choices in determining what cars to focus on at a time of rising oil prices, combined with high legacy health care and retirement costs, set the stage for record losses. The industry cut back its investment in efficiency R&D and played it safe at exactly the moment when a bold step forward in rethinking the car, and our use of oil, was most needed. As a result, the domestic industry that produced 99 percent of the world's cars in 1951 saw its market share in America drop from 73 percent in 1975 to 57 percent in 2006, with no relief in sight.[7]

It is of scant comfort to laid-off workers in Detroit that foreign competitors have hired American workers. The Michigan father laid off from Chrysler takes little satisfaction in knowing that someone has just been hired at Toyota in Tennessee. Overall there has been a net loss of millions of manufacturing jobs, along with downward pressure on wages and benefits as a result of the slipping position of automobile manufacturing. This not only hurts carmakers but also is devastating to suppliers in parts, carpet, steel, paint, and rubber.

The managerial response to this continued fall has been the same for years: contract. Through repeated rounds of "restructurings," management has eliminated or scheduled for elimination 140,000 hourly and salaried automotive jobs since 2000.[8] "They keep coming up with plans, but they never get rid of the people that put them in the hole," says Allen Wojcznski, fifty-eight, who works at a GM warehousing plant in Ypsilanti, Michigan.[9] Call this the Wojcznski Principle. It states that in the domestic auto industry, a declining company does not change strategy; it fires the people who make the cars. This is called a "Turn-Around Plan." Every time employees turn around, they're being laid off.

Management has made more than a few mistakes. That Detroit invested in the Hummer while Toyota invested in the hybrid may be one reason Toyota now has a net worth greater than GM, Ford, and Chrysler combined. To be fair, the purchase of the Hummer was immensely profitable to GM. But that profitability existed in a low-gas-price, non-carbon-constrained world—a bygone era.

Detroit loved the Hummer. The future does not.

On occasion, grand pronouncements have been made that bold leaps toward energy efficiency would be made. Ford introduced the hybrid SUV in 2006, for example, but within months retreated from its pledge to produce a quarter million by 2010. And, even as Ford was the first domestic manufacturer to market a hybrid car, the company sustained the worst greenhouse gas performance of all Big Six automakers[10] and was last in fuel economy, at 19.1 mpg in 2005—a level substantially lower than the 24 mpg of the Model-T eighty years prior. It doesn't have to be this way.

What explains Detroit's lack of foresight?

Former Merrill Lynch analyst John Casesa laments Detroit's continued assumption that fuel prices will remain low. In commenting on its failure to build smaller, more fuel-efficient cars in August 2006, he said, "It is a mistake and it's very disappointing. I just think it shows that Detroit still has a business model predicated on low energy prices.[11] Detroit has always found inefficient cars a safe harbor. Mike Walsh, formerly with the EPA and now an advisor to several nations on improving their automobile industries, goes further: "Once America removed its signals that we need to conserve fuel"—and stopped raising standards—"the SUV began to emerge as the only real profit center for the domestic manufacturers."[12]

There is plenty of evidence, though, that until now Detroit just hasn't been interested in efficiency, even when pushed by strong public policy. Consider the case of GM's electric car, the EV1. The EV1 was a sleek, quiet, super-efficient, all-electric car that could be spotted on California highways from 1995, when the state mandated its introduction, until 2003, when GM took it off the road. It was a beauty that worked like a charm and had zero emissions. Hundreds of EV1s zipped around LA freeways, beloved by their owners, technically successful, but GM killed the program.

In the documentary movie *Who Killed the Electric Car?*, Chelsea Sexton, a former GM employee in the EV1 program, blames her former employer. "Did you ever see a TV ad with handsome women draped on the hood of the EV1 and the car zooming through the desert like you do all the other cars it tries to sell? It just never really made an effort." Sexton believes the EV1 died because GM never tried to market it.[13]

The EV1s were chopped up into little pieces of steel, some of which probably ended up in the bodies of Hummers. Hammering electric cars into Hummers is not a path to peace with global warming, or to freedom from oil. Instead of building a strategy around highly efficient vehicles, GM sued to invalidate the legal requirement to make electric cars. As we shall see, that corporate attitude is thankfully changing.

Ironically, an American, David Hermance, a California executive engineer for Toyota, was the father of the American hybrid on which Japanese automakers are now building industry dominance. He designed the improvements to the Toyota Prius that allowed it to catch on in the American market.

Why did Detroit ignore this homegrown talent? As Walter McManus, director of the University of Michigan Transportation Research Institute, puts it, "Detroit automakers, who have long depended on the least fuel-efficient vehicles to provide most of their profits . . . , are seeing their sales and profits evaporate, as new vehicle buyers switch to more fuel-efficient vehicles. Management apparently assumed that (1) fuel prices would stay low forever, and/or that (2) their customers would not change their vehicle choices because of high fuel prices. Events of the past two years have demolished both assumptions."[14] McManus concludes, "The cash cows [trucks and SUVs] are dying off."[15]

A University of Michigan study found that sustained gas prices above $2.86 a gallon put 297,000 jobs at risk—37 percent of them concentrated in just the states of Michigan, Ohio, and Indiana—and threatened the closure of sixteen plants, mostly in the Midwest, as well.[16] Clearly, the stakes are high.

There is an alternative. Detroit could take steps right now to improve fuel efficiency and to own the next generation of technology and jobs. When McManus and his team did a comprehensive study to determine whether Detroit's profits would increase along with gains in the fuel efficiency of their fleet, they reached a conclusion that would stun the boardrooms of Detroit: "Each automaker should pursue proactive improvements in fuel economy that exceed what CAFE [the federal Corporate Average Fuel Economy standard that governs automobile fuel efficiency] requires, for fuel prices between $2/gallon and $3.10/gallon and consumer discount rates between 0% and 7%." McManus found that profits for the Big Three could actually rise by as much as $2 billion. This conclusion was not preordained. McManus says, "The results of our simulations were surprising, even to us." The study concludes that 15,000–35,000 jobs would even be created.[17]

But if the hybrid cars and advanced diesel engines are supplied through imports—the path of least resistance—40,000 to over 200,000 existing and potential American jobs would be lost to overseas competitors.

Management at the Big Three sometimes blames unions for their inability to be competitive, but it was not the workers who decided on a product mix heavy in poor-mileage vehicles. And, in recent years, the United Auto Workers has championed loan guarantees to automakers to convert domestic plants to produce hybrids and other advanced, fuel-efficient cars. Nonetheless, it is true that the cost of labor hurts U.S. firms. Domestic manufacturers pay about 20 percent more in wages than their foreign competitors,[18] but the real culprit is the absence of a national system for health care and retirement security. This failure places the entire burden for legacy benefit programs for retirees on the shoulders of workers and companies, a huge competitive disadvantage for the Big Three. GM has legacy costs, for example, of $1,500 per car. U.S. automakers spend more on health care than they do on steel, with more than $6.7 billion going just to retiree health care in 2005.[19] In Europe and Asia, the government picks up the bill.

In 2006 Senator Barack Obama proposed swapping "health care for hybrids," giving assistance with legacy health care costs in exchange for retooling U.S. plants to produce fuel-efficient vehicles.[20] It is one commonsense solution to a hydra-headed problem. But whatever the final answer, to preserve American manufacturing we must require our cars to use less oil *and* level the playing field of health care and retirement costs on which U.S. workers and industry compete with the rest of the world.

Mike Walsh believes that the survival of a car company now is as dependent on international conditions as on any domestic market.[21] What happens in China may be as important as what happens in the United States. Five years ago China was just a blip on the screen—now it is the third-largest automobile market in the world, and demand is growing at the unbelievable rate of 20 percent annually. It will be the world's largest auto market in ten years.

Some use the threat of competition from Chinese manufacturers as a reason to keep our costs low and avoid investments in efficiency. But that turns reality on its head. China has imposed efficiency standards higher than our own and even levies a tax on gas guzzlers. When U.S. firms move to expand their base in China, they will face tougher fuel economy standards than in the United States.

In fact, failure to reduce oil consumption could become a major barrier to global competitiveness for U.S. manufacturers. Over 60 percent of global car sales in 2002 were in countries that are party to the Kyoto Protocol and have carbon emission management programs in place.[22] Considering that the average GM SUV emits 41 percent more carbon per kilometer traveled than the average Honda SUV,[23] we can clearly say, "Detroit, we have a problem."

Other parts of the world have found a way to inspire fuel efficiency. We have not. The rest of the world's auto manufacturers are growing. Ours are not. There is a connection between these facts. We need new thinking from Detroit so that we do not have an economic replay of the political debate in the 1950s: Who lost China?

## Will a New Day Dawn in Detroit?

Will Detroit find a way to win over China and save oil in the United States at the same time? It has a chance. The first signs appeared at the Los Angeles Auto Show in 2006.

We've all heard that old dogs can't learn new tricks, but old corporations quite possibly can. That thought must have crossed the minds of the assembled crowd in Los Angeles on November 29, 2006, when CEO Rick Wagoner boldly announced that GM was going to produce hybrid cars, including some that would actually plug in. "We intend to bring our substantial global resources to bear on this issue starting yesterday," he said. "It is highly unlikely that oil alone is going to supply all of the world's rapidly growing automotive energy requirements."[24]

If GM is serious, the world could change. GM's goal is to run its Volt plug-in hybrid on batteries alone for the first forty miles. That would make it even more efficient than the CalCar. The question is whether, given its track record, GM is serious about commercializing the car. Wagoner did not go so far as announcing a production date but said, "I can tell you that this is a top-priority program for GM, given the huge potential it offers for fuel-economy improvement."[25]

Is this dog truly learning a new trick—in fact, a new bag of tricks?

There are some reasons to believe it is the former. First, Wagoner and other GM executives have publicly recognized that they misunderstood the impact of Toyota's launch of the hybrid Prius in 1999. Moreover, Wagoner's announcement about plug-in hybrids was accompanied by his equally important announcement that GM would begin to produce its Vue model using its current hybrid system to achieve 20 percent better fuel efficiency, as well as a second model with improvements that would allow 45 percent better mileage. That could mean GM truly gets it.

More important, GM has made real business commitments dedicated to perfecting the technology needed to bring its Volt to market. In January 2007 it signed two agreements with battery developers to prove the reliability of lithium ion batteries. One of them, the A123 Company, described the batteries as merely needing engineering improvements to be ready for the road. They already power a wide variety of Black & Decker power tools; they just need to be configured for safety and reliability in a car.

For now, Chelsea Sexton is cautiously optimistic. "They have come full circle and are trying to do better," she says. "They are starting to see how much enthusiasm there is for that technology."[26] Felix Kramer adds, "I think Detroit is starting to get it. We consider it a victory for the grassroots, CalCars, and the Internet-led effort."[27]

"We must—as a business necessity—develop alternative sources of propulsion," says Wagoner.[28] But GM has much catching up to do. Sales

The electric car has come full circle from the 1830s, when Robert Anderson of Scotland invented the first electric carriage, to today's plug-in-hybrids. Shown here: Thomas Edison poses alongside the electric Bailey roadster; GM unveils the plug-in Volt in 2006. (U.S. Department of the Interior, National Park Service, Edison Historical Site, 14.625/12 neg. 214; General Motors Corp. Used with permission, GM Media Archives.)

of Toyota's hybrids already exceed the entire sales of GM's Saturn models, and sales of hybrids are expected to rise from 200,000 in 2006 to 535,000 in 2011, according to J. D. Powers and Associates.[29]

There is no doubt that GM is committed to hybrids in China. GM's Chinese sales increased 36 percent in 2005 and, on November 6, 2006, Wagoner announced that the company will build Chinese hybrids in collaboration with a local partner, Shanghai Automotive Industry Corporation.

GM is not alone in starting down the hybrid path. At the same Los Angeles Auto Show, Ford announced that it has redesigned its Escape hybrid to be quieter and less expensive, and Nissan announced its intention to build hybrids. But right now GM and Ford are staring into the abyss of a financial crisis. Both have had to mortgage their plants for operating capital. Attitudes may indeed be changing—impending demise has a way of focusing the mind.

When twenty-one new alternative-fuel vehicles were showcased at the LA Auto Show in November 2006, it was clear that the tectonic plates of the international auto industry were moving. "It sort of feels like the early part of the twentieth century, when everyone was trying to figure out whether to go with steam or electricity or gasoline," says

Gavin Conway, editor of *Automobile* magazine. "People are saying, do we go with electric, hybrids, diesel, or what?"[30]

Whatever the direction, the production infrastructure is already being put in place, with leadership from rank-and-file members of the industry. A prime mover in these efforts is Charles Griffith, head of the automobile program for the Ann Arbor–based Ecology Center and a member of the Michigan Apollo Alliance. He launched the Green Machines Tour, a series of research projects and events drawing attention to the auto jobs that are being created today in plants across America's manufacturing Rust Belt through energy efficiency. Workers are already building advanced transmissions, hybrid drive trains, and more efficient gasoline and diesel engines and working with lightweight composite materials and other elements of the cars of the future.

In Michigan alone, Griffith has identified fifteen different plants producing technology that improves fuel efficiency. He can point to $1.5 billion of investment in new manufacturing technology, money that will go into building the next generation of product, investments that will create or preserve more than 2,300 jobs and increase fuel efficiency up to 20 percent.[31]

Describing these investment levels, Griffith says, "Yes, the industry is reeling now, but they also are making huge investments in the next generation of products. Toyota is not going to march in and take over all of these plants and save the day for these communities. It is going to have to come down to the Big Three investing in these new technologies that make transportation more efficient."

These plant upgrades are saving real jobs. In Ypsilanti, Michigan, in a factory on the edge of closing, GM invested $450 million in a new, highly efficient, six-speed transmission that will improve fuel economy by as much as 10 percent over a standard four-speed transmission.[32] That investment saved 650 jobs. Ford invested $170 million in its Livonia transmission plant, which since 2005 has been producing over 100,000 of those high-efficiency transmissions a year to put in its Mustangs, Explorers, and other lines.

"Displacement on demand" technology saves from 5 to 20 percent of fuel by allowing half the cylinders in an eight-cylinder engine to shut

down when driving conditions are not demanding, turning a gas guz-
zler into a more efficient, four-cylinder engine much of the time. Another 5 percent gain can be squeezed out of engines using "dual vari-
able valve timing," a technology creating five hundred new union jobs
and built at a new joint venture of DaimlerChrysler, Hyundai, and Mit-
subishi in Dundee, Michigan.[33] Numbers like these explain why UAW
president Ron Gettelfinger has said, "Retooling our auto industry to
produce cleaner, greener vehicles has to be part of any comprehensive
energy and jobs strategy for Michigan."[34]

These are not only blue-collar, assembly-line jobs. Recently, GM,
DaimlerChrysler, and BMW launched the new Hybrid Development
Center in Troy, Michigan—which employs over five hundred engineers,
technicians, and other specialists—to speed up the development and
deployment of hybrid technology.[35] In an industry that sells over 16
million cars and trucks a year in the United States, each of these changes
is small, but with billions of dollars flowing to new fuel-saving technology and research, there is hope that this is more than window dressing;
and in every community where a plant is saved, the impact is enormous.
Only time will tell whether a comprehensive change in strategy is truly
coming to Detroit.

We need more than promises. But should they succeed, the companies that gave us the Corvette, the Mustang, and the GTO will be part
of the new, clean-energy future. If they do not, other companies will.

Let's pull for the home team. It's a good play for Chevrolet.

## A Look down the Road

Many U.S. companies are now investing in worthwhile, incremental,
energy-saving changes, but the most we can get out of those changes is
a reduction in the use of gasoline, not the wholesale revolution required
for the 80 percent reduction in $CO_2$ emissions the planet needs to protect the climate. Where will the true revolution in cars and oil savings
come from?

In some cultures the future is predicted by reading sheep entrails. In others, palm reading will do. But if you want an exciting vision of the possible future of the car, a soft-spoken visionary in Snowmass, Colorado, named Amory Lovins is available to provide it.

Lovins is an engineer who has spent the last twenty years designing the future of energy, a future that is rapidly becoming reality. Founder of the Rocky Mountain Institute and the winner of a MacArthur Fellowship "genius" award, he is both a breaker of molds and a voice calling us to stretch our imaginations when it comes to cars.

He rages at the machine. His rage is justified, he says, because the technology of the car has made such modest improvement in one hundred years. "After more than a century of devoted engineering effort, today's cars use less than 1 percent of their fuel energy to move the driver. Only 13 percent of the fuel energy reaches the wheels, and just 6 percent accelerates the vehicle—95 percent of the weight it pushes is its own, not the driver's."[36]

Given these pathetically inefficient numbers, even the best modern car may be fairly considered an energy hog. If the aeronautics industry had advanced in airplanes at the same rate the auto industry has advanced in efficiency, we would still be flying propeller-driven biplanes. The comparison, though, is unfair. In truth, the auto industry has produced spectacular advances in technology over the last twenty years, improving performance about 2 percent per year.[37] The problem is that, until recently, almost none of those improvements were dedicated to improving energy efficiency, because they haven't had to be. Cars in America have become safer, they have become more powerful, they even made the huge technological leap forward of the cup holder, but they have not become more efficient.

It does not help to know that the modern car releases its own weight in carbon dioxide annually. It's not comforting to know that each day the average car consumes gasoline made from one hundred times its own weight in ancient plants. These facts portend great changes for the car of the future.

In improving efficiency, Lovins focuses on weight: "Two-thirds . . . of the fuel use is caused by the car's weight. . . . Obviously, then, the most powerful way to reduce fuel use and emissions of cars is to reduce their mass radically—say, by half."[38]

Steps in that direction are being taken in Glenwood Springs, Colorado, at the Fiberforge company—a spin-off of the Hypercar project—which was launched by Lovins to demonstrate the potential to profitably mass-produce cars that achieve radical increases in energy efficiency, Fiberforge is now building spare-tire wells and strut towers out of composite materials. These seem like small items, trinkets almost, but the advanced manufacturing techniques the people at Fiberforge have developed may allow the creation of a car with a 50 percent reduction of its present body weight without sacrificing strength or safety. When that happens, fuel efficiency could skyrocket.

High-tech composites are well known—they are used in everything from tennis rackets to the new Boeing 787. But industry has not focused until now on developing manufacturing techniques that get away from essentially doing the work of producing high-tech composites by hand. Fiberforge has patented a process to quicken the pace of production and radically reduce waste.

Fiberforge's system is a ways from application on major parts of the car body, but the potential in composite manufacturing techniques for strong lightweight cars is tremendous. Fiberforge's carbon-nylon composite is sixteen times stronger than stamped steel and four times as stiff but vastly lighter. It is no wonder that Fiberforge was in talks with one of the Big Three's competitors as of late 2006.

Revolutions sometimes happen overnight with a bang and sometimes take more time and develop quietly. The revolution in the weight and aerodynamics of the new car is of the second type, but its impact will be no less profound.

Engineers like Tadge Juechter, assistant chief engineer of Chevrolet, are excited about a slew of technologies coming on line to save weight throughout the car. "Polycarbonate glazing will be in production within ten years," Juechter says. "To an ice scraper or car wash it will look like glass, but you have a 50 percent weight reduction."[39] The weight of tires will also come down, with one company, Dymag, cutting their weight by 5 kgs, a savings that is magnified by 50 percent when the tire is rotating.[40]

A change in the shape of cars, too, is the shape of things to come. "The aerodynamics become a factor exponentially the faster you go," says Nissan's Richard Plavetich. The air is four times harder to push at 16 mph than at 8 mph. So we can look forward to cars that appear more upright and slender.[41]

Lovins's vision is a mix of obvious applications of existing technologies and some yet to be achieved. He sees the near-term path as a series of steps, each of which will significantly improve mileage per gallon of gas. No single step requires technology more than five years off; most are here today. When they are assembled, a stunning improvement in miles per gallon of gas is possible—decreasing oil use by a factor of ten. This vision mirrors the industry's own strategic plans in many respects and captures an emerging consensus on how we can break the grip of oil. Here it is:

- First, we broadly employ existing hybrid technology like that used in the Ford Escape, Toyota Prius, and Honda Civic. This can roughly double fuel economy nationally.

- Second, we deploy lighter and stronger carbon composite materials for car frames and bodies. This step cannot be guaranteed, as mass production of these materials is still in development; but the advances made in composites have been stunning in just the last ten years. The combination of reduced weight and reduced drag will again double mileage per gallon. At this point we have quadrupled gas mileage.

- Third, we install flex-fuel capability in hybrid engines, so that they can burn E85 (a blend of 85 percent ethanol and 15 percent gasoline) when the engine demands an assist from the internal combustion engine or the batteries are drained. This quadruples the mileage per gallon of oil, because at that point the car is running on either electricity or 85 percent biofuel.

. The best way to drastically increase the miles generated per gallon of gas in a car is to not burn gas in the first place.

• Fourth, we employ plug-in technology to radically increase the storage of electricity in the batteries and dramatically cut the use of fuel. This also allows the smart electrical grid to use the batteries as a storage reservoir for power.

When these steps are implemented together, the amount of gas required for an American car to go one mile will be reduced by 97 percent. This exercise demonstrates an amazing potential. It has been calculated that just running a plug-in hybrid on E85 ethanol could get an effective fuel economy approaching five hundred miles for every gallon of gas. Even a fraction of that savings could break our reliance on oil and radically improve our carbon footprint.

When all these pieces come together, the result will not be just a car, it will be an industrial revolution. For a moment, pause and consider what the world will look like in this scenario. Farmers will produce the new fuels for drivers to use in their tanks. Solar energy, wind energy, geothermal and tidal energy, and coal with sequestered carbon will produce the electricity that feeds into the batteries overnight. These will all be $CO_2$ free. Well-paid Americans will produce the composite bodies of the cars using advanced technology. A plug-in, flex-fuel, composite-body, hybrid car is the ultimate internal-combustion-engine car that not only will reorder our streets, but also will rebuild our nation's manufacturing and agricultural base.

These are not outlandish steps. Two of them—flex-fuel cars and hybrid cars—are already on the road in cars straight from the manufacturer. Plug-in hybrids are already being driven using modification kits. Only composites are not present in large quantities on the streets today, although the BMW M3 now sports a carbon fiber roof.

No one step in isolation will realize this potential. All of them cumulatively can.

Because the U.S. automobile fleet takes sixteen years to turn over, it is possible to envision a fleet that is entirely hybrid and flexible-fuel enabled, with half of those engines including plug-in capability, by 2027. Making just those two changes in the fleet would reduce projected national oil consumption of 21 million barrels per day by 12 million barrels, or over half, according to Anne Korin, a national security and energy expert.[42]

Korin notes that in the 1970s much of our electricity was generated by oil. After the oil shocks, we moved to alternatives, and now oil accounts for only 2 percent of electricity production. We've done it before, and we can do it again, this time in transportation. The job impacts would be significant, too, no less significant than the climate and security benefits. As Korin asks, "Do we think it's important that there be a U.S. auto industry? If we do, then we must ask how to help the industry help itself without breaking the bank. Plug-ins with flexible fuel are a very attractive option."[43]

Work remains to be done, of course, but the plug-in hybrid battery acceptable for mass production, the key step, is close. "The fundamental tool kit—the weight, volumetric efficiency, the demonstration of life in a lab basis, and safety through extensive testing—have all been demonstrated," says David Vieau, president and CEO of A123 Systems.[44] A123's battery is already powering hybrid plug-in conversions manufactured by the Hymotion Company in Ontario. Only time and scale are obstacles to full deployment of plug-ins. To fully integrate hundreds of individual lithium cells into a single cell takes time, but it has already been done by A123 in the nickel-metal hydride battery in use on GM's hybrids.

"Sure, we have $60 million in financing, but we are just small fry to GM," says Vieau. "It takes a while to get a big outfit like GM to really place a big bet on a new one like us. But we'll get there. This new contract we have with GM says we are the real deal."[45] When you have a battery three times as powerful as that used in the GM EV1 just eight years ago, good things happen.

Those good things are already being realized in California at the EnergyCS company, where they are converting hybrids into plug-ins to put cars on the road today that "really turn heads," as CEO Peter

Norman likes to say. "These batteries cost more than a normal hybrid, but I believe it's entirely realistic to project that economies of scale will get them down to only $1,500. Since your car will get 150 miles a gallon, you'll make that back over the life of the car in saved fuel costs—easy."[46]

If we're to realize that possibility, though, we need to do more than rely on voluntary technology changes by industry. Only by legislating guarantees that fuel is saved across our fleet will the cost and scale barriers be rapidly overcome to ensure that Americans receive the option of plug-in hybrids, new composite materials, and flex-fuel vehicles. We must change the policy incentives to change the market for a new generation of cars and fuels. The existing market, in which there is no cost for putting $CO_2$ out the tailpipe, simply does not require manufacturers to produce the cars needed to dramatically reduce emissions. Yet even if a cap-and-trade system is implemented to produce price signals on carbon, the transportation sector will need additional policies to drive higher efficiency and a new range of fuels, as the market has been remarkably inelastic, with surprisingly small responses to shifts in gas prices.

For years, Congress has snatched defeat from the jaws of victory by rejecting all meaningful efforts to achieve oil savings. The original CAFE standard requiring improved fuel economy required doubling mileage from 13.5 miles per gallon to 27.5 miles per gallon. As a result, our dependence on foreign oil dropped from 46.5 percent in 1977 to 27 percent in 1985. It happened for the same reason seat belts were installed, air bags were installed, and catalytic converters were installed—Congress mandated it. If we had continued making progress at the rate we were during the Carter administration, we would be free of oil imports from Saudi Arabia today.[47] Updating standards to guarantee greater oil savings and require less carbon in our fuels could drive the revolution in technology that is just waiting to be deployed.

With all this potential, our fleet of private vehicles today gets lower gas mileage than it did in 1982. During the time we invented the Internet, mapped the human genome, and saw into the farthest reaches of the universe, Congress did not move a muscle to break America's dependence on oil. As a result, we are stuck in the same mileage rut as when we used rotary dial phones and the closest thing to a cellular phone was Maxwell Smart's shoe phone. If today we show one tenth of the optimism and confidence John F. Kennedy showed in the 1960s, we can break our dependence on oil.

## Fuel Cells: Making Water—And Energy

One sunny day in January 2007, at the intersection of Capitol and C streets in Washington, D.C., a short, shiny, sexy little GM coupe sat at the curb and made history. It was the first plug-in hybrid car to be displayed for members of the U.S. House of Representatives. The crowd of congressmen, media types, and passersby ogled the little number with the excitement one would expect when the first car that could run 40 miles on an overnight charge, slash $CO_2$ emissions, and get 150 miles per gallon was available for inspection.

Then a curious thing happened. A Ford experimental SUV, powered by a fuel cell and also capable of being plugged in, drove by, with big letters on its side proclaiming its technology. The crowd instantly swung their heads around to follow that jazzy number down the street, and several folks headed that way to take a gander at the Ford version of the future. After all, here was another technology that could cut $CO_2$ emissions and move away from oil. The crowd was tugged in two directions, one toward the GM plug-in hybrid that could run on gas or ethanol as a backup fuel, and the other toward the Ford electric car that could also be plugged in but would use a fuel cell to "recharge."

The moment crystallized the emergence of a tantalizing question: Which breakthrough technology will rescue both the planet and the auto industry?

There are many who believe that the future is in fuel cells—though today that takes something of a leap of faith. J. Byron McCormick, who leads GM's efforts to develop a fuel-cell car, is one believer.

McCormick is inspired by the elegance of the fuel cell. It uses the energy of the universe's most abundant element, hydrogen, which constitutes 75 percent of all matter, silently combining two hydrogen atoms with one oxygen atom and in the process stripping off an electron, which then creates a current, to run an electric motor and perhaps power the GM cars of the future. The products of this reaction are electric power, water vapor, and heat. The only emission out of the tailpipe is water, purer than your grandmother's well water.

According to McCormick, the fuel-cell system is twice as powerful as battery-powered electric systems. It excites him for the same reason it was used on *Apollo*—it's a powerful way to store energy. But many challenges remain. "Storage is the big deal," McCormick says.[48] His team has to design a way to compress hydrogen into a space and configuration such that the car does not have to look like the Goodyear blimp to carry enough hydrogen for adequate range.

The fuel-cell effort, however, is a radical departure from GM's past. The company that fought CAFE standards and ceded the efficient car market to the Japanese now recognizes that there are 6 billion people with 750 million cars chasing a depleting pool of petroleum in a rapidly warming atmosphere. "It's not sustainable. We simply must mobilize our energy resources. We think the electrification of the car is the best way to do this," says McCormick.

There are substantial reasons to have doubts about the commercial viability of fuel cells. First, the estimated 50,000–90,000 service stations throughout America would have to be retrofitted with completely new pumps, a monumental task. Second, if hydrogen is produced off site, it will need to be delivered to the stations using new technology independent of existing oil delivery infrastructure. Estimates assume an infrastructure investment of approximately $500 billion. On-site production of hydrogen at the station helps avoid the cost of major investments in pipeline and tanker-truck infrastructure, but questions remain as to what original fuel could be used.

Despite these challenges, GM is serious when it discusses "electrification of the car." Its plug-in designs and its fuel-cell car will share one virtue: The only connection driving the wheels will be an electric motor.

The only new clean-car energy effort we have seen from the Bush administration, its discussion of the fuel-cell car, however, treats hydrogen as a near-term certainty. We cannot allow that illusion to become a diversionary tactic to stop meaningful requirements in improving fuel efficiency. Hybrids and biofuels are near to being ready today. While hydrogen may be the perfect fuel, many questions remain about its practical application, and its use as an excuse for inaction on fuel economy, hybrid development, or any other more current car technology would be an abomination. Forgoing development of the DC 3 in the 1940s in the hope a 747 could be perfected in the 1960s would have been a titanic national error. America cannot wait for hydrogen.

But McCormick's goal to have 100,000 fuel-cell cars on the road in 2015 can't be ruled out. It has investment and energy behind it. As he says, "Can we make it? Yes. Can we make it in time? I believe so." That sense that "failure is not an option"—and a bunch of duct tape—is what got the original *Apollo 13* astronauts home. It may just work for GM, but it won't be a simple trip.

So when will fuel cells become commercially viable? Here are three opinions from folks in the know:

- Lawrence Burns, vice president in charge of research at GM, says, "We are going to prove to ourselves and the world that a fuel-cell propulsion system can go head to head with the internal combustion engine," and he believes that by 2010 GM will likely have a fuel-cell car that has the same range and durability as an internal-combustion engine.[49]

- Ben Knight, vice president of research and development at Honda, says, "We see [fuel cells] right now as the most promising technology to lower greenhouse gas." He adds, however, that it is "too hard to put a date on" the beginning of large-scale production.[50]

- Joe Romm, assistant secretary of energy in the Clinton administration and author of *The Hype about Hydrogen*, says, "We're either talking several decades or never."[51]

This range of opinions may be the equivalent of opinions that were bandied about when the original car was being developed. Would diesels dominate? Would gas prove uneconomical? Was electric best? Perhaps the car just needs to be reinvented every century, and doubt and debate are as intrinsic to the automobile as a pair of dice hanging from the rearview mirror.

The challenges facing the development of fuel cells mirror those faced in building a biofuels economy, as we shall see, but fuel cells carry even greater technological uncertainty and greater investment challenges. In both cases, though, the most pressing problem is implementing a strategy of distributing the fuel. Large investments are being made in cellulosic ethanol, for example, but very little by oil companies in putting in E85 ethanol pumps. Large investments are being made by Honda and GM in the hydrogen car but little by the gas companies in designing a hydrogen distribution system. The chickens are doing all right; the eggs are lagging. Or is it vice versa? This is one reason the vision of the plug-in hybrid has proved so compelling, with its use of existing infrastructure to swap out electricity for liquid fuel. One way or another, here is a place where government has a pivotal role in creating the conditions for the necessary private partnerships to bloom.

But all of these low-carbon cars offer a future of transportation that is easy to love. After all, falling in love with cars—isn't that what Americans do best? What clean cars will we fall for tomorrow? The future remains to be invented.

## Becoming Mahatma

You must become the change you seek in the world.
—*Mahatma Gandhi*

Redmond, Washington, is one of the grayest, wettest, most soaked places in America. It is so wet that one time when Al Gore arrived in Seattle and asked a boy if it always rained in Washington, he received the reply, "I don't know, sir. I'm only eleven."

Mike Town is a teacher of environmental science at Redmond High School with a special passion for energy conservation, as he tells it, "ever since my brother and I couldn't run our paper route during the oil embargoes of the 1970s because we couldn't get gas for our old clunker. I had even built a passive solar house in 1992, and I thought I was doing pretty well. But then the kids got to me."[1]

The "kids" in Mike's classes had listened to him for years extolling the necessity of dealing with global warming and the virtues of renewable energy. They loved him and his classroom, bedecked by posters of America's wilderness areas. They loved his lectures about the virtues of renewable energy. They even clamored to see his passive solar house. But one day they broke him down and lit him up, all at once.

"I had been going on about how we just have to incorporate solar energy into our lives if we are going to stop ruinous global warming that will damage these areas we love. I knew this field, so I was cruising along feeling pretty good about my efforts, but then one kid brought up me up short. 'If solar electricity is so hot, why don't you put solar panels on your house, Mr. Town?' she said. 'You've been talking about this for two years . . . and I don't see you doing anything about it. Why not?'

"She had me. I realized right then that there was no way I could have integrity in teaching these kids to act if I was not going to. I had to put my money where my mouth was. I decided right there to build a solar-powered home, I didn't care how rainy it was."

So Mike went out and built a 1,600-square-foot home for himself and his wife in a nice spot—if you like a constant drizzly rain and low gray clouds scudding up to the Cascade Mountains. He epoxied strips of American-made Unisolar amorphous silicon solar cells onto the metal sheets of his roof in about two hours, hooked it up to an inverter, and turned on the lights.

And against the conventional wisdom, it worked. Ever since, his electricity costs have effectively been reduced to zero. His hundred square feet of solar cells, lying nicely on his southerly facing roof, produce a thousand kilowatt-hours per year of clean electricity, which results in a modest $10 to $20 monthly utility bill. That bill is netted to zero when he gets the credit for the net metered power he feeds back into the grid. He did have to pay for the purchase and installation of the system, a cost of about $5,000, but since he avoided putting in a furnace by using passive solar, he figures he saved an equivalent $5,000. He is able to keep a comfortable home with just a tiny propane heater when it gets cold.

Forget what you've heard about solar panels. If a teacher can light his home in one of the soggiest places on earth, imagine what can be done where the sun actually shines.

And forget what you've heard about the Kyoto emissions targets being too tough to reach. Mike has taken his commitment into his school, helping it meet the equivalent of its portion of the Kyoto target by changing the entire direction of the school's energy use. After swapping out its lighting, controlling the temperature of its rooms, and installing a high-performance, in-ground geothermal heat pump, Redmond High is a better-quality workplace and has reduced its $CO_2$ emissions 27 percent below Kyoto targets with ease. Now the high school in Microsoft's hometown will be a beacon for energy efficiency in schools, treating energy transformation as a natural extension of the innovation brought about through the software revolution.

We can't allow ourselves to be trapped in the tyranny of the present. Mike didn't, and now the future is on the rain-beaten roof of an inspirational teacher in Redmond.

Mike and Meg Town pose in front of their zero-energy solar home that feeds electricity back onto the grid. Clean solar energy is here today and working cost-effectively and reliably all across the country.

CHAPTER 3

# Waking Up to the New Solar Dawn

What happens to a dream deferred?
Does it dry up like a raisin in the sun?

—*Langston Hughes*

Solar power was once an American dream. But today as we wake to a new solar reality, the future is rising in the East. We're used to thinking of China as laggard when it comes to developing clean energy. But, while Chinese leaders may be behind the curve on civil rights, they have been forced to look over the horizon on energy. China's energy consumption is predicted to explode from 45 quadrillion Btus in 2003 to 139 quadrillion Btus by 2030. It is estimated that 64 percent (89 quadrillion Btus) of this energy in 2030 will be provided by carbon-emitting traditional coal plants.[1] The combination of rapid growth and polluting energy has left China with air so filthy that observers can no longer even see the Chinese flag when it is raised over Tiananmen Square on National Day. As one young American who tried to witness the event, Sara Wise, said, "Not only could we not see the flag, we couldn't even see the sun rise. We could only tell it was time for the flag raising by looking at our watches."[2]

In the face of this looming catastrophe, however, China has now acted in ways America has not. In early 2005 China passed landmark renewable energy legislation pledging to produce 10 percent of the country's total energy from renewable sources by 2020.[3] This legislation is set to create a huge market demand for renewable energy products, including solar technologies. China already has a burgeoning domestic solar industry, ready to compete for its market share.

In 2004 CLSA Asia-Pacific, a large Hong Kong–based global investment bank, said in its "Solar Power Sector Outlook," "Initially skeptical, we have become enthusiastic about solar power because it has realistic prospects for revenue to expand from U.S. $7 billion to U.S. $30 billion by 2020," while an industry report from the clean-tech research and publishing firm Clean Edge predicts growth to over $69.3 billion by 2016.[4]

Someone, some nation, will provide the Chinese with the ability to harness the sun. Bringing solar power to China may be the biggest potential market for American products since the entire world became a market for Coca-Cola. Americans invented the photovoltaic cell, but, just as solar is coming of age, America has lost its edge in the industry. In 1980 U.S. solar power manufacturers captured 80 percent of the world solar market; by 2005, American companies provided a paltry 9 percent of that market even as the industry grew.[5] We have lost the lead in an industry whose technology we invented. But the game is far from over.

We can recapture the future of solar energy, according to a soft-spoken physicist named Richard Blieden. Dr. Blieden began his quest for the secret of economical solar power in the early 1970s. He has never stopped. Now, after decades of effort, his dream is on the cusp of becoming a reality. When it does, America will experience a burst of growth in its export of solar technology that will rival its growth in aerospace exports.

Blieden was director of the Office of Solar Electric Applications at the Energy Research and Development Administration in the mid-1970s. At the time, hopes were high that this new technology could free us from the restraints of fossil fuels. Solar panels went up on the White House roof, and research budgets went up in federal labs. But to become competitive, solar costs would have had to come down by a factor of three hundred. The industry soldiered on, however, and from 1974 to 1984 solar panel production went from 1.3 million to 17.2 million square feet.[6] Bleiden left government and joined the industry, and both federal researchers and his team at Arco Solar knew there was too much energy to ignore and too many innovative Americans capable of improving the technology.

Then it all came crashing down. Ronald Reagan had different ideas. The solar panels came off the White House roof and went into storage in a General Services Administration warehouse in Franconia, Virginia. Research budgets were slashed. As far as the federal government was concerned, the dream of solar energy was put under the shadow of official neglect.

But Dr. Blieden did not allow his dream to die. He has led efforts to develop solar cells at a series of progressively more successful companies, always getting closer to the tangible goal of making solar-generated electricity at the same cost as other electricity. His efforts and those of his colleagues have continually increased the efficiency of solar power and lowered its costs, from about $2 per kilowatt-hour in the 1970s to $0.18 to $0.23 per kilowatt-hour in 2006.[7] The cost is now about the same as peak-power costs in expensive markets like California and cheaper than grid-based power in Hawaii. That steady if unspectacular improvement has justified Dr. Blieden's underlying confidence that as the volume of solar power increased, costs would decline too due to economies of scale and technological improvement. Tom Woodward of the San Francisco energy technology investment firm Nth Power says, "Basically every three years, the overall solar industry volume doubles, and for every doubling of volume you reduce costs 18 percent."[8]

Now Dr. Blieden is a leader with United Solar Ovonic, the largest manufacturer of amorphous silicon solar cells in the nation. He loves his cells. "You can shoot a bullet through them and cut them up, and they will still work. They are tough as nails. They are less expensive because they use less silicon. They work well in cloudy conditions. They are very, very, effective," he says.[9]

Blieden's cells can now be seen on the roofs of large elementary schools in California and small houses in Australia. But most impressively, they are about to blossom in a place formerly known for its demand for rice: China. "We see real prospects in China," he says, with more than a bit of understatement.

As we shall see, American solar is emerging as big business and appears poised for dramatic changes in cost structure and commercial availability. It is just in time, not just because of pressing environmental needs, but also in order to preserve our international competitiveness. We're in a war. Not the one in Iraq, which is ultimately a diversion from our deeper energy and security challenges, but in China, to supply its vast and expanding energy needs, and elsewhere, to supply clean energy to the exploding markets around the world. To win that war, we'll have to think long term. We'll need to seek more than short-term market share and gain a deeper understanding of tomorrow's possibilities.

## Can We Do It?

A significant reason for optimism is the embrace of solar by American businesses—not just as generators, but also as consumers. If you were to do a flyover of the largest companies in the nation, you would be struck by the number—including Ford, Pepsi, Whole Foods, FedEx, Google, and Toyota—that now sport shiny roofs providing those businesses with reliable, low-maintenance electricity. Without any apparent sense of irony, BP is installing solar roofs on its service stations to power its gasoline pumps. The low maintenance cost of solar can be demonstrated by the fact that the nation's first three-hundred-kilowatt roof installation, built at Georgetown University in Washington, D.C., in 1975, is still going strong, pumping out clean energy. While detractors point out that solar is cost effective in few places as yet, it is nevertheless growing at the rate of 20–25 percent annually in the developed world,[10] and it is increasingly economical when compared to the cost of peak electric power as global demand pushes natural gas prices ever higher—not to mention the public benefits of increasing the stability of the electric grid.

In Silicon Valley there is a group of men who are working to change the economics of solar for good. They are what we can call the "Thin Men," named after a combination of that thirties mystery classic and the thin-film solar cells they are cooking up in their labs. The Thin Men are rushing to perfect both a new type of solar cell and its manufacturing process, which may be the final step in the long journey of getting solar energy to cost-effectiveness. The development of solar electricity has been akin to the production of the solar cells themselves, with layer upon layer of new technologies being built upon the previous incarnation of the photovoltaic cell, just as layer upon layer of silicon is bonded to its substrate to form the cake-like solar cell.

Ultimately, solar cells convert electricity in a process we could consider to be the human equivalent of photosynthesis, used to great effect by the potato to convert sunlight into carbohydrates and by sugarcane to build sugar. Humankind's solar technique is to use sunlight to generate a stream of electrons in the elements of a photovoltaic cell via the power of physics, thereby creating an electric current. The human method of converting sunlight to usable energy does not involve the chemistry of sugars, like the plant method, but the perfectly clean electricity it creates is just as sweet.

The Thin Men were born out of the intellectual ferment of Silicon Valley in the year 2006. The goal of creating a cost-effective solar cell is the same for all the Thin Men, but their concepts of how to do it are as distinctive as their fingerprints.

Martin Roscheisen and Brian Sager are the founders of Nanosolar, a Palo Alto firm now ready to build the largest thin-film manufacturing plant in the world. Their brilliance lies not in the large size of their plant, however, but in the thinness of their film and their magnificently low expected manufacturing cost. The cost is so low that their plant could be producing grid-competitive electricity in a matter of a few years.

The pedigree of these two inventors describes the perfect arc of innovation. In 2000, Roscheisen was a Silicon Valley whiz kid who founded and eventually sold three software companies that had netted over a billion dollars for his investors. Sager, a biologist by training, had done well in several biotech start-ups. They were both looking for the next great adventure and jointly decided to seek the largest convention-shattering and world-changing technology they could possibly find: solar energy.

It may seem surprising, but Roscheisen describes solar energy as "old technology." In the time frame of the Silicon Valley entrepreneur, the thirty-five years that solar cells have kicked around in labs world-wide, enjoying marginal improvements every year, make them seem like ancient science to these two men in their thirties who have been accustomed to changing the world. So they started from scratch, on a quest to determine how they could kick-start a whole new system in solar cell manufacturing. Given that they had precisely zero experience in the solar energy industry, this was an ambitious effort, bordering on hubris. They were cagey, too, originally naming their company Nano-dyne to hide their intention to build a nanotechnology solar cell.

According to Roscheisen, their inexperience is exactly what allowed them the intellectual freedom to break from the history of what they considered failures in solar energy. What they saw when they reviewed the literature of solar energy was an unbroken chain of efforts to make solar cells more productive. For over three decades, developers had been struggling to squeeze more electricity out of each square meter of solar cell, pouring their creative talents into making tiny, marginal improvements in the efficiency of the cells and never achieving anything close to a breakthrough. Every few years, they wrestled another fraction of a percent of the hundred watts per square meter of sunlight falling on the earth into usable electricity, but they never developed a commercially competitive solar cell because they never significantly reduced the manufacturing costs of the cells.

Roscheisen and Sager decided to turn that whole strategy upside down. Unfettered by decades in the business, they decided the real key to success in solar was to radically reduce the cost of manufacturing the cells. So they set off on an adventure in designing the cheapest method in the world to build a thin-film solar cell. Now they are constructing the world's first plant in Palo Alto to do just that.

Roscheisen and Sager describe themselves as having a wholly new assumption set in tackling this problem. They found that the fundamental roadblock to achieving cost-effectiveness was the incredibly lethargic "throughput" of the solar cell manufacturing process. Simply put, it took way too long to construct a solar cell. Roscheisen and Sager quickly realized that as long as that glacial pace was the standard in the industry, solar energy would remain the province of consumers who buy just to *be* green rather than those who buy to save green.

So they developed a complex manufacturing process that can produce a hundred feet of continuously rolled solar cell per minute, an improvement that, as it moves to commercial scale, should make solar cell–produced electricity as cheap as that taken off the grid today. Speed doesn't necessarily kill; in this case, it brings a whole new industry to life.

Roscheisen and Sager also decided to abandon what they considered to be a historical accident that had seriously delayed growth of the industry. That accident was the choice of silicon as the basic material to build the cell. Silicon is brittle, expensive to handle, and not particularly productive of energy, but it was the material we knew how to use to make semiconductors, which is what solar cells really are. These Thin Men saw beyond that technology and made several bold steps to use an entirely new material, CIGS, a combination of four elements—copper, indium, gallium, and selenium—with properties better suited to their mass production goals.

First, they mastered the fine art of using nanotechnology to assemble the CIGS particles in the precise ratios of the constituent metals that must be maintained to ensure the efficiency of the thin cell. This is magical, of course, since the process involves manipulating particles that are one-billionth of a meter in diameter. This feat is accomplished in part because of the characteristics of these particles to "self assemble." Their ability to improve a solar cell comes in part because at these minute dimensions there is a spectacular increase in surface area of the particles as a ratio to their volume. This vastly increases their effectiveness in turning sunlight into excited electrons.

The problem of how to manipulate these tiny items has bedeviled those who faced it before, but the Nanosolar team designed ways to manipulate the particles into the exact alignment demanded by the physics of the cell. When asked who thought they were nuts to try such an audacious act, Sager replied, "Anybody who knew anything about nanotechnology in the year 2000."[11]

Second, the Nanosolar group perfected a means of using existing printing technology to essentially spray the CIGS material onto a proprietary metal alloy of very light weight in a continuous process, improving the throughput of the cells by a factor of up to 100. Roscheisen contrasts this printing process with what he considers a much more challenging and difficult-to-perfect process being developed by the Miasolé Company, of sputtering the CIGS material onto the substrate using magnetic fields. All inventors love their tools. The Wright Brothers loved their wind tunnel. Roscheisen loves his tools for printing CIGS. The exact ratios of the CIGS particles are premixed before their application onto the metal sheet, making the printing much more controllable, he believes. The payoff could be remarkable. When completed, the Nanosolar cell will return the energy required to make it in three weeks. The current cell takes three years.

Asked why they were willing to take such a different approach than their predecessors in the field, Roscheisen says simply, "They were academicians; we were businessmen. To us, cost was everything."[12] That willingness to break with hoary old practices was one reason the two founders of Google, Sergey Brin and Larry Page, wrote the first two checks to get Nanosolar started. If Roscheisen and Sager succeed, this will surely be a case where the openness of the inexperienced mind has trumped the single-mindedness of experience.

When asked his motivation for tackling such a tough technological mountain to climb, Roscheisen's answer is quick, direct, and telling. "I have made money—and I admit it's a good thing—but I want to change the world," he says. "I want to have a positive impact. We can harvest energy in a way that is totally benign, from our sunlight. I intend to have a positive impact on a fundamental problem with a small amount of capital in a short period of time."

Competition stimulates innovation, and another Thin Man, Dave Pearce, has developed an entirely different way of manufacturing a thin-cell photovoltaic. His company, Miasolé, uses a magnetic field to control the disposition of the CIGS material onto the surface of the cell. Which Thin Man's technology will grab the brass ring and dominate the new world of solar energy, the sputtering process of Dave Pearce and Miasolé or the nanotechnology of Roscheisen and Sager? Only time will tell, but in either case, the world may finally see the quantum advance that will bring the sun down to earth and harness its power by transforming it into energy.

Dave Pearce's eyes are on the East, where China offers a five-year holiday from taxes to lure companies like his into its market, and on the West, where Germany offers 50 percent outright grants to new photovoltaic plants and strong incentives for consumers to install solar panels and feed that energy back into the grid. Such policies have caused a boom in solar growth in a country with a solar potential far less than our own, and have allowed Germany to dominate the world market, accounting for 55 percent of all installed solar photovoltaic capacity.[13] Japan, also benefiting from strong government policies, leads the world in solar photovoltaic manufacturing, with 39 percent of the market share. This is a sad state of affairs for America, and for potential manufacturing jobs, since the basic science of photovoltaics was invented here.[14]

So Pearce now asks the obvious question: Where is the American government as Germany, Japan, and China soak up the talent and investment to maximize this vast economic potential? The sad answer is that Congress is in the thrall of old energy industries. Federal research in solar power is now one-fourth what it was, adjusted for inflation, in 1975. In contrast, in the same time span, medical research has quadrupled (to $28 billion) and military R&D has gone up 260 percent (to $75 billion).[15] But the government has invested heavily in fossil fuels, handing out $7 billion in tax breaks to oil and gas just in 2006. Pearce makes a simple request: Can't the U.S. Congress extend the Investment Tax Credit to the manufacture of solar cells, a boost that could cement thousands of those jobs in America instead of in China and Germany? Even better, why couldn't Congress impose a $CO_2$ cap-and-trade system to level the playing field with fossil fuels, a development that would recognize the economic value of clean energy and could immediately make solar power competitive, even with a fraction of the improvements Pearce expects to achieve?

We have a long road to travel. In 2005, Japan made 824, Europe 515, and the United States 155 megawatts of solar electricity.[16] That is what 1960s politicians might call a "solar gap," and it is a direct result of the failure of Congress to assist in the development of this emerging industry in ways the Japanese and German governments have done so effectively.

## Unexpected Sources of Innovation

Ironically, we are even further behind in adopting these new technologies than much of the developing world, where having light of any kind, from any source, is a life-changing event. It is easy to forget that two billion people on this planet live in "energy poverty," without steady access to reliable energy.[17] Far from being on the electric grid, two billion people have to either burn kerosene in their lamps and use dung or scavenged biomass for fuel, or go without light and heat in the darkness, as deserts expand when robbed of plant matter. The scope of this tragedy is both hard to imagine from a perch in the developed world, and a hard and stunning fact that must be addressed.

For those two billion people, finding locally produced electricity means the difference between the light of day and the dark of night. For the past decade or so, there has been a strong demand for solar energy in the developing world because those people face a situation where the cost of grid-based power is infinite and the supply is zero. As a result, around 70 percent of U.S. solar cell production is exported, mostly to developing countries.[18] Here is a situation where the demands of the low-tech world have served as the foundation for growth of a high-tech industry.

The joy of light is sure to drive a continued wave of solar across the developing world. According to Neville Williams, the man most responsible for the spread of solar lighting in India, China, and the Congo, it is a rapturous sight to see a young mother in a rural village in India who has clean, safe lighting in her kitchen, free from the hazards and odor of kerosene, for the first time in her life.[19] Williams should know, because he is directly responsible for the founding of the Solar Electric Light Fund (SELF), a nonprofit international agency that has had the delightful honor of bringing solar-powered lighting and cooking to millions of families in the developing world in the last twenty years. The photos in Williams's journal include repeated shots showing the joy of rural villagers posed in their kitchens and doorways, as the first clean light produced by solar power shines on their families. In this way, perhaps solar power in a rural village can be considered a dual power generator, first from the solar cell, and second from the incandescent smiles of people enjoying new access to opportunity.

Williams's journey to spread solar in the developing world may make him the solar equivalent of Johnny Appleseed. He thinks he's just a "normal chap." But if you ask the locals of the settlement of Morapatawa, in the northwest corner of Sri Lanka, where he helped establish a co-op that brought power to a group of cashew growers at the end of a five-kilometer dirt track, he is a blooming genius.

## Getting to Work

Still another approach has been taken by Andrew Beebe and Bill Gross of EI Solutions. They are not focused on the Hail Mary pass into the end zone to get the big clean-energy play from thin film. EI (for Energy Innovations) has focused on its rushing game instead, making steady incremental gains to bring about more efficient power. Its strategy is bearing fruit. Recently, the firm installed the largest commercial solar installation in the country, the second largest in the world. Nearly 200,000 square feet of solar panels now cover four acres at the headquarters of Google in Silicon Valley. At 1.6 megawatts, the array covers everything from the roofs of six buildings on Google's campus to two canopies in the car parks, producing over 2.5 million kilowatt-hours annually for a cost savings of nearly $400,000 each year.[20] That's money that would otherwise be spent on fossil energy. Instead of producing pollution, this installation actually cuts greenhouse gas emissions by 3.6 million pounds each year for the twenty-five-year life of the installation. That is the yearly carbon equivalent of driving a car over 4.25 million miles, reduced through that one installation.[21]

Google's motivation for investing in EI's product is the desire to be good global citizens and get ahead of impending carbon constraints that the company believes are coming at a global level. But the company also will see a financial return. Google's estimated payback will be seven or eight years for a product with a life of twenty-five years. That gives eighteen years of a steady revenue stream of hundreds of thousands of dollars in saved energy generated each year, real power with substantial value. What's more, if you believe power prices are going to go up, the value proposition of solar is even greater, as Google's energy bills will remain stable and predictable. After all, the cost of solar is fixed at the installation; solar requires little maintenance and its fuel is free. The global demand for panels today is so tight, with the exploding growth in the industry, that there is even a secondary market for used panels developing, so the installation truly is a no-regrets affair.

The five-year-old EI has made its technology work by using the same technique the humble sunflower uses. The sunflower turns its head and tracks the path of the sun across the sky throughout the day. Beebe and Gross's solar cells do the same, using a handy piece of technology that tracks the sun on two axes and concentrates its rays on a small area of solar panels, allowing the company to use radically smaller amounts of material to make the same amount of power. Their equivalent of the sunflower uses lenses pointed directly at the sun to bend the light and concentrate it into a one-centimeter square of panel, reducing the number of cells needed, so the cost of cells is driven down to about 10 percent of the cost of the unit. This allows EI to get effective efficiencies of 38 percent from its cells using gallium arsenide panels made by a division of Boeing called Spectra Lab. As good a number as that is, Beebe believes that area efficiency is a red herring because what the customer really cares about is the cost per kilowatt-hour. People want a cost-effective solution, and they are helping to deliver one.

Currently, in California corporate power rates are high, averaging about $.13 a kilowatt-hour. Using the EI "sunflower" without any policy incentives today costs about $.18, but that cost is driven down to $.09 with the benefit of the California solar program—a pretty good deal, and a price that will never rise. EI's business model, however, is not to rely on subsidies for the long haul. It sees policies like financial incentives for installation as a critical first step in creating the market, but it wants policies that make those benefits decline over time as solar reaches its potential as a major source of energy.

Beebe and Gross are excited not just about the technology or about delivering zero-carbon solutions to their clients. They are also inspired by the jobs they are creating. Besides the fifty people in their company who do the work, there are one hundred people who performed the installation at Google from three different trades over three months.

In many places the International Brotherhood of Electrical Workers (IBEW), the chief electricians' union, now offers training in solar installation as part of its apprenticeship programs. The growing demand is also creating manufacturing jobs that can provide products for export, boosting demand for skilled labor as demand for solar grows. One of the largest U.S. plants is owned by Sharp Solar in Tennessee, and it has grown along with the booming market, creating hundreds more jobs for IBEW workers.

For the near term, Beebe believes it is essential to extend and deepen the federal tax credit for solar to help grow the market. Right now the solar market is concentrated in California and New Jersey, where electricity supplies are constrained and solar programs are generous. But the renewables space is a crazy quilt of utility-based and state-based policies and incentives. A federal approach is a no-brainer for bringing the utility industry seriously into renewable generation.

Sometimes the most important thing is just getting things built. That is exactly what this fast-out-of-the-gate company is doing.

## Putting the Sizzle in the Solar Steak

One day in July 2006, Mrs. Alicia Resch, a resident of Washington, D.C., went shopping for something she had never bought before, a solar roof. Purchasing something so exotic and foreign would seem a daunting challenge, but Mrs. Resch has the advantage of being married to Rhone Resch, director of SEIA, the Solar Energy Industries Association. So Mrs. Resch, even though she was a first-time buyer, was well armed with facts and figures about the attributes of all the competing technologies in the marketplace. Since Mr. Resch was duty bound to be scrupulously fair to all his organization's members, she could be assured of getting the straight scoop.

The decision on which type of panels to purchase was not just a matter of comparing the specifications of the panels; there was also the matter of aesthetic appeal. The Resches had looked at several home installations, and Mrs. Resch had a clear favorite. It was the shiniest, blackest, sleekest, flattest, most stylistically modern panel she could find, made by the SunPower Corporation of San Jose, California.

So the sale was made, just the way most car deals are closed in America: based, in part, on how the machine looks, what image it projects, and how it makes the customer feel. The Corvette did not dominate the minds of teenagers in the sixties based on its statistical attributes. Now solar cell technology purchases will be based in part on their style and image. This is a lesson that should keep solar geeks from assuming that the industry will blossom based just on good numbers.

The SunPower cell is also one of the most efficient cells now in the retail market, achieving efficiencies of over 20 percent,[22] a huge improvement over cells that typically run at 14–15 percent. So now the

Resches pay for their roof panels by incorporating the cost of $50 per month into their mortgage, while their average utility bill has gone down $100 each month. Plus, they have the thrill of watching their meter run backward, as they feed excess power into the grid much of the time. This is possible because the District of Columbia allows "net metering," meaning consumers offset their use of electricity from the grid against their contribution of excess energy to the grid. Consumers' meters, therefore, literally run backward when they are producing more electricity than they are using. In addition, the District of Columbia provides a 50 percent capital grant to solar consumers.

More fundamentally, the Resches' installation was made possible by the genius and perseverance of a former Stanford professor, Dr. Richard Swanson, the founder of the SunPower Corporation, which was to become, in the words of one observer, the BMW of the solar cell industry. How Swanson and his team built one of the most efficient and aesthetically pleasing solar panels is the story of a solar pioneer with a very different strategy from those of the companies we have met before.

When Dr. Swanson left Stanford and formed his company in 1985, he was determined to build a solar cell with radically improved efficiency. As time went on, he not only increased efficiency by about 60 percent but also brought down costs significantly.

When asked what his "secret sauce" is, he laughs, because he wishes there were just one. What he and his original team of thirty scientists found was that multiple improvements were necessary. They had to find a way to locate the ugly metal electrodes only on the bottom of the cell; they had to change the refraction characteristics so that light not absorbed by the panel got reflected and could be absorbed somewhere else; they had to figure out how to roughen the surface of the cell to increase absorption. He calls this process "total internal absorption," which sounds like a type of Zen meditation but is the prescription for wringing the most out of every photon of light and, not coincidentally, for building the fastest-growing tech company in America. The firm produces one hundred megawatts of power a year, with $680 million cash on hand, and is listed as *the* blue chip stock in the solar energy field, one that Wall Street analysts feel has to be in any renewable energy portfolio.[23]

SunPower's products are truly flying high, not just figuratively but literally, since their high-efficiency solar cells powered the *Helios* solar airplane to 94,000 feet fueled completely by the sun. Swanson has certainly done better than Icarus.

But you ain't seen nothin' yet. The company plans on tripling its production in the next two years and thereafter. It plans on building multiple manufacturing sites for its panels around the world, because being close to its markets makes sense economically. It has a 14 percent market share in just its third year of production.[24]

Could SunPower be the Microsoft of solar energy? We do not know, but we do know that its success is dramatic enough to warrant listening to the lessons Swanson has learned:

- First, in the field of solar energy, like life, perseverance pays. SunPower had to go through five rounds of layoffs to get to its current position.

- Second, it pays to strike alliances. SunPower really became competitive on a cost basis only when it teamed with the Cypress Company, a semiconductor manufacturer, and obtained the Cypress manufacturing skill set in working with silicon, which allowed a radical reduction in SunPower's manufacturing costs.

- Third, diversification will pay off in the field of renewables, just as it does in investing. Swanson sees the need for a variety of solar cells for a variety of applications. For rooftops, for example, where space is at a premium, his product is ideal due to its high efficiency and consequent ability to use less space. But it may not have the cheapest cost when new thin-film products come on line or when other manufacturing or design breakthroughs drive down prices. So in applications where space is not at a premium, like industrial solar plants with huge arrays of cells across acres of ground, cheaper panels may be best even if they never get beyond 14 percent efficiency. In Swanson's future, not all solar cells are created equal, but all are useful—all have a place.

In fact, he is almost lyrical in describing what he sees as the elegance of having so many choices in renewable energy. "The beauty of renewables is their diversity," he says, "and this makes up a wonderful ecosystem of energy. Once people have a deep understanding of this, the world will change in ways people will embrace quickly."[25]

Swanson recognizes that his product still is not at grid parity in cost, but he believes it is reasonable to believe it will be in five years or so. He sees efficiencies of 25 percent as a realistic goal for silicon-based cells—a 25 percent improvement over today's number—coupled with 40 percent improvements in manufacturing costs just from economies of scale, and both contributing to make his product competitive with the grid.

Other competitors are in the hunt as well. RoseStreet Labs Energy (RSL), of Phoenix, is preparing to commercialize a next-generation technology that will use the full spectrum of light to produce a cell that can perhaps achieve efficiencies of 48 percent.[26] Current cells use only a fairly narrow part of the broad spectrum of frequencies that make up a ray of sunlight. Should RSL succeed in using the whole band, it would be the equivalent of doubling the available energy from a given photon of light.

## One Million Rooftops

Our rooftops may become our Saudi Arabia of solar energy. Even using today's panels, America could produce its entire electrical load via our available rooftops. We do not need a hundred-square-mile plot of desert with wall-to-wall solar panels. Our rooftops will do nicely. It is more efficient, in any event, for our energy to be generated in a distributed fashion, in a multitude of places, to avoid the costs and inefficiencies of lengthy transmission systems; an average of 7 percent of the energy is lost in transmission.[27]

Neither will we all have to pick up and follow the Beverly Hillbillies to California to be able to enjoy the fruits of solar energy. While Washington, D.C., has 1,600 kilowatt-hours of potential solar energy per year (the number of hours the sun can produce 1 kilowatt of electricity), Seattle, Washington, gets 1,300—not that much of a difference. Things do get dicey when one reaches Barrow, Alaska, of course, where the sun does not shine for several months of the year, but even in Arctic Village, Alaska, a remote outpost two hundred miles north of the arctic circle, the locals have put solar panels on top of their community washhouse to run the washers and dryers. They understand that global warming is melting the tundra on which their houses are built, so even in the far north they are doing their part.

The possibilities are enhanced when tracking systems are used to follow the sun across the sky. In 2006, the city of Chico, California, enjoyed its first year of successful operation of a 1.1-megawatt solar-tracking power plant, now powering the city's wastewater treatment plant with clean, renewable energy. Tracking systems can obtain 7 to 20 percent greater efficiency by capturing the full power of the sun's rays as it courses through its heavenly arc. Chico has done that while also preventing the release of 1.6 million pounds of $CO_2$ per year.[28]

So in the near term, solar is booming, as both a boost for consumers and a shot in the arm for the economy. The number of people now working in the solar industry, estimated to be 20,000, is expected to double in the next several years. The market for solar is predicted to grow from a $15.6 billion industry in 2006 to a $69.3 billion industry by 2016.[29] It is a great sign for the industry that the biggest cloud on the horizon is a shortage of silicon.

It is a boom time. The American solar industry has been growing at rates of about 20–40 percent a year for the last several years. By the end of 2005, nationwide solar photovoltaic capacity was 425 megawatts.[30] Whereas twelve hundred people attended the national solar conference in 2005, seven thousand journeyed to San Jose for the conference in 2006, including that famous solar fan, Governor Arnold Schwarzenegger.

## The Rise of Solar Thermal

Photovoltaic panels that make electricity from sunlight are not the only strategy the human mind has created to bend the sun to our purposes. A whole different technology called solar thermal is now ready to take off. This technology concentrates the sun's rays onto a molten metallic substance whose heat is used to create massive amounts of steam, which can power an electricity-generating turbine.

This vision is now turning into glass and steel in the desert of Nevada, where Solargenix Energy is building a sixty-four-megawatt solar thermal electricity–generating plant using parabolic trough technology. This technology uses parabolic mirrors arranged in long troughs to generate heat that eventually spins a turbine. It will result in the largest solar power plant built in the past fourteen years, the third-largest solar plant in the world. Solargenix believes there is a realistic opportunity to produce power at grid parity costs in several years using its new system. If that happens, Nevada may benefit from a total of 7,000 jobs resulting from the construction of facilities to generate a thousand megawatts of clean power in the state with the creation of nearly five hundred permanent jobs.[31]

Another approach is under way in California, where the utility Pacific Gas & Electric (PG&E) has entered into a contract with the LUZ II company to buy five hundred megawatts, enough to power 350,000 customers, produced by a hybrid solar-and-gas system.[32] The system uses a solar concentrator to drive a turbine during the day and a co-located gas turbine generator to produce electricity at night. Some predict that this type of system may be the "sleeper" solar technology, because having a solar plant and a gas plant "share" a turbine allows a significant reduction in costs. Akin to the way cogeneration steam plants work, this twinning of productive capacity can radically improve the cost-effectiveness of these systems and transform solar energy into

The Ausra solar thermal system produces one megawatt of electricity from every two acres of mirrors. (Ausra, Inc.)

reliable base-load power while slashing carbon emissions. As a bonus, because these plants heat molten metal to temperatures of 1050°F, they can generate electricity even after the sun goes down.

The advantages of this system have caught the eye of one of America's brightest lights, Vinod Khosla, who purchased the Australian company Solar Heat and Power in February 2007 and is setting up its new operations in the United States under the name Ausra. This technology may yield electricity in the $.08-per-kilowatt range, a spectacular price, making it competitive with grid base load in most of the United States. The company already has contracts for several plants in California and Arizona. Clean, cheap solar energy promises to bring new opportunities to all corners of this planet while giving it a few more years of health.

## Here Comes the Sun: A Realistic View

Is solar for real, finally?

One veteran of the renewable energy world, Scott Sklar, speaks of the future of solar with the calm wisdom of an old salt. Sklar, president

of the Stella Group, a renewable energy consulting firm, has been helping to develop renewable companies for decades, believing that their
time would come. His views are as mature as his big gray beard, since he
has worked in virtually all of the renewable fields. He says that, indeed,
the time for solar has arrived. He holds this view not necessarily due to
whiz-bang new giant leaps in the basic science of solar, but due to the
inexorable march of improved efficiencies throughout the solar world.
He points out that the cost of the solar cell itself is only 40 percent of
the total cost of residential solar power, so improvements in all the infrastructure required—including the panel mounts, the inverter, and other
accoutrements—can bring down the total cost.[33] Those "connectors"
will become more efficient, Sklar says, just from economies of scale, and
in some cases they will be eliminated as solar becomes integrated right
into building materials.

When that happens, and a home builder sees the same price for
grid-based power as for putting in solar cells integrated with the shingles, solar's percentage of our electricity will be limited only by the rate
at which old capital investments can be replaced by the new. We cannot
expect all Americans to rush out and put up solar cells, but it is reasonable to believe that in the very near future, a substantial portion of new
construction will include solar. Utilities will reduce their projections for
grid-based capacity accordingly. Sklar believes that solar's costs will
come down by half in the next decade because of these efficiencies and
market trends alone.

It is Sklar's prediction, therefore, that 5–7 percent of our nation's
new electric power will come from solar in the next twenty-five years
and a total of 25–33 percent from renewables as a whole.[34] All bets are
off, according to Sklar, however, when the fossil fuels industry finally has
to pay for the right to release carbon into the air. When that happens,
he believes, solar will be at parity with the grid in a matter of years, not
decades.

As the result of persistence and plenty of American ingenuity, solar
energy, which for too many years progressed at a crawl, is now ready to

walk. Soon, driven by smart policies and global demand, it could be at an all-out run. Then we can be reminded of Benjamin Franklin's comment when he heard an observer of the first manned balloon flight state that such a contraption had no "purpose"; Franklin retorted, "And what are the uses of a baby?"

## When Energy Markets Go Wrong: Surviving Enron

*Jay Inslee*

It took a while, but the truth finally dawned on me: Enron owned
the White House. One would think I would have figured that out
earlier. After all, the White House had refused to help solve the western energy crisis, even though electricity prices had gone up sometimes 1,000 percent in my congressional district in Washington State.
This had happened because Enron and its fellows had figured out a
way to constrict the supply of electricity in the West, both by literally
turning off generators and by creating transmission bottlenecks that
produced artificial shortages. The fine folks at Enron were later
caught on tape describing their plans under such colorful names as
"Death Star" and "Throw Momma from the Train." I had fought for
a year with every tool at my disposal to get the Bush administration
to rein in Enron, to no avail. Obviously, Enron had some sway over
them.

But it took a meeting with Dick Cheney to realize how malig-
nant that conspiracy of inaction was.

That morning, a bipartisan group of congressmen were to meet
with the vice president in HC-5, one of the general-purpose meeting rooms in the basement of the Capitol Building. It was my first
meeting with Mr. Cheney, and an important one, since we were there
to try to talk him into lifting a finger, any finger, to stop Enron from
bleeding our constituents dry.

On walking into the room, my first impression was that Mr.
Cheney was on time and I was not. I felt a little embarrassed
but quickly recovered when I remembered that he had kept my

constituents waiting for about four months already in trying to get relief from Enron's gouging.

After Mr. Cheney had shaken hands with the twenty assembled members of Congress and engaged in the usual pleasantries, we got down to the business at hand. Several members gently described the dire circumstances caused by the 1,000 percent increases in the spot power market—for example, the elderly having to go without heat during power shortages and the stoplights going out in California. These were down-home stories that one would think would appeal to a man who once served as the congressman from Wyoming.

It quickly became apparent, however, that the stories of suffering had about as much effect in melting the vice president's heart as the arctic blasts that scour the high plains of Wyoming have on the frozen ice fields of the Grand Teton Mountain. He wasn't merely unmoved, he was so unresponsive and callously indifferent that I half expected him to say, "Let them eat Sterno."

So I decided to take a more economically demonstrable approach, using facts and figures. Surely, facts and figures would appeal to this former CEO of Halliburton. I launched into the facts regarding the energy market. The markets had never experienced such volatility. The price explosions were unprecedented. Fully 32 percent of the generators in the western market were turned off, creating huge price hikes, when typically only 2 percent were down for maintenance at any one time. I told him only one conclusion could be drawn from this data—someone was consciously diminishing supply to drive up prices, and was succeeding, given the vertical climb of prices on the spot market. The evidence was incontrovertible, and he and the president were the only people in America standing between my constituents and fiscal ruin. I asked him to help us.

He looked straight at me, and his reply had all the subtlety of being slapped in the face with a flounder. He said, in a voice dripping with arrogance, "You know what your trouble is? You just don't understand economics."

I came close to responding, "You're right, Mr. Vice President, I don't understand economics, but I do understand a rip-off when I see one." But, given the dignity of our respective offices, I did not. Neither did I say that I would match my degree in economics from the University of Washington with what was probably his in ballistics from the University of Wyoming any day. Instead, I simply responded that the facts were clear, and that when the truth emerged, what Enron was doing would be a scandal.

The vice president did not tell me to "go [expletive deleted]," as he once told a colleague on the floor of the Senate, but the message was the same. Of course, this was a vice president who had gone into a room with a hundred oil and gas lobbyists and written an energy policy that basically deeded the nation's crown jewels to the oil and gas industry. But given the obvious chicanery being committed by Enron, it was still disappointing when the vice president of the United States ignored an economic emergency and topped it off by suggesting that I was dumber than a post.

So when Mr. Cheney's own Federal Energy Regulatory Commission (FERC) finally examined the evidence three years later, in 2005, and reached the obvious conclusion that Enron had been stealing the West blind, it should have been satisfying to know that my constituents and I did, indeed, know something about economics. We just did not understand "Enronomics." It should have been a tasty dish, a lightly salted serving of Enron crow presented on the vice president's finest china at his lushly appointed home in the U.S. Naval Observatory. Instead, with the exception of a few convictions, little has changed. Ratepayers, shareholders, and retirees have been left holding the bag, and the American people remain vulnerable to future manipulation.

The Enron scandal was the crowning jewel of a school of thought that hoped to place the private sector beyond all public controls. Enron CEO Ken Lay, nicknamed "Kenny Boy" by the president himself, was a top donor to the president's campaign, served on the transition team for the Department of Energy, and was even responsible for the selection of two nominees to FERC who would oversee the regulation of his industry.[1]

In truth, the Enron scandal and the energy crisis that came along with it were the result of a systematic scheme that dismantled the rules and incentives that protected the public interest in a market where power is concentrated in the hands of industry. Not only is the concentration of power we've seen over the past six years antithetical to democracy, it's also bad for business and bad for the climate.

The clean-energy revolution will not succeed if power is concentrated, for the simple reason that there are no silver bullets. No one industry has the answer, or even half of the answer. In Dick Cheney's worldview, concentration among a few favored companies is the way the game is played. The future belongs to different ideas.

## CHAPTER 4

# Energy Efficiency: The Distributed Power of Democracy

When Enron's managers declared bankruptcy in 2001, they left 20,000 employees short $1.3 billion in pension funds. Employees' entire life savings were liquidated as stock plans were frozen, and nearly 5,000 people were immediately out of work. Individual and institutional investors were soaked for another estimated $60 billion—money that vanished from the retirement savings and pension funds of countless citizens.

In the end, this spiral into bankruptcy brought down not only Enron but also many others. Manufacturing workers in northwestern industrial firms lost their jobs by the thousands as the result of the unpredictable explosion in energy prices. It is estimated that during that lawless period, Enron managers and their co-conspirators rigged energy supplies and pricing with such ruthless efficiency that they destroyed 100,000 jobs in the Pacific Northwest and sucked a staggering $1.1 billion out of the economy of the western states.[1] These were not hypothetical dollars but the deferred earnings of workers and pensioners, real pennies saved for a rainy day by a generation of hardworking Americans.

Vice President Cheney, the author of a number of painful lessons in democratic governance, taught us another in his handling of Enron: Energy and political power go hand in hand. He also tried to stop progress by teaching this lesson: "Conservation may be a sign of personal virtue, but it is not a sufficient basis for a sound, comprehensive energy policy."[2] Not a sound policy for him and his friends, at any rate. But for the rest of us, energy conservation may hold the key to taking back our democracy.

## America's First Fuel: Discovering Energy Efficiency

When some of us think of energy, our first thought is of giant gas turbines and huge hydroelectric dams, massive structures turning out megawatts of electricity. If you've ever stood under a 50,000-volt transmission line, you have felt the thrumming power of a thousand tons of falling water concentrated into a four-inch-thick high-tension line. But the power on that transmission line can be rivaled by the power of the silent absence of wasted energy. Fifty thousand air conditioners running on one less kilowatt each because of increased efficiency are just as powerful as a power plant churning out 50,000 kilowatts of power. The only difference is that the conserved energy is quieter, safer, and almost always cheaper.

But when it comes to the energy we produce, whether from a gallon of gas or a ton of coal, today's American economy is a wasteful energy hog. As long as dead dinosaurs and fossilized plants are doing the pushing, we are content to use inefficient engines, inefficient fans, and inefficient electrical systems. We drive bloated cars that could get hugely improved mileage with the use of known technology. We live in homes that leak heat like sieves. We work in buildings that waste enormous amounts of energy trying to heat and cool their poor designs, while they are lit with ancient lighting technology that wastes 90 percent of the electricity it uses.[3]

This is, ironically, good news: We live atop a vast reserve of energy efficiency. Take the example of California. It initiated a bold efficiency plan in the 1990s. Speaking about that plan, Brian Prusnek of California's Energy Commission predicted success, saying, "This efficiency campaign will avoid the need to build three generating plants. In terms of greenhouse gas emissions, that's the equivalent of taking 650,000 cars off the road. How many other investments yield a 50 percent financial return and reduce pollution?"[4]

In the wake of the 2001 energy crisis, California launched the "Flex Your Power" campaign and immediately reduced electricity demand by 5,000 megawatts by swapping out millions of incandescent lightbulbs with compact fluorescent bulbs, installing light-emitting diode (LED) traffic lights to replace standard signals, and creating incentives to upgrade inefficient appliances. This strategy freed up existing power that was being wasted for other essential uses, spreading the benefits of efficiency and cost savings across the economy.

California's campaigns followed directly from an epiphany by physicist Art Rosenfeld, who, after the oil embargo of 1973, calculated that with the same rate of consumption as Europe and Japan, the U.S. could have been an oil exporter instead of mired in crisis. That awakening led directly to the modern movement for energy efficiency. Rosenfeld's great energy "discovery" three decades ago exposed a fundamental truth: We have enormous savings available through efficiency. "By the end of the first week [of studying the energy problem], we realized that we had blundered into one of the world's largest oil and gas fields. The energy was buried, in effect, in the buildings of our cities, the vehicles on our roads, and the machines in our factories," Rosenfeld said.[5]

Efficiency is a form of energy itself, in other words. This hidden and easily accessible energy has been called "negawatts" by energy visionary Amory Lovins. We could also call this power "selectricity," since we are about to build an economy where we select the electricity we actually use, instead of having excess wattage foisted upon us by inefficient appliances and wasteful building systems.

Following this discovery of the resource of efficiency in the 1970s, California adopted some commonsense measures to capture its value. It adopted an aggressive building code, Title 24 of DOE-2, encouraging the use of insulation and better lighting, a provision that the California Energy Commission estimates is now saving Californians $5 billion in electricity a year.[6] It adopted a tough energy-efficiency standard for appliances. It helped develop a new window coating that helps maintain the temperature of a building, as well as a new technology—the compact fluorescent lamp, an incredibly efficient lighting system. Most important, the state adopted a utility policy that started to reward power generators for efficiency improvements rather than for selling more electricity. This practice, known as "decoupling," separated the profits of a utility from the need to sell more juice. Now utilities make money saving energy rather than selling it. One way they do that is by paying consumers to make their houses more energy efficient instead of paying power plants to make more energy and churn out more emissions. You get the same comfort in your home but a smaller electricity bill at the end of the month—and fewer bad air-quality days to boot.

The results of this comprehensive efficiency plan were spectacular. Today, a typical Japanese citizen uses 4,000 kilowatt-hours of electricity.[7] The typical European uses 6,000 kilowatt-hours of electricity; and in California they use 7,000. But nationwide, Americans use nearly twice that amount or 13,000. This is actually an opportunity.[8] California's efficiency vision "produced" more energy through savings than could possibly have been cost-effectively produced by bringing fossil fuel–generating plants on line—all with no pollution.

As important, this miracle of efficiency took place amid a continuation of the California lifestyle. People in California still use hot tubs in Marin County, make movies in Hollywood, and churn out cutting-edge products in Silicon Valley, all while using nearly half the energy per person as the rest of the U.S. population. It is not "California Dreamin'," it's California reality. It is a reality because some visionary California leaders dreamed of using efficiency to grow their state. Rather than resigning themselves to feeding more energy into a leaky pipe, they decided to fix the leaks.

In 2005, Americans spent nearly $300 billion on electricity,[9] but just using *current* technology, most buildings and factories could immediately reduce their consumption by at least 25 percent, with a payback of under four years.[10] In fact, energy efficiency has already played an essential role in meeting our energy demand in recent decades. Americans have cut the energy required to produce every dollar of our gross national product by 49 percent since 1970.[11] The cumulative savings produced by energy efficiency since 1973 make that source of energy larger than any other single source, including oil.

That is why we really ought to consider efficiency as our "first fuel." We need to reverse our current thinking that immediately looks for more power, always increasing capacity to meet demand, and instead take a close look at what is driving that demand from the outset, cut the energy it takes to get the job done, and recognize the power of saving energy as the first fuel of choice to keep our economy growing.

In places like California we have started that process, but the savings still to be harvested remain vast. Even with our dramatic reductions over the last three decades, U.S. energy use per dollar of GNP remains nearly double that of several other industrial countries, and over two-thirds of the fossil fuel we use is lost in the form of waste heat.[12]

California is not the only place utilities have enjoyed great success in efficiency. Seattle City Light has reduced electrical consumption by 10 percent through active conservation; that is enough energy to power 100,000 homes, saving more carbon than taking 80,000 cars off the road and saving consumers $63 million on their energy bills.[13] That is the power of efficiency at just one utility in one city. Imagine the change that is possible for a nation committed to saving energy. Puget Sound Energy similarly has achieved substantial savings and is willing to try new ideas like "real-time pricing," which allows consumers to save money by using more energy when it is cheaper to produce, at night. When consumers do their wash in the evening rather than during peak load hours, both the consumer and the utility save money.

The savings from these and a slew of other strategies can be huge. Just the implementation of new efficiency standards for clothes washers and water heaters will avoid the necessity of building 127 new 300-megawatt power plants. If we simply required the higher efficiency standards (called SEER Level 13) for air conditioners approved in the Clinton administration, instead of the Level 12 standards proposed by the Bush administration, we would supplant the need for another 43 new 300-megawatt plants. Adopting sensible building codes and making modest improvements of one kilowatt per home would prevent the need for another 170 power plants.[14]

Here is a total of 340 power plants in the palm of our hand, ready to be saved. The benefits are so obvious that even in New Jersey, the state where Edison invented the lightbulb, a bill has been introduced to ban the incandescent bulb. If Edison knew this, he would not be rolling over in his grave, he would be standing and applauding. What would he think if he knew we were still relying on a technology that was 127 years old when we had new and better ones at our disposal?

## Reforming Industrial Practice: From Pariah to an Energy Star

Efficiency is not merely a private virtue. It is also a hard-nosed business proposition. The chemical industry is too often an environmental pariah. In the 1960's, Dow Chemical Company was widely reviled for its role in producing agent orange, which defoliated the environmentally devastated country of Vietnam. In 2001, Dow purchased the Union Carbide Company, which in 1984 had been a part of one of the worlds worst industrial disasters in Bhopal India. For many, a company like Dow is simply a part of our environmental problems.[15]

The company made changes because it realized that energy efficiency is good business. As John Dearborn, energy business vice president, said, "We recognize that all energy consumers have a role to play in effectively managing the world's precious energy resources, and focusing on energy efficiency is the best near-term action that all of us can take to be part of the solution." This follows Dow's stated position on global warming: "We believe that climate change is one of the most serious issues our society faces today."[16] This unambiguous statement led to an unambiguous success in energy efficiency.

The people at Dow did it the old-fashioned way. They set numerical targets and held managers accountable for meeting them, they measured their progress, and they publicized their results. They exceeded their goal of a 20 percent improvement between 1994 and 2005 because they knew their feet would be held to the fire. Now on the Dow Web site, anyone can see the company's goal of another 25 percent improvement by 2015 and a daily tracking report of its progress.[17]

This company meant business. Energy efficiency was not a public relations statement; it became a fundamental cultural component of the whole enterprise. It has paid off in Dow's relationship with the investor community, witnessed by its being named "Best in Class" by the Carbon Disclosure Project, a coalition of global investors with more than $31 trillion in assets. It has also paid off on the bottom line, with $4 billion in cumulative energy savings over the life of the project.[18]

Dow's success was based on a whole slew of small improvements, not any one silver bullet. Perhaps its biggest single leap forward was its growth in cogeneration for electricity and heat. At Dow's new Plaquemine, Louisiana, plant, both electricity and heat are produced by burning natural gas, thereby achieving a 20–40 percent increase in efficiency. No strangers to the concept, one of the nation's first cogeneration plants was designed by the team of Herbert Dow and George Westinghouse in the early 1900s. Efficiency often just means adapting techniques we already have to the current setting. Dow has proven that principle with cogeneration.

Large efforts like cogeneration were matched with small ones like using energy-efficient lighting and reducing waste in literally thousands of manufacturing processes. All of these individual actions had a huge cumulative impact, saving 900 trillion Btus of energy, enough to fulfill all the electrical needs for residential users in California for one year.[19] That is no small feat.

Why Dow? Its CEO, Andrew Liveris, answers candidly, "The chemical industry is a leader in the efficient use of energy. We have to be, because we use petroleum and natural gas as both a fuel and raw material." Now Dow is staking out a position as a global advocate for change. "We can do more to leverage our experience in energy efficiency by convincing others that it's a win-win for the environment and the economy," says Liveris.[20]

Dow's commitment to achieve another 25 percent improvement is a powerful statement that it is not just depending upon the low-hanging fruit of efficiency. In fact, experience suggests that the deeper a business looks, the more efficiency it is able to achieve. "Opportunities in energy efficiency re-grow over time," says Neal Elliott of the American Council for an Energy-Efficient Economy. "In other words, the more you look for energy-efficient opportunities, the more you'll find."[21]

Multinational companies have the internal resources to make such changes, but small businesses, local governments, and individuals often need help, incentives, and better information. However, opportunities to bring efforts like Dow's to scale for the nation as a whole have been hurt by a reduction in federal efforts. Appropriations for efficiency research were cut 17 percent in 2006. Some programs that could have helped the industry obtain efficiency were cut 30 percent. If we fail to invest in energy efficiency, "We would be leaving a lot of energy on the table," says Peter Molinaro, vice president of Dow.[22] While business leadership is important, it is no substitute for public investment in research or regulations like efficiency standards that only government can provide.

The impact of scaling back federal leadership on energy efficiency cascades through the economy in both wasted energy and missed business opportunities. Charles Bates is an Alabama engineer who has been perfecting a casting technique that uses 30 percent less energy than traditional techniques, but in 2006 he faced a cutoff of the funds that were helping his technology get off the ground. "We've been making progress by leaps and bounds," he said.[23] "It's a great program, and we'd be sorry to see it go," said Bryan Baker of Vulcan Engineering, a company that supplies casting equipment to the auto industry.[24] Programs like Public Benefits Funds, which put state money into building retrofits, and Industrial Assessment Centers, which help small businesses find efficiency improvements, are critical to help smaller companies that do not have the assets the Dow Chemicals of the world can employ.

Increasingly, companies are relying on efficiency to cut costs and meet demand. Major firms like DuPont, BP America, and 3M have all been leaders with the Alliance to Save Energy and have success stories to tell. 3M has enjoyed a spectacular 77 percent improvement in efficiency since 1973, in part by replacing 280 conventional electric motors with 50 adjustable-speed drive motors at 3M headquarters.[25] Energy efficiency is becoming part of the corporate culture. Society may no longer tolerate the business executive who pooh-poohs energy efficiency.

The principle is also becoming interwoven in our professions. For instance, Christine McEntee, president of the American Institute of Architects, has taken a strong stand on efficiency. "To address this, our board of directors approved a resolution promoting high-performance building design with a goal of reaching a 50 percent fossil fuel reduction in buildings by 2010 and carbon-neutral buildings by 2030," she says. When presidents of professional organizations talk about carbon-neutral buildings in twenty-five years, we know progress is on the march. "The fact is, the technology and the tools to bring energy use down are already out there; we just need to do more to educate designers, builders, owners, and the public about how to use those tools," McEntee says.[26]

She is right about the need for more work in this field. Despite the fact that energy efficiency costs on average $.038 per kilowatt-hour compared to an average $.074 for purchased electricity, utilities still do not concentrate on this effort.[27] One statistic in particular stands out: According to Steve Wright of Bonneville Power, utilities spend less annually on efficiency research than the food industry spends on research regarding dog food.[28] That glaring oversight could change if our federal and state laws would require utilities to adopt what is called "integrated planning" in anticipating new demand, requiring them to look first to efficiency, as many progressive utilities are now doing, rather than focusing only on producing more electricity.

Utilities around the country have discovered that it is much cheaper to "buy" power by funding conservation efforts that free up energy that would otherwise be wasted than to buy additional power to feed into the system or build additional plants. Is it too much to ask, then, that a

utility be required to show that it cannot obtain savings through efficiency before it builds new plants? Shouldn't a utility have to explore
programs to help its consumers pay for better lighting or pumps before
it spends billions on more expensive nuclear or other large-scale generation that takes years to come on line?

## Affordable Green: Efficiency for the People

Green and efficient energy strategies are not just for well-heeled companies. At the Green Institute, an eco-industrial park that is redeveloping an old area of Phillips, one of the poorest and most ethnically diverse neighborhoods in Minneapolis, there is no furnace. Nonetheless,
this state-of-the-art green office park and light manufacturing facility is
comfortable through the long, cold Minnesota winters. Instead of turning to a conventional boiler, when executive director Michael Krause
was designing his headquarters, he chose a simple and elegant machine
to heat and cool the center; it is just a pump and fan, really, with two
large iron pipes sunk deep into the ground: It's a geothermal heat pump,
or ground-source heat exchanger.

A geothermal heat pump is a beautiful thing. It works on a simple principle. While the air above ground fluctuates wildly with the
seasons—with documented temperatures as low as −70°F in Montana
and reaching a record high of 134°F in Death Valley, California—just
below the surface of the earth, a few feet beneath the frost line, the temperature is relatively constant and moderate the world over, ranging at
most from 45°F to 70°F. By sending fluid through a closed loop of pipe
down into this friendly climate and back up again, the heat pump ex-
tracts heating or cooling from the crust of the earth and runs it through
a simple heat exchanger like a home HVAC system, providing a stable,
reliable, and comfortable indoor environment in all seasons.

The system is exciting as much for what it lacks as for what it does.
There is no pilot light, because there is nothing to burn. There is no
boiler, no noise, no soot or $CO_2$, no contribution to childhood asthma
or bad air days, and no fuel bill, except for the electricity to circulate the

pump and run the fan. By using something as simple as the earth's surface temperature to derive energy and provide a basic service like heating a Minnesota office building in the dead of winter, this machine not only blurs the lines between energy efficiency and renewable energy, but also shines a stark light on all the pollution, waste, and needless cycling of energy we take for granted in a modern city.

Congressman Ed Markey from Massachusetts is fond of saying that energy independence and climate solutions go together like peanut butter and jelly. The same could be said about energy efficiency and renewable energy. They are both clean, restorative energy solutions that break dependence on imported and polluting energy, and frequently savings from energy efficiency allow green buildings to invest in greater capital costs up front for clean-energy systems that cut long-term energy bills. From an economic perspective and in practice, it is clear that energy efficiency is at the center of making a clean-energy transition work. Efficiency and renewables are best when they go together, hand in hand.

Green building is full of efficient and renewable technologies—simple, elegant, and clean—that underscore the excitement of our coming clean-energy revolution. Building-integrated photovoltaics are one example that puts solar panels right into a building's skin of windows, facade, and shingles, turning the structure itself into a generator of clean, renewable energy. When you move through a green building, you see for yourself what can be done, cast in bricks and mortar, bamboo and glass. Green buildings speak to what is possible and make efficiency come alive in a real place, enhancing the quality of life for the people inside.

These buildings are not just laboratory specimens. In the heart of New York City's historic Harlem neighborhood, Carlton Brown is the private-sector developer of a multifamily, mixed-income housing development, 1400 on 5th. It was the first of what is now a string of energy-efficient, affordable, and neighborhood-scale developments that Brown has undertaken, using renewable energy and good design to uplift communities from Trenton, New Jersey, to Jackson, Mississippi, and soon New Orleans and Baltimore.

Guiding Brown's work is a simple if ambitious set of goals designed to bring green affordable housing to the people who need it most. "We start out with a core set of beliefs," he says. "Otherwise, you are just doing stuff."[29] He sets clear benchmarks for his projects to make a difference. They use 50 percent less energy than the building code dictates. They cost 10 percent below the index of median housing prices. They improve indoor air quality for the residents of the building, and they involve the community in setting design goals. As president of Full Spectrum New York, Brown—a steady, thoughtful leader and tireless champion in a nearly ever present porkpie hat—is proving every day that green building can be affordable; and that modern, advanced, energy-saving construction is for everyone; that clean energy can empower community and, indeed, is the future of our cities.

To make his point on radically improving the energy and resource efficiency of construction, Brown looks to other industries. Airplanes, ships, automobiles, and computers all demonstrate different models for design. "A 747 probably has as many parts as a 250,000-square-foot apartment building," he muses, "yet you expect defects in a new building. In an airplane you expect everything to work right from the start." Brown has learned from these carefully modeled design processes. He

With projects like the mixed-use, mixed-income development 1400 on 5th in New York City's Harlem neighborhood, developer Carlton Brown is demonstrating that high-performance green building and affordable housing can go hand in hand. (Harold E. Rhynie.)

proofs out his buildings before he ever breaks ground, using computerized 3-D design, to optimize energy use, reduce waste, decrease cost, and maximize efficiency. He makes the most of everything, from lumber to labor and the energy, air, and water that circulate through the structure during the life of the building. Green high-performance construction has become a staple of luxury buildings, but Full Spectrum has proven that the same tools can be applied for low-income and minority communities.

Starting from community-based design, Brown builds all his components in a modular factory setting off site according to the community's specifications, from the walls and building superstructure to the plumbing systems. In the process, he improves indoor air quality and creates good jobs. In the manufacturing sector, he points out, you can . train someone in six weeks for a living-wage job that it would take them five years to attain in a traditional construction context. He works as a partner with the labor unions who erect the buildings and uses community benefits agreements that connect him to local hiring and training. He has helped the modular construction industry see the potential of green building, working, for example, with a company in Minden, Louisiana, that manufactures precast modular units for prisons, demonstrating how to build green housing with no PVC, low volatile organic compounds, and energy-efficient design to rebuild the Gulf Coast with high-quality housing. "It is kind of strange sometimes how transformations can happen," he says.

Brown has applied his holistic "systems thinking" to the social dynamics of the communities he works in. "Making a community green is just a piece of the sustainability puzzle. You need the human dimensions as well: jobs, indoor air quality, energy use, and honoring the culture of the community with an inclusive process," he says. Regarding his goal of cutting energy use by 50 percent, he points out that "in communities of color, often most buildings aren't even up to code, so you are really talking about an 80 to 90 percent cut in energy and emissions." For low- and moderate-income residents of his developments, this is serious business. You can look at it as a climate issue, but you can just as easily see it in a family's finances. Cutting monthly energy bills by a few hundred dollars is very visible when you are living on $30,000 a year.

At 1400 on 5th, the results really add up. The average unit is typically saving $1,200 to $1,300 every year. Brown calculates that the net present value from the energy cost savings he will achieve in his four hundred units in two developments in Harlem will be $78 million over the next thirty years, all while cutting greenhouse gas emissions by 1,100 tons a year. That's not chump change; it's money that will be invested in local spending, savings, or family vacations, but not in wasted energy.

In Jackson, Mississippi, Brown is taking this approach to scale in a 40-acre downtown redevelopment over twelve square blocks. Using $100 million in tax increment financing (TIF) and backed by the conservative Republican governor, Haley Barbour, and the mayor, it will be the largest green project in the state. The project is incorporating a whole suite of integrated strategies for efficiency and clean energy, from green roofs, to light shelves that bounce sunlight deeper into the units and cut electricity use, to building-integrated photovoltaics and the use of stationary fuel cells developed for NASA and the navy, to cut peak energy use and triple efficiency. The fuel cells will be powered by biodiesel made from local soybean and cotton growers, who would otherwise be producing subsidized crops that would flood African markets and kill local farming in the third world. Fuel will even be made from waste from catfish farming. And of course all of the units use geothermal heat pumps.

Carlton Brown is making a real impact on big issues like childhood asthma, global development, and climate change, and he's doing it by making millions of small changes on the ground, with green, energy-efficient, affordable housing. He is making homes for families and jobs for blue-collar workers, bricks and mortar you can touch and feel, investment in the heart of communities that need it. He is also proving the economics of energy-efficient and high-performance building. When he built 1400 on 5th, financing was hard to come by. But he proved that building to the U.S. Green Building Council's Leadership in Energy and Environmental Design (LEED) Gold Standard for low-income residents made sense, and that passing a high threshold for energy-efficient and healthful building materials could improve communities, save money, and create new markets for quality housing, along with high-skill jobs. Afterward, when he built the sustainable condominium complex called the Kalahari down the street, Goldman Sachs was knocking at his door.

Brown believes that too much development is shaped by a politics and policy of scarcity, grounded in the belief that there isn't enough to go around. He doesn't buy it and worries that that way of thinking leads to gentrification and the notion that to improve a neighborhood you must move one group of people out and move another group in. Instead, he is building places that people want to live in, making it attractive for middle-class families to move in and making it possible for low-income families to stay and build wealth. He is doing this using the tools of energy efficiency and renewable energy. Is this a green strategy? As Brown says, "If you don't deal with the social construct, you will never get to the biological one."

We know the power of the slogan "Safety First" for industry. Now we need the slogan "Efficiency First" for utilities and businesses. If we adopt this approach, many a nuclear plant will be avoided, not because of an arguably valid distrust of nuclear energy, but because of an inarguable trust in efficiency. Before we start plugging in nuclear plants, we first ought to start plugging in energy-efficient lightbulbs and retooling our homes and factories.

But there's a key political construct here as well: Efficiency is just another word for freedom. Increasing efficiency means decreasing the concentration of power, both economic and political, in the industrial megaliths that often dominate the economy. Every kilowatt-hour saved through efficiency is one less kilowatt's worth of economic power that is translated into the kind of political power that allowed Enron to run rampant, and one more kilowatt of economic power for consumers to spend in their local neighborhoods.

The concentration of economic power that derives from an absence of energy efficiency can infect any government of any party, while the broad distribution of that same economic power—and the new choices that come with smart energy use and saved resources—can increase the power of our democracy. All of us have a legitimate and real interest in seeing a reduction of the unwholesome consolidation of power that comes with poor energy choices. By increasing efficiency, we build a stronger society.

We know what we have to do. We have to squeeze the stupefying amount of wasted energy out of our system. The good news is that there is a deep well of wasted energy into which we can drill. We have already squeezed four quadrillion Btus of wasted power from our economy each year through demand management programs,[30] but we can go much further. A few more quadrillion, and we'll have our problem licked.

GREEN-COLLAR JOBS: FROM THE SOUTH BRONX TO OAKLAND

*Bracken Hendricks*

As the founding executive director of the Apollo Alliance, I have had the opportunity to meet many of the people who are using clean energy to rebuild their communities and take power to shape their destinies—everywhere from union halls in Appalachia to center cities from New York to California.

Majora Carter stands out among this growing movement of leaders and organizers, though she is by no means alone. I first met Carter while she was chatting with Colin Powell at a high-toned event sponsored by President Clinton, her youthful and energetic presence belied by a few gray hairs in her dreadlocks that spoke to her hard-won experience. Grounded by her roots in the South Bronx, she moves easily between the two worlds, one where geopolitical power is part of the air in the room, and one where power is re-earned daily through the hard work of bringing people together to claim their voices in our democracy. She is as comfortable chatting with world leaders as she is training single mothers and returning felons who are reentering society to care for shade trees or build green roofs on energy-efficient buildings. Carter believes in the restorative power of clean energy to create good "green-collar jobs" that drive opportunity deeply into the economy.

The South Bronx is a community cut off from the rest of New York by highways, the great monuments to the automobile-based engineering of Robert Moses's 1960s-era urban renewal. From the roof of Carter's offices at Sustainable South Bronx, looking in one direction you see the Brookner Expressway—a great highway that cuts through the Hunts Point community, isolating it from the rest of the Bronx—and the steady flow of cars that symbolize the current oil economy flowing through the area on their way into Manhattan. Sixty thousand diesel trucks go in and out of this peninsula each week. Looking in the other direction, you can see the smokestacks of the sewage-pelletizing facility and several new power plants recently located in the area, more noxious land uses in an area that has suffered the psychological and environmental health impacts of much of the energy infrastructure and pollution that bring prosperity to the rest of New York. Perhaps most important, you can see houses, where the industrial and residential land uses butt against each other.

This daily exposure takes a toll on residents. Scanning the area, you can see the sources of tremendous energy demand, terrible air quality, and the paved surfaces that send storm-water runoff from the sewers into rivers laden with oil and pollution in 450 places across New York each time it rains. You can see the clear hallmarks of poverty and economic neglect. However, you can also see the potential of the entire Hunts Point peninsula, the Manhattan skyline beyond, and the estuary near where the Harlem and Bronx rivers converge.

Carter has created a program to train local residents for the jobs of a green economy. To her this work is about organizing her community to reclaim an active role in shaping the future. It is also about learning to see things differently.

"You have to train yourself to see it as an opportunity, or it will go right by you," she tells me. She got her start mobilizing her neighborhood to fight the siting of an incinerator—yet another waste facility that would make her poor community a further dumping ground for the unwanted by-products of the economy. But, as she puts it, "If they only looked at our waterfront as a place to put garbage, it was up to us to look at it as something to inspire."[1]

Carter sees huge potential within this view of the South Bronx. She sees the seeds of a new economy, one that restores its connection to the land and digs deep local roots, valuing people as it tackles some of the most intractable social, energy, and environmental problems of our day. Although she started Sustainable South Bronx to challenge the construction of a waste-to-energy project, it quickly became clear that it would be far more effective in the long run to fight for new opportunities and positive alternatives. She began to find the overlooked resources in the land, in the people, and in the built and natural environments.

Greening the community became her rallying cry. As she began to acquire the habit of making her own opportunities, they kept coming. She moved from organizing against dumps to organizing to build parks. And as she saw those parks being constructed, she realized that the workers were coming in from elsewhere, so she organized to train unemployed local residents, many of whom were ex-offenders shunned by the traditional job market, and she spun golden opportunities from those overlooked resources as well. "What better way to create a sense of ownership," she says, "than to build it yourself from within your own community?"

She now has a program that turns the Bronx River into a training program for the emerging sector of green-collar jobs, turning out a new class of trainees each year. From riverfront parks restoration, she is moving to create work in brownfield redevelopment, installing green roofs, green industrialization, and soon solar panel installation. All these emerging industries represent new markets for jobs and training for those who need them most.

"Green-collar jobs" is not an abstraction. The environmental sector of the economy is bigger than the biggest Fortune 500 company, representing $341 billion in industry sales and 5.3 million jobs in 2005.[2] It represents three times more jobs than the chemical industry, six times the workers in apparel, and ten times the number of people in the pharmaceutical industry. From machinists to clerks, from designers to mechanical engineers to laborers, *green* quite simply means jobs—it has been an unrecognized sector of the economy for too long. Now, with the arrival of clean technology and the work of solving our climate crisis, it may get the respect it deserves.

The Bronx is not alone. In Oakland, Mayor Ron Dellums and the Oakland Apollo Alliance, ably led by the dynamic Van Jones, are also pursuing the power of green jobs to change communities. They are developing the California Youth Energy Services to train and pay young adults to conduct energy audits. They are partnering with developers to build green buildings on the site of a once toxic brownfield. They are laying the groundwork for "green enterprise zones," where businesses are given incentives to locate sustainable enterprises that hire local residents. Their efforts are even creating a "Green Job Corps," a training partnership that builds a pipeline with local labor unions, Peralta Community College, and the City of Oakland to train and employ residents in the new green economy.

As Van Jones puts it, "The 'green economy' is exploding into a billion-dollar sector—with more growth predicted. Before we find ourselves left behind and left out, those of us working to uplift urban America see now as a good time to ask who is going to benefit from this massive economic growth."[3]

Majora Carter and Van Jones are working to see that a clean-energy revolution takes place not only on Wall Street but on Main Streets everywhere. We need the skills, talents, and underutilized resources of every American and every community. Everybody Needs to Get on the Bus.

CHAPTER 5

# Reenergizing Our Communities,
# One Project at a Time

We've got trouble, right here in River City.

—*Professor Harold Hill,* The Music Man

Today in American towns, cities, and neighborhoods, from the South Bronx to South Dakota, we are failing to invest in our people and in the places we call home, and many communities are hurting. Even amid growth and prosperity, we are failing to invest in the basic infrastructure that makes our cities function. From transit and rail to schools, parks, roads, and energy systems, basic investments are deferred at a high price to our competitiveness and long-term prosperity. The oldest and largest association of professional engineers in the country, the American Society of Civil Engineers, gave America a "poor" grade of D for an estimated $1.6 trillion in unmet infrastructure needs for 2005.[1] As a proportion of gross domestic product, our investment rates are declining. For example, while population, GDP, and demand increased markedly in recent decades, annual investment in electrical transmission infrastructure actually declined by 60 percent, resulting in a major shortfall in capacity between 1975 and 2000.[2]

America's rail system was once the envy of the world; today we fight for basic funding to keep it afloat. In rural communities and inner cities, our schools and public buildings are in disrepair—underfunded, over-crowded, and aging. But reconstruction of our public buildings offers a chance to modernize with energy efficiency, renewable energy, and green construction. We rely on an electric grid that uses nineteenth-century technology to power a twenty-first-century economy. From New York to Los Angeles our roads and bridges, wastewater treatment plants, ports, and transit systems go begging for maintenance funds—wasting energy and losing business opportunities. Concrete is not being poured, steel is not being tied, and investments in public works are being allowed to crumble. The bustling and friendly Main Streets of midwestern mythology are becoming the shuttered relics of a bygone age as factories close and longtime residents see their children seek opportunities elsewhere.

According to Apollo Alliance cofounder Joel Rogers, executive director of the Center on Wisconsin Strategy, "The U.S. is virtually unique among developing countries in not distinguishing between capital accounts and operating budgets."[3] This sounds like the rhetoric of a revolutionary accountant, but it is exactly that failure to distinguish revenue-positive investments, like infrastructure, from wasteful spending that impoverishes our legacy of reconstruction in communities and sinks us ever deeper into climate crisis. "There was a time when America made long-term, large-scale investments that secured a prosperous future, from the Louisiana Purchase to the Erie Canal, to the transcontinental railroad, the GI Bill, and the Interstate Highway System. These were all big-ticket items, but they paid for themselves in the long run," Rogers says. As he points out, "Jefferson didn't have the money lying around for the Louisiana Purchase. A new Apollo Project for energy is appealing because it is part of a class of investments that pay for themselves—it is not merely redistribution of wealth—and it makes our whole country better off."

Rogers notes that in today's economy there are two distinct ways to make money, but only one is accountable to workers and responsible to the environment and communities. One is centered only on commodity prices and the cheapest production of goods, while the other is focused on adding value, distinctiveness, and quality. "A low-road economy treats people like roadkill and the earth like the sewer. It is empirically bad for workers and the environment, but it is most certainly profitable. A high road, however, can also be profitable; indeed, for an advanced economy it is the only way for the long term," says Rogers.

A new Apollo Project for energy presents us with exactly this choice between two diverging paths to accumulation and profitability, but if we rely just on individual firms that are not committed to sustaining the broader national economy or improving living standards for the public at large, it will take too long to save the economy or the climate. "You won't have the society left to reconstruct if you wait for firms alone to act," says Rogers. "The choice is a social choice and a political choice."

A high-road economy judges economic performance not just by increasing prosperity, but also by sharing the fruits of that prosperity. By that measure the United States succeeded very well from its founding until the early 1970s. The U.S. economy not only grew like crazy, but it also shared the benefits, opportunities, and final results in broad ways, creating the largest middle class the world had ever known. Furthermore, it relied on institutions and rules, like trade unions and policies, to share that "productivity dividend" to keep a society fit to live in. A new Apollo Project is not only about fighting climate change; it is about turning our whole economy in a new direction.

Metropolitan areas are one of the natural pillars of both clean energy and a high-road economy. They share denser infrastructure, provide ports of entry, and are the locus of new industries and the leading lights of a new and changing economy. Metropolitan regions are also much more energy efficient than sprawling cities and offer large opportunities for improvement by rebuilding modern infrastructure. As Rogers says, "In the past, it was the same politics that beat back climate solutions that have defeated metro areas, dividing a mostly white labor movement from people of color, separating environmental interests from the functioning of successful and responsible businesses. Clean energy can claim opportunity for people who have been excluded from the old energy economy. It gives environmentalists a way to move beyond end-of-pipe solutions and avoid disaster in the first place. And it shows high-road businesses that their real enemy is not regulation in the public interest but low-road predatory businesses that are profiting off of lower standards and eating away at workers, communities, and the global environment."

Creating energy independence can arrest this downward spiral and reinvigorate both inner cities and rural America. New jobs are being created today in emerging industries, from manufacturing energy-saving technologies, to producing biofuels and wind turbines, to building a new generation of transit infrastructure, constructing high-performance green schools, and rewiring the electric grid. These are jobs that cannot easily be outsourced because they represent investments in our communities through construction of infrastructure, shifting from imported to domestic energy resources, and manufacturing close to local markets. These are jobs that cross the economic spectrum, from architects and engineers to craftspeople and laborers. Energy independence and climate solutions mean real investment.

We will see this principle in action. Communities are on the verge of a new economic growth, to be achieved by harnessing the power of new technology and renewed productive investment. According to research by Clean Edge, investments in biofuels, wind, solar, and hydrogen fuel-cell technology together will mushroom from $55 billion in 2006 to $226 billion in the next decade.[4] By using community hiring, apprenticeship programs, local ownership, and other smart forms of economic development, those investments can drive their benefits deep into communities that have been bypassed by past expansions.

Capital is currently leaving local economies to buy imported energy. Reinvesting that capital creates new opportunity for communities and can put communities back on track across America.

## The Portland Story: It's Not All about the Car

The design of the interstate freeway system did not come down from Mount Sinai on stone tablets. Neither did the design of the automobile come from the Old or New Testament. Their designs came from Dwight Eisenhower and Henry Ford, respectively, two mortals whose contributions were wonderful and productive but also capable of improvement.

Our addiction to oil has many costs, especially when it comes to America's communities. Automobile dependence has fragmented urban neighborhoods with freeways. It has added to public health problems, decreasing exercise and increasing smog; and growing congestion eats up ever more of our free time in commuting. When it comes to climate, the United States alone produces 25 percent of the world's carbon emissions, and because nearly 80 percent of the U.S. population lives in cities, the way we build our transportation system and the energy we consume daily in cars disproportionately affect global climate change.[5]

With 5.3 pounds of carbon in every gallon of gas, the average U.S. household with two midsize cars sends over ten tons of $CO_2$ into the atmosphere each year. Increasing sprawl means we drive farther to perform the simple tasks in daily life: getting to work, shopping for groceries, and taking kids to soccer games. Americans drove 2.6 trillion miles in 2004, the equivalent of 10 million trips to the moon and back.[6] The way we design and build our cities may be one of the most important parts of stopping global warming and breaking our addiction to oil. Turning to new modes of transit may be one of the best things we can do to restore our communities.

For fresh thinking about the future of transportation, we need only to look to Portland, Oregon, known as the Rose City. Portland's 1.8 million residents exalt in TriMet, one of the most advanced transportation systems in the United States. It has broken the back of dependence on the freeway and the car, the twin forces so fundamentally responsible for global warming. The car may be a symbol of independence in much of the country, but the people of Portland asserted the independence of their community by changing their transportation habits to save the essence of their hometown.

While some older East Coast cities, such as Boston and New York, grew up around their transit hubs, cities in the West have typically sprawled. In spite of that, the people of Portland have succeeded in building one of the most successful modern light-rail and streetcar systems in the country, and their community has flourished as a result. Now Portland can also claim to be the first city in the nation to actually have reduced its $CO_2$ emissions below the 1990 levels prescribed by the Kyoto Protocol. This is in large part because 97,000 Oregonians are commuting in light-rail cars powered by electricity, mostly from clean hydroelectric dams, instead of driving on clogged freeways, spewing tons of $CO_2$ into the atmosphere. The rail system connects the neighboring cities of Gresham, Beaverton, and Hillsboro to Portland as well, so the victory is a regional one.

Portland has demonstrated that the cleanest car is the one not driven. The "cars" Portlanders ride hold 174 passengers in comfort and style. The system, warmly called the Max (Metropolitan Area Express), is so beloved by Portlanders that it has been expanded three times by public vote; it is now streamlined with a bus and streetcar system downtown that carries 32 million riders annually.[7]

In a manner of speaking, the Max may be the Yankees franchise of public transit systems—envied, unequaled, and a bit cocky. Much as other teams try to figure out how to compete with the Yankees, other cities can learn from the story of how Portland got its light rail.

"We didn't start out to solve global warming," says Rick Gustafson, former director of TriMet and now a transportation project developer. "In the 1970s we in Portland made a big decision. We decided to take our federal money usually allotted for freeway development and plow it into public transit and urban development rather than let new freeways plow through our town and destroy its character. Our decision was meant to save Portland, not the world." Their decision turned out to be good for the long-term health of the city and the planet. Transit-oriented development has become an economic magnet and has built a livable community, even as it cut emissions and saved oil.

Other cities, however, have remained slaves to the freeway. "I went up to Seattle in the late 1970s and tried to get them to see the beauty of light rail," says Gustafson, "but they stuck with freeways. Now they are building a light-rail system twenty years after Portland. We are in our third generation of extensions on our lines."

In Portland, the shiny white Max cars cruise almost silently on forty-four miles of tracks. Electrically driven rail cars leave only a gentle "whoosh" in their wake, no sound of belching diesel or roaring gas turbines. Portlanders love their Max for many reasons—its reliability, its cost, its safety—but its silence is a major factor. That style of reliable cleanliness and quiet efficiency lures people out of their automobiles. Its riders are not simply moving out of buses and into rail cars. The system's ridership is 100 percent higher than that of the bus lines it replaced.

Most important, 77 percent of the Max's riders are "choice riders," who own a car but choose to ride the Max. Let those pessimists who believe it is impossible to coax well-heeled Americans out of their cars go to Portland. They will see a transit future riding the rails today. Portland has done transit right. It is no wonder that while the city has a service area that ranks twenty-ninth in population nationally, it is thirteenth in total ridership on its transit system.[8]

Laying the tracks for light rail was only one piece of the Portland puzzle. "The rail system itself is part of a much bigger achievement," says Rick Gustafson. "Light rail could not have been successful in achieving our community's goals without robust and effective efforts to make higher-density living a preferred alternative for Portlanders. We met a huge goal last year. We were the first city in the country to reduce the per capita vehicle miles traveled per year. That means that people in our city actually reduced the amount they are driving after it has been going up for three decades. Prior to our success, we drove over twice as many miles per person per year compared to 1970. Now it's coming down. That means we have a chance to save our city—and help on global warming, too."

In the long run, the only way to keep our cities livable is to reduce the environmental damage of cars by reducing their use. Portland's citizens have done just that by making denser living a preferred choice. Since the light-rail project began in 1986, smart land-use planning has created attractive living environments in denser configurations. The Pearl District, for example, is a thriving neighborhood where residents can walk to forty restaurants, bringing life to the abandoned warehouses of twenty years ago. Now 25 percent of all trips in Portland are walking trips, accompanied by all the attendant health benefits.[9]

Gustafson says three elements are needed to achieve this kind of improvement. "First, you need to create high-quality access opportunities with transit. We did that with light rail and our streetcar. Second, you need to have good urban design. People want a human scale with lots of windows, broad sidewalks, and inviting shops on the ground floor. Now strolling in Portland is a recreation. Third, you need the other amenities you associate with a great city, restaurants and the like. When it's all there, it works like a charm."

Nationally, suburban household members travel twenty-one miles a day on average; people in Portland's core travel only nine. Chalk up those twelve saved miles as a big bite out of global warming and a massive cut in imported oil.

The growth in Portland's business parallels the reduction in oil and $CO_2$. Just along Interstate Avenue, one stretch on the Yellow Line, the number of businesses opening has increased 50 percent.[10] "In addition to strong ridership, we've seen tremendous excitement about the revitalized community that's a more attractive place to do business and live," says TriMet general manager Fred Hansen. TriMet is not just building transit; it is building hundreds of business opportunities in the golden real estate next to its lines, and according to Hansen, "that number continues to grow."

Portland recognizes that the real competition in the global high-tech economy is between urban metropolitan regions, not nation-states. Portland is a winner in that competition because of its "new urbanist" strategy, for which the Max is pivotal. An article titled "Slicker Cities" in *Business Week* pointed out, "They don't talk much about declining competitiveness in Portland, Oregon, which is enjoying a huge influx of designers, engineers, and entrepreneurs drawn by its funky neighborhoods, miles of bike paths, and recreation options. These are exactly the amenities that Portland has developed to complement its transit system and make its high-density, high-transit matrix work."[11]

In ten years Portland's economy has grown at a steady 5.5 percent annually with companies like Ziba Design, which services tech firms, including Intel. Ziba founder Sohrab Vossoughi says the stimulating city center is critical to being able to hire the twenty new designers he needs a year. "The values of this generation are in line with the DNA of this city," he says.[12]

Similarly, the values of the new energy economy are in line with the DNA of the organically growing high-tech economy in America. The Max system in Portland does not just deliver workers to work; it delivers a wholly invigorated economic base to a major city. New energy in transportation translates to new energy in economic development. The story also means greater social equity, as low-wage workers have more transportation options and greater ease reaching jobs; plus, new construction of dense urban centers creates a boom in demand for high-skill blue-collar workers.

The Portland story has a moral, as all good stories do. It demonstrates that to accomplish grand visions in transportation, the system must be considered as a whole ecosystem, not just in constituent parts. While the construction of the Max would have been impressive in any event, its full flowering took place through integration with a comprehensive plan not only to reduce commuters' travel time and distance while improving the quality of trips, but also to revitalize the urban core, along with the quality of life for its residents. Instead of listening to traffic reports on their car radios, Max passengers can now read the morning paper and attend to more important things.

## From Green Timber to Green Fuels

A clean-energy revolution promises not just to renew big cities; clean energy is having a big impact on small-town American as well. Grays Harbor, a small hamlet on the coast of Washington State, was a dying timber town twenty years ago. Built on the abundant riches of the massive timber on the Olympic Peninsula, it enjoyed a century of harvesting, sawing, processing, and shipping lumber all over the world. For six generations of families, choker setters had gone into the woods, green chain pullers had gone into the mills, and small business owners had cashed their paychecks. It was a happy community of 41,000 souls living in the yearly hundred inches of rain that watered the forest canopy on which they depended.

Then a small, feathered bomb hit the town, in the form of the spotted owl. Rulings by the federal courts designed to protect the endangered creature forced timber companies to abandon the forests that were its critical habitats. This radically reduced timber harvests at the same time that the market was opening to global competition for raw logs and milled forest products. In a matter of years, the timber supply dried up, the mill workers were laid off, and the longshoremen who loaded ships bound across the world sat waiting for the call to join a dockside crew. The call never came.

These are proud and hardworking people: the Swedes of Hoquiam, the Scots of Aberdeen, and the Slavic community in Cosmopolis. They had built a place where work and family were enough. The town had a rough optimism and brawling temper not far removed from the timber camps. Labor was king and work was hard, but the trees would always be there. When the economic heart was ripped from this one-industry community, the visible disintegration of small businesses being shuttered and mills rusting away was bad enough. Far worse was the invisible pain of families whose breadwinner sat idle.

Because Grays Harbor is literally at the end of the road, well away from other employment centers, folks had nowhere to turn. The few tourists who missed the road to the best clam-digging beaches farther south were not much help.

Like many communities suffering from economic dislocation, Grays Harbor began to cast about for ways to bring back the jobs that had been so productive for generations. They tried the conventional routes, attempting to lure light manufacturing and call centers to the area, to little effect. They even tried a plan to make Grays Harbor a historic seaport, filled with sailing ships, museums, and tourists with disposable dollars. It fit the area's sailing tradition and excited the community, but the tourists never came.

Then, serendipitously, the town discovered another renewable resource: biofuels. More accurately, biodiesel discovered Grays Harbor.

It began one day in 2005 when Gary Nelson, director of the Grays Harbor Port District, got a call from John Plaza, founder and president of a company called Imperium Renewables, which makes biodiesel. Plaza had carefully researched potential locations for a huge expansion of his refinery operations and needed a spot with both rail and seaborne access. He had a vision for a plant that could use feed stocks from midwestern soybeans and oil crops around the world while the market for local crops like mustard seed from nearby farmers developed. The demands of the emerging biodiesel market warranted building a plant that could ride out shortages and price spikes in any oil market, and port transportation was key.

The courtship between the community and the company was brief but exciting. Financing was successful, and by November 2006, construction had begun on a 100-million-gallon-per-year plant that will make Grays Harbor the center of the largest biodiesel refinery in North America. With the imposing physical presence of an oil refinery but none of its toxic emissions, it will boast nine two-million-gallon tanks.

Soon, the several hundred well-paid construction workers building this $60 million plant will be replaced by sixty-five to seventy-five refinery workers with steady, well-paid work displacing fossil fuels. Since manufacturing jobs of this quality spin off 7.5 indirect jobs each, this plant will generate about 500 new jobs, many in Grays Harbor. Hundreds of railway workers will deliver thousands of rail cars a year of midwestern soy oil, and scores of tug operators will barge biodiesel to Seattle. That's a lot of jobs in a small town, and the difference between a functioning community and a dot on a map.

Imperium values the skills of workers from the local paper industry, people who are used to processes akin to refining biodiesel. The men and women who brewed up pulp for paper will soon brew biofuels. The company now receives twenty to thirty résumés a week from people drawn by the promise of a local future. Port commissioner Gary Nelson says, "These guys have done it right. They have diversified their operations in feed stock and in their market. I'm impressed with them, and when you are as eager as we are for growth, you make sure things are for real before signing up. We aren't out of the woods yet, because we lost 2,000 jobs in the last five years and we're still not back to even. But we are real hopeful around here now."[13] In a town like Grays Harbor, hope is a precious commodity.

Despite the good news, the transformation cost at least one man his job. Any transition causes dislocation, but in this case the victim was a state representative who spoke poorly of the biodiesel plan and was promptly thrown out of office by his angry constituents. Voters do not like a naysayer, particularly one giving short shrift to economic recovery and the potential of clean energy.

In Grays Harbor, Washington, Imperium Renewables is tapping demand for renewable energy to bring jobs and hope back to a hard-hit mill town.

John Plaza looks at renewable energy as rising above partisan politics. "Biodiesel is a red-blue uniter," he says. "It can unite the country and head us in a new direction in energy. I believe it has the capacity to change the world eventually. Sure, we can't grow our entire supply of fuels using soy-based biodiesel. But we should use what we have, and it's turning this community around economically."[14] In the future, Plaza envisions an even more cutting-edge source of energy: algae, which he believes could produce 650 gallons of biofuel per acre. "When that happens, we can seriously obtain energy independence using just .2 percent of our land mass," he says. His efforts are both building the necessary infrastructure bridge to higher forms of biofuels and reviving the fortunes of a hungry town. "I'm happy with that," he says. He should be.

Grays Harbor is not a one-trick pony, however, when it comes to green industrial development. The biodiesel plant has attracted three other green industries: Grays Harbor Paper produces 100 percent recycled paper; Sierra Pacific burns "hog fuel," the sawdust from the mill; and the Pane Trek Company is building green paneling. Furthermore, these companies have discovered cogeneration; Grays Harbor Paper and Sierra Pacific are burning biofuel to produce both heat for their operations and electricity that is fed back into the grid. This doubles the efficiency of their power operations.

Together, Imperium and those green companies now form the core of the future for Grays Harbor's economy. The sudden concentration of green industry—unimaginable in an area where spotted-owl stew was featured on many restaurant menus in the 1990s—may represent a pattern to be duplicated across small-town America. Green has come to mean jobs—not job destruction—for Grays Harbor.

## A Newer Newark: From Brownfields to Green Buildings

Newark, New Jersey, is not always associated with hope, green strategies, or opportunity. Too often, renewal for cities like Newark has meant the cynical urban renewal of the 1960s, which broke up communities and left them scarred with massive impersonal projects or block after block of demolished buildings. Those were sacrifice zones carved by highways to funnel commuters through the inner city from suburban homes to work downtown without interference. Newark's image is scarred, too; it's more famous for its riots and insurance fires than for its history as a transportation crossroads and a cradle of industry, or for the rich ecological heritage of the Garden State.

But in the heart of Newark a community organizer named Baye Adofo-Wilson is taking a green tack to rebuild his economically distressed neighborhood. As executive director of the Lincoln Park Coast Cultural District, he is bringing new life to the Lincoln Park neighborhood, known locally as the "Bottom." It's a name with a double meaning: the bottom of a hill in the center city and the bottom of the economic ladder. The latter meaning is not lost on the community's residents, and as Wilson says, "When they say you're at the bottom of Newark, you're pretty far down."[15] But there is tremendous hope there as well, hope that Newark and the Bottom are on their way up. Wilson and clean energy are in the thick of an effort to make that a reality.

Wilson is a focused, energetic man who knows how to get things done. He's a person who can pull together a complex project like rebuilding an entire neighborhood with three hundred units of housing and a cultural arts center, and learn green development as he goes.

Like many neglected urban neighborhoods, Lincoln Park has tremendous forgotten history and abandoned assets. Beginning two blocks from City Hall, it is a bridge between the rest of the city and its downtown. It was part of the 1666 footprint of Newark. In the nineteenth century it was one of the more affluent neighborhoods in New Jersey, home to two governors and the founders of Prudential Insurance and Ballantine Beer.

But the area fell victim to the troubles that hit many American inner cities in the 1950s and 1960s. With redlining by banks and urban flight strangling new investment, poverty set in, historic brownstones collapsed, maintenance was deferred, and the neighborhood deteriorated.

While Wilson is green by training and inclination, his passion is also for people. He has come to clean energy not only to do the right thing for the planet, but as a strategy for social justice. "Coming out of a poor community, the environment wasn't part of the central conversation on poverty," he says. When energy and the environment came up, it was about siting hazardous land uses and Superfund sites near poor, black, and vulnerable populations. Those are important issues, but not part of the inspirational solution he wanted to build. Recently, however, his passion for energy and environmental issues has been rekindled by the opportunities he sees as a nonprofit developer to build a green workforce, create homeownership and affordability, and provide new clean-air solutions.

Wilson is redeveloping Lincoln Park. He has assembled an eleven-acre site in the center of the downtown and is preparing to build three hundred units of new housing surrounding a new Museum of African American Music. The project uses culture and history as a centerpiece of the renaissance of the community. And Wilson has decided that he wants the museum to be the greenest building in the state of New Jersey, a testament to sustainability. He and his colleagues felt that in Newark the decline had been so deep that anything new had to be at the cutting edge, to leapfrog over current practices. Green building aligns their project with the future.

They plan to make the museum a teaching tool, first educating the community on its history and culture and then opening a window to green issues, materials, and industries. "You can get them into the room with hip-hop and DJ and house music and educate them on other issues like energy by letting the building itself speak. It creates a new way for them to listen."

As the project grew, the ideas expanded and became more ambitious. With three hundred units, the opportunity to make a difference was too great. Now they are making all the housing units high-performance buildings, registered as meeting the LEED Gold Standard. They are building in solar panels to cut long-term energy costs. They have launched a partnership with the New Jersey chapter of the U.S.

Green Building Council to develop new design standards to meet the needs of multi-unit dwellings, pushing the envelope to be more inclusive of mixed-use and urban homes. They are helping to write the rules on how urban areas go green.

As Wilson says, "At the end of the day, this is what we should all be doing in the city." There is a moral commitment to the green dimensions of the project, because this effort will invest $170 million in a neighborhood desperately in need of capital improvement. This scale of development by definition will have an environmental impact on the community, and he wants to make sure it is a good one. He is pulling out all the stops on rethinking materials by using green roofs; pervious paving to allow rainwater to pass through the surface; bamboo flooring that grows in a season, whereas other wood takes years; wheat-board cabinetry that is both nontoxic and easily grown; and low-flow bathroom fixtures that greatly increase both energy and water conservation.

Wilson and his colleagues are in the process of developing strategies to quantify the savings from energy efficiency and the reductions in their greenhouse gas impacts, even exploring how to use carbon credits for urban redevelopment. Ultimately, he hopes to produce zero-energy buildings, with no net energy use, through aggressive implementation of efficiency and renewables. That is a pretty impressive goal for a mixed-income urban redevelopment project with substantial amounts of affordable housing. But there is no reason that environmental sensitivity and deep social equity should not go hand in hand.

Wilson makes it clear that public policy has been essential in making this effort possible. When developers build in a greenfield—land never before developed—they have none of the cleanup costs that urban developers have. An urban site's costs, however, are borne as extra overhead costs by the developer, even though the benefits to the community and the state are great from reusing existing high-quality infrastructure for smart growth. It is appropriate that public policy helps development move from sprawl back to investing in the urban core. In Lincoln Park, for example, the developers were able to tap federal and state brownfield assistance for cleanup of contaminated groundwater from leaking underground storage tanks.

In turning brownfields to green buildings, access to public resources has been critical. As leaders in the field, Wilson and Lincoln Park are also bringing the trades up the learning curve as contractors master the skills of green construction and programs like YouthBuild train young people in the construction jobs of the future.

It has been a long journey from the project's beginnings in a community charrette in 1999, when residents started to map their destiny, to the acquisition and assembly of thirty lots from the state to make the vision possible. Now they have broken ground, bringing the dream of a new home closer to three hundred families and enriching the community with a new cultural resource.

The best news is that Lincoln Park families get safer streets, homeowners get energy cost savings, and young folks will find new jobs and skills. The community will see the cultural fabric of the neighborhood restored and a stronger legacy created for future generations. Whatever their vantage point, the citizens of Lincoln Park are coming to believe in the promise of a green future for their old neighborhood. Clean, efficient energy and strong communities truly go hand in hand.

## The Greenest City in America

> My goal is to make Chicago an example of how a densely populated city can live in harmony with the environment and nature.
>
> —*Mayor Richard Daley, 2006*

What Lincoln Park has undertaken in a single neighborhood is being taken up elsewhere across whole metropolitan regions, in both affluent communities and those that have seen hard times. We need only look to Chicago, where visionary leadership has launched a new direction for one of America's great metropolises, claiming the mantle as one of America's leaders on clean energy and green development.

Chicago is a town with a gritty, rough-and-tumble reputation, known for fading industry, hardball politics, Al Capone, and in modern times the expansive neglect of its South Side. Mayor Richard Daley is a tough politician and one of the last people you'd expect to be a tree hugger. But seven years ago, Mayor Daley realized that more trees were being removed than planted in his city. The fact struck a chord with him as exactly the sort of thing he was trying to change in his efforts to fight crime, rebuild industry, lure new investment, and keep residents from leaving the city. The mayor faced far bigger problems in transforming this city of three million from the capital of the Rust Belt into a high-tech powerhouse, but he saw a connection between the city's struggles and its trees.

Daley's plan for revitalizing Chicago was as dramatic as it was simple. He just decided to make Chicago the greenest city in the nation. He didn't do it to take on energy independence or climate change. His goals were economic and social more than environmental. But building a green city could have multiple benefits, all creating an energetic and vibrant quality of life that would attract business, even as it cut carbon emissions and got people out of their cars.

Greening would be a cornerstone of turning around the reputation of the city. According to Sadhu Johnston, the city's dynamic secretary of the environment, that meant everything from changing the city's automobile fleet, to evaluating the supplies purchased, to using renovation of public buildings to promote efficiency and renewable energy. Creating a program for green buildings became a visible symbol of transformation.

Daley demonstrated his commitment by installing a living "green roof" on City Hall, a high-tech sod planting of wild local grasses and wildflowers. The combination of plants and walkways covers 20,300 square feet of the roof and includes an increased layer of insulation. An irrigation system distributes water during the cooling season, and shade from the plants reduces the sunlight striking the building by 25 percent.[16] The benefits were clear. The green roof reduced the temperatures by 50°F or more on the rooftop, reducing the air temperature above City Hall by 10° to 15°F. The roof saves City Hall $3,600 every year and cuts energy use by 9,272 kilowatt-hours of electricity and 7,372 therms of natural gas for heating annually.[17]

Johnston and the mayor went further and dreamed of taking the project to scale across the city. Today, Chicago has over 2.5 million square feet of green roofs on over two hundred public and private buildings. Reducing the average temperature throughout the city by 1°F—an achievable goal—by using green infrastructure like green roofs and shade trees is calculated to cut cooling costs by $150 million a year.[18]

Daley is using public buildings to lead by example. What started with City Hall became a template for new schools, fire stations, and museums—all high-performance, green, and efficient buildings—to demonstrate stewardship of energy and show the private sector what could be achieved. In Chicago, as in Newark, the buildings have become the teachers.

The importance of green buildings goes well beyond the energy savings and the iconic value of green roofs. Green building is a central strategy for addressing our energy addiction and responding to the climate crisis. In the United States today, design, construction, and operation of buildings account for 20 percent of all economic activity. Buildings consume 65 percent of all electricity, 35 percent of total energy, and 40 percent of raw material; and they produce 30 percent of all our greenhouse gas emissions.[19] Green building and green infrastructure can slash the environmental impact of development and wasted energy.

To date, Chicago has retrofitted 15 million square feet of city office space, saving $4 million in energy costs. And the private sector is getting involved in a major way, drawn by expedited permitting and incentives, like financing for design and certification costs worth as much as $50,000, and grants for green roof construction and solar thermal projects. The number of green building permit applications has more than tripled, and in 2006 over ninety major construction projects were pursuing LEED certification, which requires energy-efficient construction, alternative energy sources, and improved use of resources and can mean cutting energy use in half.

Daley and Johnston have used the greening of Chicago not only to generate jobs and tax revenue indirectly by improving quality of life, but also to recruit clean-energy businesses directly. They can point to the growing Solargenix Company, which moved its manufacturing plant to the city in part because of the city's multimillion-dollar commitment to solar power. The strategy is also creating new markets in the construction industry for skilled craftsmen, laborers, and energy auditors; and the electricians' union and the local utility have created a partnership for solar installation and apprenticeship training.

Johnston is excited by how the green strategies that the mayor has put in place often solve many problems with one solution. Every year 20,000 ex-offenders are released from prison into Chicago. Recidivism is high for those people, who typically have trouble finding work and rebuilding their lives and too often end up back behind bars. A truly sustainable city must provide work for the least employable; restoring social balance is every bit as important as restoring ecological balance. Mayor Daley, recognizing this, created a number of programs to take on the problem of job placement for ex-offenders and simultaneously develop a green-jobs base of skill-building work in a clean-energy economy. The city has created Greencorps, which offers a range of regenerative job training and placement options for ex-offenders, including weatherization of homes to save energy and heating costs and rebuild the housing stock even as it rebuilds people's lives.

## The Industry That Devoured Marsh Fork Hollow

If smart energy investments can rebuild a community, thoughtless ones can tear a community apart. The legacy of wasteful energy use is having a tremendous impact on communities in Appalachia today.

It is a peculiar attribute of the modern coal industry that it can both provide for and devour the communities that nourish it. The former residents of Marsh Fork, West Virginia, will tell you that the industry that sustained their town for over one hundred years is the same one that today is eating it alive. This is the result of a new type of coal mining called mountaintop removal, a process in which whole swathes of mountains are torn down to reach the coal, and whole regions are destroyed in the process. It's not your father's coal mining anymore.

Julia Bonds is a Marsh Fork grandmother whose ancestors lived there for ten generations. Now she has only fond memories of her children swimming in the creeks of her beloved "holler" to tie her to a place that is no more. Beginning in 1997, the coal dust spreading inexorably over every inch of her home, the toxics leaching into the creeks, and the constant threat of a breach in the upstream impoundment dam slowly but convincingly forced every living resident of Marsh Fork Hollow, and its adjacent communities of Packetville and Birch Hollow, to abandon their histories and homes and flee.

Julia Bonds was a child of the coal mines; her father spent his life in the mines, as did his father before him. That both of them died of black lung disease did not, perhaps surprisingly, embitter her to the thought of coal. She says that was simply the way of the mining life in the past. When asked, she will tell you she is a "coal miner's daughter" with a tone of pride.

But when she began to see the black residue in her home, on her car, and on her child, she became concerned about the mining that was literally shaving the top off of the hills a few miles from her home. It is not surprising that she began to see the impact in her home, as this type of mining chops off hundreds of acres of the hills that sheltered those West Virginia towns, pulverizing the coal so that the slightest touch stirs it up into a swirling dust cloud and storing millions of gallons of toxic blue stew behind temporary earthen dams perched tenuously above the communities.

Bonds's pleasant memory of her grandson fishing in the creek is now replaced with the memory of the day he came home commenting on the strange color of the creek that had once supported a good stock of keepers. Worse, her memories now include listening to her grandson wheezing, because he had an increase in asthma attacks, attacks that virtually disappeared after their move just five miles away to Rock Creek.

As the insults became worse, the residents of the hollows began to contemplate the simple necessity of leaving. It was not an easy decision. Their lives were bound to friends and family, their vocational prospects were limited, and they had no way to get fair-market value for their homes, since even if the coal company made them an offer, the value was lessened due to the mountaintop removal.

Ultimately, they had no choice. One by one, the families succumbed to mountaintop mining and abandoned their homes. Now the only living souls in the three hollow communities are the guards posted by the coal company.

Julia Bonds has a clear opinion about what happened to her and her community, the place where she enjoyed her neighbors, the fresh air, the clean water, and the simple life in a frenzied world. She knows the value of coal because her family mined it for generations, but that was in underground mining that did not chew up the surface. "Our feeling is that we were sacrificed," she says. "We were sacrificed for cheap energy. Well, in my book, there is nothing cheap about what happened to us."[20]

These are not the paranoid ravings of a woman with an ax to grind. She will show you a copy of the coal company's depopulation plan, a plan to move whole communities from their valleys, refugees from mountaintop mining. Even the company recognizes the impact of this type of mining to be incompatible with adjacent human habitation.

Bonds's view is clear. Coal can be of value. It can supply heat for the home and employment for whole communities. "But," she says, "if they can't do it without destroying whole hollers, creeks, and communities like ours, they shouldn't do it at all." Each time her house shakes from the four million pounds of explosives blown every day, she is reminded to keep working on the organization she has started in an effort to move Congress and confront presidential inaction, the Coal River Mountain Watch.

She is involved for the long haul. Her empty home still stands in Marsh Fork Hollow, and her kin are buried there. But the job of saving Marsh Fork is formidable. It pits her against powerful forces like the

Massey Coal Mining Company and its president, Don Blankenship, who turned $3 million of slashing television attacks toward politicians who opposed mountaintop removal in the West Virginia legislature before the 2006 election. He hoped to bring down those who insisted on the people's right to protect air and water, health and safety.

While the fight over protecting communities was played out as a partisan war over the rules the mines would face, it must have been disappointing to Blankenship on election night, when the good people of West Virginia turned against his PR blitz and voted to increase the number of opponents of mountaintop removal.

Julia Bonds does not believe we should shed any tears for Mr. Blankenship, not when his mining practices caused her neighbors' children to have to sleep with their clothes on when it rained in case the jury-rigged dams above their homes collapsed and the family had to make a run for it. Or when her neighbors' dinner table conversation changed from Little League games to the best escape routes out of their hollow. Or when her tight-knit community scattered to the four winds.

The electoral victory for the people of the hollows demonstrates a fundamental principle of American politics. When big-money interests can do their work in the dark, in the back rooms and corridors of power, they frequently succeed. When they are exposed to the public, as the Massey Company was in the election of 2006, their efforts are usually rejected.

The work of opposing the mountaintop mining will continue because the damage continues. According to federal agencies, mountaintop mining buried more than 72 miles of Appalachian streams between 1985 and 2001.[21] Without additional protections, 2,200 square miles of forest will be eliminated, and at least 2,400 miles of streams will be wiped out or harmed by 2013 if changes are not made. The final version of the Bush administration's mountaintop removal study, however, proposed streamlining the permit process rather than protecting the streams. "This is just a rehash of what the federal agencies have been doing for the last five years, ignoring the clear scientific evidence of irreparable harm to West Virginia," said Joe Lovett, director of the Appalachian Center for the Economy and the Environment.[22]

"We deserve better than this," says Julia Bonds. Indeed, they do.

## Grabbing the Reins: Community-Based Ownership

In Marsh Fork, the survival of an entire community may depend upon creating smarter ways of producing and using our energy. In other small towns in America, the coming of clean energy has meant an economic rebirth.

On the back roads of Minnesota and around the country, farm communities have been fighting off decline, with foreclosures, local businesses boarding up shop, and entire communities threatening to vanish. In the face of this outflow of capital, both human and economic, and the threat of losing their way of life, the people of Minnesota are fighting back.

In 1993, the Minnesota state legislature passed a simple bill to create incentives for small ethanol plants, with a 15-million-gallon-a-year capacity, to be built and owned by local farmers and their neighbors.[23] These refineries were to be farmer-owned cooperatives—an alternative to the absentee ownership that is sweeping rural America—creating value-added production, making farmers more than price-taking producers of commodity crops on a global market, and reviving hometowns in the process.

While corn ethanol is not the final solution to our energy dependence, it is a part of the transition to advanced biofuels and away from oil, and the new models of cooperative ownership pioneered in Minnesota offer a way of making sure that the clean-energy revolution benefits not only corporate giants—replacing Exxon with Cargill—but also small towns and family-owned operations.

The Minnesota story is about community spirit inspiring community investment. The co-op approach is as old as the farmers' grange societies, built to pool their capital to settle the nation's heartland. Today's co-op pioneers reached Benson, Minnesota, 131 years after the original pioneer, Ole Corneiliusen, a Norwegian immigrant, arrived on foot and planted the Scandinavian cooperative ethic, which eventually blossomed into an ethanol co-op there.[24]

One of today's pioneers is Bill Lee, plant manager of Chippewa Valley Ethanol Company, a farmer-owned co-op and one of the first four plants built under the program. Today there are over one hundred. After ten years of operation, over 950 local farmers and community investors are owners, and the benefits to Benson are far reaching. The city has become a renewable energy powerhouse, and the boom has spread new wealth.

In the mid-1990s, the Rural Electric Cooperative of Benson decided to choose a bold plan instead of accepting slow death. The board of directors saw that without some boost to the economy, there would be no electrical consumers left in their town. The board went to work to create a farmer-owned biorefinery from scratch. Using Minnesota's incentives, the board members started lining up local investors, a process that was hard at first. Trust takes time. People were used to Amway parties, but drawing investors into a new product like biofuels was a tough sell.

The people of Benson were driven by a powerful alchemical combination of desperation and determination. Their desperation arose from seeing no jobs for their kids, a population in decline, low grain prices, and a general economic malaise. Their determination came from the local tradition of citizens stepping forward together when times were tough—as for an old-time barn raising. The icon for the new resurgence of the farm economy may be the capital drive for an ethanol co-op.

The Chippewa Valley cooperative started operations in 1995 with a state-of-the-art, 15-million-gallon ethanol refinery. It has expanded to a 45-million-gallon-a-year plant today, and the co-op is preparing for a further expansion to 85 million gallons a year.[25] In the next round of investment co-op members are taking the technology further, using agricultural wastes like wheat straw and cornstalks to produce biomass energy. This will allow them to turn off the natural gas and reduce the climate impact, creating a smaller $CO_2$ footprint.

Investing in biomass gasification will also help them prepare to participate in the coming market for next-generation cellulosic ethanol, made from the woody fiber of plants, as they learn to create markets for a new commodity—biomass—and to collect, store, and use it profitably. They understand that they are now in the first phase of a two-phase transformation. They intend to be ready for the second phase, of cellulosic ethanol.

But innovations are happening not only in technology; the business model, too, is evolving and producing exciting new potentials. Benson shows that the farmer-owned model is working well. Most of the investors live within fifty miles of the plant, and ownership comes with a responsibility to grow feed stocks for the fuel production. Two-thirds of the corn used at the plant comes from local farms. So not only the dividends and profits but also the money spent on supplies are all recirculating within the local economy with a very positive effect, which will be amplified with the switch to cellulose.

At another community-owned co-op, the CORN-er Stone Ethanol Cooperative of Luverne, Minnesota, which began in 1995, the whole community is welcome to invest, not just farmers. It took a long two and a half years for the team of Luverne community leaders to raise the $9 million needed to build their facility. They raised $3.4 million of community money, pieced together USDA loan guarantees and personal guarantees, and even went to the contractor to help finance the project. Today they have over 220 investors, all from within the community. What started as a 12-million-gallon plant is running at 21 million gallons a year, with better technology.[26]

Benson and Luverne demonstrate that in cooperative facilities, the value of local ownership is substantially greater than wealth that comes from remote ownership. The Luverne plant generates nearly $50 million in revenue, most of which circulates within the community, paying for grain, local bankers, and labor. The only money that leaves goes to buy natural gas, electricity, and insurance. All other expenses stay within the community.

In the eight years since the Luverne co-op started operations, community owners have received dividends of five times their original investment, and the original equity stake has gone up in value five and a half times. The minimum investment was $5,000 and the average $17,000; today the typical investor has gotten over $85,000 in cash and is sitting on stock worth $94,000.

For Dave Kolsrud, the CEO, CORN-er Stone is also a market for his crops. He is a fourth-generation farmer who owns five hundred acres on Beaver Creek that he is handing down to his son, Chris. "You know what this co-op means to me?" he asks. "It means my son can stay on the farm. The amount of corn I send to the co-op is not huge, but it's a huge deal to me to keep my son farming."[27]

Today in Luverne and Benson the implement dealers are doing well again, and local residents are paying down debt. Real estate and land values have risen as people purchase more land for production. Locals are driving nicer vehicles and spending more at local businesses. In the neighborhoods there are new roads.

In Benson, Lee finds it remarkable that the town of 35,000 people is commissioning a study on preserving the architectural integrity of the downtown business district, not something a town in decline has the luxury to think about. Benson also just completed the construction of a new swimming pool and recreation center to replace the old WPA vintage pool. The newfound prosperity brought by the co-op has created the opportunity for a new generation of investment that hadn't been seen since the Works Progress Administration of the Great Depression.

The benefits generated in Benson and Luverne have not been limited to those towns. The Luverne consortium has invested in three other facilities, as far away as Nebraska and Kansas, that share its community-based model. These successful pioneers are reaching out to spread the word and share their investments in similar communities struggling to raise capital.

Community ownership is now spreading to wind power as well. It may seem a leap from ethanol to wind, but as Kolsrud says, "Once you get into this renewables business, you really get involved." These people are hooked.

One project spawned by capital from the co-op's profits is Minwind Energy, a community-based wind farm also in Luverne, spun off by the co-op investors. Eleven massive wind towers have been built in Luverne, with turbines ranging from 950 kilowatts to 1.65 megawatts. This wind farm is all community owned, by people within fifty miles. Together, they have invested over $14 million in turbines, all the money coming from within the community.

Lee sees historical and mythological precedents here. "I think of it as bringing into being Thomas Jefferson's vision of an empowered yeomanry," he says, "more democratic, more engaged, with citizens able to live well off the land for which they are the stewards. It's good for democracy." He also puts it another way: "We co-ops can play Prometheus to the petroleum industry's Saturn. It's an epic battle of taking control of your destiny and looking out for the little guy."

Yet the Minnesota plants would not have gotten off the ground without the state's policy and the support they received from USDA in finding mechanisms to facilitate financing. In addition, the Renewable Fuel Standard enacted in 2005 was a major push for opening up the market nationally, giving confidence to investors. Now perhaps most important is increasing the alternative fuels infrastructure, so that drivers can always find a pump; and certifying higher blends of ethanol in regular fuel to get standard gasoline blended up to E20 will also pay immediate dividends.

In the wind industry, the policy incentives have not been as strong as they have been in the ethanol industry for helping community-based projects. The production tax credit that offers an incentive for wind farms helps only entities with large profits that need tax deductions and works less well for co-ops. A new system is warranted to help these co-ops. Kolsrud says, "When you put a tower in that is owned by the community, they become beautiful. Farmers say, 'I own 5 percent of that turbine, and I'm doing my part for energy independence.' It is a real emotional high. People really love their towers. They feel part of changing America's energy path." He believes that if you could level the play-ing field of incentives, community wind would take off.

With the right policies, we could see a clean-energy revolution be-come a community investment revolution to boot. If so, we will realize Thomas Jefferson's dreams of vibrant and independent farmers ensur-ing the health of American democracy. As Jefferson said, "Small land-owners are the most precious part of a state."[28]

## Putting the Commons into Community

The seeds of the new energy economy are sprouting all across the na-tion. Where they have landed, economies are changing rapidly. As we have seen, they can sprout in all kinds of soil.

New Jersey, Minnesota, Oregon, and West Virginia all have towns and neighborhoods that have embraced a new energy future as a way to fight for their communities and rebuild their economies. Their actions have come from the bottom up, not the top down. Farmers in Min-nesota decided to create a new model for community-owned energy. Urban developers are rebuilding their own neighborhoods using energy-efficient measures as a rallying cry in Newark. The seeds of these efforts were found not in some boardroom in a distant big city but in the communities themselves, and the benefits flowed back into new models of development: green cities and towns that are strong, prosper-ous, and vibrant.

These groups of people have embodied the root value of the word *community*: to hold in common. The voices of the people we have met who have done this pioneering work carry an undertone of consider-able pride in what they have done for their hometowns. Whether the fi-nancial equity is in private, public, or cooperatively shared hands, the community has been given a stake in the development process.

Financial equity matters, but when it comes to restoring our small towns and inner cities, we should also value what may be termed "hopeful equity." To restore a small midwestern town, you need the town's people to hold hope that their bank, their clinic, and their movie

theater will be there in five years. They need to hold a stake in the equity of hope in their community's future. New energy industries can
make a big deposit in that account.

A clean-energy revolution can be a catalyst for restoring the frayed
fabric of America's communities. It represents a shift in power in two
ways. First, power is being distributed in the sense that the refineries,
wind turbines, and other productive centers of renewable energy are
being geographically dispersed and decentralized. Distributed energy
generation means local investment. Second, the power to make decisions and the power to make investments are being shared between the
Wall Streets of the world and the Main Streets of the world. Both ways
are important and revolutionary.

The real power of a new, clean energy future is giving people a sense
of power over their own lives. It is one thing to switch on a light. It is
quite another to switch on a community's sense of self-reliance and
optimism.

## "WE DON'T NEED OIL"

### Jay Inslee

"We don't need oil," announced the confidence-exuding, silver-haired executive as he walked into a basement meeting room of the Capitol to greet a group of congressmen. He looked like a successful software entrepreneur, wearing a soft cashmere sweater, dark slacks, and a cell phone on his belt, the way gunslingers wore their Colt 45s. "We don't need hydrogen," he told us. "We don't need new car and engine designs. We don't need new distribution systems or waiting ten years to solve this problem. Most importantly, we don't need oil. We need ethanol.

"I am not here to talk about your little experiments in collecting vegetable oil from the french fry stand and running your Volkswagen with it. I am not interested in your neighborhood experiments in biofuels. I am only interested in technologies and products that can be scaled up to serve a major market, the United States of America. I am only interested in technologies that can both solve our energy woes and create a profitable industry."[1]

His name was Vinod Khosla, and his presentation was spellbinding. My friend and fellow congressman Republican Zach Wamp heard the message. The next morning he approached me and said that he was ready to join me in a full-bore effort to jump-start the production of cellulosic ethanol. Zach wasn't just eager, he was suddenly a house afire, wanting to introduce a cellulosic ethanol bill "asap."

In one hour, Vinod Khosla had presented a level-headed, understandable, and technologically achievable plan for effectively weaning our way off of foreign oil by ultimately producing cellulosic ethanol, an alcohol made not from corn, but from the woody cellulose material of plants.

The congressmen in that meeting haven't been the same since.

Before Khosla arrived, ethanol made from the kernels of corn was considered to be a nice, but limited, fuel source. By the time he left, we had a vision of an entirely new energy horizon, with cellulosic ethanol supplanting vast amounts of petroleum.

Khosla was an "army brat," the son of an Indian officer who moved continually from town to town in northern India. Khosla wowed his family with his penchant for reading newspapers at age three and building electronics at age ten. He moved to America; founded Sun Microsystems, where he pioneered open systems and commercial RISC processors; became a leading venture capitalist; and along the way became one of the wealthiest men in the world.

The eight members around the table listening to him were rapt, as rapt as any herd of congressmen I had ever seen. Members usually are a fidgety bunch, glancing at their BackBerries, reading op-eds,

Vinod Khosla led in software; now he is leading in biofuels.

and whispering to their staff. But this group did not whisper, rustle, or breathe heavily. He owned them.

He was not timid. He addressed our fear of failure right up front. "Do not reject this idea just because it seems beyond our grasp at the moment. All new ideas seem preposterous at first. Ten years ago, who among you could have predicted you would be living via e-mail? Now every single one of you is addicted to your CrackBerries, right?" Then he asked, "How many of you have cell phones that weigh five pounds? None, right? Well that's how much they weighed fifteen years ago."

As a younger man, Khosla had predicted the rise of Internet protocol technology, way ahead of the curve. He went on to create hugely successful companies and was well stocked with credibility. A decade ago, he heavily invested in certain technologies that would be useful in the telecommunications industry, while the dominant industry totally missed the oncoming technology. Sound familiar?

To those who say we might get only twenty tons of biomass per acre in 2020 rather than his projected twenty-seven tons, Khosla replies, "Well, that means we will just replace all our imported oil, rather than replacing all our oil. Isn't that good enough? Isn't replacing 60 percent of our oil worth the risk?"

He has invested in three corn ethanol plants, three cellulosic ethanol companies, and two companies that are working to develop over-the-horizon means of creating ethanol using even more distant technologies. In February 2007, he announced the opening in Georgia of the world's first cellulosic ethanol plant to use wood fibers from trees. One might liken his personal investment commitment to short, medium, and long-range strategies for the whole country, a combination our nation could follow.

Khosla is the Captain Cook of venture capitalists, so six congressmen—four Democrats and two Republicans—have joined his voyage to discover an ethanol economy. We have banded together in a series of meetings to try to develop a suite of legislative proposals we hope to boil into one bill designed to accelerate both the production and use of cellulosic ethanol. Our ideas range from raising the tax credit for cellulosic ethanol to requiring cars to be flex-fuel capable to requiring a certain number of E85 ethanol pumps in service stations.

But the truth is that no matter what policy Congress adopts, without the energy and insight of entrepreneurs like Khosla, we will accomplish little. Sometimes the private sector has to inspire us in Congress. Government can't do it alone.

# CHAPTER 6

# *Homegrown Energy*

Why didn't you and I invest heavily in Microsoft in 1986? Our $1,000 down payment would be worth nearly $350,000 today.[1] But we missed the opportunity. Why? Because we walked to work in the old economy, treading a familiar path, unaware of the changes on the horizon, not seeing what was coming, while wide-eyed and wild-haired computer geeks mined the mother lode of emerging potential, racing to program new languages and whole new modes of communication, spinning silicon into gold as they forged a new digital economy. We heard the predictions of a radically changing world but had trouble distinguishing the coming reality from the science fiction musings of futurists.

It was a quietly frenzied time for those involved, focused and practical yet radically transformative, with computer keys clacking all night as whole new industries and fortunes were built by digital geniuses in their garages and venture capitalists in their suites. It all occurred right beneath our noses, as we, the vast majority, remained oblivious to the birth of a new world.

A new world is being born again today.

The venture capitalists who brought us the Internet and the telecommunications revolution are well on their way to answering the shot across the bow of climate change with a new suite of low-carbon technologies. You don't have to listen to their pronouncements; you can follow their actions in the financial pages instead.

According to research by Clean Edge, which tracks trends in the industry, investment in wind is predicted to grow by 240 percent by 2016. In the same time period, growth in solar investment will explode by 344 percent.[2] These are booming technologies that are rapidly advancing in price and productivity, moving forward in scale at a rapid clip driven by policy, sound engineering, urgent need, and a public that has finally opened its eyes to the limits of our atmospheric dumping ground. The same visionaries who saw the revolution in computing and communications have put their chips on a winner a second time, but this time the stakes are far higher, and the consequences for our lives may be still more profound.

But clean energy also includes fuels, and the market for biofuels has exploded as well. It hit $20.5 billion globally in 2006, growing more than 30 percent from the previous year. Even without additional federal incentives, global manufacture and wholesale pricing of biofuels (both ethanol and biodiesel) are forecast to grow nearly 300 percent in ten years, to $80.9 billion by 2016.[3] Federal policy to stimulate this market further, as well as to promote developments that will improve its sustainability, is a near certainty, making this a conservative growth estimate.

On the ground, all this investment translates into bricks and mortar: new products and a new suite of choices for energy. In January 2006, Seattle Biodiesel, now Imperium Renewables, made news by attracting $7.5 million from venture capitalists betting on a technology most Americans had never heard of: biodiesel fuel. Why was that front-page material in one Seattle paper? One of those investors was Microsoft billionaire Paul Allen. And what about his even more famous partner, Bill Gates? Gates's investment firm had plunked down over $30 million the week before on a nascent biofuels company in California.

"The greatest fortunes in the history of the world will be made in this new energy business," says Ted Turner, the man who won the America's Cup, founded CNN, and made $1 billion in the process.[4] The biggest energy business going is oil, and finding an alternative has become job number one for many. Following the logic of Turner's prediction, climate solutions are not only good for the planet; increasingly, they are good business as well. Investing in renewable energy not only drives down carbon emission but also drives up earnings. Gone are the days when the move away from carbon-based energy could credibly be called a threat to our economy. We are facing a massive transition, and an abundant harvest will be reaped by those with foresight, capital, and a better way of trapping energy. To be sure, as with any technology, there will be something of a bubble with all this capital chasing new clean energy; some firms will flourish, and some will fail. But our lives, our workplaces, and our communities will be remade once again by the coming clean-energy revolution.

It is not the fortunes that will be made that ultimately are of consequence here, however; it is the explosive growth of a new fuel. Rockefeller's fuel (gasoline) changed America far more than it changed his fortune. We are about to experience such a sea change as we democratize and decarbonize energy through wind, sun, and biofuels. The day is coming when we will be able to get our fuel from midwestern farmers rather than Middle Eastern sheiks—in fact, not just from farmers in the Midwest but also from pulp mills in Maine and Georgia, landfills in Chicago and LA, and wheat farms in Idaho.

## Spinners of Straw into Gold

Ray Hess is a farmer who has made his living growing wheat and potatoes. Now he also sows the seeds of hope on his ranch in the Upper Snake River Valley of Idaho. Hess looks out over his 1,400 acres and sees the farm his grandfather started by laboriously breaking the ground of a sagebrush-covered plateau seventy years ago, and he wonders if his two sons will be able to keep the farm. Like so many farmers, he has been hit hard by the twin demons of skyrocketing fuel prices and low commodity prices. Farm incomes have been in decline. Hess has dreaded even contemplating selling off his ancestral ground.

But an opportunity to stay on his land has come along. Two years ago he started talking to the Iogen Corporation about building a refinery that could take farm wastes and spin them into a clear alcohol—cellulosic ethanol—to power cars. Iogen makes the next generation of ethanol, made from cellulose, or woody plant matter, using everything from cornstalks and wheat straw to rice hulls and switchgrass, transforming agricultural residues and dedicated energy crops into a new low-carbon, high-value fuel.

Hess went to work to sign up three hundred farmers to contracts for providing their straw to Iogen at prices that varied from $8 to $25 per ton, depending on the price of crude oil. The higher oil prices go, the higher the return to the farmer. Hess was successful in part because, as president of the Idaho Potato Growers Association, he is a credible leader and because Iogen is the only company in the world that has produced cellulosic ethanol from straw in large quantities, almost 780,000 gallons a year already, with plans to build plants to produce closer to 80 million gallons a year in coming years.[5]

So now three hundred farmers over a fifty-mile radius centered around Blackfoot are chomping at the bit to start baling their waste straw and cashing those checks from Iogen. That $25 to $40 per-acre additional revenue could mean the difference, for this whole generation of farmers, between keeping their kids on the land and seeing multiple generations of tradition go the way of the sideboard plow.

Hess has done his homework. He has devised a game plan for the actual nuts and bolts of the growing, harvesting, and transportation of the straw that would make logistics planners at the Pentagon envious. He knows that his valley has just the right infrastructure to make it the perfect place for an entirely new industry to take root.

He has also looked at the growing demand for ethanol, driven by a national imperative for new sources of clean fuel, and has reached the powerful conclusion that cellulosic ethanol is the only type of ethanol that could sustainably meet that demand. Relying on first-generation corn ethanol over the long term would put too much pressure on commodity prices and natural resources to be tenable. Everyone is waiting for cellulosic ethanol to provide the next wave of supply, because farms can produce several times the amount of energy from an acre of soil by using cellulosic ethanol technology than by using only the first-generation ethanol from corn. Corn ethanol uses only the kernel of the plant. Cellulosic ethanol uses the carbohydrates of the entire plant—kernel, stalk, leaves, and all—not only of corn but of a variety of crops (including Hess's wheat straw). Perhaps most important, Hess has looked closely at the economics and at Iogen's projection that it will be able to produce ethanol for between $.90 and $1.20 per gallon, including the cost of the feed stock. He knows that at costs anywhere close to those numbers, drivers will be beating a path to Iogen's door and to his fields.

It is true that Hess is just tickled to see a fuel developed not from oil but from corn stover, straw, grasses, or even "your shirt off your back," as he delights in saying. But he is also a hard-hearted capitalist who knows how to count, and he counts on real cash from cellulosic ethanol. Eventually, with better economics and better $CO_2$ emissions, Ray Hess and his sons can stay on his farm and we can stay on the earth.

## The New Edisons: From Dot-Com Millionaires to Biofuel Pioneers

Fortunes built on the foundations of chips consisting of strings of silicon atoms are now building businesses based on creating chains of carbon atoms. Silicon makes a dandy medium for computer chips, but if you put a match to it, it melts with virtually no flame and leaves an ugly black residue. Carbon atoms, in contrast, burn with a vengeance when hooked together in long chains. We have built our economy on the energy contained in those chains, in the form of coal and oil. But now we are ready to put into our service whole new combinations of carbon atoms, this time arranged by living plants rather than by the compression of the earth's dead crust.

Biofuels are a new generation of carbon chains and may be fairly considered fresh energy sources. They are fresh in the sense that they are not the product of millions of years of compression beneath millions of tons of metamorphic rock, which is what it takes to mint a gallon of oil or a ton of coal. Instead, they represent a benign marriage of chlorophyll molecules with the sun's own rays falling silently on our farmers' fields. That marriage produces carbohydrates, which can be refined by companies now being founded by software millionaires and farmer-owned cooperatives alike.

Biofuels are based on the principle that humankind can break apart what photosynthesis has put together. Unlike fossilized carbon, which must be mined from the earth and then is sent into the atmosphere, biofuels pull carbon from the air, recycling it back into plant matter as they build the sugars and fibers that become fuel. That wonderful process, in which chlorophyll acts as a matchmaker between carbon dioxide and sunlight, is the foundation of life on this planet. With no photosynthesis, there is no food.

Carbohydrates are like vegetable energy-storage packets. That's why we eat them. But new technologies allow us to break up the cells encapsulating the precious carbon and burn that carbon in the form of ethanol, biodiesel, butanol, and other exotic fuels. Some of those technologies involve distillation, some involve stripping certain components off the plant's molecules; but at their heart they all depend on taking the carbon used to make cornstalks or wheat shoots, concentrating that stored energy, and burning it. And because they use the natural carbon cycle instead of pulling up fossils from deep beneath the earth, if done right, they can dramatically cut our carbon emissions.

Not that this idea is entirely new. In 1896 Henry Ford produced his first vehicle to run on straight ethanol. Still earlier, in 1893, a German inventor named Rudolf Diesel constructed his first eponymously named engine to run on oil extracted not from crude oil, but from peanuts. But each time biofuels have begun to take root, so to speak, some circumstance—from war to oil monopolies—has interfered. This time, however, the vision shared by Ford and Khosla may just become a reality.

That forthcoming reality is being hastened by the realization that ethanol, particularly cellulosic ethanol, can come to compete with gasoline in price. With corn at $2 a bushel, ethanol is economically competitive with gasoline (at the current federal subsidy of $.51 per gallon) when oil costs $30 a barrel or more. Without the subsidy, it is competitive with gasoline when oil costs $50 a barrel or more. Yet as demand has risen, so has the price of corn. At $3 a bushel, ethanol competes with gasoline without a subsidy when oil costs $70 a barrel or more.[6] The day is coming, however, when the decreased costs of processing cellulosic ethanol, in combination with the increasing cost of oil, will make this second-generation fuel attractive based just on price. The National Renewable Energy Laboratory has a goal of reducing the cost of producing cellulosic ethanol from $2.25 a gallon in 2005 to $1.07 by 2012.[7]

Currently, starches from corn kernels and the juice extracted from sugarcane are used to make ethanol in the United States and Brazil. These were used to produce 4.86 billion gallons of ethanol in the United States and over 4.3 billion gallons in Brazil in 2006.[8] But ethanol produced from those sources is just the warm-up act in the biofuels revolution. The show will hit the big time when the more sophisticated process of making ethanol from the woody cellulose of the plant fibers themselves is commercialized. If corn ethanol is the Wright Flyer of biofuels, cellulosic ethanol is the Boeing 787.

Cellulose is a compound found in the cell walls of all plant life, or *biomass*. Producing ethanol from cellulose is the holy grail of ethanol advocates. Using the woody cellulose material to produce fuel vastly expands the amount of organic material from which we can distill energy. It opens up a wide range of waste products, from straw to rice hulls to corn stover and perennial grasses and fast-growing trees, that can be grown as dedicated energy crops. These dedicated biomass crops—like switchgrass, hybrid poplar trees, and many native grasses—require fewer energy inputs in their cultivation, less fertilizer and water, and fewer pesticides and herbicides than corn.[9] As perennials, most biomass crops also promote a healthy ecosystem by reducing soil erosion and improving soil fertility.

One persistent concern about biofuels has been the "energy balance" of ethanol production. Repeated claims that more energy goes

Switchgrass is just one of the many crops that can be used to produce cellulosic ethanol.

into the production of a gallon of ethanol than is embodied in the resultant fuel have hurt the reputation of this energy source. Ten years ago, 1 Btu (British thermal unit) of energy was required to make .87 Btus of energy in the form of ethanol. Now all evaluations show improvements, but a wide variety of ratios remains in the twenty studies that have examined this issue. The most credible are the ones conducted by the Argonne National Laboratory and the USDA, which, respectively, concluded that first-generation corn ethanol has a net energy return of 26 percent[10] and 34 percent.[11] In 2006 the Natural Resources Defense Council (NRDC) commissioned a review of studies on the energy return on investment from corn ethanol and found that all but one resulted in a positive net energy balance, ranging from 29 percent to 65 percent.[12] And the horizon is rapidly expanding for ethanol's efficiency. Even using existing technology, as farms and processing plants begin to apply what are today's best practices, net returns should rise further. Brazil has increased the productivity of sugarcane ethanol to eight times the energy input, and estimates on cellulosic ethanol range from an energy balance of between 4.40 and 6.61 units returned for every unit of energy input.[13]

Huge leaps forward may be in the offing. Techniques that substitute biomass for fossil inputs to produce ethanol currently yield returns as high as 46.6 units of energy for each Btu of fossil fuel input,[14] demonstrating the tremendous potential for improvements in efficiency of production if the measurement is not merely energy efficiency but also reducing the carbon footprint of the fuel. Argonne National Laboratory finds that cellulosic ethanol reduces fossil fuel energy use by 90 percent.[15] With commercial cellulosic feed stocks for ethanol on the horizon, and use of biomass in the production process increasing, the energy and environmental profile of ethanol can continue to improve.

It is essential, as well, to have the infrastructure in place that will allow drivers to use the fuel across the country. Already today, a surprising number of cars can run on E85 ethanol—the blend of 85 percent ethanol and 15 percent gasoline that is emerging as a standard. There are over five million flex-fuel vehicles that can run on high blends of ethanol on the road[16]—a market roughly the size of that for diesel automobiles—but many car owners are not aware that they can already fill their tanks with it. Owners can discover whether their car can run on E85 by consulting their driver's manual, but until now, auto manufacturers have not lifted a finger to advertise this capability. Millions of gallons of gas are also now blended with a variety of percentages of corn ethanol, from E6 to E20, but the leap has yet to be made to providing substantial amounts of E85 to American drivers.

An engine built to run on this blend of 85 percent ethanol costs roughly $100 more at the factory, the cost of a sensor and upgraded fuel lines, and still allows drivers to use regular gasoline as necessary. The cost to gas station owners of installing an E85 pump ranges from $10,000 to $50,000[17] and can be done easily at existing facilities—unlike the adaptations for hydrogen or natural gas—and that cost can be reduced through federal and state incentives. So ethanol enjoys an enormous advantage over other alternative liquid fuels. It works with the transportation and fueling infrastructure already in place in the United States with only minor modifications.

Even more important than price and efficiency, the true beauty of ethanol is its ability to tackle emissions of $CO_2$. Even production of first-generation corn ethanol reduces greenhouse gas (GHG) emissions by one-third compared to gasoline.[18] With the introduction of cellulosic ethanol, the reduction of $CO_2$ can reach more than 90 percent below the emissions produced by an equivalent amount of gasoline.[19] Because growing biomass removes from the atmosphere an amount of greenhouse gases roughly equivalent to the amount ethanol gives off when it is burned as fuel, biofuels are a "closed loop" of carbon. The only net increase in atmospheric $CO_2$ is from the energy used in production.[20]

Currently, the extra greenhouse gas emissions from the ethanol cycle are limited to $CO_2$ that is produced from the fossil fuels used in growing the feed stocks and processing the ethanol. When burned, gasoline emits approximately twenty-five to thirty pounds of carbon dioxide per gallon. This figure does not consider the substantial amounts of fossil fuel used in the oil extraction and refining processes. Corn ethanol releases around twenty pounds per gallon,[21] and that number will only get better as production technologies improve. Therefore, as fossil fuels are substituted out of production and efficiencies increase, the climate impacts of ethanol can be reduced more substantially than those of gasoline alone could ever be. In short, gas will always be dirty. Ethanol has the potential to become even cleaner than it is now.

When biomass energy rather than fossil fuel is used in the refining process, corn ethanol emits only about eight pounds of carbon per gallon. Advanced cellulosic ethanol, using biomass energy in the refining process, will release a mere three pounds of carbon per gallon, almost an order of magnitude less than an equal volume of gasoline.

In its most advanced form of production, ethanol can even cause a net reduction of $CO_2$ in the atmosphere. When the carbon is captured and stored underground during the manufacturing process, corn-based ethanol can actually reduce the net amount of carbon in the air by two pounds as the corn plant grows. Cellulosic ethanol does even better, se-questering a net total of over five pounds of carbon for every gallon burned if the carbon is captured. The sequestration process is expensive but could become economically attractive when manufacturers have to pay a price for their carbon emissions, or when federal standards reward low carbon fuels. This potential to actually clean the air is extremely ex-citing to ethanol's supporters.

The biomass feed stocks that can be used to make cellulosic ethanol are widely diverse, as mentioned. Fast-growing trees and grasses, animal waste, residue from paper mills, and urban demolition materials are all examples of biomass. In early 2007 Vinod Khosla announced a major investment in a project to use wood fiber to produce ethanol in Geor-gia, and virtually every region of the country can take part in supplying feed stocks for this fuel. The by-product of cellulosic ethanol produc-tion, lignin, can also be used to generate electricity.[22]

For all these reasons, investment and speculation in both current and next-generation ethanol are booming. In the race to make cellu-losic ethanol efficient and profitable, companies are competing for re-search grants, loan guarantees, and future market share. Companies that have developed bacteria that digest biomass to produce ethanol include Iogen and Arkansas-based Bioengineering Resources Inc. Investment firm Goldman Sachs has poured $27 million into Canadian biotech company Iogen.[23] Iogen has also entered into a partnership with Volk-swagen and Royal Dutch Shell to explore the feasibility of opening a cellulosic ethanol biorefinery in Germany. Vancouver-based Syntec Biofuel has invested in a method of ethanol production involving gasi-fication of organic material rather than bacteria. In addition to Khosla and Gates, Virgin Group chairman Sir Richard Branson is investing $300 to $400 million in ethanol production facilities in the United States.

As interest in ethanol has grown, however, so have concerns about the environmental consequences of growing ethanol crops. Certainly if ethanol follows a technology path that requires increasing natural gas or coal for process heat and increasing the use of chemical fertilizers for corn, the environmental benefits would at a minimum be diminished, with the possibility of harms. These are real concerns. However, the growth of the biofuels industry will not and should not be simply an expansion of current ethanol technology. Instead, several forces are pushing ethanol development in a very different direction. First is the growth of cellulosic ethanol and the introduction of a much more diverse, low-impact, and high-yield set of feed stocks that use fewer inputs of energy and water. Second is the very promising development of new policies like the California low-carbon fuel standard, which rewards reductions in the amount of $CO_2$ in fuels, thereby recognizing biofuels produced using renewable energy—like methane or gasified cellulose—instead of natural gas. While their net environmental impact remains to be seen, based on our future technology choices and regulations, biofuels—unlike gasoline—can be produced sustainably, and that should not be taken lightly.

A particularly persistent criticism of ethanol production has centered on fears that land consumption would damage food supplies. If we ramped up our capacity to refine biodiesel, for instance, but expected productivity increases didn't materialize, resulting in a net reduction in the production of soybeans dedicated to food, what would that do to our nation's food supply? In a word, nothing.

The fact is that today we export fully 58 percent of our wheat, 34 percent of our soybeans, and 18 percent of our corn.[24] We export mountains of heavily subsidized U.S. agricultural products, a practice that has had some very negative effects on agriculture in developing countries. When subsidized U.S. food commodities are dumped in third world markets, they can drive food prices below the costs of local agricultural production, making it uneconomical for farmers to produce, driving poor farmers from their land, and devastating local economies.

For instance, the 2002 Farm Bill increased agricultural subsidies by $83 billion over a period of ten years, raising subsidies to cotton growers by 60 percent.[25] This effectively shut cotton grown in Africa out of the U.S. market. World Bank studies suggest that U.S. subsidies reduce West African annual revenues by $250 million a year.[26] Switching from subsidized food and fiber exports to environmentally beneficial energy crops in the United States would be a boon for both American energy security and the world's subsistence farmers.

In a very real sense as well, our export crops are grown to feed our rapacious hunger for foreign oil. Oil imports are the single-largest share of the U.S. trade deficit. In addition, a large share of the price of those bushels of soybeans that are exported flows out of our farm economies and out of the country. Some experts estimate that as much as 40 percent of the price of those export crops goes to pay the shipping costs to send them overseas. Much of the money for our crops is going to multinational exporters rather than American farmers, a situation that can be alleviated by moving to more domestic and localized energy and agricultural production.

In short, our agricultural system today generates export revenues that simply flow out of our economy to sustain payment obligations to the Middle East, rather than serving as primary investments in the foundation of our own domestic economy and homegrown sources of energy.

What can we realistically expect from the development of the next generation of biofuels? The possibilities are impressive. Studies by the NRDC demonstrate that in combination with aggressive efficiency measures and smart-growth policies, the use of switchgrass for cellulosic ethanol production could shrink our demand for gasoline to just 6 billion gallons per year in 2050, compared to the 290 billion gallons expected under business as usual. Assuming improvements in yields, this scenario would require 114 million acres of land, a demand that could be met using a portion of the 120 million acres that are currently dedicated to export crop production and the Conservation Reserve Program (CRP), which pays farmers to leave lands fallow—often by planting them in perennial switchgrass already—while still protecting both food production and land conservation goals.[27] Other studies show as little as 50 million acres being needed.[28] These studies show that even if we fall short on conservation and smart-growth goals, we could nonetheless replace all the oil we now import from the Middle East by

2050. Sweden has already set a goal of eliminating its oil use altogether; we can, too.

At the same time, it is crucial not to minimize the importance of requiring substantial improvements in production practices. Some estimate that producing just half of U.S. automotive fuel—for example, using only existing corn ethanol methods with no improvement in crop yields—could use 80 percent of the nation's cropland, with severe impacts on commodity prices and food supplies. The biodiesel industry is already encountering serious environmental concerns about the impacts of tropical palm oil and soybean plantations on biodiversity, and more issues are sure to follow unless standards are developed within the industry to certify the sustainable production of fuels, as well as monitor their carbon impacts. Such certification programs are well under way in the European Union and are beginning to be developed in the United States. The stakes are high for getting it right. Biofuels are the best option for our liquid fuels, but finding the balance of technology, policy, and environmental issues is not a lead-pipe cinch.

## Brazil: Energy Star in the Southern Cross

Brazil has the world's longest river and its grandest rain forest. Its greatest distinction now, however, may be its latest: becoming energy independent, a feat it achieved in 2006. Brazil is now totally energy independent, in large part because 40 percent of its transportation energy is from ethanol grown and processed right in Brazil.[29]

Brazil is the world's first biofuels economy. America could be the second.

When a Brazilian driver pulls up to a local fuel station, he or she chooses what fuel to use, gas or ethanol. The flex-fuel cars operate on either one, and the drivers force the suppliers to battle for their business by keeping prices reasonable. In Brazil, the ethanol circle has been closed, the sugarcane growers growing the feed stock, the ethanol refiners brewing ethanol, the auto manufacturers building and selling flex-fuel vehicles, and the service station owners providing billions of liters of ethanol a year to pleased drivers.

Brazil is testament to the practical reality of ethanol. But it took thirty years to obtain such ethanol penetration into its market. We need to learn from Brazil if we are to move more quickly.

As Eduardo Carvalho, the president of UNICA, the Brazilian consortium of ethanol producers, tells it, Brazilian oil companies fought tooth and nail to avoid installing E85 pumps in their stations, since those companies did not control the production of ethanol. Today those same firms are erecting artificial barriers in the United States. Carvalho suggests that until the oil companies are themselves involved in producing ethanol, they will claim that installing the pumps will cause every problem from fuel leakage to gum disease. The lesson from Brazil is clear: Only a mandate of some form will get the pumps into the stations. We do not have the thirty years it took Brazil to use a host of subsidies, tax treatment, and government jawboning to get companies to install E85 pumps.

One hundred percent of Brazilian stations now feature at least one ethanol pump. In the United States, out of 170,000 stations, just 873 have one. This paucity is not surprising since no major oil company has entered the ethanol market in a serious way to date, although in May 2007 BP announced forthcoming investments in ethanol. We cannot wait for the major oil companies to surrender to ethanol, running the risk that they never will. We need to heed the lesson from Brazil and require that Americans be given the freedom of access to E85 pumps.

Brazil has another important lesson for us, about deploying the cars capable of running on E85 ethanol. Brazil increased its percentage of new cars with flex-fuel capability from 4 percent to 70 percent in only three years, simply by mandating that manufacturers make the change.[30] It occurred at minimal cost and had maximum impact. We should be able to do the same.

We may have trouble beating Brazil in soccer. We should have no trouble at least tying Brazil in ethanol use.

## Biodigesters: Using the Southern End of a Northbound Cow

The biofuels revolution cannot be just an intellectual discourse. There is the actual matter of building with bricks and mortar, of making an innovative commercial enterprise pay. In that enterprise, few have come further than Dennis Langley, a Nebraska cattle farmer, ethanol producer, and one of the founders of an innovative energy start-up firm called E3 BioSolution.

When Langley steps onto his Nebraska feedlot, he is confronted by the same problem vexing other farmers—namely, a pile of cow manure roughly the size of Mount McKinley. His 30,000 head of cattle generate an amount of manure and solid waste comparable to that of a city with a population of 300,000, producing tons of pollutants and flashing methane, a greenhouse gas twenty-one times more powerful than carbon dioxide, into the atmosphere. That is a major environmental and logistical challenge, and it triggers significant regulatory oversight under the EPA.[31]

But to Langley, it is also a source of economic advantage. Through an innovative design, he combined his feedlot with a solid-waste management facility and a traditional corn ethanol plant, creating huge environmental and economic advantages in the process. By way of a specially designed floor in the feedlot, he is able to harvest the manure every fifteen minutes and send it to an anaerobic digester, which captures the methane before it reaches the atmosphere. Instead of worsening global warming, the methane is used as replacement energy for the ethanol plant, entirely eliminating the need for fossil fuel inputs into the ethanol production process. That reduces nitrogen pollution from the manure by 70 percent and produces ethanol with an energy balance of 46.6 units of ethanol for every unit of fossil fuel energy, all while cutting the cost of production.

The ethanol plant in turn produces a waste product called distillers grain, which consists of the high-protein residue of the corn used to make the fuel. The wet feed is returned to the feed lot and reduces the methane produced in the cows' digestive tracts, which otherwise would be released into the atmosphere (a source of jokes but a serious problem for greenhouse gases)—providing benefits at every stage of the process.

The most profound benefits are economic. This 50-million-gallon facility is able to save $15 million a year in avoided energy costs while producing additional marketable by-products of organic nitrogen fertilizer worth $3 million. Five more plants are on the way.

That's some cow pie.

## From Entrepreneurs to Civil Servants: Getting a Second Opinion

As in Brazil, the fruition of ethanol's future in the United States depends, in part, on new action by our government. One key player in that effort will be the Department of Agriculture. The "new" USDA is typified by Dr. Hosein Shapouri, an expert economist who was instrumental in assessing whether biofuels could be a real economic success rather than a pipe dream. Dr. Shapouri is far from a starry-eyed dreamer. He exposed the proposed projections of the benefits of ethanol to the harsh inspection of his team of hawk-eyed economists.

What they saw was a relatively direct path to the United States being able to produce 1.3 billion tons of feed stock by the year 2030 without significant dislocation of the existing production of food. That prodigious number translates to the ability to supplant 30 percent of U.S. oil consumption in just two decades, without undermining our food production, without damaging our environment, and without depending on technological leaps equivalent to splitting the atom.[32]

Dr. Shapouri and his team found three fundamental American strengths favoring a bright prognosis for ethanol. First, we enjoy multiple sources of feed stocks. While Brazil is totally dependent on one crop, sugarcane, for its feed stock, Dr. Shapouri's team found that we could produce 400 million tons from forest products, 400 million tons from energy crops, and 400 million tons from crop residues consisting of the fibrous material left over after a crop is processed. We can "spread the risk" in that way.

Second, America is awash in innovative talent. The very talent that improved corn production threefold is now poised to increase ethanol production sevenfold. As evidence of the power of intellectual horsepower, Dr. Shapouri points to the twentyfold decrease in the cost of producing the critical enzymes used in the production of cellulosic ethanol already obtained and the two- to threefold improvement expected in the near future. That is why he believes that the current estimated cost of cellulosic ethanol production of $2.30 a gallon could be reduced to the range of $1.07 in fairly short order.[33]

Third, we have existing automotive technology that can maximize the virtues of ethanol. While ethanol traditionally produces only two-thirds of the mileage per gallon that can be achieved from a gallon of gasoline in standard engines, the Saab Company has already built and demonstrated an engine with technology that can take advantage of ethanol's higher octane rating to coax the same energy out of a gallon of ethanol as a gallon of gasoline.[34] Brazilians driving on E85 may have a somewhat more limited range on one tank of ethanol now, but it is realistic to project that the gap between ethanol and gasoline will be considerably narrowed, if not eliminated, in the near future using the turbocharging techniques pioneered by Saab.

Improvements can also be expected in the field, not just in the refinery. Dr. Shapouri's working assumption is that twofold improvements are achievable over existing yields of feed stocks per acre. He points to Sheridan Valley, Iowa, farmers who have improved their production from two to four tons in just two years and to Dr. David Bransby of Auburn University, who has produced ten tons in test plots of switchgrass.

Dr. Bransby is keen on switchgrass having the honor of being the nation's next big crop, not just because it is highly productive, yielding up to ten tons per acre, but also because it is native to our Great Plains, avoiding concerns about invasive exotic species. Switchgrass is as American as apple pie.

With switchgrass in the mix, Dr. Bransby believes that the USDA study is eminently reasonable in concluding that we can produce 377 million tons of feed stock per year on 55 million acres.[35] He believes we can do better than that because we will be able to use even more productive stocks, like "energy cane," which can grow much farther north than sugarcane. Even more enticing are crops like *Arundo donax*—now being developed by Nile Fiber, a Tacoma, Washington, company—which can produce twice the tons per acre as switchgrass. If the projections of these crops are realized, the estimates of the USDA that we could produce 30 percent of our liquid fuel from biofuels could double.

Huge strides can be made on the refining end as well. It is always exciting to learn of a quantum leap in technology, and Mascoma Inc. and its leading scientist, Lee Lynd, are making one. These folks, focusing on science developed at Dartmouth, aim to combine two steps involved in making cellulosic ethanol into one. They are close to raising a bacterium that can break down the cells of plant matter and also ferment the carbohydrates freed from the cell, in one bacterial action. This will produce ethanol at a cost savings of perhaps 20 percent per gallon, a titanic advantage.[36]

If this pans out, all bets are off—the USDA estimates will be seen one day as wildly pessimistic, and we will name the Mascoma product our national bacteria.

## Seattle Biodiesel: Homegrown Fuel Takes Root

Just as the PC has the Mac, and the Yankees have the Red Sox, ethanol has a competitor in biodiesel, diesel fuel refined from plant seeds. Two titans of Silicon Valley who have done battle in the Google versus Microsoft wars have now moved over to the competition in biofuels. Vinod Khosla, as discussed previously, is banking on cellulosic ethanol; Martin Tobias is backing biodiesel. They both ended up being right in software. The extent to which each will be right in the competition for the dominant biofuel "operating system" will be a fascinating tale to watch unfold.

Soybeans grown in the Midwest have historically gone to feed hogs. Now, thanks to a former software developer, they are feeding beetles—Volkswagen Beetles, to be exact. Powering Martin Tobias's Beetle seems a higher purpose for the humble soybean than making Jimmy Dean's pork sausages.

It was a seemingly long jump for this emerging energy guru: from the clean and orderly campus of Microsoft to the next industrial age, hard by the brown water of the Duwamish River. But according to Tobias, the same lust for innovation and capacity for risk taking applies in building a biofuels company as in pushing the boundaries of software. His company, Imperium Energy, is now building the largest biodiesel plant in the Western Hemisphere.

His process is simple. It involves crushing the beans and shipping the oil by rail to Seattle, where the glycerin is removed in a quiet, nontoxic, low-emission process, resulting in a steadily improving quantity of gallons of biodiesel produced per acre of planted soybeans. There are no tall cracking towers, no residual tar, and no chance of *Exxon Valdez*–like oil spills with this super-clean technology. Tobias considers his process to be the real McCoy of biofuels production processes, capable of producing five million gallons per year with a longer shelf life and purer characteristics than other biofuels, due to its advanced refining technology.

The purity also is a selling point. His firm is now talking with several school districts about running their school buses on clean-burning biodiesel. Parents may appreciate his fuel when it is pointed out that the accumulation of diesel pollutants inside an average school bus is sixteen times higher than the toxic parts per million in the air outside the bus.[37]

Tobias had two weapons at his disposal in producing a biodiesel that could go head to head with petrochemicals. One handicap that biodiesel fuels have faced is that they tend to thicken or congeal in colder temperatures. Imperium believes that its process can solve that problem in two ways. First, Imperium employs a "cold filtering" system, similar to that used in cold filtering beer, in which the triglycerides that cause the congealing problem precipitate out before the fuel leaves the refinery. Second, when his company refines oils from the seeds of canola and mustard plants grown in Washington State, congealing problems will disappear. But even before that happy day, biodiesel made from soybeans is already in use at −25°F temperatures in Yellowstone National Park with the aid of simple heating devices on the gas tanks. Better to warm diesel lines than to warm our planet.

When it comes to biofuels, cleanliness is next to godliness. Imperium is negotiating with Seattle City Light to sell biodiesel at a premium price, allowing the utility to take advantage of a credit for the use of low-emission biodiesel. This "premium pricing" presages exactly the type of economic arrangement that will blossom in the future on a grander scale once a cap on total national greenhouse gas emissions drives these transactions. What is happening on the shores of the Duwamish River today may be happening nationwide in the future: one business entity paying another to clean up its act.

This team is now selling all the fuel it can produce, even though it's more expensive than regular diesel, even with the excise tax benefit. The cost of biodiesel dipped below the price of regular for just a brief period in the summer of 2005. Compared to that of regular diesel, the future of biodiesel looks bright, though, since the last dinosaur died some time ago and the price of oil over the long term can hardly be predicted to go down. In contrast, we are just starting to plant canola and drive down biofuel costs as we reach scale and increase the efficiency of production.

At the moment, consumers are flocking to pay a bit more for biodiesel, leading to a growth in sales in recent years. From 500,000 gallons in 1999 to 250 million gallons in 2006, a five-hundred-fold increase in five years, the rate of growth may be faster than that of any fuel in history.[38] The customers of Imperium are buying environmental sanity, energy independence, and the confidence that they are helping solve a global concern.

But to reach the ultimate market, the masterminds at Imperium will have to one day produce biodiesel at a cost competitive with that of regular diesel. They cannot be satisfied with the easy pickings. They have already significantly reduced their operating costs. Their progress is not as rapid as Moore's Law prescribes for computer chips, but Tobias, a veteran of the software world, sees the same path to success with a fuel involving photosynthesis as with an industry involving software synthesis.

Several fundamental factors warrant optimism. First, biodiesel has the advantage that it can be woven into the web of the distribution system for today's fuels, because it can be injected directly into the stream of regular diesel being delivered by pipeline. Second, blends at low levels have been widely endorsed and accepted by major manufacturers. Third, the improved lubricity of biodiesel is just what the doctor ordered for reducing engine wear. These intrinsic benefits make realistic the estimate that biodiesel can contribute 2–10 percent of our diesel needs in a matter of several years—a small percentage to be sure, but a solid and rapid start on the road to biodiesel's becoming a significant part of the biofuels revolution.[39]

Biodiesel does have detractors. Some suggest that its use could increase emissions of nitrous oxide. Studies point to different conclusions in that regard.[40]

Energy balance questions are also raised. In a head-to-head comparison between biodiesel and traditional diesel fuel, however, biodiesel eats regular diesel alive, with a fossil fuel energy balance rating of 3.2 to 1, well ahead of petroleum diesel's 0.83 to 1.[41] Cellulosic ethanol could have a ratio of energy inputs to outputs several times that figure.

The biggest jump in productivity may come when the right feed stocks are in use. The canola that Imperium will one day use will reduce transportation costs by virtue of being grown closer to the plant; plus, canola produces roughly a hundred gallons per acre compared to fifty to sixty gallons per acre from soybeans.[42] Mustard, a beautiful bright yellow plant now starting to cover eastern Washington farms, is similarly productive at a hundred gallons per acre.[43]

Investment guru Nancy Floyd points out that locating refineries close to eco-friendly markets on the West Coast can save as much as $.50 a gallon by reducing the shipping costs of feed stock, now being hauled in by rail from the Midwest. Nth Power, her venture capital firm, is investing in Imperium, which is planning to expand its operations in

Washington to serve clients in close proximity to the Seattle area. "We have seen a lot of deals in biodiesel and in ethanol, and what attracted us to this deal was their strategy of building low [cost] refineries in places where the customers are, and then moving upstream to develop low-cost local feed stock," Floyd says.[44]

Imperium and Tobias depend on the $.99 biodiesel excise tax credit and curse its limited term. Congress provided this credit for only two years. So when Tobias goes to investors to look for capital, he cannot guarantee them that the credit will last much longer. This undermines the point of the credit by scaring away investors who need to take a long-range approach. Congress would do well to quit playing games and set up credits for meaningful and predictable lengths of time.

Not surprisingly, Tobias sees biodiesel as having distinct advantages over cellulosic ethanol. First, he contends that no commercially available cellulosic ethanol will be produced for five years. Cellulosic is late to the party, according to this gung-ho entrepreneur. Second, it gets 20 to 33 percent less mileage on a conventionally designed engine, and he believes consumers will eventually respond negatively to that.

In Tobias's vision, the Europeans will shortly enter the American market with higher-efficiency diesel cars, and the Japanese will continue their onslaught with hybrids, setting up an industrial-size street brawl between biodiesel and hybrids. He is placing his bets on biodiesel, big time. Of course, in the future, these two technologies could be implemented together, to run hybrid drive trains on biofuels.

But if biodiesel and cellulosic ethanol are to be seen as distinct competitors, which they are, cellulosic clearly holds one indisputable trump card. It puts to work the entire carbohydrate storage of the plant. Biodiesel frees for human use only the carbohydrates stored in the fruit of the plant, be it palm oil, soybeans, or canola.

It is no surprise then that, anticipating improvements in yields, cellulosic is projected to produce between 1,000 and 1,500 gallons of ethanol per acre,[45] while the most productive domestic biodiesel feed stocks (canola and mustard) currently do not exceed 100–150 gallons per acre. This 1,000 percent advantage is huge, especially when we realize that cropland is limited, even in the Midwest. And, while cellulosic now produces less mileage per gallon than biodiesel, the rates are likely to be equalized when technology created by Saab and others eliminates the mileage penalty of ethanol.

Given that cellulosic has such a markedly greater per-acre capacity, it is hard to see how it would not eventually produce a much larger percentage of America's biofuels than biodiesel. But this assumes that it will overcome the "chicken and egg" problem of a lack of pumps and flex-fuel vehicles. If Congress does not act to push both along, biodiesel may be out of the gate so far ahead that the progress of cellulosic is delayed.

Quantum leaps may be possible in biodiesel production as well; a day may come when canola and soybeans are seen as the chimps of the space-flight age, acting as temporary organic substitutes for what may become the dominant feed stock for biodiesel: algae. Algae are perhaps the humblest members of the plant kingdom, being single-celled organisms with no fruit, no stalk, no flower, and very little poetry dedicated to their visage. They have, however, a prodigious ability to grow in limited amounts of space while producing gigantic quantities of oil. What has dominated the bottom of the ocean's food chain could one day dominate the biodiesel industry, according to research conducted by the National Renewable Energy Laboratory.[46]

In 1996, that research demonstrated theoretical production capabilities of 2,640 gallons of oil per year produced in a thousand square meters of space—in the case of the study, in small ponds. Even high-yield canola plants can produce only 50 gallons per year in a similar space.[47] At least in theory, then, algae could produce over forty times the oil out of the same space as the highest-producing alternative crop. Even if the algae yields only 10 percent of its potential, it would produce over four times as much oil, given the same amount of growing space. Recent trials by private "algaculture" start-ups estimate potential yields of 10,000 gallons per acre or more.[48]

In addition to that strength of oil production, algae have a bonus for us. The gas we now seek to remove from the atmosphere, $CO_2$, is what algae feeds on. This creates the possibility of locating algae production facilities next to fossil fuel–based plants and using the $CO_2$ emanating from their stacks to feed the algae ponds. This was tested by the National Renewable Energy Lab in New Mexico, and it worked. This tandem usage could be one of the most satisfying "two-fers" in the energy world. An MIT-based consortium is testing such a pilot facility now at a coal plant. As an alternative, waste treatment plants could serve to provide carbon for our algae farms. The national lab concluded that its research "should not be seen as an ending, but as a beginning."[49] Evolution began with single-cell organisms from the sea, so why shouldn't an energy revolution?

Together, these transformations are making it possible to realize the original dreams of Rudolf Diesel, who envisioned his engine being powered everywhere in the world by fuel made from vegetable matter. His first vehicle's peanut oil engine, developed in 1893, led him to say in 1912, "The use of vegetable oils for engine fuels may seem insignificant today, but such oils may become, in the course of time, as important as petroleum and the coal-tar products of the present time."[50] Like fine wine, some great ideas need time to mature.

Biofuel's future is now being decided on the highways and back roads of America. Performance counts, and on that score, biodiesel is hitting home runs, with B20—20 percent biodiesel and 80 percent regular diesel—proving to have fuel consumption, horsepower, torque, and haulage rates as high as those of conventional diesel. It is winning where the rubber, and in this case the vegetable matter, meets the road. When one American suburban neighbor sees another getting better mileage, the age of biodiesel will arrive, one block at a time.

## Concerns and Showstoppers: What Could Make It All Go Bust

For all the power and importance of entrepreneurs and private-sector capital, governments and policy profoundly shape the markets that sustain our businesses. Without good policy, these efforts—as strong as they are—could founder.

In show business, more Broadway musicals close than become hits. In energy, not every technology will live up to its promise, even the most exciting ones. So we would do well to step back a moment and take a close look at what "showstoppers" could darken the horizon of clean biofuels.

The first, and potentially most fatal, threat to biofuels would be that they have simply come too late. If global warming strikes with a vengeance, it could destroy the ecosystems on which agriculture depends, strangling the birth of the very fuel that has a chance to reduce our emissions of $CO_2$.

As the name suggests, biofuels are the product of a living biosphere, one composed of an intricately intermeshed tapestry of water, sunlight, topsoil, pollinating insects, and temperature of the atmosphere. If that system is interrupted in fundamental ways by global warming, no biofuels technology in the world can save us.

The impact of climate change on water availability is one of the most menacing aspects of this threat. As this is being written, 67 percent of the counties in America are in drought. The snowpack on which irrigated agriculture in the West depends is rapidly dwindling year by year. High temperatures, which cause parching of the soils, are increasing. Agriculture is already threatened by global warming.

But the deeper news is worse. Recent research strongly suggests the possibility that as the earth gets to levels of $CO_2$ in the range of 500 ppm, about twice preindustrial levels, massive amounts of methane may be released by melting tundra, and the rate of accumulation of global warming gases will skyrocket above anything the earth has experienced.[51] Scientific consensus is clear that we are headed to those levels unless our energy world changes dramatically. When such a tipping point is reached, it will not matter what cellulosic ethanol technology we subsequently invent, because the agricultural base will be effectively gutted by a combination of drought, high temperatures, lack of irrigation, and potential dustbowl conditions.

Should that occur, history will record biofuels as interesting technologies that could have helped save the planet had they been employed in time, something like the lifeboats left on the dock when the *Titanic* sailed. But this potential showstopper doesn't merit ignoring biofuels; it merits accelerating their application in tandem with a whole suite of climate solutions.

Second, biofuels could suffer the fate of old age if the status of their basic technology turns out to be mature rather than just developing. All of the rosy forecasts of their promoters, from Vinod Khosla to Martin Tobias, depend on the assumption that technological improvements will continue to be made on a variety of fronts. Khosla assumes that yields per acre will grow substantially and that the price of enzymes will continue to come down. Everyone assumes that since the Brazilians reduced their cost of sugarcane–based ethanol by 80 percent, we can make significant strides as well. In short, we all assume that biofuels are an infant industry with huge potential for technological growth, rather than an advanced technology in which quantum leaps of progress cannot be expected.

Perhaps we have plucked the technological low-hanging fruit.

But if we increase per-acre yields of feed stocks by only 30 percent, as one analysis projects, rather than the tripling that Vinod Khosla predicts, we still end up replacing all our imported oil (rather than all our oil). This does not argue against urgently moving to biofuels. It makes sense to head in that direction whether we achieve a replacement of 30 percent of our fuels from this source, or 60 percent, especially considering the alternative of continued reliance on oil.

The most dangerous showstopper is one within our control. The only truly existential threat to the growth and sustainability of biofuels is the possibility that we do not adopt the policies necessary to develop them. That is the principal condition now existing that, if not changed, will kill biofuels. If we continue to let the oil and gas industry strangle Congress and stymie real progress on deploying renewable energy, much as they long delayed progress in Brazil, the development of biofuels will limp along at a fraction of the pace it could achieve if we put the national pedal to the national metal.

Strong policies are especially important in transforming the biofuels revolution already under way, to move beyond corn ethanol to cellulosic ethanol and to ensure that is done in a way that reduces the impact on our natural resources. Government alone cannot create the market—it depends on the innovation and investment of scientists, farmers, and entrepreneurs—but government is an essential partner in leveling the playing field for a new technology to overcome the barriers to entry and ensuring sustainable production. Markets alone will not bear the risks or higher initial prices that come with cellulosic ethanol or driving down carbon content, yet it is only by moving away from corn-based biofuels that we will realize the full potential of cellulosic to both reduce oil dependence and slow global warming. We need to ensure that the mandate for fuel from cellulose within the Renewable Fuel Standard is enforced and strengthened and that private markets are given the signals of certain growing demand to encourage investment.

We need to make sure also that Congress appropriates the funds for loan guarantees to enable innovative firms to bring these fuels to market at scale. We need to ensure that criteria for low-carbon fuels and sustainable biofuel production are put in place to guarantee that new producers of ethanol not only respond to price signals but also work within our environmental limits, breaking our addiction to oil in a manner that protects the global climate. And we need to ensure that besides new fuels, our strategy includes more efficiency in the energy we do use. Policy will help create and shape these markets, but business will do the heavy lifting if the signals are right.

The threat of these showstoppers is a wake-up call. The concerns they raise mostly demonstrate why we should move more quickly to deploy biofuels. At worst, the concerns are that biofuels will solve only half our problems. At best, they demonstrate just how much our fate is under our own control.

The one thing that we can be certain will stop the biofuels revolution is our own inaction. The most productive agricultural nation in human history, America, is not going to let that happen. Biofuels are on their way.

Today wind power is competitive with electricity from natural gas turbines in many parts of the country. But it has not always been so. Producing wind energy at a competitive commercial scale requires big towers and long blades that can withstand highly volatile winds. Factor in the maverick culture of wind power and a shifting policy environment, and the industry has had its share of catastrophic failures on the road to eventual acceptance.

Jim Dehlsen, CEO of Clipper Windpower, Inc., remembers what he saw one day at Palm Springs in the early 1980s: a wind turbine that could have been a guillotine. "We had all gone down to Palm Springs to see the whiz-bang Alcoa vertical-wing turbine that was supposed to be the next big thing. Those were exciting days, and most of the movers and shakers in the industry had gathered to see a demonstration of a kind of turbine I had never encountered first-hand. This one was radically different, with three wind vanes revolving around a vertical shaft about eighty feet tall."[1]

There was a reason for Dehlsen to be excited. He had been committed to wind energy for some time and had sold another company to found a wind energy firm named Zond. He had gone to work building the company and evaluating various turbine designs. In those early days, all kinds of ideas were floating around. "The Alcoa contraption we were looking at in Palm Springs looked like a big eggbeater. It had these elliptical blades that would spin around this tall vertical shaft that was guyed from the ground. It was certainly worth a look, so a pretty big group of us who were pushing the envelope were all eagerly awaiting the demonstration at a hotel in Palm Springs to go out and see it whirling around."

Before they quite got to see it in action, however, things went slightly awry. "In those days, we were all trying to figure out just what types of stresses the blade roots would be exposed to when they were spinning. That was sometimes an uncertain prospect. It sure was that day, because before we got there, a bolt broke, and one of the blades took off spinning around like the blade of a scythe. An eighty-foot blade ripping around without any way to stop it is a bit disturbing. If we had just gotten there a little earlier, it could have decapitated the whole industry! There would have been a certain irony in that."

Dehlsen still has the bolt that broke, as well as memories of other tribulations. In those days, disaster was not unusual. Dehlsen's senior vice president, Bob Gates, tells the story of the time at the Tehachapi Wind Project in California when he went out to inspect the site and found a big hole in the ground where a seventy-foot turbine tower had been. In an all too common incident, a blade had flown off, and the tower had become unbalanced and had come crashing down, ripping out its foundation. When he called the manufacturer, the Storm Master Company in San Diego, and reported the event, the fellow there patiently explained that that was impossible, because Storm Master blades just didn't do that. Gates responded, "Perhaps not, but they sure found some way to plow up a fifteen-foot hole in the ground."[2]

Despite the multiple failures, the industry continued slowly to develop, learning all the time. "You learn," says Gates. "The improvements were mostly made by the smaller companies. At the very start the big outfits had sizable government contracts and tried to do the equivalent of building a 747 before building a DC-3. So when Boeing attempted huge 250-foot-tall turbines in Washington, it wasn't a surprise they failed. The learning curve is important. We gradually built up the size of our turbines, starting at 550 kilowatts and working up to multi-megawatt machines."

Then the bottom fell out. "In the mid-1980s the federal government terminated the tax credit that had been sustaining these companies. In just a couple of years, 90 percent of the forty or fifty companies were out of business," says Dehlsen. "We just barely hung on, by the skin of our teeth."

But recently, from the ashes, a wind industry phoenix has arisen, led by companies like Clipper.

"We made a huge breakthrough when we started to develop a tidal turbine in lieu of wind," Dehlsen explains. "But in developing that turbine, we discovered a new technique to make a turbine that could handle vastly greater torque. That allowed us to now build fantastic 2.5-megawatt turbines, towers that stand 240 feet high, with blades 288 feet in diameter, the largest in the world. This year, we have sold enough of them to produce 5,000 megawatts of power, and they can produce power at roughly the same cost as natural gas–powered turbines, taking into consideration the tax credits."

Each one of those turbines can power eight hundred homes. They are the real McCoy of large-scale, mainstream wind energy production. Today there are four hundred Americans working at Clipper, two hundred of them churning out those turbines at a plant in Cedar Rapids, Iowa. The plant was formerly used for manufacturing cranes, until the company folded. Here is a textbook example of the power of new energy to replace the jobs that are being lost, right in the heartland of Iowa. Now a site is being developed for a nest of those turbines at an abandoned steel mill by Lake Erie. The Rust Belt is becoming a Wind Belt, this alternative technology blowing new life into old industrial graveyards.

Clipper calls its premier turbine the Liberty. It exists only because repeated failures led to new approaches. Eventually one worked, and now it is a leader in a mainstream American industry with glowing prospects. This shows that when it comes to technological development, failure is an option. In fact, it's a certainty, and we can't let it become an excuse for inaction. We need to see it for what it is: a step toward success. The spirit of Thomas Edison is alive in the wind industry today. In reference to his numerous experiments, Edison once said, "I didn't fail. I discovered three thousand ways not to make a lightbulb."

## CHAPTER 7

# Sailing in a Sea of Energy

We are a nation rich in wind energy potential. The earth is awash with a sea of fluid energy. Swaddled in an atmosphere of swirling winds, from zephyrs to gale-force tree snappers, the earth feels the energy of the sun translated into the fluid dynamics of wind on a daily basis. When we see the Kansas wheat fields rippling in a fifteen-mile-an-hour westerly, we are seeing air rushing from a high-pressure area created by the sun's heat into a low-pressure area that is not so warm. When our caps are blown off in New York City by a gust rushing up Fifth Avenue, we are the victims of the serendipity of an unequal distribution of energy from the sun that created different pressures in the atmosphere above the Atlantic.

Created by differences in atmosphere pressure driven by the rays of the sun, wind is solar energy in a different form. Wind power could rightly be called "secondary solar."

When sailors harnessed wind energy in their sails centuries ago to traverse the globe, they learned to take advantage of atmospheric pressure differences caused by the sun. When Dutch farmers turned those sails to the task of making mechanical energy to grind their grain, the windmill was born. But wind energy is not merely a product of poetry, a quaint natural phenomenon fit only for powering eighteenth-century sailing ships and ancient Dutch windmills.

Wind is powerful because of a simple fact of physics. Any moving fluid's force increases with its increasing speed—not linearly, but exponentially. A four-mile-an-hour wind has four times, not twice, as much energy as a two-mile-an-hour wind. Anyone who has ridden a bicycle and felt the benefits of catching the slipstream of the leading rider knows this principle well. Tremendous energy is swirling about us just for the taking. In fact, wind potential is one of our nation's most abundant energy resources; fully a quarter of our land area possesses winds strong enough to generate electricity at a price competitive with today's prices of natural gas. Just three states—North Dakota, Texas, and Kansas—together have the theoretical capacity to produce enough energy to meet the nation's entire current electricity needs. While just at the beginning of its development, wind already supplies enough energy to power the needs of 2.3 million U.S. households.

Wind energy has come a long way from the early experiments of Clipper Wind and other pioneers. Today a modern community-owned wind turbine rises hundreds of feet above the farms near Iowa Lakes Community College, where it also serves as a teaching tool for wind technicians.

Today in America, a wind energy industry is springing up, ready to exploit the tremendous potential. The westerly winds blowing across the Plains states that drove the sodbusters nearly to distraction in the 1800s are now powering those dirt farmers' descendants' turbines, and the wind energy industry is emerging as perhaps the most rapidly rising star in America's clean-energy firmament. From the dry hills of eastern Washington to the Badlands of the Dakotas, farmers are using the wind that formerly just pollinated their crops to grow a new cash crop: electricity. From Iowa's Spirit Lake Community School District to the town of Hull, Massachusetts, local governments are funding services with new revenues from the wind, and in each case creating jobs.

## Proving the Power of Wind in the "Show Me" State

There are two breeds of people in America who cannot be fooled with pie-in-the-sky promises: farmers and Missourians. Now farmers from Missouri have embraced wind energy.

In 2008, one hundred towering wind turbines will be standing in the fields of soybeans and on the pig farms of Atchison, Gentry, and Nodaway counties, powering 45,000 homes as they spin. Their construction is driven by declining farm revenues, industrial vision, and the steady promise of the wind.

"There's not a lot of money in rural America. We're not going to get another factory," says Frank Schieber, who, as a fourth-generation farmer, should know. "It's a shot in the arm." Schieber recognized the reality so many of his fellow farmers have grasped: It is a lot easier to walk out to the mailbox and collect a check each month from the utility to which they are leasing the right to site a wind turbine on their fields than it is to plow, fertilize, sow, and harvest a crop that may bring declining prices. The farmers in this project will typically receive $3,000 to $5,000 (per turbine) a year, depending on the amount of electricity generated over the life of a twenty-five-year contract.[1] Better yet, they have almost no costs, since they can continue to farm or graze the land right up to the fifteen-foot-wide perimeter of the two-hundred-ton towers.

To American farmers, wind power is like finding money in the street. Some estimate that wind energy produces up to $1 million in local property tax revenue, two hundred construction jobs, and two to five permanent jobs for every hundred megawatts of capacity built, without displacing other employment.[2]

This new relationship between the farmer and the wind is catching on across the country. In Washington State's Columbia Gorge, one of the nation's windiest places, wheat farmers John and Iva Grabner have detested the wind for years. It repeatedly blew away the clouds that might otherwise have provided the rain on which their crops depended. "We felt so cheated," Iva says.[3] Now they are reaping the benefits of those breezes to the tune of $160,000 annually in royalty payments for the electricity generated by the thirty-story wind turbines spread across their fields.

It is not just farmers who are inheriting the wind. Columbia was once the poorest county in eastern Washington State, having difficulty providing even basic services, but it now receives an additional $1 million in tax revenues a year because of the bumper crop of wind towers adorning the fields formerly monopolized by wheat. To its west, on the Pacific Coast, longshoremen in Grays Harbor County have raked in over 70,000 hours of well-paid work unloading the turbines to be installed.[4] In this new industry, the spin-offs are as economically fruitful as the main product.

## Retaking the Initiative in Turbine Manufacturing

Wind can be an economic producer in cities as well as in the fields. Remember the Ford Twin Cities Assembly Plant (TCAP), the auto plant slated for closure, discussed in Chapter 2? TCAP's union and the community are actively exploring the possibility of converting the auto plant to a manufacturer of wind turbines.

TCAP union leader Lynn Hinkle is enthralled by a deeply poetic opportunity on the table as he faces the closure of the historic auto plant in a long-standing manufacturing town. If that plant, which is powered by hydroelectricity from the Mississippi River, were converted to manufacture wind technology, the water turbines that harness the Mississippi would help capture energy from the wind whipping off the plains. It is almost too elegant for words.

Wind turbines are the product of large-scale, high-technology industrial production. Could wind generate a resurgence in U.S. manufacturing?

The wind industry's jobs are already prized in Denmark and Spain as being on a par with their advanced automobile manufacturing jobs. In Germany wind energy employs 64,000 workers.[5] In the United States the industry is growing at a rate of 35 percent a year. According to the Renewable Energy Policy Project, to produce an ambitious but achievable 74,000 megawatts of renewables, primarily from wind but also from solar and geothermal energy, in the United States would require 380,000 new manufacturing jobs for component parts; 36,000 U.S. firms—concentrated in states as diverse as California, Texas, Illinois, and Ohio—already produce similar products that could serve the growing market.[6] In short, wind represents a new wave of good jobs for workers throughout America's heartland—still in the familiar energy sector; still in heavy manufacturing; and utilizing the tremendous base of skills, infrastructure, and advanced high technology that the region currently known as the Rust Belt has taken over a century to develop.

A study by the European Wind Energy Association found that every megawatt of wind energy installed produces twenty-two job-years of employment, both directly through manufacturing and installing wind energy equipment and indirectly through job creation among suppliers to the industry.[7] Hinkle calculates that the state of Minnesota already has 812 megawatts of installed wind capacity, so even if only half of the projected jobs could be realized, that amount of installed capacity could generate nearly 9,000 jobs in Minnesota—more than four plants the size of TCAP, which at its peak employed 2,000.[8]

We could be much further along in generating those jobs than we are today. In the early days of the modern wind industry, in 1980, the United States led the world in wind energy capacity, but a shifting patchwork of policies caused the market to collapse and resulted in difficulty securing long-term financing for wind projects. An extension of the wind energy production tax credit through 2007 caused 2005 to be a record year for new installed capacity in the United States, which beat out all other countries (with over 2,400 megawatts) for the first time in ten years.[9] We are now making up ground lost since the 1980s.

The potential is even more impressive, particularly when you look at the track record of other countries and consider that Minnesota has over ten times the wind-generating capacity of Germany, for example, which today has 16,000 megawatts of installed capacity. Conservatively, that is enough wind capacity to create demand for well over a thousand TCAPs to meet the growth in employment demand.[10] Expanding the projections to the Dakotas and Iowa, it is easy to see why renewables are attracting so much industrial capital. Today such major manufacturers as GE and Siemens are deeply involved in producing turbines, and states are fighting for the growing number of manufacturing plants in the industry.

Duluth's Buffalo Ridge development is one example. After importing blades from India, the developers of the project were able to persuade the Indian manufacturer, Suzlon Energy, of the economic advantages of local manufacturing. Suzlon now has 235 Americans hard at work and another 40 coming on in the summer of 2007.[11] Recently, this Indian company has opened a blade manufacturing center in Pipestown, Minnesota, a bittersweet irony in the face of so many jobs being outsourced to India. To Hinkle's way of thinking, major wind farms "should be close to where they are building the turbines. That should be right here in the Twin Cities. They are beating us to our own markets in this country. The Chinese are making solar panels, and the Indians are making turbines. They are beating us. We shouldn't be letting this happen."[12]

If we can bring clean-energy manufacturing to this country, it could be like what happened in the auto industry after World War II. When Detroit brought new auto plants to the region, it was not just jobs in assembly that were created. It was steel mills at River Rouge, stamping facilities, wire looms, engine fabrication, glass and rubber jobs. No single city or state has positioned itself to be the next Detroit. If Hinkle has his way, America's heartland—with its skilled workforce and transportation infrastructure—will make a run for the good jobs in these new industries.

After thirty years of watching the auto industry's slow contraction, Hinkle notes, "Quite honestly, the reason manufacturing is growing into the green economy is because that is the only economy that can grow. If you are really serious, as we are, about converting a manufacturing facility today into something with longevity, you want to position yourself to be at the leading edge of the growth curve, and green manufacturing is that leading edge. We cannot allow the next economy to be built on Wal-Mart jobs that suck life out of communities. Solving climate needs to be about creating family-sustaining jobs."

For now, the TCAP plant is still churning out Ford Rangers and positioning itself for what will come next in a midwestern industrial economy where change is a certainty, but hope takes hard work and a careful plan. Each day, when Lynn Hinkle walks into his plant and sees the photo of a UAW worker proudly spraying Paul Wellstone's bus green, it gives him chills. "It's time to get back on the green bus," he says.

That message is seconded by Dan Wergin, founder of the wind turbine tower firm Tower Tech Systems of Manitowoc, Wisconsin, whose company is now employing ninety-four people in an industry that did not exist ten years ago. "If we could produce a thousand of these towers, we could sell them," he says.[13] Green manufacturing is now a growing force in the land of the Green Bay Packers.

## How Much of the Climate Solution Can Wind Supply?

According to a study by the EnerNex Corporation mandated by the Minnesota legislature, 25 percent of our power can be reliably integrated into the electricity grid in the Midwest from wind, with just minor additional costs of less than half a cent per kilowatt-hour.[14] At that level, wind would provide the same percentage of power as natural gas and hydroelectric combined.[15]

Even George W. Bush has opined that wind can one day be 20 percent of our electricity,[16] and in 2006, the U.S. Department of Energy committed to an action plan for reaching that goal. The American Wind Energy Association believes it can be achieved by 2030, but our competitors in the European Union are closing in on the same goal today. Denmark and several regions in Europe have already reached 20 percent.

Wind is only 1 percent of total electricity generation in the United States today, but with 2,454 megawatts having come on line in 2006, enough to power the state of Rhode Island, it is America's second-largest source of new power for the second year in a row.[17] Farmers in Missouri who now provide electricity as well as hogs can one day feed a substantial amount of our appetite for energy, as well as our appetite for bacon.

Wind energy is not without its environmental concerns, however. In some locations, turbines have killed significant numbers of birds and bats, although with slower rotating blades and better siting, those impacts are being dramatically reduced, and at its worst, wind energy is a smaller threat to wildlife than are house cats or motor vehicles. In spite of the real concern over proper siting, consensus has been reached that wind power is indeed "green." The Audubon Society has stated that it "strongly supports wind power as a clean alternative energy source." President John Flicker summed up the issue with stark frankness: "When you look at a wind turbine, you can find the bird carcasses and count them. With a coal-fired power plant, you can't count the carcasses, but it's going to kill a lot more birds."[18]

This is a position the Audubon Society did not reach easily. Wind turbines, like other power sources, are not entirely environmentally benign. But the avalanche of information about global warming "creates a sense of urgency beyond anything we have seen before," says Flicker. Looking at the broader climate impacts in 2005 alone, the wind turbines already operating in the United States offset 3.5 million tons of $CO_2$ emissions and reduced demand for natural gas by 4–5 percent (helping moderate prices). Flicker stresses that wind turbines need to be sited with care, of course: "Modern wind turbines are much safer for birds than their predecessors, but if they are located in the wrong places, they can still be hazardous and can fragment critical habitat."[19] Any policy expanding wind power must take our avian friends into consideration.

Siting decisions often draw opposition because no one has yet invented a way to make wind turbines invisible. Many otherwise environmentally progressive citizens of Massachusetts have done all in their power to block the construction of wind turbines off the scenic coast of Cape Cod. When it comes to energy, however, there is no free environmental lunch, only a series of trade-offs. The Department of Energy (DOE) estimates that America's offshore wind resource could support close to the total current U.S. electric capacity, or 90,000 megawatts of power. That is a lot of clean energy close to where people live. We must ask ourselves whether we are ready to trade interrupting the flow of the wind for interrupting the climatic system of the earth. For the citizens of Massachusetts the choice may come down to protecting an unaltered view or having the ocean in their living room as sea levels rise. We must proceed with care if we build in sensitive places, but the cost of inaction is also grave.

Wind turbine blades are not silent, either. At a distance of a hundred yards they can be heard making a steady whir. But Jaime Steve of the American Wind Energy Association sums up the argument for wind by quoting an old farmer he once met who loved his new wind turbine and declared, "Sure, it makes a little old sound, but it's the sound of money being made."[20] The key is reducing this impact on communities while meeting the urgent need for clean and carbon-free energy.

Doubters of wind energy sometimes point out that the only place the wind blows constantly is in the Congress. They argue that wind can, therefore, never be a significant part of a utility's energy portfolio. People need electricity even when the wind fails, of course.

Fortunately, wind is tied into a massive grid with a host of other generators powering that grid as well, so when the wind is fickle, other sources of energy can be tapped. This process is called *integration*, for obvious reasons. In the Pacific Northwest, when the wind dies down, more water can be put to work in the hydroelectric system. In the Midwest, natural gas turbines can be cranked up. In Montana, where the state is divided into two separate windsheds, wind energy can even be firmed up with more wind from another part of the state. Those who doubt the ability of wind to play a significant role in our energy future forget the glorious ability of the grid to swap electrons across regions and across many generating technologies. For instance, a combination of solar, wind, and gas-fired turbines can provide reliable energy and confidence that at least two sources of energy will be available at any one time.

More important than the wind blowing constantly is federal policy staying constant. General Electric has sold out its orders for wind turbines through 2007, but the market could have dived if Congress had not extended the $01.9 per kilowatt tax credit. "If the production tax credit for renewable energy hadn't passed, it would have been a tremendous amount of pain for the industry," says Victor Abate, vice president for renewables for General Electric. "The reality is you need to do this for a long time."[21] Wind dodged the bullet when the tax credit was extended for one year. As we have seen, tax credits work to build new markets when they are long term and do not when they are not. Congress needs to hunker down and pass a wind energy tax credit for at least five years. "Even a company with the size of General Electric has a hard time getting subcontractors to commit to casting the parts when the tax credit is only for a year at a time," says Jaime Steve.[22]

Production tax credits for wind have been a good investment, judging by the steadily decreasing costs of wind power. Wind in the early 1980s cost $.30 a kilowatt-hour, but since that time the price has dropped 80 percent due to both economies of scale and technological advances in turbines.[23] There is no reason to believe that trend will not be sustained. Improvements in the control mechanisms of the blades, which manage their orientation to the wind; the size of the blades; and general efficiency will all make the difference. In the 1980s the average turbine turned out 100 kilowatts of electricity. Today turbines are more than ten times that size, averaging 1.2 megawatts, with 5-megawatt turbines on the horizon. A wind turbine's output rises exponentially with the length of its blades, so the new technologies allowing construction of composite blades have translated into huge improvements as the size of a modern turbine reaches a three-hundred-foot wingspan, 50 percent larger than an average jumbo jet.

The cost of construction of turbine towers has recently gone up, but so have the costs of construction of coal and gas plants. The difference is that the cost of the wind itself has not gone up. For that reason, every time a state establishes a goal for wind, it is quickly surpassed. When Texas set a goal for wind to provide 2,000 megawatts by 2009, that goal was busted in 2005. Now Texas has set a new goal of 5,000 megawatts, but everyone knows that that goal will be shattered as well, and that the state is likely to have 15 percent of its power from wind by 2015.[24] The Texas example shows both the effectiveness of renewable portfolio standards—state policies that require electricity providers to obtain a minimum percentage of their power from renewable energy resources by a certain date—and the advisability of setting their targets high.

Today wind is generating over 11,000 megawatts of power, enough for 2.9 million homes, while reducing $CO_2$ emissions by 23 million tons. But that is only 1 percent of our power, and that is just today. The DOE's "Wind Powering America" program has the stated goal of increasing the use of wind energy in the United States to an eventual 100,000 megawatts by 2020. The DOE estimates that achieving this goal will create $60 billion in capital investment in rural America, provide $1.2 billion in new income for farmers and rural landowners, and create 80,000 new jobs.[25]

From its early failures, wind has become a renewable energy success story. Ultimately, it can supply as large a portion of our energy as we are willing to let it supply. It's as much a matter of aesthetics and political will as economics.

So what do people think of this enormous source of power? E. D. Pieniazec, of Berkshire, England, was asked about the Cold Northcott Wind Farm in England: "How would you describe these wind turbines?"

"Visions of the future," he said. "Give it fifty years, and no one will think twice when they see one."[26]

## Ocean Power

Wind is not the only technology involving the capture of a fluid's power. Wave power and tidal power are both just over the horizon. Wave

A prototype Finavera buoy generates power from the sea, while director of ocean energy Alla Weinstein explores a hundred-megawatt "power plant" of buoys off the coast of Coos County, Oregon.

power is a perfect complement to wind. Since water is a thousand times more dense than air, its movement packs a much greater wallop and allows us to create vast amounts of energy with a smaller "footprint," or in this case "web footprint." Unlike wind, the waves are relatively constant, and equipment already in the water is generating electricity. The Finavera Company has become the first to obtain permits for the installation of electricity-generating buoys off the Oregon coast. The real challenge for wave power is to build equipment that can survive the awesome force of a swell that seems to have been designed to destroy anything made by man. Another wave power company, Ocean Power Technologies, is built on software that can tamp down the movements of the buoys that would otherwise destroy them in heavy seas.

While wave power is truly in its infancy, its potential is considerable. There is enough wave energy in a section of our coastline ten miles wide and ten miles long to entirely supply California's grid.[27] Even a "wave park" one mile wide and ten miles long could produce 10 percent of California's power. Testimony before the U.S. House of Representatives Resources Committee by several federal agencies suggests that wave and tidal power have the capacity to one day provide 6 to 20 percent of the country's electricity. Anyone who has watched the waves tossing around a thousand-ton ship can understand the enormous potential in those waves. Wave power buoys capture this energy by compressing water or air as they bob up and down, and then use that fluid pressure to drive an electrical generator.

Tidal energy is also being put to useful purposes today. The Verdant Power Company now has turbines in New York's East River generating real electricity for real customers. The company's technology could find a home wherever the tide runs in tight quarters, including the narrow straits of Puget Sound, where the Snohomish County Public Utility District (PUD) has applied for FERC permits for a hundred megawatts of power.

Here we have the completion of what could be considered the Holy Trinity of exquisitely renewable energy. Solar energy will be captured in the first instance by photovoltaics and solar thermal and in the second by wind power, which turns solar power into wind and then into electricity. The third branch of the Trinity is actually lunar power, expressed through the tides. By these means, humankind will have figured out how to use all the free and pristine energy sent from the far reaches of space. Think of it as accepting gifts from the cosmos.

Most impressive, the Electric Power Research Institute (EPRI) has concluded that the economics of wave power could be at least as attractive as wind if the same resources were invested in this emerging technology. Wave power is where wind power was a decade or so ago. Wind and waves are united in their source and will likely be united eventually in their utility to a country starved for clean energy.

## A Mind Opened about Mined Coal

It was a strange sight. Longtime environmentalist and coal enemy David Hawkins sat testifying before a congressional hearing in March 2007, saying we needed to find a way to burn coal in the future. Hearing Hawkins testify for coal was a bit like hearing a Red Sox fan cheer for the Yankees.

But Hawkins has an answer to the question of when we have to make common cause with people we have opposed: "When we have to."[1]

Since Hawkins joined the Natural Resources Defense Council in 1971, he has been on the front lines of multiple battles with the black fuel, leading the fight to reduce its sulfur dioxide emissions and consequent acid rain throughout the 1980s and bringing recent litigation to force the EPA to reduce the deadly outpouring of mercury in the present decade. His only break from these private skirmishes was in the late 1970s when he was fighting public ones while in charge of the EPA's air quality program under President Jimmy Carter.

But in the late 1990s David had a slow but powerful epiphany. "In the short term, the next few decades, we don't have any real choice. We can do a huge amount with efficiency. We can do a huge amount with renewables. But the numbers are clear. Coal is going to be around for a good while, so we better figure out how to burn it responsibly, meaning with no $CO_2$ emissions."

He considers this a fundamental necessity. "If we don't, the 1,800 gigawatts of coal plants that will come on line by 2030 will send 30 percent more $CO_2$ into the atmosphere than all the coal that has ever been burned in human history, 750 billion tons of $CO_2$. If that happens, any effort to stop global warming is doomed."

His gloom about the problem was lifted somewhat when he got a call from his friend Professor Robert Socolow at Princeton, who told David there was a possibility of burning coal and storing its $CO_2$ underground permanently. "Here was some hope," says David. "Now after studying the technology for a decade, I believe it is likely we can burn coal and store its $CO_2$ underground in a way that is technically feasible, done at large scale, done permanently, and done safely."

"You can't argue with science," he says. "We have no choice but to stop global warming, and we have to start now. We can't wait fifty years. That means doing the best we can with what we have right now."

This conversion has not been without cost to David. He is regularly flamed on the Internet by folks in the environmental movement who do not appreciate him "going over to the dark side." "Yes, I get that," he says, with none of the bitterness you might expect from an environmental champion accused of making a huge error in judgment. "Both sides have to understand that the other is not going away. The coal side has to realize that global warming is not going away. The global warming team has to realize that coal is not simply going away overnight. When that happens, we can make some emergent progress."

Whether he's right or wrong about coal, Hawkins has a lesson to teach us: We have to break free of our prejudices if we are going to find all of the solutions we need in time. Hawkins made one solution happen recently: He just helped negotiate a deal to require new coal plants in Texas to be built with the capability to capture and sequester $CO_2$. He doesn't just think outside the box, he's helping to construct new boxes.

CHAPTER 8

# Can Coal or Nuclear Be Part
# of the Solution?

You load sixteen tons, what do you get?
Another day older and deeper in debt.

—*Written by Merle Travis (1947),*
*later recorded by Tennessee Ernie Ford (1955)*

In 2004, two Princeton University scientists, Stephen Pacala and Robert Socolow, decided to take a careful look at what it would take to change the course of global warming. Most scientists had concluded that in order to avoid unprecedented and potentially cataclysmic impacts from global warming, we would have to hold the rise in global temperatures to 2° Celsius. And to do that, we'd have to stabilize atmospheric $CO_2$ concentrations at about 500 parts per million (PPM) molecules in the atmosphere. That's a little short of double "preindustrial" levels, the concentrations we had in the air before the Industrial Revolution.

Pacala and Socolow looked at the trends and saw that if we continued with business as usual, we would end up with three times the preindustrial levels of $CO_2$. That would clearly be unacceptable. So they calculated how much carbon we'd have to cut to keep to just twice preindustrial levels. Their conclusion? We must cut projected annual worldwide carbon emissions in half by 2050, from about 14 billion tons to 7 billion tons in order to stabilize atmospheric carbon (this is the equivalent of reducing projected $CO_2$ emissions from 50 billion metric tons to 25 billion).

For the world to make those cuts, industrial nations would have to reduce emissions by 60 to 80 percent in fifty years—a dramatic reduction but one for which the necessity is well grounded in science. It is not practical to expect the citizens of Kenya to cut emissions to the same degree as Germans or Americans; a U.S. citizen, for example, emits nearly eighty times as many metric tons of $CO_2$ every day as the average Kenyan.[1]

Pacala and Socolow looked for a way to cut emissions in half. They identified fifteen available technologies that could be brought to scale globally, each reducing one billion tons of carbon over fifty years. The good news is that, taken together, just seven of those billion-ton wedges could stabilize the climate below twice preindustrial levels of $CO_2$. The

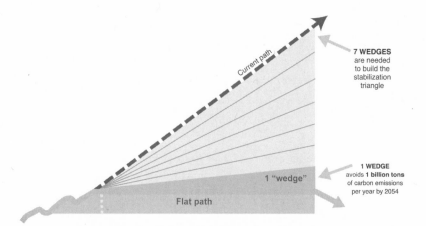

In their landmark August 2004 *Science* magazine article, Socolow and Pacala proposed that, to stabilize atmospheric carbon at 400 ppm by 2050 (the bottom curve of the graph), we would have to reduce annual $CO_2$ emissions from the business-as-usual scenario (the top curve) by 7 billion tons. They depicted these reductions in the graph as a set of wedges, each representing a technology portfolio capable of reducing $CO_2$ emissions by 1 billion tons per year by 2050. Socolow and Pacala offered 15 possible portfolios that are available today. We discuss on the next page what would be involved in seven of those options. (Courtesy of the Carbon Mitigation Initiative, Princeton University.)

sobering news, however, is that we'd have to reach the full potential of each of those technologies in a short time, and there are real uncertainties associated with each. Here are the wedges we focus on in this book:[2]

- Wind. To get a one-billion-ton reduction of $CO_2$ emissions from wind would require an increase of fiftyfold over our current capacity and production of wind energy on an area of land the size of Germany. That's doable but a big reach.

- Solar. A billion-ton reduction from solar would come from increasing installed capacity of photovoltaic electricity seven-hundred-fold, ramping up the rate of installations to sixty times what we undertake today, and covering a surface area the size of New Jersey. That's a lot of rooftops and, again, would take rapid commercialization at a level we haven't begun to approach.

- Efficiency. A third billion-ton wedge could come from increasing energy efficiency by 25 percent in every home. There is tremendous waste in our economy now, and efficiency investments would provide many benefits, but capturing them would require massive and rapid scaling of our efforts as well as time to turn over housing stock.

- Automobiles. Increasing the fuel economy of the world's cars to sixty miles per gallon over that fifty-year period offers another billion, and another stretch goal.

- Biofuels. Another billion tons are available if we increase global ethanol production fifty times, to 34 million barrels a day, and do it using no fossil fuels in the process. We'd need to have cellulosic ethanol in our arsenal, produced using biomass and methane digesters. This gives us a rapid, and sobering, timeframe in which to achieve mass penetration of the technologies.

- Redesigning our communities. Improving land use to reduce by half the vehicle miles traveled by every commuter in the world each day would provide a sixth wedge. Again, this solution would provide tremendous benefits to society, but in nearly all parts of the world, trends are moving in the opposite direction. Implementing this solution would also require immediate action, as infrastructure takes a long time to change.

In addition to these six, we could get a final wedge of one billion tons of carbon by using conservation tillage on every single acre of global cropland currently under cultivation, or by stopping all deforestation—clearly, no small feat.

Each of these goals is achievable, but each represents a tremendous leap of both faith and commitment, requiring bold action and pushing the bounds of anything ever attempted. The Princeton study concluded that we have the technologies available, but the analysis was done without regard to cost. While we could build a solar-based electrical grid today, it would be at substantially higher cost than fossil fuels–based electricity. There is also no guarantee that any single wedge could be attained to its full extent, much less all of them simultaneously.

Because of this, we cannot leave any stone unturned. Clearly, we have to pursue every wedge—the stakes are too high to permit gambling the globe's future on any one strategy, or any seven.

So far, we have looked at energy and technology innovation principally through the lenses of efficiency and renewable energy. Yet the foundation of our energy today comes from nonrenewable resources, and those too must be part of the solution.

In fact, five of the fifteen wedges that Socolow and Pacala looked at involve nonrenewable power, either coal or nuclear; but there, too, the scale is massive. To reduce carbon by one wedge through carbon capture and sequestration (CCS) at power plants would require capturing and permanently storing all the carbon emissions from eight hundred gigawatt-size coal plants. Today only three such underground storage facilities exist in the world—in Norway, Canada, and Algeria—and they store a modest 1 million tons of carbon each year.[3] To realize a coal-related wedge would require an increase from 3 million tons of stored carbon a year to 3,500 million tons per year over fifty years, a massive scaling operation. Nuclear requires clearing similarly large hurdles, as we will see later.

Nonetheless, we must take all of these fuels seriously, and examine the potential of each wedge, if we hope to find solutions to our climate and energy challenges.

## Taking a Second Look at Coal

Some people love coal. Some believe it is the answer to our energy woes. After all, black coal from deep below is really stored, fossilized sunshine from up above. In no other fuel are the sun's rays stored in such an efficiently combustible manner. It is such a power-packed rock that people go 4,000 feet below the earth and pick at it with grimy tools in 120° heat, generation after generation, to get it. When the mines explode and their friends are buried, they go right back down for the next shift. Their courage, muscle, and sinew brought to the surface the coal that powered the lighting of America's homes and the Industrial Revolution. Coal provided the bulk of industrial energy throughout the nineteenth century and still fires 53 percent of our electricity, and supplies remain to last for several hundred years.[4]

American industry has been built on the majesty of King Coal. It's easy to burn, easy to store, easy to transport, and easy to turn into hot steam. Thousands of jobs and regional economies depend on it, from the hills of West Virginia to the high mesas of Wyoming. It is a vital part of our economic history. Mother Jones was a hell-raising coal miner's widow who gave us the progressive movement. And coal provided the steam and heat to drive assembly lines and smelters, fuel the railroads to link our coasts, build the steel industry, and make the modern city possible.

Coal is powerful, efficient, cheap, and abundant. But it's also killing us. There are the 1,500 miners who die of black lung disease every year, one every six hours.[5] Mike South, former president of the National Black Lung Association, was himself a miner and victim of the disease. There are also the 20,000 Americans it kills through deadly particulates, mercury, and sulfur dioxide, but those are only the most obvious victims of King Coal as we produce and use it today.[6] The larger victim is the climate system of the earth.

Should we fail to restrain the growth of $CO_2$ emissions, all six billion of us on this little spaceship are at risk, not just those of us who die of respiratory diseases. Coal accounts for 35 percent of our $CO_2$ emissions now, and because it is so cheap, it will become a much larger piece of the global warming problem in the future, unless we figure out how to eliminate carbon from our coal plant emissions.[7] American coal-fired plants emit more $CO_2$ than those of any other nation on earth, except China.[8]

It is true that a lump of coal could one day become a diamond with enough pressure, but it is not a girl's best friend. Coal is in a race with cars to be the greatest danger to our climate. But with new technology and a new set of rules, it could also be one of the greatest contributors to any solution that offers a future for carbon-free energy.

There is a coal boom under way, and new plants will have lots to burn. It is estimated that the nation has a 250-year supply of coal.[9] That may seem like good news at first. But unless we change the way we use coal, less than one-fifth of the way through that stock of fuel, the planet will have become encumbered with double the atmospheric concentrations of $CO_2$ that existed before coal began to be burned. If that happens and the Arctic melts and the deserts expand, our grandchildren will curse the very word.

Coal is a promising fuel. It promises to light our homes with cheap energy for centuries. If the carbon in that coal is released to the atmosphere, though, it also promises to make those centuries unbearably hot, the seas unbearably acidic, and severe weather unbearably frequent. Which promise will be realized?

In this light, Merle Travis's lyrics take on a new meaning. When he says that coal mining will leave us deeper in debt, we might interpret that to mean that burning coal in the usual way, and continuing the rise in carbon emissions, will leave us deeper in debt to our progeny for fouling up the only planet available to them.

Can coal ever be clean?

Paul Anderson, the sixty-one-year-old CEO of Duke Energy Corporation, believes that it can. Anderson would be a typical buttoned-down business leader except for one thing: He wants to change the world.

To do that, he wants to discover the previously unthinkable—a way to make coal clean from a climate perspective—and he is willing to enlist the help of putting a price on carbon. He proposes that the federal government cap the allowable level of $CO_2$ emissions and charge for emissions of $CO_2$ as the most effective and fair way to prevent global warming and spur the development of new and innovative coal technology. "If we approach this rationally, it will not be disruptive to the economy and will not turn the world upside down, and will, at the same time, address the problem," says Anderson.[10] From a Bush backer and member of the President's Council of Advisors on Science and Technology, this is a stunning statement.

Not surprisingly, this statement of vision earned Anderson the enmity of Rush Limbaugh and threats of an "exorcism" from fellow industry leaders. So why did he say it?

He said it because he realizes two things: First, unlike the current Bush administration, he knows the world demands regulated $CO_2$ emissions. Second, he knows that his industry needs a clear vision of the future in order to move toward clean coal. If coal is to remain a long-term part of our energy future, the physics of our climate demand that coal come clean.

Despite that last fact, traditional coal is booming. The Chinese are building the equivalent of two 500-megawatt coal-fired plants every week, while in America, at least 150 plants are either in development or under consideration.[11] Every 500-megawatt coal-fired plant creates roughly three million tons of carbon dioxide a year; 1,000-megawatt plants produce six million tons. Based on those estimates, using conventional technology in 150 new plants will increase American global warming emissions from electricity at least 20 percent, a growth ranging from 450 to 840 million metric tons a year (depending on the size of the plants).[12] What's more, these plants, once built, will last for fifty years, promising decades of $CO_2$ emissions.

The ultimate question becomes—can coal clean up its act?

Anderson and many experts argue that it can if we capture $CO_2$ and other pollutants and inject them into deep underground storage. Several processes can achieve that, but the most cost-competitive and likely contender today is integrated gasification and combined-cycle technology (IGCC) paired with carbon capture and sequestration. IGCC involves using steam and oxygen to react with the carbon-rich coal to produce a fuel stream that can accommodate removal of the $CO_2$ that would otherwise escape into the atmosphere when the coal is burned. While many questions remain on its safety, its durability, and the rules that would guide its implementation, the need to reconcile coal and climate has many people, from executives to activists, giving this technology a careful look.

## Completing the Carbon Cycle: From $CO_2$ to Bedrock

If coal is to have a future in a world with climate change, it will be through the ability to put back into the ground the carbon we dug out of it. In one year, a single thousand-megawatt plant requires the volume of 50 million barrels of $CO_2$ to be sequestered underground, and in the U.S. alone, new coal-fired plants with the capacity of an additional 145 gigawatts are being planned.[13] This raises the question of whether there is sufficient space in caverns and crevices below ground to accommodate these enormous quantities of $CO_2$—the equivalent of three Empire State buildings every year for every coal plant.[14]

"We have enough room, probably, but the question is whether we have the right techniques and procedures for using it," says Dr. Ernie Moniz, a plainspoken professor of physics at MIT and former undersecretary of energy, who led an authoritative study of the possibilities of clean coal that was released in 2007.[15] "We need about one billion tons per year of storage capacity, and we think we have got it, with a couple of big caveats. First, scale is everything, and we have never tested to see if cracks would present a problem when we pump $CO_2$ under pressure into the saline fluid–filled layers deep underground. Second, we have no idea what regulatory mechanism would be needed to monitor these sites for long periods to assure their integrity. This whole area is just crying out for R&D."

IGCC plants have not yet been built at commercial scale with $CO_2$ sequestration, much less with the second-generation technology project known as FutureGen. The Bush administration proposed FutureGen and has given it a billion-dollar budget. Its objective is to build a zero-emissions coal plant that uses gasification and sequestration technologies. Its goals are twofold: to build the first plant designed to accomplish long-term sequestration in locations other than oil fields, and to improve efficiency and reduce costs dramatically. But FutureGen would be just one plant, and according to Moniz, "These areas [of research] need at least three or five times the number of sites to be tested to give us confidence."

The biggest problem with FutureGen is that as an ambitious, expensive federal initiative, it suggests that the technology for CCS won't be ready until the project is complete, thus discouraging separate private-sector research, development, and deployment. Meanwhile, a few regional sequestration initiatives have emerged, supported by state tax incentives to promote CCS technology, but these are underfunded because the federal government has put most of its eggs in the FutureGen basket.

Costs of experimental technologies always exceed the costs of current practices. IGCC first-generation plants cost in the range of $1,400 per kilowatt, compared with $1,000 per kilowatt to build a conventional plant. What the cost would be for a FutureGen plant, including costs of sequestering $CO_2$ underground permanently, is unknown. But even groups advocating for advanced coal research have estimated that costs would exceed those of alternatives such as wind. For instance, a report by the Electric Power Research Institute concluded that the true cost of clean coal would be approximately $0.055 to $0.065 per kilowatt in 2020, compared to costs in the range of $.04 to $.06 per kilowatt now for wind power and $.03 for efficiency programs.[16]

To be truly clean, coal plants have to be able to permanently sequester their $CO_2$. Advocates for clean coal point out that $CO_2$ has been pumped into the ground for years for the purpose of pushing out oil from depleted wells, without appreciable problems. One plant in North Dakota gasifies a feed stock similar to coal and then sells its pressurized $CO_2$ to Canadian oil fields, where it is used to pump out additional oil.[17] But using those small amounts of $CO_2$ in oil fields is a fundamentally different kettle of fish than trying to permanently lock away $CO_2$ across the whole country.

Can $CO_2$ be permanently sequestered below ground? Certainly, gases under high pressure can be kept trapped in rock for millions of years, since that is how long natural gas deposits have lain dormant underground. The idea behind clean coal is to recreate those conditions. Recent studies have shown promise but also some troubling findings—for instance, that $CO_2$'s acidity degrades the saline conditions of salt mine storage and the cement materials used to cap the wells into which the $CO_2$ is pumped.[18]

One would hope that humankind could devise a way to store a material below ground, given enough time and money, but the essential issue of advanced coal is that unless a cost-effective means can be developed to transport and store $CO_2$ for centuries, coal might be gasified, but it will not be sequestered. The difficulty of this challenge is demonstrated by the ignominious end of plans to sequester $CO_2$ in the deep ocean, plans that sounded promising until it was realized that $CO_2$ being absorbed from the atmosphere was already acidifying the oceans, killing any plans to use them as a carbon sink, except perhaps for sequestration in the deeper ocean sediments.

Simply throwing money at coal will not make it clean. The Bush administration is devoting $1 billion over ten years to FutureGen.[19] That money exists, but the question is whether it will be appropriately allocated without being spread too thin to be effective. FutureGen represents an enormous societal investment, and the project's execution needs to reflect the gravity of its mission.

The FutureGen project should be operational by 2012, but there are substantial and legitimate fears that it will suspend the deployment and use of IGCC with carbon capture and storage.[20] The comprehensive study that MIT did on coal expresses concern over the project's inadequate funding and ambiguous purpose. Rather than declaring the project a demonstration effort, the Department of Energy insists that FutureGen is for research. But for the sake of the climate and our utilities industry, we need the technology to spread and commercialize faster than mere research implies.

The current FutureGen project puts all of its eggs in one technological basket by building just one plant. Given the huge uncertainties involved, we need more experiments of greater diversity and sufficient funding. By requiring three or more geologic sequestration experiments to compete to successfully store one million tons of $CO_2$, the odds of success will increase. Attempting to prove the long-term stability of carbon sequestration in only one site will not build the necessary confidence in utilities, consumers, or policy makers. Simply put, to slow global warming and change our use of coal, the federal government should help create multiple commercial-scale plants with carbon capture and storage.

There are many ways to spend government money, and they are not all created equal. The current model gives an overly generous 75 percent subsidy to the private partners of FutureGen without a corresponding production requirement, and that creates no incentive to reduce costs. We can do better both for the taxpayer and for the future of clean coal.[21] An alternative strategy is available if we adopt measures that point us in that direction.

The government should use federal funds as a production credit rather than a giveaway. As with the wind production credit, we should grant federal payments based on actual electricity generation with sequestration of carbon rather than simple installation of equipment. This is a lesson learned from California, where an installation credit for solar panels inspires just construction, not maximized production of electricity. It is electricity and carbon reductions we want, not only capital investment. This also creates a greater incentive for industry to produce on a cost-effective basis.

It is as if the current administration is spending $1 billion of taxpayers' money to create a technology that, abiding by its own policies, would never be built—since the administration conducts its policies as if there will be no near-term regulation. No IGCC plant sequestering $CO_2$ will be able to compete with carbon-emitting coal as long as unlimited $CO_2$ can be released into the atmosphere for no cost. Why would any utility spend millions on a more expensive technology when it can continue to release emissions into the skies for free? To make carbon capture and sequestration work, we need some cost and a cap to be imposed on $CO_2$ emissions to make it economically viable to bury them in the ground. Smokestacks are cheap. $CO_2$ sequestration is not. Yet, in the early stages of a cap-and-trade system, the price for carbon may still be too low and the increased cost of carbon capture and sequestration too high to drive implementation. Additional requirements, such as a low-carbon standard for new plant construction, may be needed to drive the application of critical technology to capture carbon emissions from power plants. The Bush administration's policy in this regard is at war with itself because cutting emissions is voluntary, emitting is costless, and investments to promote change are too low. If such policies continue, there may come a day when sequestration is demonstrated but no one uses it because there is no incentive to do so.

There is a different way, of course. In Norway the government both taxes $CO_2$ emissions and operates under an overall cap in emissions, so the Statoil company is today pumping $CO_2$ into permanent storage below the sea floor. A technology without a reason to use it is just an expensive hood ornament. Norway has both the technology and the policy. We may have the technology one day, but we will need a change in policy to bring it to bear.

Nonetheless, enormous effort is being invested in the FutureGen project. The project has promised $750 million to a consortium of utilities and power producers, which will match that investment with another $250 million of private capital to be used to build the world's first IGCC plant that sequesters $CO_2$. The project is a mammoth undertaking, given the technological challenges in both processing the fuel and developing geological storage. But it will take more than substantial breakthroughs in technology to bring any such plant on line. Major forces will have to come into play to get any utility to buy into this new technology. Though there are at least twenty-six such projects world-wide, including FutureGen and a project called BP Carson, most utilities are still waiting for an incentive to include "carbon capture–ready" plants in their planning.[22]

"The bottom line is there is no incentive for any utility—regulated or unregulated—to do anything new," says Neville Holt, technical fellow with the Electric Power Research Institute. "There is no reward for the risk. . . . If you are an independent power producer, you want the lowest capital cost to reduce your financial exposure."[23]

Holt has put his finger on a huge barrier to truly revolutionizing coal: the utilities' reluctance to make a change. "We've got 320 gigawatts of coal-fired plants running, and air emissions of only 100 gigawatts are scrubbed. The utilities' costs to generate electricity are about $20 a megawatt-hour, and they will keep going as long as possible," he says. Continuing to use dirty coal without removing pollution is not a minor matter, according to Holt; "it is a tremendous economic advantage."[24]

Even the most energetic proponents of carbon capture recognize the hurdles. Dale Heydlauff, a senior vice president for governmental and environmental affairs at American Electric Power, says it will take a large subsidization to bring IGCC close to being competitive. "Without it," he says, "AEP will build gas units in the near term. . . . If there are only purely economic drivers, we will turn to gas and maybe some wind energy."[25] And the 50 percent of our electricity derived from coal will continue to emit its carbon.

Traditional coal enjoys an overlooked subsidy that puts the cost burden on society; it's what the economists would call an externality—the public health and environmental damage engendered by burning coal. It is no wonder, then, that while 40 percent of the plants now under consideration would incorporate gasification technology, very few are planning to install carbon storage (CCS).[26] What is more depressing, only one of them, the FutureGen plant, is actually planning to immediately deploy $CO_2$ storage. Cleaning up coal is a two-step dance: first gasifying it, then sequestering the $CO_2$. Without both steps, it can never be the "Clean Coal Waltz"; it will always be the "Old Coal Two-Step."

The coal industry might welcome the inducement of a subsidy for IGCC, and it may be needed to accelerate development, even with a price on carbon; but will it be enough to truly drive this tectonic shift in the coal industry? The whole system has to be tested, not just its glamorous parts. It will be of no meaningful value if we spend $1 billion of public money and then cannot find a way to sequester $CO_2$. Here is one instance when congressional spending for a hole in the ground would actually be of public benefit.

Even if we find suitable storage technology, we should not expect IGCC to be as inexpensive as pulverized coal is today. Dr. Moniz estimates that with sequestration IGCC will sell electricity at about 50 percent higher cost than current coal plants. This is because it takes energy to compress $CO_2$ for storage, on the order of needing a separate plant to produce power to handle the sequestration needs of two other plants.[27] Unless technologies can be commercialized—as in the Ramgen Company's effort to compress $CO_2$ at 30 percent less cost—it is difficult to see how coal with sequestered carbon could become cost competitive against carbon-emitting coal plants unless there is a high price on emissions or a mandate to deploy storage technology. Clearly, CCS is not a route to cheaper energy, but it is the only route to using our enormous coal reserves while burying $CO_2$.

## Taking Another Tack with Fuels?

Rentech, Inc., of Denver, Colorado, recently received a capital infusion in the form of a loan guarantee dedicated for use of a process called Fischer-Tropsch to convert coal to diesel fuel, a process that has been used for decades with proven results. Germany ran its war machine on oil processed from coal this way, and South Africa, forced by sanctions, did the same during the apartheid era.

"If South Africa can do this, there is no reason we cannot," Hunt Ramsbottom, CEO of Rentech, says. "We use a different catalyst than they do, but the process is very similar. We have publicly stated that as long as oil stays in the $40- to $45-a-barrel range, we will be able to make diesel for competitive prices, while still removing the $CO_2$ created during the processing."[28]

Should this come to pass, America would have the capacity to replace Saudi Arabian oil with domestic coal-bred diesel, the United States then having the coal equivalent of 963 billion barrels of oil compared to estimates of 685 billion barrels in the Middle East. From an energy independence perspective, this could equal the freedom potentially gained through development of a biofuels economy. We would finally be able to rely upon good old red-blooded American dead biological material rather than foreign dead dinosaurs.

While the Rentech fuel would give us independence from Saudi Arabia, it would not give us freedom from global warming. If we turn to that type of fuel, we will still be emitting massive quantities of $CO_2$ for every gallon of coal-derived diesel we burn. For while Ramsbottom's assurances that Rentech will scrub the $CO_2$ out of its processing system are sincere and sequestration may be achievable, when the ultimate diesel product is burned, $CO_2$ nevertheless comes rushing out of the tailpipes of our vehicles. Liquid fuel from coal produces nearly double the $CO_2$ emissions of gasoline, and even if 90 percent of the carbon were removed during manufacturing and stored underground, the resulting coal-based fuel would still have 8 percent more $CO_2$ than gas, according to a Princeton study.[29]

An alternative approach, developed by GreatPoint Energy in Cambridge, Massachusetts, shows greater promise: It gasifies coal into a natural gas product that it argues could reduce $CO_2$ by 60 percent, but it receives no federal support.[30]

A coal-to-liquids program can make fuels for our cars' tanks and solve one energy security problem, but it creates a new set of concerns for the climate. In contrast, using our coal to produce electricity with IGCC and carbon capture to run plug-in hybrid cars may solve both concerns. The same ton of coal being used to produce a gallon of diesel fuel could be used to produce kilowatts of electricity for the most efficient type of engine we know of, an electric engine, and still provide a transportation fuel using existing infrastructure—the grid. When we evaluate our transportation fuel based on its carbon footprint, we will make the right decisions, not only in biofuels but, importantly, in taking on the questions associated with the future of coal.

So how should we place our bets? Given a choice between the coal-to-liquid program and an advanced coal electricity program with carbon capture and storage, we should look to performance. We face two threats: to security and to climate. When one of those threats—global warming—is existential, the answer is clear. We should choose the technology that solves both problems: IGCC with sequestration.

If America intends to accept the environmental price of coal mining, it ought to do so in the service of a vision that can address the challenges of oil dependence and climate at once. Producing electricity from coal while capturing and storing the carbon should be our priority. It could help free us from both Saudi Arabia and the threat of abrupt climatic change.

We are at an important crossroads in the futures of both coal and climate. If we adopt policies that channel coal into a burgeoning new industry in coal-based liquid fuels—a technology that does nothing to solve the threat of global warming—we will have invested substantial new infrastructure in an industry that accelerates the threat to our atmosphere.

That is a path we cannot afford to take. Once that industry is created, it will require too much time and global risk to transfer those billions of dollars of investment into a true clean-coal technology that captures and sequesters carbon.

Even the hope for IGCC rests, of course, on the unproven assumption that all those gigatons of $CO_2$ can be stored underground safely and economically. Here is where we should place our efforts and energy in tackling the challenges of the future of coal.

## Can We Do It?

Advanced coal technology just may work. But we need to clean up our policies first. First, we need to send a signal that we will not grandfather the right to future carbon emissions for the 150 traditional plants planned for development—planned now partly out of their developers' desire to beat out climate regulation and not be exposed to carbon costs. "We need to send a message to the developers right now that they can't build a dirty plant in 2007 and avoid a $CO_2$ cost in 2009," says Steve Clemmer of the Union of Concerned Scientists. "$CO_2$ stays in the atmosphere for one hundred years. It is the gift that keeps on giving. We must fire a warning shot across the bow of those that want to build dirty plants now so they can escape responsibility. That means no grandfather clauses, or at least minimal ones."[31]

Second, we need to recognize that incentives are not enough. Right now, the coal industry is being offered a $1 billion carrot in the form of federal support for clean-coal R&D. Is that carrot big enough, powerful enough, and dynamic enough to drive a fundamental shift away from pulverized coal and toward clean coal across our entire energy system? In a word, no.

This is too big a rabbit to coax out of its hole just by subsidizing research. In nature, coal can be transformed from a black lump of carbon into a crystalline diamond. In politics it is the same. Both require pressure.

"Only when the Clean Air Act mandated a 50 percent $SO_2$ reduction did anything happen," says Dallas Burtraw, senior fellow at Resources for the Future, of America's experience with reducing sulfur dioxide pollution. He points to research from the University of California demonstrating that despite decades of generous subsidies to the industry to help it develop cleaner coal technology to reduce sulfur dioxide, improvements simply were not made until a federal mandate in 1990 required them.[32]

"With a mix of the carrot and stick, the stick turns out to be a very important instrument," Burtraw says. "Forcing regulations don't need to be big, but they must start soon. They begin a process to influence investments and change industry expectations. They can lead to more public- and private-sector research and many small improvements on the margin that matter."

The Bush administration insists on trying to fight this battle with one hand tied behind Uncle Sam's back. It refuses to take even the mildest regulatory steps to protect the public's health against the ravages of $CO_2$. It is passionate in favor of handing out tax-cut goodies to the industry and equally passionate about refusing to require industry action on $CO_2$ in exchange for those handouts.

We need laws that create a legal cost for using up the capacity of our climate to absorb more carbon. We also need laws that give the industry certainty about what behavior is acceptable and what is not. To fail at this places our economy and our environment at risk.

The rush to build traditional coal plants may also expose utilities to financial costs. By 2030 even conservative analysis suggests that utilities could pay at least $20 to $50 per ton in emissions charges under $CO_2$ regulations.[33] The utilities that are charging ahead with even the most modern pulverized-coal plants that do nothing to limit carbon emissions are making high profits today but exposing their investors and customers to enormous risk of a known threat very shortly. That is why shareholders are passing resolutions in corporate meetings to require consideration of $CO_2$ impacts in planning—a prudent move.

So Mr. Anderson and his Duke Power are not alone. The major West Coast utility, PG&E, has joined his call for federal action, as have BP and the major industrial energy user Alcoa, preferring to deal with one federal $CO_2$ cost constraint rather than a fifty-state hash of inconsistent ones. "The worst scenario would be if all fifty states took separate action and we have to comply with fifty different laws," says Anderson.[34]

Anderson's colleague Jim Rogers agrees, but with a caveat: "We cannot have fifty state cap-and-trade systems," he says. "We need one consistent standard, but one that recognizes the different situations of different regions of the country." He argues that any cap must take into account the dramatic differences in the energy situations of the various states. "The geology of Indiana, with all its limestone, may accommodate in-ground sequestration of $CO_2$ with ease, while that of North Carolina will probably not. We might have to do chilled ammonia rather than IGCC in the Carolinas. If so, the system has to give some break to the Carolinas. Coal is 50 percent of our energy but is 70 percent in some regions. Those regions need some leeway on the costs imposed by a cap. We provided such relief to more deeply affected utilities with the sulfur dioxide cap, and we need to do the same in $CO_2$." Finally, with the acceptance of an inevitable limit to our carbon emissions, these utility executives will be able to move on to deeper issues about how such a policy might be designed.

The power that attracted a Bush administration backer to the cause of a $CO_2$ cap is certainty. When a utility considers spending $300 million for a five-hundred-megawatt electricity plant that will last for fifty years, it wants to have the base economics locked in, fixed, and not subject to the whims of fifty state legislatures. Anderson has taken the unprecedented step of suggesting a cost be imposed on his industry because of the certainty of global warming and the benefits of certainty when making investment decisions.

Anderson's position is revealing. It shows that incentives to the coal industry will not be enough to induce the type of fundamental shift in planning that global warming demands. We should note that he has suggested a $CO_2$ cost, not just some tax incentive for coal plants that use IGCC technology. When a major utility suggests such an action, it should tell us that only the tough step of imposing a cap on carbon, likely coupled with mandates to store carbon, will do the trick of accomplishing a shift to the next generation of advanced coal technology and the future of coal itself.

These businessmen know one pivotal rule: Incentives come and go with Congresses, but regulating $CO_2$ would be permanent, and they can plan on that.

"Uncertainties can kill you," says Paul Fischbeck, a Carnegie Mellon University professor who has developed a model of uncertainty in the economic climate for utilities. He sees the delay in implementing $CO_2$ regulations as counterproductive. "We run seminars with utility executives and ask them to raise their hands if they don't expect carbon regulation in twenty years, and in a room of two hundred we get about two or three hands. They expect something, but they don't have any idea what shape or form it will take or when it might be enacted."[35]

Jim Rogers has the realistic view that if we meld action and fairness, the task is achievable. "If we do this right, we can get to 1990 emission levels by 2030. We can get this job done. We just need a fair cap-and-trade system and the right mix of what I would call development and deployment investment."[36] The cut he proposes is a weak one, but the movement is in the right direction.

His point is only reasonable. Any utility executive in 2007 who does not see a carbon cap coming is not reading the newspapers. If they choose to build for the past, it is out of a conscious irresponsibility, not out of surprise.

However, even a rigorous cap-and-trade system, during its crucial first few years, is not likely to establish a market price for emissions high enough to incentivize construction of new coal plants that capture and store carbon (most analysts believe that carbon price would be in the range of $25 to $30 per ton of $CO_2$). In this case, a technology mandate may be necessary, requiring all new coal plants to be capable of capturing and actually sequestering emissions by a certain future date.[37]

We have tons of coal. We have tons of innovative energy. We may be able to combine both for a couple of centuries of coal without the carbon, but only if we pick the right places to mine America's rich vein of innovative talent.

One way or another, coal will be part of our near-term future. It is up to us to see that it is used in a way that ensures we have a future that is long term.

## Splitting the Atom Instead of Splitting the Atmosphere

Coal is the largest source of base-load energy in the United States, and it deserves special attention in our efforts to ensure a sound energy future, a safe planet, and a stable climate. But there is another major player in the world of base-load electrical energy. Nuclear power is the third-largest source of electricity in the United States, behind coal and natural gas, and because it emits no carbon, it has increasingly become a topic of discussion in the world of climate and energy.

What killed the growth of nuclear energy in America? Was it Chernobyl, Three Mile Island, or Jane Fonda in *The China Syndrome*—or simply high costs and difficult financing? Whatever the cause, building nuclear reactors for civilian energy stopped dead in the 1970s, when the last reactors were commissioned. In 1996, one of the two units in the last plant commissioned, the Watts Bar plant in Chattanooga, Tennessee, went live. The other was killed. The combination of fear of radiation and fear of huge construction and operation costs effectively put nuclear energy in mothballs.

Now at least the idea of nuclear energy is getting a good airing. This is not surprising since a nuclear reactor emits no $CO_2$. No other characteristic is more important in today's energy world. Today, 441 reactors are operating around the world, providing 17 percent of all electrical production, and 32 reactors are under construction worldwide.[38] Despite that, doubts and fears about nuclear energy are broad and deep. The eighth Energy Enlightenment, however, states that we all have to put aside our prejudices and take a fresh look at the world if we are going to defeat global warming. That imperative has no greater importance than when discussing nuclear energy.

It may not be easy to do, however. No energy source produces a substance so toxic that a few specks of its fuel or its residue can kill. No other source leaves a by-product that can linger for tens of thousands of years and still be deadly. No other technology is so incredibly capital intensive, so expensive that the collapse of reactor building projects in Washington State led to the largest bond default in world history in the 1980s.[39]

On the other hand, no other technology can take a tiny amount of fuel and produce such prodigious amounts of energy. No other existing technology can provide such a huge base load of electricity on a steady basis without emitting a whiff of $CO_2$. With this technology, tiny pellets of uranium oxide can power whole cities.

But they, or their offspring, can also destroy cities. A benign nuclear reactor in France may be technically similar to one in North Korea, but the difference in the effect on our ability to sleep at night is enormous. We may justifiably have confidence in our nation's ability to maintain effective safeguards over our own nuclear material, but our failure to develop other technologies that the world could use in the place of nuclear energy would unavoidably increase the risk of proliferation of nuclear technology for weaponization. Spreading solar technology around the world does not present a security threat. Spreading nuclear technology around the world does. The world contains too many unstable regimes and too many groups eager to obtain fissile material to conclude otherwise.

That risk may be manageable, it may be necessary, but it cannot be ignored. It is true that we lived under the threat of thousands of Soviet thermonuclear warheads thirty minutes away and survived. We cannot forget, however, that the ultimate nightmare scenario is an angry group with fissile material and access to plans now on the Internet. No biofuel, no wind turbine will ever take out an American city. Nuclear energy could.

So nuclear energy is the alpha and the omega of energy. It represents both the best and the worst of energy technology. If reactors can become standardized systems that can operate economically and gain the confidence of the American people, and we can find a way to substantially reduce their deadly waste, they may be part of our energy future. Otherwise, they could eventually represent a technology that thrived for a few decades and faded away in the face of lost public acceptance and the absence of a waste storage system.

## The Storage Problem

A pile of hot radioactive waste the size of a small hillock stands between nuclear energy and growth. Currently, 52,000 tons of highly radioactive waste from civilian reactors are stored around America in what is euphemistically termed "temporary storage."[40] Some of it has been in temporary storage, in huge pools of water and above ground in large dry casks, for three decades. The industry has been bedeviled for that time with a lack of a permanent storage technology. Until one is found, the industry will not be able to grow.

The federal government was legally obligated to take responsibility for this waste, but it did not do so for a simple reason—it doesn't have a solution for long-term storage. As federal agencies have failed repeatedly to make adequate progress on the Yucca Mountain underground storage facility in Nevada, utilities have been stuck holding the bag of storing this dangerous material. Now utilities have sued the federal government for millions in damages they have incurred in having to care for this waste. The failure at Yucca Mountain is so glaring that the DOE entered into an agreement with the Skull Valley Band of the Goshutes Native American nation in Utah for that tribe to accept the nation's tens of thousands of tons of radioactive waste. But even that stopgap measure went down in flames when two federal agencies nullified the agreement and stopped hauling the waste across federal lands.[41]

The inherent problem of trying to instill confidence that radiation cannot escape underground for 10,000 years is obvious. In January 2006, for example, researchers at the University of Cambridge found that zircon, a material used to encapsulate waste, may not be as stable over thousands of years as originally believed. "We need to take this into account because most of these materials will degrade more rapidly than we had thought," said Ian Farnan, one of the lead researchers.[42]

Yucca Mountain was originally scheduled to open in 1998, but technical problems combined with political challenges have postponed its opening until at least 2017. Although tunnels have been dug 350 meters below the surface at Yucca, it cannot be said that a storage solution is now available. It cannot be said that one is even close. Until it is, large-scale growth in the industry is impossible. It is true that 161 million Americans live within seventy-five miles of temporary storage sites today, so one could think that nuclear energy by now would be considered a good neighbor. But Americans understand the concept of tens of thousands of years of toxic material ready to leach into America's groundwater, so they will insist upon a permanent solution before they embrace a full-scale growth program for nuclear energy.

More important, even if the Yucca site is finally approved, it will not be the complete answer. After it is in full operation, and is full, there will still be an additional 61,000 metric tons of waste in "temporary storage" at nuclear plants across the country.[43]

Options may exist to reduce the storage problems with much more sophisticated technology than digging a hole in the ground. It may be possible to substantially reduce the volume of waste through several means of reprocessing the material. The Bush administration has committed the nation to an international effort, the Global Nuclear Energy Partnership, to develop ways to reprocess spent fuel rods to recover usable plutonium and uranium and separate out long-lived radioactive elements known as actinides.[44]

The country's previous experience with reprocessing was ugly, though. Several sites experienced major equipment failures, chronic breakdowns, and even fires. The efforts were largely terminated in the late 1970s. But some countries—for example, Japan, China, and Russia—have active or pilot reprocessing programs.[45] It seems that the failures of the past should not terminate the prospect that a new technology can be developed.

## The Security Problem

Reprocessing technologies have a major challenge. When nuclear waste is reprocessed, the fissionable elements have to be recovered in a way that prevents them from being used to produce weapons. Part of the commitment of the administration's program is to develop proliferation-resistant technologies. It intends to take waste from one country and ship it to another for reprocessing. Under that plan, waste material will be flying across the globe. If that is to occur, the technology will have to result in materials that are not suitable for an Al-Qaida bomb. When such technologies do become available, they will be incredibly expensive, with just one plant estimated to cost on the order of $7.5 to $30 billion.[46] In the end, no matter how many times the fuel is reprocessed, we will still need long-term underground storage, the scope of which would depend on which reprocessing technique is chosen.

Should the United States spend any funds on reprocessing technology research in the next three years, as the DOE has requested? In light of the nonproliferation concerns, the huge cost involved, and the poor track record in this country, we should do so only if we are in a situation that involves a global threat and demands immediate action with no silver bullet available.

Which is exactly our current situation.

This research should be somewhere near the bottom of the totem pole, however—hundreds of other projects are more worthy. But given the risk of global warming, it is reasonable to continue this work. Nuclear energy will never be "clean" in the sense of being pristine, but we cannot eliminate from consideration the possibility that it could one day be a part of the solution, especially if climate problems turn out to be worse than currently anticipated.

To assume a significant role, nuclear reactors will have to become more standardized and more passively safe. Perhaps the biggest reason the industry has been stagnant for years and is actually expected to decline in the next decade, however, is cost. To build the last twenty U.S. reactors cost $3 to $4 billion, or about $3,000 to $4,000 per kilowatt of capacity. This compares to $400 to $600 per kilowatt for the latest gas-fired combined-cycle plants. Six U.S. reactors have actually closed due to their costs of operation.[47]

One reason reactors are so awesomely expensive is that each one is a customized product. They will become more affordable only when they become more standardized. Westinghouse recently sold China four of its new AP1000 reactors, which can produce 1,100 megawatts with 35 percent fewer pumps, 50 percent fewer valves, and 80 percent less piping. This is unusually good news for our exports picture. Only two major products are sold to China from the United States: jets and nuclear reactors.[48]

But to become a major factor in the new energy world, nuclear plants would have to be in design now, even before the perfection of new technologies or the resolution of disposal and proliferation concerns, because of the incredibly long permitting and design process. Nuclear plants take many years from conception to first power production. If nuclear reactors are to become a meaningful player in the next two decades, Americans would have to accept them now.

If we do continue research in nuclear, we must also take into consideration the fact that the industry already enjoys an enormous subsidy. The American government has assumed the huge risk of indemnifying the industry for its liabilities in the event of a catastrophe. At some point, a nation can no longer justify continuing to carry an industry on its financial shoulders. We are at that point regarding the nuclear industry. If it comes to a choice between subsidies for new, pristine, and nonthreatening technologies such as wind and solar, which are still moving down their cost curve, and a heavily subsidized and always toxic mature technology like nuclear, our support should go to the newest, cleanest technologies first.

Nonetheless, we cannot ignore the fact that the second most powerful force in the universe is the power keeping an atomic nucleus intact. The first most powerful is the human intellect. If we play our cards right, it may one day be possible to split the former cleanly and safely by using the latter.

Ultimately, the question of whether to pursue nuclear research comes down to one issue: Do we have enough guaranteed renewable sources of energy to obviate all our non-$CO_2$ options? The answer is the same as for the question we faced on coal. We have many options, but we do not yet have the guarantees we need. The only guarantee we have is that global warming will eat us alive if we do not call for all hands on deck.

With nuclear energy, however, such major questions persist regarding large-scale deployment that while it may not be unreasonable to continue basic research into their resolution, a wholesale crash program for current deployment would be irresponsible. Returning to the "Princeton wedges" of Pacala and Socolow, to achieve a one-billion-ton reduction using nuclear fission would require tripling total global capacity from the current 17 percent of electricity. This growth would add several thousand tons of plutonium to the world's current stock of approximately 1,000 tons. Such a tripling of disposal and proliferation threats is a major price to pay, and the world does not seem prepared to take on such a challenge wholeheartedly when other, more promising options are waiting in the wings.

So what should we do on this voyage of energy discovery? When the ship is sinking, the wise captain brings all the lifeboats on deck and asks the ship's carpenter to try to make them all seaworthy, even those with dry rot and holes from target practice. As we exhaust the potential of renewable and efficient technologies, coal and nuclear may be lifeboats we need. We ought to find out if they can be made seaworthy. If not, we ought to move on to other boats.

## The Apollo Alliance: New Coalitions for Change

*Bracken Hendricks*

In April 2003 I helped launch the Apollo Alliance at the Campaign for America's Future's annual conference to "Take Back America" in Washington, D.C., a gathering of grassroots activists convened each year under the leadership of Apollo cofounder Robert Borosage. As executive director and a cofounder of this new coalition, I stepped to the microphone to announce the coming together of a dozen labor unions and a broad cross section of environmental organizations to declare common cause in demanding the jobs, investment, and opportunity at the heart of a clean-energy economy. It was an exciting moment, to bring these powerful movements together, representing millions of people on the ground, machinists and electricians, environmental activists and sportsmen. It was time for a new coalition and a new voice for jobs *and* the environment.

The response was swift and enthusiastic. There was tremendous hunger for a discussion of our climate and jobs crises that was rooted in a positive vision for moving the country forward. I became convinced at that moment that our months of hard work in building the alliance had laid the groundwork for a politically powerful realignment with the clean-energy revolution at its heart.

What started as a loose coalition of labor and environmentalists has today grown to include 22 unions and the International AFL-CIO, almost all the major national environmental organizations, 150 businesses, 150 community-based organizations, and formal Alliance chapters in ten states. It has won bipartisan legislative victories and gotten membership groups working together for a shared message, creating jobs in clean energy.

It is increasingly clear that succeeding in an energy revolution will take a political revolution as well. Uniting the labor and environmental movements; a business voice; and community, faith, and civil rights groups is a key part of creating that revolution. These new alliances are grounded in shared interests and a shared vision for a "high road" national economy. In an economic study conducted for the Alliance, the nonpartisan Texas-based economist Ray Perryman calculated that a rapid conversion to clean energy that invested $300 billion over ten years (one quarter the cost of the Iraq war in the last four years) would create over three million jobs concentrated in the manufacturing and construction sectors and offer billions of dollars of stimulus to the economy in new earnings and investment.[1]

A seminal moment in the formation of the Apollo Alliance was the transmission of a catalytic memo written by political strategist and Apollo cofounder Dan Carol in the immediate aftermath of the tragedy of 9/11. The "moonshot" memo called for an *Apollo*-scale effort linking economic stimulus with ending dependence on oil, and calling for an alliance of strange bedfellows to get the job done. Carol's vision for broadening the coalition on climate and energy solutions through a focus on economic transformation is at the heart of a political movement that is finally emerging as a new politics for the country, linking concern over climate change, national security, and energy to hope for good jobs, stronger communities, and a more robust democracy.

Broadening the constituency for clean energy from an environmental base to a core economic and security audience was at the heart of forming the Alliance. As Steelworkers president Leo Gerard said at the time, "In the face of a trading system that's devastating both workers and the environment, an Apollo Project for energy independence has the potential to unite trade unionists and environmentalists in building an economy that values every worker's right to bargain for a decent living and every citizen's right to live in a healthier world."[2] The two are connected. Our economy either builds a broadly shared and lasting prosperity on a sustainable footing, or it doesn't.

The new Apollo Project for energy, by emphasizing the link between green strategies and long-term economic growth that creates good jobs, has laid out a critical piece of the political equation for healing long-standing rifts between environmental advocates and champions of workers' rights, and has also paved the way for collaboration with progressive businesses and advocates for social justice.

Today Jerome Ringo is president of the Apollo Alliance, and he is working to continue expanding that base of coalition partners. Ringo started his work in the Louisiana petrochemical industry; as an oil and chemical worker, he led health and safety fights in the refining industry. Once he had secured protective equipment for the workers in the plant, he began to talk to folks "outside the fence." His rich experience inside and outside the energy industry impressed on him the need to build broad coalitions.

Ringo looks to Martin Luther King Jr. as a guide. The civil rights movement was one of the last truly successful broad-based popular movements in the United States. What is most important about King is that he turned decades-old civil rights battles into a movement by bringing people of all backgrounds together around a common cause. Racial justice ceased to be the issue of one class of citizens, faced alone by individuals, and became everyone's concern.

Ringo believes that no issue is as powerful today, or as common to everyone, as that of climate and energy. The new Apollo vision of a renewed environment; millions of good jobs; and stronger, more secure communities can be the spark that unites a truly common movement. As Ringo says, this is "not a Democrat or Republican issue, not a rich man's or poor man's issue; it is not something just for politics or the faith community. It is something that touches all of us and will have to be resolved by all of us."[3] The current crisis, he says, "can't be solved by a segment of the people—everyone has to have a place at the table."

The Apollo Alliance is creating organizing tools to bring people together around this vision, launching a national Apollo Challenge to motivate and mobilize voters, organizing businesses and community leaders around state legislation, and crafting new policies to show what's possible. It is also taking the long view by trying to creatively engage the very young with a Young Apollo program. "Just as elementary and middle school students prompted their parents to recycle and quit smoking," Carol says, "organizing youth, even before they hit college—a clean-energy Boy and Girl Scouts—can start to speak to the conscience of adults and truly change citizen and consumer behavior at the scale we need."[4]

Ringo waxes eloquent on the threats we are facing and their potential to unite us if we can rise to the occasion. As he said recently while strategizing over coffee, "I have stood at the base of Kilimanjaro and seen the melting glaciers; I have stood in an Arctic village and seen the melting of the permafrost. I am an evacuee of Hurricane Rita. I have seen storms take out refineries in my home state and double the price of gas. Tomorrow may be too late. I recognize a sense of urgency, but more, I recognize a need for involvement from everybody."

Kennedy didn't have a template for how to reach the moon, but he had a strategy for marshaling the resources of the country to solve the task at hand. With a united country, he was able to achieve the unbelievable, the unsupportable, the impossible, and do it in a relatively short period of time.

So can we. We need to bring America together around a vision of hope. A new and unifying politic. We cannot afford to waste the talent or lose the contributions of any part of our society. It is time for a new political movement.

CHAPTER 9

# What's It Going to Take?

You can't ignore politics, no matter how much you'd
like to.

*—Molly Ivins*

In the summer of 1969 the Cuyahoga River caught fire. Pools of oil, de-
bris, and chemical pollution burst into flames beneath a railroad trestle
in downtown Cleveland along the gritty urban waterfront near Lake
Erie. The fire raged briefly, leaping some five stories from the surface of
the winding industrial river.

A river was on fire in America, and what at first attracted little attention in the city of Cleveland—no police were called to the scene—
grew slowly into a national story. *Time* magazine ran a photo of the
Cuyahoga on fire, bright jets of water set against a roiling backdrop of
smoke as steam engulfed a riverboat, a line of flame defining the rippling surface of the water.

The degradation of the Cuyahoga slowly grew into the stuff of
myth and folk song. It captured untapped public concern over the poi-
soned state of waterways in people's own cities all across the country
and a deeper sense that the planet was in disrepair. The damage of industrial growth was coming home to roost. Our prosperity had a down-
side that was becoming all too apparent.

Since the river had burned before, only small stories ran in the Cleveland papers. But this fire somehow mattered in the public imagination. It touched a nerve. The image of a burning river on the cover of *Time* gave form to a foreboding sense of imbalance. Water was not supposed to burn—especially not in America. Like the troubling footage of a naked, napalmed girl in flames in Vietnam, this image crept into the national consciousness as a symbol that something had gone deeply wrong.

When a shift like this happens, it has the power to build momentum, tapping the best American traditions of hard work and belief in reform. This fire sparked a movement.

Change had been set in motion, and lawmakers responded. A period of environmental consciousness and federal activism was ushered in that saw the birth of the EPA, the National Oceanic and Atmospheric Administration, and the Clean Water and Clean Air acts. More important, a national environmental movement was emerging. When a river is burning, it is time to act.

Today there are deeper problems brewing. You can see it not only in the melting Arctic ice, or Middle East wars, but closer to home. People are asking about the daffodils and cherry blossoms blooming in December in Washington, D.C., the droughts across the high plains, wildfires sweeping the West that from 2000 to 2006 consumed an area the size of Illinois, and weather patterns that seem all wrong. You can see it, too, in the anger of consumers at the gas pump and the persistence of concern over our energy dependence tracked in the national polls by pundits and politicians.

What isn't clear yet is what spark will ignite this unease and sense of foreboding into a flame of public outrage and the willingness to make deep changes. The scientific debate about global warming is over, our oil dependence is widely acknowledged, but what will change the politics? What will make this issue take fire, like that grimy oil slick in Cleveland? To conquer a global problem of this magnitude, we need a global movement for the global environment—and for our economic, social, and national security as well. And if scientists are right, we need it fast, within the decade.

Perhaps the human tragedy of Hurricane Katrina will in time become a touchstone for this larger, preventable disaster. The scenes are indelible of desperate citizens lifted from rooftops by helicopter and the tragedy of the bodies of those who didn't make it floating unattended. Perhaps in time their stories will begin to merge with those of other environmental refugees living at the edges of a changing climate. Americans may come to feel for Aleutian hunters trapped on shifting ice floes and the people of abandoned northern villages as the thawing tundra destroys the very foundation beneath their homes. We may consider the plight of Pacific Islanders losing entire nations to the sea, or closer to home the losses of farmers and ranchers in yet another season of drought and wildfires. Perhaps the volatility of gas prices will wear down American voters.

But alone even those stories will not be enough. Real and disturbing as those images are, they can be overcome by four powerful forces, what we might call the "Four Horsemen of the Energy Apocalypse." The first is the power of inertia. We cannot forget that the ideas represented in the new Apollo Project represent change, change in investments, change in policies, and even some change of behavior. Inertia in the course of human events has worn down many an effort to change the status quo.

The second enemy force is the largest cabal of special interests ever arrayed against positive change in the history of the U.S. Congress. We should never forget that the change we seek will in one way or another step on the toes of the most gargantuan group of profitable industries and economic interests ever assembled: oil companies, utilities, refiners, and all the related financial industries that have supported them. These groups can unleash on Congress, and the American people, a bombardment of lobbying and publicity worthy of Verdun. When that happens, there are more than a few members of Congress who could be affected more by the science of their reelection than by the science of global warming. Fortunately, fissures in that wall of resistance are developing, as a growing number of companies are recognizing the advisability, and inevitability, of a sea change in energy, as well as the economic opportunities for jobs and growth. But any industry with cash reserves in the mega-billions is a force to be reckoned with.

The third horseman of the Energy Apocalypse is the specter of policy makers being blinded by the miasma of ideology rather than enlightened by the light of science. It is a political tragedy that global warming and clean energy have become issues viewed through an ideological prism rather than through a scientific, pragmatic one. Too many politicians and pundits began to see global warming as a communist plot designed by partisan politicians rather than as a scientific challenge demanding rational analysis and decisive action. There is also ideological resistance to the solutions that global warming will require, from tax breaks to public investment to direct regulation and the imposition of fees. The virus of ideology has infected many an otherwise rational member of Congress and turned them into something less, at least on this issue. Now it is our task to scrub ideology out of the energy discussion, so we can make bipartisan progress toward investing in a shared and better future.

The fourth horseman is simple: fear—fear that we cannot adopt policies that can succeed, fear that there is no clear path forward. Fear breeds inaction. It was "cold unreasoning fear" that led Franklin Roosevelt to say, "The only thing we have to fear is fear itself." He could have been speaking of our energy challenges today.

Without a plan of action grounded in a deep belief in a positive vision, a growing fear of disaster will only cause retrenchment and further atomization at just the moment when we most need to rally together. We must look to the seeds of solution, even as we face squarely the growing problems that surround us. We must plan a different future and organize around a different kind of politics.

The mission of a new Apollo Project for energy is to offer such a galvanizing story and organizing opportunity. The original Apollo Project reminds us of our ability to persevere and transcend our limits. It reminds us of the potential of hope.

We can see it in the personal stories of the many Americans with a role in this revolution. Their roles are diverse: the venture capitalist in clean energy, the farmer with a crop for cellulosic ethanol, the community organizer uniting neighbors in a shared campaign, and the autoworker building hybrid drive trains. Each is playing a part in the clean-energy revolution, seeing a future not only for the planet, but also for their loved ones. And so our story continues with the hope for the birth of a movement. We look now at some of the possible roots of such a deep political change.

## From Steel Mills to Windmills: It's All about Jobs

One of the central political lessons of the original Apollo mission is that bold and decisive leadership makes a difference in setting the country's direction. In the absence of federal action on energy, governors across the country are taking the lead. They have done extraordinary things. Arnold Schwarzenegger has taken bold action in creating the country's first state climate change policy, capping carbon emissions as well as promoting the installation of solar energy in California. Brian Schweitzer has done groundbreaking work on biofuels and wind in Montana. Kathleen Sebelius from Kansas and Dave Heineman from Nebraska have led the bipartisan Governors' Ethanol Coalition nationally.

Two governors from fossil fuel–rich states have shown how to move beyond carbon-based energy powered by new technology. Governor Ed Rendell is the leader of Pennsylvania, the Quaker State, the home of the first oil rush in the United States, and long a leader in coal production. Governor Bill Richardson from New Mexico also heads a state known for its history in mining, oil, and extractive industries. These two leaders have shown that the path to clean, renewable, and efficient energy can create jobs—and wealth—and fits squarely with the deep traditions of an energy state.

Building a clean-energy economy as a source of good jobs is no longer just a matter of theory. Pennsylvania is well along the path of using policy to create markets for clean energy and good jobs. Governor Rendell has turned to his advisor Kathleen McGinty, secretary of the environment for the Commonwealth of Pennsylvania, for leadership in this area.

The sort of leadership she and others provide is helping to shape the political prism through which Americans see the issue of clean energy. Pennsylvania is showing that solving climate change is not just an environmental policy problem. It is core economic strategy, creating new markets and new investment.

While in the White House and other quarters, leaders still operate in a world of jobs vs. the environment, or environment vs. the economy, in the Pennsylvania governor's mansion, leaders have embraced the environment as a central organizing principle of economic revitalization. Governor Rendell has used it to attract the better part of a billion dollars of new investment and create literally thousands of jobs during his tenure.

"Pennsylvania is a manufacturing state, and in manufacturing, you depend on having customers," says McGinty. "To the extent that government can use its purchasing power to be a force facilitating energy patriotism, we have enabled the private sector to step into these emerging markets, knowing there will be demand for their product."[1] This changes the game for clean energy, from a niche market to a mainstream energy resource. The governor welcomes those in other states who minimize alternative energy as a limited or trendy market, as that creates more opportunity for Pennsylvania to have the field to itself.

The governor has created his own political space for moving an energy agenda through a combination of inspiration and vision, and a deft assemblage of constituencies. His vision has been way out ahead of the curve. He announced his Energy Harvest plan in the year 2000. He found a way to articulate how a state that led the world into the age of oil could now lead it into an age of new energy. He did it by investing a huge amount of his personal capital in the campaign, by using concepts like the Ben Franklin Technology Partners to link the history of Pennsylvania with its future. He fulfilled the first responsibility of a leader: He defined a vision.

Governor Rendell also built a political coalition on the self-interests of a multitude of players. He was able to demonstrate to utilities, unions, communities, miners, and investors why it was in their personal interest to buy into this vision. He was fortunate in having a progressive labor leadership that intuitively understood the power of clean energy to build well-paying jobs.

Finally, he understood that he needed successes to build on. He set realistic goals early in his program, met them, and has now vastly expanded his program; in February 2007 he announced a major expansion of his energy independence initiative designed to save consumers $10 billion over ten years.

Along the way, he has run a tight ship. As with any leader, his true power has come from his ability to attract talent and to let it run. In Pennsylvania's case the talent is Katie McGinty, and she has run with the ball, working closely with the Department of Economic Development to recruit clean-energy businesses and create a dedicated clean-energy finance authority to cut the cost of capital for businesses locating in the commonwealth. Pennsylvania under Rendell has also passed an ambitious Alternative Energy Portfolio Standard that mandates that renewable and advanced energy sources will supply 18 percent of the energy in the state within fifteen years. The strategy has worked.

In 2004, Rendell and McGinty were able to recruit the Spanish wind turbine manufacturer Gamesa to locate its first North American plant in Johnstown, Pennsylvania, to manufacture the massive blades for state-of-the-art wind turbines. The plant is now up and running, and the workers are represented by the United Steel Workers of America, making good on the promise that President Leo Gerard staked his reputation on, that clean energy can create good manufacturing jobs with high wages. Gamesa is currently building three more manufacturing facilities on the site of a closed steel mill and is investing in eighteen wind farms around the commonwealth, all of which is forecast to create over a thousand jobs during the next five years.[2]

Gamesa is not just a flash in the pan. Recently, Pennsylvania wooed the German solar firm Connergy and convinced it to locate its next manufacturing plant in the state to access the market for solar energy that is being created by the ambitious dedicated solar power set-asides in the state's alternative energy standard.

The successes don't stop there. Bilbao-based Iberdrola, owner of renewables giant Scottish Power, is one of the leading private electric utilities in the world and the largest renewable energy operator on the planet, with over 3,500 megawatts of wind energy in operation in 2006. Iberdrola, too, is locating its North American headquarters in Pennsylvania.

At the same time, Pennsylvania is in negotiations with a Canadian company that produces battery systems for hybrid vehicles and futuristic fuel-cell energy systems, to locate a new plant in Pennsylvania to be close to the emerging market there. All this while Governor Rendell is still celebrating a new $250 million investment in biofuels in Clearfields County, an area of the state that has not seen that kind of new business location in years. These investments did not happen by accident. They were the result of political will.

The Rendell administration is also committed to building jobs through energy efficiency. It expects to attract business opportunities in every part of the energy conservation value chain, from information technology to smart electric meters and the skilled technologists needed to operate those systems.

Energy efficiency is serviced not only by large international firms like Honeywell, but also by homegrown start-ups like the Pennsylvania-based enterprise Enerwise, an energy management company that offers hardware and software and makes money by reducing energy use. Information technologies dedicated to energy have found a home in Pennsylvania. Moving forward, Pennsylvania is gunning to get more into the game of solar manufacturing by luring companies now going to the solar-friendly German market.

The governor has also created a program called Growing Greener 2, which makes tax-free bond financing available to fund new bricks-and-mortar clean-energy projects, and launched the PennSecurity Fuels Initiative to build a market for biofuels producers in the commonwealth.

How has Pennsylvania made these strides when it has been so dependent on fossil fuels for so long? How did the governor push through measures for such a progressive agenda? He is a dynamic leader, but he also knew that once an economic base for these new technologies was created, they would form a political base to push for even more such visionary policies. He has created a virtuous political cycle.

Pennsylvania is not the only state that has found the right matrix to move clean energy forward. Two other states in particular, New Mexico and California, have shown what bold state leadership combined with technology can achieve. New Mexico has new energy because it has an energetic and committed leader, Governor Bill Richardson. California has a governor who has not only helped renew his state's energy policy, but also renewed his governorship in the process. If Pennsylvania shows the power of treating clean energy as a source of economic development, those two very different states offer insights into what is possible by tackling climate change directly, making it a centerpiece of a competitive economy.

The experience of those two states demonstrates both that clean energy has a bipartisan appeal and that a dedicated clean-energy policy can succeed in wildly different economies. They do not make many movies in New Mexico, and California is a net energy importer, but the states have achieved the same revolution in clean energy. They share bold leadership and a sense of optimism in their people.

New Mexico is an oil and coal–producing state that historically has exported nearly 50 percent of its electricity from fossil fuels, yet under Bill Richardson's leadership, it is looking to clean energy as it looks toward the future. Richardson saw a huge national void that he wanted to fill "for New Mexico, for the West, and for the nation." His secretary of the environment, Ron Curry, puts it this way: "The important thing to understand about climate actions in New Mexico is the critical role of the leadership of the governor. He would rather have cabinet secretaries who err on the side of being bold rather than sitting on our hands."[3]

Working in a bipartisan partnership with Governor Schwarzenegger, Richardson and other western governors are taking a bold and systematic approach to reducing greenhouse gas emissions across the West. They have laid the groundwork for a new economy with a plan to advance a host of clean-energy and renewable technologies as a serious centerpiece of energy policy, bringing almost all of the governors west of the Mississippi into the dialogue. Richardson launched the Southwest Climate Change Initiative with neighboring Arizona governor Janet Napolitano and pledged to reduce New Mexico's greenhouse gas emissions to 2000 levels by 2012, to 10 percent below that by 2020, and cut emissions 75 percent by 2050. That consortium grew in February 2007, when five states agreed to a pact that will ultimately lead to a cap-and-trade system among all the state partners.[4]

In the absence of a mandatory national policy to cap carbon emissions, New Mexico chose to become the first state to join the voluntary carbon trading market of the Chicago Climate Exchange as well, gaining valuable experience in establishing baseline inventories and meeting reduction targets across state government. The Chicago Climate Exchange now has two hundred members, and cumulatively they have reduced greenhouse gas emissions by 32 million metric tons, or the equivalent of two New Mexico coal plants. Secretary Curry says they "can still do much more, but the point is that this is happening right now, in the absence of any national policy. The governor is putting meat on the bone today."

The governors have learned that one secret to success, as in any endeavor, is constant improvement. Governor Richardson already has laurels to rest upon, having saved consumers $2 billion and the atmosphere 267 million tons of $CO_2$ with these actions, but he is just getting started.[5] He plans to expand his renewable portfolio standard to a 25 percent goal by 2020. Similarly, while California already leads the nation in efficiency, Governor Schwarzenegger joined his legislature in adopting an absolute cap on transportation $CO_2$ emissions in 2007.

Both states plan to export their ideas. New Mexico intends to become a center of providing renewable energy to the whole multistate region. It is focusing on utility-scale concentrated solar and major wind farms—things done on a very large scale to produce a significant quantity of energy that can be exported from the state. Says Economic Development Secretary Rick Homans, "This is an opportunity coming very soon, the demand is very real, and New Mexico doesn't want to be caught flat-footed." Homans goes further, outlining a plan for dedicated transmission grid capacity for renewable energy and stating, "If you accept the economics of a renewable energy transmission authority, it means that a lot of things have happened to create a whole new industry."[6] He clearly sees clean energy as a major future market for the state. California is doing the same, building a record of achievement that will soon have to be followed by a Congress that cannot withstand success for too much longer.

Local leaders have shown themselves to be just as visionary as state officials. Over five hundred mayors from across the country, both Republicans and Democrats, have signed a pledge to have their cities meet Kyoto $CO_2$ emission targets, sparked by a challenge originally issued by Seattle's mayor, Greg Nickels. County officials likewise are providing the nation with models of how to structure government action to promote energy efficiency, such as the energy-use plan generated under the leadership of King County, Washington, executive Ron Sims.

This grassfire of local action has now, finally, caught on at the highest national level, a dynamic made most evident when Senator Hillary Clinton announced early in her presidential campaign that she would promote an "Apollo-like" energy plan if elected and followed up by unveiling a comprehensive plan in the spring of 2007. Several other candidates set out aggressive energy plans in 2007 that embody various aspects of the ideas we have reviewed here. America has a good chance of seeing the type of leadership previously seen only in the Statehouses and city halls of the country brought to bear in the White House in 2009.

## Keeping It Real: Working the Grassroots

Building a movement to drive clean energy is not just about top-down leadership or changing the path of federal or state policy; it is also about building the politics to get there—creating a groundswell for change from the grassroots, a politics and a popular voice that can't be ignored.

The struggle for civil rights was one of the most powerful social movements in the history of this country. It was a coming together of people that sprang from the fight against injustice but built toward a higher vision and made America more true to its ideals. Churches and union halls were the birthing centers of a powerful force for cultural change. It was local congregations and the sanitation workers and bus drivers coming together under the banner of the American Federation of State, County and Municipal Employees that created a new voice for social justice that reverberated even to the hallowed halls of Washington. It was the power of people in community, finding a common voice that crossed lines of division and articulated a clear moral demand on the conscience of a nation that created the mandate for change. Today we face challenges as radically fundamental to our well-being and our future as a people. Today we need a new movement.

In communities around the country activism is already brewing, a new consciousness percolating on the issues of green jobs, alternative energy, and climate stewardship. Clean energy is emerging as a tool for community organizing, connecting with the real concerns of voters and building real grassroots political power.

A striking example of this is taking place in Los Angeles, where a community-based organization is demanding that the city government adopt green-energy policies for the benefit of local neighborhoods. Anthony Thigpenn is the thoughtful and dedicated president of Strategic Concepts in Organizing and Policy Education (SCOPE), a grassroots organization that draws members from the poorest communities of LA. Mostly poor; mostly black, Asian, and Latino; and from neighborhoods that have been passed by all too often by waves of prosperity and economic development, the members of SCOPE understand what it means to bear the costs of development without sharing in the benefits.

Thigpenn is leading the charge in forming the LA Apollo Alliance, at the intersection of community and energy policy, and the level of enthusiasm he has found has surprised even him. He is a broad-minded guy who intuitively got the connection between a green economy and social justice. He is experimental by nature and was willing to try organizing via a clean-energy message in his poor communities of color.

The LA Apollo Alliance brought together partners like the International Brotherhood of Electrical Workers Local 11, which represents private-sector construction electricians; the Service Employees International Union Local 347, which represents city workers; and the Piping Industry Progress and Education (PIPE) Trust Fund, which invests in training and educating plumbers and pipe fitters; along with the major local environmental groups and community organizations that were fighting for improved economic and living conditions in the neighborhoods.

When they had built this institutional infrastructure, they hit the streets, doing what they do best, bringing strong messages to the people. And it is there that Thigpenn and his lead organizer, Jennifer Ito, found something that caught them off guard. SCOPE set out to work within communities like South LA, Hollywood, Echo Park, and Koreatown, doing door-to-door organizing as they have done on many issues. They felt confident about their message of putting communities first, emphasizing jobs and training, and using that to produce a skilled workforce. But they were uncertain whether a message about energy and a green economy would resonate with their voters. After thousands of hours of doorknocking, however, they found that the idea of using clean energy to build economic opportunity in their neighborhoods struck a deep chord.

Oreatha Ensley, a local Apollo organizer, education activist, and grandmother who went door to door, put it this way: "In South Los Angeles, disinvestment of resources and jobs has crippled the community." She says, "I wasn't sure what my community's response would be to an initiative that puts jobs, training, and improving the environment together as top-priority solutions to the poverty that our families experience every day. I expected some folks to tell me that jobs are number one and cleaning our environment is just a nice wish. Instead, they told me that it's about time we reinvest in our community, because we are slipping away further into poverty and getting sicker because of it."[7]

The groundswell built further. They took their Apollo Challenge directly to the mayor, holding a major community meeting. It turned into a celebration that drew five hundred people from around LA, where Mayor Antonio Villaraigosa participated in a signing ceremony endorsing the Apollo Challenge and committing to an initiative focused on greening deteriorating city buildings to create jobs and improve the health of communities. Mayor Villaraigosa was joined in signing the pledge by LA City Council member Herb Wesson and City Council president Eric Garcetti.[8]

In addition, the mayor pledged to develop a program to provide career ladders for job training, building on an analysis of green-tech jobs that identified opportunities to address poverty in LA by focusing on green building construction and maintenance and harnessing green building materials manufacturing and supply within the region, as well as exploring new financing tools to make it happen. The people of South Central LA are making this message their own.

## Faith: The Other Renewable Energy

> God said, "Let there be light. And there was light."
>
> —*Genesis 1*

The Bible says that God spoke first of energy. According to the Bible, it was light, the purest, most heavenly form of energy, that was present at the creation. All the rest followed this divine radiance. Now we are engaged in an effort to capture energy as pristine as that first light. The effort is based on the universal spirit of all creeds to honor and respect God's creation: the earth.

This fundamental value invests all faiths and their surrounding communities as they strive to care for God's handiwork and save it from the wrath of global warming. Faith-based communities are an essential element of the national effort to build a new clean-energy nation, following the path of other successful movements, from abolition to the labor movement to the peace movement. They organize in the basement, then sing hymns upstairs, and share commitments and values at all levels.

A new clean-energy movement is uniting all points of the religious compass. Catholics, Jews, Protestants, and Muslims are joining hands. This work must succeed if the earth is to be saved. While these faiths may disagree on the age and origins of the planet, they agree that as our home, it deserves our devoted stewardship. Church offers a moral center for millions of Americans and a point of departure for engaging in good works in the world. Today, the alliance of the faith community and secularists may be the planet's best chance for survival. In the past, it has been one of the most powerful alliances for change this country has ever known.

All faiths contain a central thread of our responsibility to care for God's work. The Koran is replete with references to the precious resources of air, water, and land.[9] Native American tribes invoke the Creator's spirit in their efforts to preserve the salmon in our western rivers. Environmentalist Robert Kennedy Jr. has pointed out that most faiths describe the wilderness as a place to seek spiritual enlightenment and renewal.[10]

But until recently, faith communities have not been powerfully engaged in the effort to create a clean-energy world and stop global warming. The task was left to those who have maintained a secular belief that the first light described in Genesis was really the big bang. But now the faith community has arrived, a cavalry from Calvary. The Creator's creation is now being protected by those who believe in Him, a troop of energy angels. They have arrived just in time.

One of those energy angels is Paul Gorman, executive director of the National Religious Partnership for the Environment, an organization whose member groups represent 100 million people of faith. One hundred million people can get a politician's attention. Gorman's principle is simple: "The environmental movement has been a solely secular movement for too long. Every national movement from abolition of slavery on has been based on a deep resolve based upon faith. It takes deep faith to move mountains."[11]

This insight led Gorman to join others to establish a national movement in the cause they call "creation care."

"We represent a diverse coalition, from the Jewish community to the Christian Evangelical community to Catholics and the mainline Protestant groups," he explains. "But no matter where they fall on the orthodoxy scale, they all contain some kernel of the concept that man has a responsibility to tend to [God's] garden." He is right on that, since the Bible says, "The Lord God then took the man and settled him in the Garden of Eden, to cultivate and care for it" (Gen. 2:15). Notice that God's direction to "care" for his creation was not optional.

So Gorman and his tribe went forth over fifteen years ago and began to build a politically active national coalition to bring down to earth, and to Washington, D.C., God's admonition to care for his work and to turn faith into action. Now the groups in Gorman's coalition are forging a national consensus among those of faith to demand attention to the problems of the planet. One of their primary successes is getting members of Congress to understand that they will have a large faith community with them if they support the environment. Gorman quotes one conservative Republican senator as telling him, "You guys are really helpful. I get the science of global warming, but I've got to talk with my Southern Baptists. I want to help on climate change and by getting those folks on board; it is a huge help."

Their success comes because they mix the profound with the prosaic. Gorman says eloquently, "The care of the earth is a part of our search for a deeper understanding of human purpose." They also use edgy marketing campaigns to capture the fleeting interest of the general public. Among them are the "What Would Jesus Drive?" and "How Many Jews Does It Take to Change a Lightbulb?" campaigns. (The answers are, respectively: "Any fuel-efficient car" and "Two—one to screw it in and one to count the electrical savings of using a compact fluorescent bulb.")

More important, the campaigns have given the clean-energy movement a values-based voice. "Morality matters on the environment, but the environmental community has sometimes lacked a vocabulary to express that morality. We have helped integrate that central tenet into the policy discussion," says Gorman. Perhaps because Gorman is the product of an Irish Catholic mother and a Russian Jewish father, he is particularly adept at melding diverse moralities. Now he is "broadening the base" with organizers in an expanding universe of states, including North Carolina, New Mexico, and Kansas.

Gorman knew he was achieving success when one day on a lobbying visit, a congressman asked an older woman in the group how long she had been an environmentalist and she indignantly replied, "Why, young man, I've been a Christian all my life!" Gorman's organization now delivers that message to congressmen through the power of e-mail. And the power of prayer.

Gorman has a comrade-in-arms, Richard Cizik, who works in the vineyard of public opinion to spread the gospel found in Psalms 24:1–2: "The earth is the Lord's and all that it holds, the world and its inhabitants. For he founded it upon the ocean, set it on the nether-streams."

Cizik is vice president for Governmental Affairs of the National Association of Evangelicals, and he now dedicates his life to stopping the destruction of the world and its inhabitants. He was moved to action by a meeting in 2006 with Harvard's E. O. Wilson, who told Cizik and his group that if humankind does not change, 50 percent of the world's species will be extinct by the turn of the century. Seeing that prospect, Cizik shares this prediction: "When the Creator comes to judge you, what will he ask? Will he ask you how you were created? No. He will ask you, 'What did you do with my creation?' "[12]

So Cizik has mounted a national campaign to share his community's view that humankind must deal with global warming as an act of grace. He has produced a movie, *The Great Warming,* narrated by Keanu Reeves, and has sent DVDs to 50,000 churches across the country. He now focuses on Republicans with the message that the evangelical community will consider them "unjust doers" if they do not face global warming. He minces no words in saying that if Republicans do not accept that responsibility, it would be "the biggest Republican failure since civil rights." But he says he is making progress in that regard. "My friends in the Republican Party are starting to accept science again. That will eliminate the stigma of the Scopes trial. It will be a great advance for both the evangelical community and the Republican Party."

That is pretty good work for a fellow who wanted to be in the foreign service until he met Norman Vincent Peale, who told him, "God could use a few good diplomats." Now he is using his skills to keep the Genesis story blooming: "And God saw that this was good. And God said, 'Let the earth sprout vegetation: seed-bearing plants, fruit trees of every kind on earth that bear fruit with the seed in it.'"

With Paul Gorman and Rich Cizik, congregations across the country are spreading the seeds of clean energy. If those seeds sprout in the halls of Congress, they just might protect God's seeds on earth.

## Where Have All the Student Agitators Gone?

When America advanced in civil rights, when it freed itself from the Vietnam War, and when it gave birth to an environmental ethic in the 1970s, it always had one dynamic group on the streets and in the vanguard: our college students. We have always been able to depend on the passion of youth to change society. Now that the world is threatened by global warming, where are the students?

According to Billy Parish, an energetic and effective college organizer, they have arrived. Parish is the director of the most important new arrival on the political scene, Energy Action, a coalition of forty-one national student networks that has succeeded in putting together 464 student groups on college campuses to advocate for clean energy. In a brief four years his network has convinced forty-two colleges to adopt climate neutrality pledges and persuaded twenty college presidents to work on the rest of the nation's college presidents. Energy Action's leadership in launching the Campus Climate Challenge has brought all of the major student environmental groups together to organize under one big tent.

Since there are 4,000 U.S. colleges and they are responsible for 7 percent of U.S. carbon emissions,[13] Parish's group has the potential for remarkable impact, both directly, through cutting emissions, and indirectly, through organizing and education. In just one month—February 2007—the network had each member of Congress adopted by a student, held 560 college screenings of *An Inconvenient Truth*, and hosted conferences on clean energy in all ten regions of the nation. That is some effective organizing

The boat needs rocking, and Billy Parish and his coalition members are rocking it. Parish helped found the coalition following a summer away from Yale when he met scientists in the foothills of the Himalayas studying the retreat of glaciers that provide 40 percent of humanity with water. "It became clear to me we had to act. After seeing the drought and melting glaciers in India, I came home and started to organize students to push for action. It is my generation's responsibility," he says.[14]

Parish's seminal experience was unique, a point he makes about his fellow agitators. "Everybody has their own motivation. My girlfriend is a Navajo, and she is motivated because a dirty plant is wrecking her home country. But we also have 500,000 members from the Future Farmers of America, who come at this from a very different perspective. We have the group Restoring Eden, a group of students at evangelical colleges, too. Our challenge is to craft a message that unites us all.

"Maybe the biggest thing that unites us is that people want to believe they are part of a movement, something bigger than themselves.

Billy Parish and the Campus Climate Challenge are raising the stakes on college campuses with effective organizing for clean energy.

Now we are working to use social networking technology on the Internet, as well as grassroots campus organizing, to build on that motivation," he says.

Parish is young, but not too young to have worries. He worries that under Bush, Congress will adopt weak measures to deal with global warming that will stymie the real progress we need to make. "Weak measures may be worse than none at all because they could retard real efforts when Bush is gone," he says. "What is tough enough to be worth it? That is a tough question." Those in the 110th Congress who are pushing for real progress in clean energy are faced with the same tough question during the last two years of Bush's term. Congress must avoid the temptation to do the minimal and then declare victory. In this case, the imperfect can be the enemy not just of the perfect, but also of meeting the demands of the basic science of protecting the climate.

Parish also worries that we may not be sufficiently aggressive in leading Americans to accept some changes in their lives. "We might have to make some changes in our lifestyle to really get to where we need to go," he says. "We have to figure out whether we should talk about sacrifice, or focus on all the positive potential for making progress so that people do not get discouraged and give up the ship early."

There are, indeed, some tough questions. But we have a clear answer to the question of where the students are. They are with Billy Parish—and us.

## Green Politics That Cross Red and Blue States

Ernie Shea spent eighteen years running the National Association of Conservation Districts, representing community-based soil and water districts around the country, and he knows a little something about farming and the farm community. Today he runs the 25x'25 coalition, a strongly bipartisan group of farmers, ranchers, and foresters who have joined with other partners to support the goal of meeting 25 percent of America's total energy needs from renewable sources by the year 2025. This unlikely group of advocates has found a new voice and a new commitment to working together in championing clean energy, as they seek to transform the public image of the agricultural sector from one that is focused on subsidies to a forward-looking force allied with the future and an innovative economy.

Shea convened the 25x'25 group with the goal of thinking big on how to make a difference in agriculture using clean energy. They went in thinking, "This might be something big," and they came away saying, "It isn't big—it's huge!" The coalition commissioned analyses from respected economists of what this 25x'25 future would look like, and the results surprised even them. The research showed that what they were talking about was growing a new sector of the economy representing $700 billion of activity, with the potential to create five million new jobs, all while reducing $CO_2$ emissions by over one billion tons.[15] Now they have introduced resolutions supporting their goals in both the House and the Senate.

By the end of 2006 the coalition had grown from about a dozen farm leaders to represent four hundred organizations united around the single goal of achieving 25 percent renewable energy. They are now working on state-level alliances in thirty states. They have received the formal endorsement of sixteen current and six former governors from both parties and have spent the last year constructing an implementation plan to turn into a legislative demand in Washington. They have gotten over thirty senators and over ninety House members to sign on to their concurrent resolutions in the House and Senate without even working that hard to get endorsements. And most important, they have gotten the word out to farmers in America's heartland.

It is critically important that this new movement from the farm community is coming from "red state" America. Tackling climate change has been maligned as a danger to the economy and has been looked at too often through a partisan lens. But as the farm community creates an agenda of clean-energy solutions, it brings a fresh look at climate change as well—as an opportunity not a threat. Farmers are seeing that, from protecting our agricultural yields from loss of soil moisture through drought to investing in farm communities through biofuels and wind farms, energy and agricultural policy and politics are closer today than ever before. This realization is changing the politics completely.

Agriculture and energy go together like a wink and a smile. The shifting politics of clean energy have the potential to transform the national political dynamics of rural America, moving red states with green issues. There is something stirring in the Great Plains and the Mountain West, in the Sun Belt, the Farm Belt, and the nation's industrial heartland. Looking out across the vast divide of today's red and blue states, it's important to remember that America's heartland has not always been the center of conservative thought. It was red state America that gave birth to the populist movement, a radical agrarian agenda that swept like wildfire out of Texas and across the rural west of Oklahoma, Kansas, and Missouri mobilized around issues of debt, investment, and giving working farmers an ownership stake in the future of the nation. Later, it was a revolt by heartland progressives like Iowan John L. Lewis that gave America an industrial labor movement and innovations like the weekend. And it was the heartland instinct to view the economy through a moral lens that led another Iowan, Henry A. Wallace, to fight for a progressive vision of government that regulated corporate abuse and buffered economic cycles to keep family farmers on their land.[16]

You can see a clear tension in all the polling—the president's falling approval rating is coupled with the paradoxical failure of Democrats to pick up gains in public opinion; anger over corruption in Congress is pitted against distress over a general coarsening of media culture; frustration with high salaries for corporate CEOs is braced by an equal sense that personal morality and ethics are in decline. The old politics just doesn't seem to fit. The old battle lines fail to describe the current problems and are hopelessly weak at offering solutions that are likely to do any good. It is little wonder then, with so little to hope for, and so few champions, that the country is starkly divided on how to proceed. The new Apollo Project can help break this impasse.

Thomas Frank wrote about this in *What's the Matter with Kansas?* He put his finger on the political movement of heartland voters toward tough stands on moral values and correctly identified it as an effort to address a creeping discomfort with a culture and an economic system that's ever more insecure and uncaring for the fate of average folks. Yet it would be a mistake to understand this debate as a split between one camp focused on "moral values" and another offering "economic self-interest." That view misses the core of the tension for most voters in America today. In truth, our economic problems and our values crises are deeply intertwined and lead back to a crisis in our national sense of purpose. The malaise of rural poverty, a diminishing manufacturing employment base, and the creeping low-road culture of Wal-Mart jobs with discount wages all contribute to the deepening fear and insecurity driving our economic, political, and ethical landscape.

It just might be that what Americans are looking for is some way to reconcile their moral concerns with their economic insecurity, to create a positive vision for the country and the world that they can believe in again, a vision that offers both prosperity and justice, that makes us all safer and restores the chance for an ennobling future. What appears today to be two competing ideologies—one red and one blue, one based on moral values and one on populist economic theories—could just as easily be the sign of one nation searching for deeper answers. The nation is just waiting to come together around a real vision of a future, one that marries these equally pressing national imperatives to build an economy with meaning, compassion, justice, and hope.

The candidate or party that first steps forward to articulate such a bold and unifying vision, backed by a strong commitment and clear priorities, will have something that can break the Gordian knot of the last few elections. Rather than making tactical and cautious plays for the narrow and vacillating middle, the party that steps forward with a dynamic agenda just might find a country every bit as willing to produce a landslide as it has been to date to cast votes for paper-thin margins of victory.

And that vision may well come from red state America. Consistently throughout American history, rural America has articulated a deeply moral vision of the American economy, rooted in the practical ethics of working men and women—often grounded in religious teachings and respect for the value of work and thrift and fueled by a deep concern for the common man. These leaders and their movements helped articulate an economic theory that counterposed Wall Street's market fundamentalism to Main Street's need for investment, fair rules, and a level playing field in order to grow a great nation out of the wilderness.

The original heartland progressives like Henry Wallace would have found the split between economic self-interest and moral values incomprehensible. Theirs was a pragmatic but deeply moral vision grounded in the long-term self-interest of the nation, an economic vision based on the core American principles of liberty, widely shared prosperity, reward for hard work, and equality of opportunity. That reform platform had as its bedrock a belief in science, investing in people, and playing by the rules, and it reorganized American politics and priorities. It was that prairie populism—a mainstream American notion of opportunity and possibility—that created new coalitions and a new base of political power, which linked the interests of farmers and mechanics, grange members and recent immigrants, around a constantly improving future.

Now prairie populism may have a rebirth as a popular new Apollo Project. Rebuilding our society around the central organizing principle of clean innovative energy, good jobs, and a low-carbon economy is exactly such a program of investment in people and places that expands opportunity and revitalizes industry while fulfilling our deepest moral responsibilities to each other and future generations.

## Caps, CAFE, and Conflict: The Politics of Carbon

Building a groundswell of public opinion that calls on our leaders to take us in a new direction is only one part of the struggle. Achieving success will also require changing national policy in Congress.

"Politics is a strife of interests masquerading as a contest of principles." So said Ambrose Bierce of the democratic process. Thus, during the debate in Congress about our energy future, many paeans to high-minded principles will be trumpeted. Behind them, however, will be huge economic interests with money on the line, regional economies, and the jobs of countless workers. Both principles and interests must be part of the solution to our energy challenges. Public virtue and private gain must be conjoined.

The principle of environmental stewardship advocated by the faith community will need to find a working partner in some economic interest of a large sector of the economy. The principle of energy efficiency will have to be coupled with the financial interests of workers and employees. Both alliances will have to overcome the entrenched resistance of the naysayers and flat-earth society members.

That very dynamic began to unfold in the pivotal week of January 15, 2007. That historic week started with the announcement that Exxon was abandoning its financial support of global warming–denier organizations, purveyors of propaganda schemes that Exxon had propped up with some of its profits for years. The week ended with the arrival in Washington, D.C., of the CEOs of ten of America's largest corporations, including DuPont, Alcoa, and Duke Energy, to lobby Congress in favor of a carbon cap-and-trade system. Clearly, economic interests had begun to be aligned with environmental principles. In this case, interest in saving money through energy efficiency and avoiding fifty separate state carbon caps in the face of a shifting public mood drove the action.

An even more fundamental force was at play, however, one that President Bill Clinton articulated that same month when he spoke to the House Democratic Caucus: "In this global economy you have just got to come up with a major source of new jobs every eight years, or you're sunk. In my term in office, I was lucky enough to have it be the explosion of software. Now there is one and only one easy answer on how to do it again—energy."[17]

Clinton's logic is driven by both his innate optimism and his study of the global economy. "Look at England and Denmark, the countries with the two closest economic situations to our own. They have grown their median income while they have kept unemployment down. There is only one possible explanation of how they have achieved this feat while we have been stuck with stagnant incomes—they have energy polices driving growth and we don't," he said.

He was passionate on this topic, pointing the famous Clinton index finger to emphasize the fact that Denmark is now getting almost 22 percent of its power from wind and will generate half its energy from that source within ten years. He was adamant that the energy challenge is a great gift. "We ought to pursue this relentlessly. There are millions of jobs to be created. It's like finding a bird nest on the ground," he said, bringing the first ever Arkansas homily to the energy debate.

The conjunction of the CEOs and the former president presages an alliance that will certainly propel significant steps forward in driving new investment into clean-energy technology. But tougher and more divisive issues will arise on how to move forward, especially in the matter of restraining carbon emissions.

In early 2007 the jousting began over what type of system to implement, a universal cap covering all industries that ultimately cause carbon emissions, or one that covers only point-source polluters. As could be predicted, each industry began to jockey for advantage to try to lay the responsibility for reducing $CO_2$ emissions on another. The fault lines became obvious when at the first hearing on possible improvements to CAFE standards, Joe Barton, a Republican who would normally bristle at regulation, suggested that if his oil industry was going to be constrained by a cap-and-trade system, then, "Doggone it, maybe the auto industry ought to do something more to reduce $CO_2$, too."[18] The juxtaposition of these two distinct industrial interests makes for strange bedfellows and strange adversaries. Much of the coal industry and the manufacturing sector will favor an approach in which the transportation sector is regulated beyond just a carbon cap, because they believe that only such regulation would really reduce $CO_2$ from cars. At the same time, if a cap is imposed, the auto companies would likely seek a universal strategy that drives more reductions toward utilities as the simpler regulatory target for securing verifiable emissions.

The interests that emerge will likely create a fault line between energy companies and manufacturing energy users on one side and the domestic auto industry on the other. This battle will play out in the halls of Congress.

In the face of future climate policies, industry will be split on another point as well. Some utilities, notably TXU Energy in Texas (until it radically reversed its strategy of new plant construction as a result of pressure from new investors in a buyout offer), are trying to beat the cap by rushing traditional plants into construction in the hope they will be grandfathered by any future regulation. Other utilities, like Duke Energy and American Electric Power, are taking a different tack, building what could become coal plants with carbon capture and storage, in order to prepare for a world in which they must manage their carbon emissions.

On the matter of regulating carbon, there is a third way, a "belt and suspenders" approach. We could use both a universal cap (the belt) and carefully crafted regulations for particular sectors (the suspenders) to capture oil savings from autos, require efficiency in utility planning, and mandate carbon capture in coal plants when the carbon price is not enough to cause those investments on their own. The potential coalition for such an approach could include much of the utilities industry, many manufacturers, the environmental community, the faith community, and Robert Redford; and if the provisions for promoting oil savings focus on the core jobs and competitiveness concerns of automakers, they could be brought into this strategy as well.

That alliance could set the conditions for the sort of economy President Clinton called for, with energy policy that drives growth. As he said, "We ought to pursue this relentlessly." Because, most important, this coalition will also include protection of the health and welfare of our grandchildren as a driving force.

Our commitment to new energy is also a commitment to new generations of grandchildren. We are betting now on protecting our children's children for generations to come. There are worse national endeavors to pursue.

# A Tale of Two Presidents

*Jay Inslee*

In February 2007, both George W. Bush and Bill Clinton appeared at the Democratic House Caucus retreat at a conference center in Virginia and addressed global warming. On Friday night, President Clinton wowed the audience of three hundred by demonstrating both a passion for adopting a new energy future and a commanding comprehension of the technologies available to us. When I spoke with him after his speech, President Clinton pounded his fist to drive home his point: "There is only one thing we can do to create the jobs we need—create a new energy economy." This was something clearly close to his heart, and I forgave him for stealing my speech.

The next morning I was tapped by Speaker Nancy Pelosi to address energy issues with President Bush at his meeting with the caucus. When I stood to ask my question, the president started to leave, but with caucus chairman Rahm Emanuel's gentle insistence he took my question. Whether the Decider saw me coming and headed for safety or just wanted to get on his bike, I have only a suspicion.

Having let him put me off at our first meeting on global warming years earlier, I pulled no punches this time: "Good morning, Mr. President. This morning at breakfast with my son we saw a beautiful bald eagle just above the James River. It was there because years ago a president and a Congress acted upon clear scientific evidence to save this grand bird. But then I looked at the front page of the paper this morning, and it had a picture of starving polar bears on a melting iceberg, bears that will be extinct if we do not act. The other local paper reported that Hampton Roads, Virginia, would be partially underwater this century if we do not act. Both papers reported on the unequivocal findings of the Intergovernmental Panel on Climate Change the day before.

"Some time ago I was encouraged when you and I conferred in the White House about global warming. You told me you knew you had a responsibility to act. You told me that you had the best minds in your administration working on a plan you would present. Well, Mr. President, that was six years ago, and I am still waiting. So is my son.

"We know what we have to do. We have to adopt a new Apollo type of energy project to use America's huge innovative talent to solve this problem. Yet we are only investing one-half of what we were in the late 1970s in research. Your administration is just not do-ing the job.

"So, Mr. President, here is my question: When will you join us in capping $CO_2$ and building a new Apollo energy project so that my son, and my grandchildren, can enjoy the same bounty we do?"

I did not expect him to answer, "Tomorrow," and he didn't.

His answer was disappointing but not surprising, "We'll do nu-clear energy. It's a renewable resource that gives off zero gas. Ethanol is going to be good, and cellulosic. I am putting money into these. But the rest of the world is putting out gas, too, and other countries haven't done so well that signed onto the Kyoto Treaty. India and China haven't done anything!"[1]

In other words, he would help do something real about carbon when hell froze over. His finishing statement was the one that was beyond shocking: "You shouldn't assume I don't care about global warming as much as you do," he said while placing his hand upon his Texas heart. "I care about global warming, I really do."

In the spirit of unending optimism, I talked to President Bush again later that morning and explained to him that his work was fine as far as it went but told him, "You are spending a billion on clean coal, but nobody is going to ever use it as long as they get a free lunch—if there is no cost for sending carbon up the smokestack or no limit on the amount of total emissions. You have got to have a cap to make it work." At that, he had a glimmer of recognizing my point and said, "You mean they won't be driven to it otherwise?" "Right," I responded.

I asked for a chance to meet with him about this point, but he responded by drawing near me and saying, "Working that eagle in there was really good. That was really effective," followed by the trademark snicker. Whether this president does not understand the magnitude of this threat or simply does not care is unknowable, but either way, our country deserves a response.

Afterward, one of my congressional colleagues made an astute observation: "He just has no vision on this. We won't get any help from this president. It's up to us."

All of us.

CHAPTER 10

# An American Energy Policy

In 1713 the coal mines in England were flooding. Finding a pumping solution was a national imperative. So a young Englishman took on the challenge of developing a steam engine that could power the pumps on which England's industrial future depended. His name was Thomas Newcomen, and he could be credited for designing what became the first practical steam engine, a contraption using a boiler; piping; and a long, fulcrum-mounted beam. By 1725 his engine was in common use throughout the collieries in Cornwall, Black Country, and Dudley.

Newcomen's engine was dependable, but another young fellow, a Scotsman, thought it just a rudimentary device that failed to capture the real power in steam. His name was James Watt, and he set out to use the scientific process to build a better engine. He made a critical discovery that the Newcomen engine was inefficient, wasting lots of available energy from the steam. In 1765 he built a prototype of an alternative with the critical innovation of condensing the steam in a separate chamber from the boiling system. Then he set out to find investors to help commercialize the new engine.

His efforts were difficult at first, because people could not see a reason to build another steam engine. Didn't England already have one? With the help of a group of inventors and amateur scientists later called the Lunar Men, including Erasmus Darwin, the grandfather of Charles, and Joseph Priestly, the discoverer of oxygen, he eventually was able to build and market his engine. By the 1790s the Watt engine had eclipsed the Newcomen engine, and Watt is now often erroneously credited as the sole inventor of the steam engine.

The lesson of the Newcomen–Watt story, however, is that it is not necessarily the first generation that should be locked in as the ultimate technology. Newcomen's engine did work in a rudimentary fashion, but had policies in England favored its perpetuation and squeezed out Watt, England would still have flooded mines and the steam age would never have taken off. When a new technology comes along, there may be a tendency to give it advantages that prevent further advances, a tendency that must be avoided.

So, too, in our age: Today we rely solely on oil, but that is changing, and the first response of oil companies has been to construct barriers to biofuels. These barriers must be resisted. But likewise, we must resist efforts to create protections for corn ethanol that could prevent the development of next-generation fuels like cellulosic ethanol, bio-based butenol, and others. Similarly, we must guide our energy choices by the right measures of performance, looking at their impacts on climate security, and not fall into the trap of locking in a new industry, like coal to liquids, that prevents the development of advanced coal systems, such as IGCC, that can be made to capture and sequester the carbon.

In this clean-energy revolution there will be many stops along the path forward, and the technologies and infrastructure of a true clean-energy economy will build on each other. We need to create that infrastructure, like public transit, more efficient cars, pumps to move bio-based fuels, a smart grid to drive efficiency, and renewables; but we cannot allow those investments or their political consortiums to choke off further improvements that are sure to come, improvements that make energy ever cleaner.

So, as we launch a national response to our energy crises, we must remember James Watt.

We also would do well to remember Samuel Langley and his efforts to fly. We know the Wright Brothers as "First in Flight," of course, but there were many suitors to that title, most prominent among them Langley, who in 1903 was secretary of the Smithsonian Institution. At the time, his efforts to build an airplane totally eclipsed those of the two self-financed bicycle repairmen from Dayton, Ohio.

In 1903, Langley had procured the incredible sum of $50,000 from the U.S. Army to build a flying machine. This was a major R&D grant for its day. Langley captured the imagination of the public and built an engine twice as powerful as that of the Wright Flyers. By October 7, 1903, he had constructed an elaborate and somewhat bizarre-looking craft that he mounted on a floating barge in the Potomac River, ready to be launched with the help of a catapult. The craft was called the Aerodrome, and it represented the greatest national investment in aircraft of the day.

It took off, hovered for a moment, and crashed into the muddy Potomac. The honor of inventing the airplane did not go to the well-financed, nationally favored enterprise. It went to two brothers with a bike shop.

We can't know for sure which technologies will sweep the energy market; we can't point to the innovators who will concoct them. They may come from government laboratories or industry partnerships. They will often come from the outliers, small businessmen, and regular fellows with a good idea. That is why, when we design our national R&D programs, we ought to ensure a place for the small, the new, and the cutting-edge.

The current program for the FutureGen advanced coal project puts our entire national investment in a single billion-dollar project, rather than diversifying efforts to sequester $CO_2$. Similarly, as we move to commercialize cellulosic ethanol, we should drive greater investment into a range of experiments, some at smaller scales and even locally owned, to broaden our chance of success. In solar a range of strategies can build cheaper, more efficient panels and drive down costs; the race between Miasolé and Nanosolar to commercialize thin-film panels illustrates this arc of innovation while energy efficiency proves the biggest wins can come from many small changes.

In all these ventures, we ought not to put all our national eggs in one project like Langley's Aerodrome. We have more Wright Brothers out there.

## Shaping a Policy Agenda

Crafting a new national energy policy is no walk in the park. The project involves no less a challenge than reorienting the entire U.S. economy. Several thorny issues present themselves at the outset.

First, not all new energy technologies answer the national goals of both energy independence and climate protection. Increasing our domestic use of alternative fossil fuels by harvesting tar sands and oil shales, for example, would help improve our domestic energy security but would greatly worsen $CO_2$ emissions.

Second, and similarly, we must realize that not all technologies or fuels are created equal from a climate perspective. We must, therefore, develop criteria to measure the "carbon footprint" of the technologies we advance. Different types of ethanol, for example, while chemically identical, are widely varied in their environmental impact. A gallon of fairly "dirty" ethanol made by using old technology—like corn grown with chemical fertilizers and natural gas for process heat—can have negative consequences for soil and water quality and marginal benefits for greenhouse gas reductions. Alternatively, cellulosic ethanol made without fossil fuel inputs can really benefit the climate. Our policies and markets must recognize the difference.

Third, any policy we adopt must take into account changing conditions in the future that may result from climate change. A decision to shift policies toward greater use of biofuels should anticipate, for example, prospective changes in growing seasons and soil moisture occasioned from global warming itself. If we are to have a viable transition to low-carbon fuels, it must begin before substantial climate impacts occur.

Finally, as we design a national policy, other national interests will come into play. For instance, climate and energy policies can advance or delay our legitimate desire to see small community-based enterprises. These public purposes ought to be woven into our policies. It is not only multinational corporations that should have a chance at creating a new energy future, but community-owned and cooperative businesses as well. Similarly, the good jobs benefits of all of these policies can be maximized to create new manufacturing industries, markets for skilled construction, and green-collar jobs for those who have been shut out of past booms in national prosperity.

## Policy Matters

Policy shapes demand. Policy drives investment. Policy equalizes distorted markets misshapen by information failures, inadequate environmental or labor protections, and historic subsidies. Often there is no substitute for public action.

The evidence is everywhere. We have seen policies that reduce the risk and cost of nuclear power create a market for new plants, and subsidies for oil companies drive new exploration. Today we have the experience of wind turbines springing up in the twenty-three states (and Washington, D.C.) where renewable portfolio standards (RPSs) have been put in place. The Chippewa Valley Wind Farm is a tangible testament to the power of the RPS. According to rural development expert David Morris, over half of new wind energy investments can be attributed directly to those state policies.[1] An RPS is a great equalizer.

At the same time wind power has been blowing with gale force, the interest in biofuels has been exploding, driven largely by the enactment of tax incentives and a federal requirement for the production of 7.5 billion gallons of biofuels by 2012 in the Energy Policy Act of 2005. The floodgates of new financing opened once the future market was certain. Policy will play just as important a role in the transition to next-generation biofuels made from cellulose and dedicated energy crops.

Around the country, we have also seen the explosive growth of green building and energy efficiency driven by the adoption of new efficient building codes and requirements for public buildings to meet LEED standards. As states and cities recognize that more than two-thirds of all electricity use and 38 percent of global warming emissions are the result of inefficient energy use in buildings, some localities have adopted strong energy-efficiency standards.[2]

We know we can also ensure that economic growth associated with clean energy can be captured right at home by providing incentives for industries to do their manufacturing domestically, as Washington State (under Governor Christine Gregoire's leadership) is doing to attract new solar manufacturing, and Japan has done to corner the world solar market. We must not allow a repeat of the recent solar story, in which Americans invented the technology and the Japanese and Germans commercialized it through smart policy incentives.

We can also use policy to ensure not only that we create jobs, but that those jobs create high-quality wages and benefits and the gains are shared broadly. Community benefits agreements link economic subsidies to local hiring to ensure that job gains reach the people who need them most. Support for training, skills certification, and apprenticeship programs create career ladders for workers leading to stable jobs with family-supporting benefits, and ensuring the right to organize a union helps guarantee those gains for the long term. We should be concerned with job quality as well as job creation.

It is not only government policies that matter, however. Increasingly, the rules set forward by institutional investors and in corporate governance are driving clean-energy investment. The California Public Employees' Retirement System (CalPERS), thanks to the leadership of then state treasurer Phil Angelides and CalPERS board chair and labor leader Sean Harrigan, became a pioneer in the use of pension funds to build a clean-energy economy. CalPERS created the Green Wave program, which has invested over a billion dollars in clean technology, retrofitting real estate portfolio holdings and establishing a screen for investments that directs funds toward businesses that are responsibly managing carbon emissions.[3] Both CalPERS and groups like Ceres, under the leadership of Mindy Lubber, have broken new ground in using shareholder activism to push companies to consider the financial risks associated with their climate impacts, thereby helping to accelerate investment in clean technology as a rapidly growing sector of the economy.

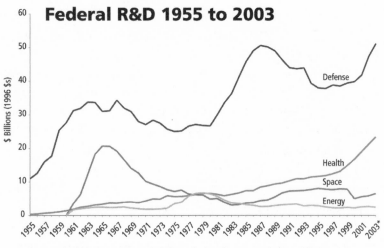

Source: National Science Foundation, Federal R&D Funding by Budget Function, Fiscal Years 2001–03.

Federal spending on research and development in energy has decreased in the last three decades, while R&D in defense has skyrocketed. We are failing to invest in real security through clean energy. (Daniel Kammen, UC Berkeley, and Andrew Pratt, Center for American Progress.)

In Pennsylvania, Tom Croft and the Heartland Labor Capital Network have pooled tens of millions of dollars in labor pension funds to invest in clean energy and manufacturing projects to rebuild a hard-hit region of the state. Croft joined Pennsylvania governor Ed Rendell, who convened a North American deal-flow network, bringing together twelve pension funds with combined assets of between $20 billion and $25 billion to promote in-state investments that retained manufacturing and supported worker- and environment-friendly companies, while meeting their fiduciary responsibilities to build their bottom lines.[4] At the same time, private equity firms like KPS have been investing in turning around domestic steel mills while also investing in energy efficiency and providing workers with a share in the ownership. The AFL-CIO Housing Investment Trust has a billion-dollar project for reconstruction in New Orleans that is investing in green manufacture of building materials. These efforts show that corporate governance setting the rules for institutional investors to be socially responsible is emerging not only as a way of doing good work, but also as a way of building real prosperity for both investors and communities.

In spite of these exciting trends in states and the investment community, as of this moment our national policies remain a mess. A failure of federal leadership has resulted in a stagnating fuel economy. The trade deficit is out of control in part because of our massive oil imports. Family gas bills soar, while bills to require oil savings and retool American plants to produce more efficient vehicles languish in Congress.

The leadership we have seen across the economy and across levels of government—from the over 500 mayors who joined the U.S. Mayors Climate Protection Agreement to regional coalitions of governors joining in compacts to create carbon markets—is exciting. But there is no substitute for federal policy. Both the size of the challenge and the need for consistent policies across the nation cry out for federal investment and sound regulation in the public interest.

Time is running out. The nation's leading climate scientist, James Hansen, says, "I think we have a very brief window of opportunity to deal with climate change . . . no longer than a decade, at the most."[5]

The question, then, is this: What are we going to do about it?

## An Integrated Agenda for a New Apollo Project

The mosaic of policies we need is not a simple matter. The original Apollo Project's *Saturn V* rocket was constructed of over a million pieces. The new Apollo energy project may not be far behind. There is truly no silver bullet. The solution will take a mix of appropriate regulation—like requirements to plan for energy efficiency and bring renewable electricity on line, as well as capping carbon and auctioning the permits to produce revenue to fund the transition. Building a rapid clean-energy transition will also take large-scale public investment in commercializing new technology, retrofitting buildings, and retooling our nation's infrastructure.

The national Apollo Alliance has put forward a plan to invest $313 billion in the productive base of our economy over ten years. This investment would dramatically cut our reliance on oil and slash carbon impacts, but it would also generate over $1.3 trillion in GDP gains, produce over 3.3 million jobs, and create nearly a trillion dollars in new personal income.[6]

Such an investment program, as the Alliance lays it out, would invest $49 billion in low-carbon and renewable energy sources and $75 billion in incentives for retooling manufacturing industries to build the cars of the future and energy-efficient appliances in more efficient factories. It would invest $90 billion in incentives and investment to build the market for green and high-performance buildings and retrofit our cities to save energy. And it would direct $99 billion toward new infrastructure for everything from smart-growth, high-speed rail and other alternatives to cars, to a modernized electrical grid that would allow real-time pricing and dramatically improved energy efficiency and the use of distributed renewable energy.

The New Apollo Energy Act, HR 2809, now pending in the U.S. House of Representatives, calls for a similar suite of investments but with a greater emphasis on leveraging private funds. The public investment will amount to at least $18 billion per year over ten years—the same amount Kennedy spent on the Apollo space program. Along with the private investment, the bill aims to mobilize even greater capital than the Apollo Alliance plan. Yet current federal investments in clean energy fall far short of the mark of what is needed.

This sort of large-scale public-private investment will be an engine to power not only a greener but also a more prosperous economy with a higher quality of life and improved public services. It will have to be focused on five key national policy priorities for confronting the challenges to our climate and energy security while building industries, strengthening communities, creating jobs, and reducing the threat of global warming.

Those five key policy priorities are (1) meeting energy demand through energy efficiency, (2) getting off oil, (3) rewarding renewables and carbon-free electricity, (4) building cities as if energy matters, and (5) capping carbon emissions. Together these approaches start to spell out a comprehensive strategy for the nation to break our addiction to oil, roll back the threat of climate change, and remake our economy, while building on existing policies and accelerating efforts in the private sector and the states.

## 1. Meeting Energy Demand through Energy Efficiency

The most critical area for immediate policy action in a new Apollo energy project is the improvement of our nation's energy efficiency. Energy efficiency has been called the "first fuel" because it is the area of our economy that offers the greatest amount of low-hanging fruit. The best energy source is the energy you don't have to use. It is energy there for the taking. Our mantra should be "It's energy efficiency, stupid!"

Progressive American businesses are using such a mantra to drive product development. Leaders at GE exhort their managers to use their "ecomaginations" in developing new energy-efficient systems. Costco is dramatically reducing its power consumption through a host of commonsense measures, from using daylight to using energy-efficient lighting systems. The MagnaDrive company near Seattle is manufacturing a transmission system that can increase the efficiency of electric motors by up to 70 percent in hundreds of industrial applications.

The majority of homes and businesses could cut electricity consumption by more than 25 percent with simple changes to such things as lighting and insulation, with rapid paybacks of under four years.[7] Much can be done to invest in improving the efficiency of our existing fleet of power plants as well. The first line of defense against climate collapse and energy insecurity must be to reduce our overall demand. Energy efficiency is like finding money in the street.

Perhaps the best example of the power of efficiency is the recent experience of the State of California. Comparing California with the rest of the nation is stunning. Nationally, electricity consumption per person grew by approximately 60 percent between 1976 and 2005. That is a staggering rate of increase. Yet in California, despite a prosperous and growing economy, per capita energy use remained exactly flat during the same period.[8] While Californians continued to enjoy their coastal lifestyle, the state adopted policies allowing them to radically reduce the electricity required to maintain that lifestyle. Nationally, we can enjoy the same success as California by tapping our national reserves of wasted energy and adopting a suite of the following policies.

A concerted program of investment as well as stronger codes and incentives for green building could save consumers money, create jobs, and generate new markets. The Apollo Alliance assessed the impact of spending $4.2 billion a year for ten years on residential, commercial, and industrial retrofits and determined that that could create over half a million good jobs and more than $235 billion in GDP gains. That major positive impact could be achieved while improving quality of life and cutting costs to consumers.[9]

SLASH ENERGY CONSUMPTION IN OUR BUILT ENVIRONMENT

*Match state public benefits funds with federal dollars.* Energy consumption in buildings uses fully two-thirds of our electricity, so finding efficiencies there is absolutely required. One critical tool for driving new investment into energy-efficient building practices is called a public benefits fund (PBF). This is a pool of public money generated by a state through a wires charge on energy use, and it could be used to finance energy-efficiency retrofits. According to the Alliance to Save Energy, a charge of one-tenth of a cent per kilowatt-hour would add only $1 to the average residential monthly electric bill but would create a pool of $3.7 billion a year to fund needed efficiency projects, driving down the cost of energy over time.[10]

States' public benefits funds already spend almost a billion dollars a year on efficiency. A number of states—such as California, Massachusetts, and New York—have become leaders in supporting the financing of energy-saving technology and building improvements through the use of these public funds. We should provide a federal dollar-for-dollar match of state expenditures on energy efficiency in all states that invest at least $8 per capita per year and drive down energy use by a minimum of 0.5 percent each year. The funds would go directly into upgrading school energy efficiency, retrofitting public buildings, and offering financing for private businesses and consumers to cut their energy use.

The Energy Future Coalition calculated that for a cost of $2.7 billion per year, a federal matching program for state PBFs alone could save $15 billion a year and result in a 5 percent savings in electricity use.[11]

*Apply the California energy efficiency model nationally.* California's Title 24 program has developed a very effective range of incentive programs and strong baseline building codes and standards to promote more efficient lighting, windows, boilers and chillers, and heating ventilation and air-conditioning systems, applying a systems-wide approach to upgrading energy efficiency. The program is able to provide energy savings at a rate of $.029 per kilowatt-hour, half the price of building new base-load power at $.058 per kilowatt-hour.[12] By helping consumers use less energy to get the same benefits, the program is able to save significant costs. Since 1970, California has driven down the cost to the state for energy by $12 billion a year, or $1,000 per family, and that avoided energy is, of course, carbon free.[13] The package of policies for utilities, consumers, building managers, and others should be applied nationally.

*Create strong incentives for green building and energy-efficient building codes.* The federal government should also provide strong incentives to those states that adopt international energy codes, that continually improve energy efficiency, and that link their building codes and public incentives to green building standards. Building codes provide a floor below which design and building practices will not fall; they also create jobs and demand for highly skilled construction labor. By using the tax code to provide incentives and federal supports for state programs, it would be possible to rapidly raise the bar on energy efficiency in buildings, and ultimately encourage zero net energy buildings.

*Improve the regulatory environment to promote efficiency.* A number of important tools have been developed that dramatically improve consumer incentives for energy efficiency. One system uses "real-time pricing" of energy to encourage load shifting away from peak hours of the day. Another uses "tiered pricing," which charges a higher rate to high-volume residential customers to encourage energy efficiency and on-site use of renewables. A third strategy, of "rate decoupling," helps utilities unlink their profitability from the volume of energy they sell. This encourages them to sell efficiency rather than power. "Energy-efficiency perform-ance standards" have also been used in some states to require that a set proportion (for example, 10 percent in Texas) of expected growth in demand is met through improving efficiency rather than constructing new power plants. The federal government could encourage such "de-mand-side management" through grants and federal regulations.

*Promote energy-efficient appliances.* The government can simply set mini-mum efficiency requirements that manufacturers must meet. We can continue to advance minimum efficiency standards for appliances, im-provements that have been blocked for years under the Bush adminis-tration. Public information through programs like Energy Star labeling plays a major role in educating consumers and promoting energy-smart appliance purchases. In fact, every federal dollar spent on the Energy Star program yields an average savings of $75 or more in consumer en-ergy bills; a reduction of about 3.7 tons of carbon dioxide emissions; an investment of $15 in private-sector capital; and a contribution of over $60 to the American economy.[14] Moreover, many states offer incentives like rebates and bounties for trading in inefficient appliances for state-of-the-art efficient ones. Properly designed, these policies are also good for American manufacturing, as energy-efficient appliances tend to be the more technologically advanced products, involving higher profit margins and using more skilled labor.

*Encourage industrial cogeneration.* The most energy-intensive industries account for 80 percent of all energy consumed in U.S. manufacturing. A plant generating both electricity and heat can be twice as efficient as a plant using just one resource. To realize the power of such plants, one need only go to Denmark to see the spectacular efficiency gains of co-generation plants championed by Danish leader Sven Auken, which are providing both electricity and residential heat for whole neighbor-hoods. Investment tax credits and other incentives for maximizing the resource of cogeneration could generate huge savings. According to the DOE, reducing energy waste in U.S. industry by 10 to 20 percent would add nearly $2 trillion to the GDP cumulatively over fifteen years and create two million new jobs.[15]

*Harness the public purchasing power of government.* The Federal Energy Management Program has been extremely successful at reducing energy consumed in federal buildings. Congress should require more stringent energy efficiency at federal facilities and as a preference for federal contracting and should assist states with building retrofits, including green building and facilities management.

*Expand manufacturing extension projects that focus on energy efficiency.* The National Institute of Standards and Technology has run a highly effective Manufacturing Extension Partnership (MEP), which provides vital consulting services to improve the operations of U.S. industrial employers. Expanding such assistance and training in energy efficiency and industrial process improvements will save money and preserve good jobs in the United States, even as it saves energy and cuts carbon emissions.

Energy efficiency creates enormous benefits. In a 2005 report, the Alliance to Save Energy proposed a suite of policies related to energy-efficient building; the report found that reducing current energy use by 14 percent and cutting growth in overall building energy use by two-thirds by 2020 would save consumers $56 billion on their energy bills.[16]

## 2. Getting Off Oil

Our cars and trucks should not be improved—they should be revolutionized. They must be made to go farther on a gallon of fuel, but we must also have more choices of fuel. We can no longer be hostages to oil. This will involve two separate and equally critical areas of policy development.

First, we should increase the mileage we get from every gallon of gas in the cars we drive through improved fuel efficiency. Second, we must develop new ways of fueling our cars and trucks to reduce carbon emissions and free ourselves from volatile oil markets, which drain the lifeblood of our economy. The new options will include a diverse range of next-generation fuels. Those include cellulosic ethanol from a wide assortment of feed stocks, from switchgrass to wood fiber. Other potential fuels are diesel from canola, soybeans, and even algae.

We need to accelerate the commercialization of plug-in hybrids. This will be good for GM if we can help it make good on the promise to be the first company to roll out a plug-in, flex-fuel model, the Volt. It will also be good for new U.S. companies like A123 Company, an MIT spin-off that is positioned to provide the incredibly powerful lithium batteries to power the Volt.

### START DEPLOYING THE NEXT GENERATION OF TRANSPORTATION TODAY

*Mandate oil savings.* It is essential that we develop rules with teeth that guarantee that American cars take less gasoline to run. We have three potentially achievable choices that would produce an immediate increase in auto efficiency; it is less important which option we choose than that we move forward in a way that mandates a reduction in oil use while applying policies that preserve jobs in the auto industry. First, we could simply increase the corporate average fuel economy, or CAFE, standard. Second, we could mandate a percentage increase for each company above its current levels. Or, third, Congress could require that oil consumption be reduced by a certain percentage each year and delegate authority for implementation to the executive branch agencies and their rule making. Each of these choices has clear environmental and energy benefits and clear political difficulties. Settling on a mechanism for requiring that we save oil will be a political negotiation, but we must have a stronger baseline requirement. Any of these approaches will be effective in saving oil, but they should also be implemented in parallel with policies that save jobs.

CAFE standards have been so highly successful in improving mileage that it would be easy to think they offer an easy policy course. After all, they raised the entire fleet average by about 60 percent in the 1970s and 1980s.[17] However, because U.S. manufacturers are now so heavily concentrated in the production of large cars and trucks and will have a harder time improving fuel economy, there is strong political opposition from U.S. industry to raising standards. But the failure of U.S. car companies to move effectively into more fuel-efficient vehicle lines could also result in the loss of jobs and market share for these same firms unless the transition is managed rapidly.

An alternative approach to raising the floor of CAFE standards would be to require each manufacturer to ratchet up the fuel economy annually for its entire fleet. This could break the congressional impasse, and it would be beneficial to full-line producers that manufacture large vehicles. Raising the bar by just 4 percent per year on a consistent basis would be good for American manufacturing, but it would face opposition from foreign car makers that are already building more fuel-efficient cars.

The third possibility, for Congress to pass a mandate that the president take such regulatory measures as required to meet designated fuel savings targets, could be a way to work around congressional opposition to touching the CAFE standard. It would depend, unfortunately, upon presidential will (or won't).

It is clear that we must act through one of these mechanisms. A voluntary approach has failed for two decades. Experience has shown that we are remarkably insensitive to rising gas prices, altering our buying choices only in the case of astronomical price spikes. Economists call this *inelasticity*. We can call it the lesson of experience—the only way mileage will go up is if it is required to. Only meaningful standards well implemented can save oil while saving jobs.

Of course, as we move toward cleaner fuels, it will no longer be enough to look at just miles per gallon. Since entirely new forms of fuel are coming into use, we will have to move toward a whole new system based on measuring carbon emissions per mile rather than miles per gallon. Former Senate majority leader Tom Daschle has proposed a new CAFE system, a "carbon alternative fuel equivalent" standard, to get at the roots of climate change. The state of California has announced its intent to create a low-carbon fuel standard, in addition to regulating tailpipe emissions of $CO_2$, a measure now challenged in court by

industry. All of these measures will reduce the climate impacts of automobile transportation.

A critical element of any increase in standards for fuel economy
will be to preserve the two-fleet rule, which calculates the fuel economy of domestically produced and imported vehicles within the same
manufacturer's fleet separately. This seeming technicality ensures that a
portion of the advanced-technology, alternative-fuel, lightweight, and
smaller cars are produced here in the United States. Without the two-
fleet rule, manufacturers would be content to move all of their high-
mileage car production offshore, since they could do so and still receive
"credit" in just one overall fleet. Measuring a company's performance
across two fleets ensures that the company will maintain a balance in
domestic production.

Analysis by the Apollo Alliance showed that $30 billion in invest-
ment tax credits and loan guarantees to accelerate retooling in the domestic auto industry (to ensure that higher standards would not mean
fewer jobs) would result in the creation or retention of nearly 130,000
jobs across the economy, with GDP gains of $42 billion over ten years.
It is possible to design policies that both improve standards for oil savings and drive new job-creating investment into the economy. With
sound investments, this is not a zero-sum game; in fact, it is the root of
sustaining our future national competitiveness.[18]

*Support the transition in industry.* It is in our national interest to help provide a bridge across troubled waters for the U.S. auto industry, both because it will help preserve companies and good jobs in the industry and
because it will help smooth the passage of these underlying policies. We
need to solve the legacy health care crisis in the auto industry. U.S. car
makers currently spend more money on health care than they do on
steel. The Health Care for Hybrids bill, now pending in both cham-
bers of Congress, is one method for taking on this issue, by leveling the
playing field with European and Asian competitors that do not have to
pay for the legacy costs of retired workers, while directing new investment into next-generation fuel-efficient cars. This bill would create a

voluntary program in which domestic automakers could receive federal financial assistance covering 10 percent of their approximately $6.2 billion in annual legacy health care costs through 2017, provided that the companies invest at least 50 percent of their health care savings in manufacturing fuel-efficient cars. That means both lower costs for business and consumers and greater investment in our productive manufacturing base.[19]

We must also provide loan guarantees or investment tax credits to manufacturers to directly help reduce the cost of capital for retooling equipment and retraining workers to produce energy-saving cars. Consumer preference for high-efficiency hybrid and advanced diesel vehicles is increasing in an era of skyrocketing gasoline prices. In 2004, the University of Michigan Transportation Research Institute estimated that a facilities conversion investment tax credit of 67 percent to incentivize production of these vehicles in the United States would cost just under $1.1 billion spread out from 2005 to 2009. The credit could switch half of all powertrains and 25 percent of vehicle imports to U.S. production, providing the treasury with $7.16 billion in new tax revenues and preserving 59,500 jobs over a ten-year period.[20]

*Require production of flexible-fuel vehicles.* Today there are six million flexible-fuel vehicles (FFVs) on the road capable of running on either gasoline or a blend of 85 percent ethanol and 15 percent gasoline; that is roughly equal to the number of diesels on the road.[21] These cars have been produced due to a loophole in the fuel economy standard that allows a credit for oil savings to cars capable of running on ethanol, regardless of whether the fuel is used. Currently, there is a chicken-and-egg problem with getting both a new fueling infrastructure and a new fleet of vehicles on the road simultaneously. Brazil, however, was able to go from virtually no FFVs on the road to over 70 percent FFVs in the new car fleet within three years.[22] A simple mandate that at least 50 to 70 percent of new cars be produced to accommodate E85, along with clear labeling of the vehicles, would go a long way toward creating a viable market for biofuels. The additional cost of about $100 to include flex-fuel capability at the time of manufacture is peanuts to the manufacturers and would prevent the sorry situation of developing the capacity to produce vast quantities of ethanol with no customers to buy it.

*Harness the purchasing power of government to create a market for plug-in hybrids and other advanced-tech vehicles.* Collectively, the federal, state, and local governments are the largest users of gasoline in the country. Government is the five-hundred-pound gorilla of procurement. It should use that power.

*Dramatically expand research, development, and deployment funding for new technology.* The lesson of the Wright Brothers is that little guys with big ideas can do grand things. The A123 Company is on the cusp of making the world's most efficient battery, but when you talk to the company's executives, they express frustration that they have to surmount the hurdles of being both small and early in the game. They have a hard time getting huge corporations to trust that they can deliver. Here is one place where targeted R&D could really make a difference. Establishing more effective grant programs is one of the best investments Uncle Sam could make.

CREATE REAL FUEL CHOICE BY KICKING THE OIL HABIT

*Require oil companies to install alternative fuel pumps.* The oil companies will not install ethanol pumps unless they are required to do so. The big oil companies are not eager to compete with Idaho farmers like Ray Hess and his cellulosic ethanol or the folks in Grays Harbor County, Washington, who are ready to sell biodiesel. The government could easily mandate that oil and gas companies that have twenty-five or more stations must install E85 pumps at 10 percent of their stations by the year 2010 and 50 percent of their stations within ten years. This simple formula would create widespread access to fueling options for owners of flexible-fuel vehicles and would make biofuels a viable choice for consumers. The financial impact of this mandate could be softened by an expanded tax break to cover a large portion of the investment necessary for the installation or conversion of a new pump, and the focus on large retail chains would prevent this mandate from creating an undue burden on mom-and-pop gas stations.

*Increase the Renewable Fuel Standard and carve-outs for cellulosic ethanol and biodiesel.* The Energy Policy Act of 2005 established the first national requirement for renewable energy. By the year 2012, 7.5 billion gallons of ethanol must be used in our nation's fuel supply, with 250 million gallons coming from cellulosic ethanol. The creation of this requirement set in motion the conditions for the growth of the industry. Refineries got financing because of the guaranteed market, farmers allocated crops for the production of grain for energy supplies, and today we are on track to meet the target substantially in advance of the deadline.

But the bar is not high enough. An analysis from the University of Tennessee estimates that ultimately we could strive for 65 to 85 billion gallons of advanced biofuels in our nation's energy system—nearly ten times the 2005 mandate as we move beyond traditional ethanol.[23]

But these sorts of numbers cannot be met using corn-based ethanol. We need to carve out a specific and robust requirement for the next generation of biofuels, increasing the portion of the mandate that is set aside for sustainably produced cellulosic ethanol and biodiesel.

*Provide loan guarantees to commercial-scale cellulosic ethanol plants.* Everyone wants to be the second investor to finance the construction of a cellulosic plant. The federal government can light the match for the cellulosic revolution by funding loan guarantees that can be the key to unlocking the financing for the first cellulosic plants. Iogen Company is ready, willing, and able to build its plant in Idaho once that guarantee is signed. Smaller-scale early commercialization plants below the current 30-million-gallon minimum should be eligible for loan guarantees as well, to encourage a diversity of technologies and business models.

Separate incentives should also be offered for traditional plants that substitute cellulosic material for natural gas as a source of process heat, to
provide an early market for cellulose as a new farm commodity.

*Create an aggressive program of incentives for local ownership of renewable en-
ergy facilities and biorefineries, following the Minnesota model.* Locally owned
wind farms and ethanol plants can provide significantly larger returns
than the status quo for communities and create meaningful economic
development for the nation's hard-hit rural communities. We saw this
clearly in the experiences of Benson and Luverne, Minnesota. Federal
incentives that are established to promote the development of biofuels
and wind should offer additional incentives and higher direct producer
payments to promote community- and farmer-owned facilities, as well
as targeting incentives to small and midsize production scales.

*Certify the sustainable production of biofuels and reward low-carbon fuels.* A
shift to renewable fuels should be accompanied by a program that cer-
tifies the sustainability of the production process of those fuels and rewards low-carbon choices. The processes that create biofuels need to be
rated for how much $CO_2$ they create. This can be done following the
model of public information tools, like the EPA Energy Star or USDA
organic labels. California has advanced a mandatory low-carbon fuels
standard that will guarantee that an increasing portion of the fuel mix in
the state will have reduced climate impacts, and that all fuels will be
graded on their carbon content. This is a critical tool for sustainably
moving away from oil dependence in our transportation fleet and
should be a major tenet of our national fuels policy.

*Expand R&D funding for over-the-horizon alternative fuels.* Great promise
has been shown in research applications for producing biofuels from very
simple plants like algae, as well as various forms of products in the urban
waste stream. A robust program for research and development should be
sustained for developing future generations of fuel that require fewer
fossil-fuel inputs and offer ever improving carbon characteristics.

## 3. Rewarding Renewables and Carbon-Free Electricity

The third major area where we must focus substantial policy attention is on developing carbon-free sources of electricity. We can do that principally by introducing new renewable energy technology, and by reducing the carbon emissions from traditional energy sources, like capturing $CO_2$ emitted from coal plants before it reaches the atmosphere and making existing plants more efficient. Both must be aggressively pursued. The Perryman analysis for the Apollo Alliance showed that new energy investments of just under $5 billion a year would yield nearly $415 billion in new GDP over ten years, while creating 932,000 jobs.[24]

### TRANSITION IMMEDIATELY TO GREATER USE AND DEPLOYMENT OF RENEWABLE ELECTRICITY

*Set a bold national goal for renewable energy production.* The nation needs to move rapidly to adopt the national goal of achieving 25 percent of all energy from renewable sources by 2025. Where significant commitments to renewable energy have been made, setting a goal and putting policies in place to get there have worked. Texas made one of the earliest commitments to a renewables standard and has since expanded the target because the state was on track to meet its original goal. In the EU, European leaders agreed in March 2007 to a binding target of 20 percent of their total energy consumption to be provided by renewables such as biomass, hydro, wind, and solar by 2020, with many nations on track to beat the goal.[25] Our nation's recent experiences in the states with the Renewable Energy Standards have also caused an explosion in the production and use of wind and solar. It is clear that setting big policy goals works to spur new markets and stimulate the economy. Recently, the University of Tennessee studied the nationwide economic impacts of a 25 percent renewable portfolio standard by 2025 and found that it would generate an additional $700 billion in economic activity annually by 2025, while creating 5 million total new jobs.[26]

*Increase and extend the production tax credit and other incentives for deploying renewables.* The federal government currently offers a production tax credit (PTC) of $.015 for every kilowatt-hour of clean energy produced. That incentive has made wind energy competitive with natural gas and other fossil energy in many markets around the country. Solar energy benefits from an investment tax credit, which encourages installation of distributed-energy systems on homes. A major problem with federal policy, however, is that it has been intermittent, not allowing for the sort of long-term planning that businesses, utilities, and governments require to finance and construct major energy projects and production facilities.

In fact, short-term extensions of these critical policies have led to wild swings in the construction of projects. The United States led the world in the production of wind energy in the 1980s, but abrupt changes in policy caused the market to collapse, and it has only recently begun to recover. Investors have one message for Congress: Do not do short-term tax breaks. Had we had long-term incentives in place, start-up firms like the Lunz Solar Thermal Company wouldn't have collapsed when the tax breaks expired, while early efforts to build a U.S. wind manufacturing industry would have been greatly accelerated. It is critical to extend any tax incentives for at least five and preferably ten years.

*Support policies for distributed generation as an increasing share of our electricity.* Getting utility-scale renewable energy installed is only half the battle. We need to build a distributed-energy system, with a substantial portion of our energy coming from generating facilities on our homes, businesses, and schools. That would minimize the strains on the transmission system and take advantage of the explosion in technology that could make us all electricity generators.

We have many ways to do this: (1) Net metering laws allow customers who produce their own energy to feed it back to the grid, running their electric meters backward, so they are billed only for the net energy they consume, or even generating revenue as home owners become small-scale energy producers. (2) Interconnection standards remove bureaucratic and financial barriers to connecting those systems safely and reliably. Establishing national technical standards for hookups will prevent consumers from being stymied in putting up their own solar cells. (3) Fair-rate design establishes mechanisms to compensate solar and other renewable producers for the fair-market value of the power. Some utilities have tried to gouge consumers by refusing to pay them market rates for their power that's fed back into the grid. (4) Financial incentives should also be offered for the installation of small distributed energy systems. In New Jersey the state has invested heavily in promoting solar installations as an alternative to managing a congested grid. Germany employs a different strategy, having established a feed-in tariff that has a guaranteed but declining price for every unit of solar electricity provided by customers to the grid. Either way works, although the feed-in tariff more reliably ensures that a payment takes place only when electricity is actually produced.

*Expand research into storage technology for intermittent renewable energy technology.* Renewable technologies are sure to grow our economy, and we should be investing in the research and technology development to expand their use and application. The General Compression company is preparing to build a compressor that can be mated with a wind turbine so that wind power can become a steady-state producer by storing its energy in compressed air below ground. It does that by making it practical to convert wind energy to compressed air that can then be released at the most beneficial moment to generate the most valuable electricity. It could potentially double the revenues of a wind farm. Another wind energy storage technology enterprise, the Ramgen Power Systems Company, is ready to build a compressor that can pressurize $CO_2$ so that clean coal can economically meet its $CO_2$ sequestration goals. Both compressor companies will create jobs. Should their technologies become commercially viable, both companies will improve technology and reduce the time it takes to save the climate—and our economy—by using wind more efficiently as a base-load energy source.

*Build a smart electrical grid.* The national electrical grid provides a back-bone for our economy. The massive Northeast blackout in August 2003, which shut down much of the Midwest and East Coast, is estimated to have cost the nation between $4 billion and $10 billion.[27] Investing in a smart grid that uses real-time information to manage energy flows would allow for innovations like real-time pricing that empower users to practice load shifting, or moving their demand to off hours to save money, while balancing the demands on the grid and reducing congestion. It would also allow the Sun Microsystems of the world to create jobs in designing the new software-heavy systems required to manage a smart electrical grid, and it would drive new investment into construction and maintenance jobs as well. A small national wires charge to fund the rewiring of the national grid system could fund the transition as the country moves from a nineteenth-century to a twenty-first-century technology to power our economic growth and prosperity. Smart-grid investments could be launched as metropolitan-area pilot projects and by building microgrids for securely providing municipal services.

*Create a clean-energy investment agency.* Modeled on successful Small Business Administration programs, a clean-energy investment agency would create good jobs through training programs and financial assistance to promote deployment of innovative energy technology. Such an authority would carry the mandate of building a domestic clean-energy industry and supporting innovators, entrepreneurs, and workers with technical and financial assistance. As Congress moves to establish a dedicated fund for renewable energy development, a clean-energy investment agency, as advocated by the Senate Clean EDGE bill and proposed by the Apollo Alliance, would provide a mechanism to get those funds into community-based investments in clean-energy technology.

*ARPA-E: Expand research, development, and deployment (RD&D) of renewables.* Federal R&D pays off. But now, at the very moment we are most in need of it, what we are spending on energy R&D is less than one-seventh of what we were spending on the original Apollo Project in the

1960s.[28] We need to invest in a major national security research and development initiative for energy, modeled after the successful Defense Advanced Research Projects Agency, which gave rise to the research that led to the backbone of the Internet. A recent National Academies report recommends funding an ARPA-E agency at $300 million per year, expanding to $1 billion per year over five years.[29]

Under the Bush administration, research spending on alternative energy consistently declined until a large political push on clean energy caused the administration to increase investment back to the levels when it took power. Instead of proposing cuts to clean-energy programs, we should be using basic research as the linchpin of a national strategy for economic competitiveness in the race to combat global warming. A quintupling of federal R&D on energy would be a good way to start.

REDUCE CARBON EMISSIONS FROM TRADITIONAL BASE-LOAD ELECTRICITY

*Invest in RD&D of advanced coal plants like IGCC with CCS.* Coal is a major source of global energy and will remain so for many years to come; 1,000 to 1,400 gigawatts of new coal plants are predicted to come on line by 2030, 154 gigawatts in the United States alone. That would add 6 to 8.4 billion tons of $CO_2$ emissions, the equivalent of the 7 billion tons the United States currently emits from all sources, to global emissions.[30] For our national security and to fight global warming, we must develop a strategy to ensure that coal used to produce base-load energy does not contribute to climate change. With a major world coal construction boom under way, we have to build plants using the best available technology for removing and permanently storing carbon emissions away from the atmosphere.

Developing a robust program of research investments into carbon capture and storage (CCS) and incentives for deployment will be essential even with the introduction of a carbon price. Cost-sharing grants, investment tax credits, and loan guarantees offered for the introduction of integrated gasification combined-cycle (IGCC) technology and carbon capture are warranted public policy investments.

They will on their own, however, be insufficient to transform the coal industry to move beyond carbon emissions. The market alone will not assume the full risk of making publicly beneficial technologies like CCS available. We need a disciplined investment of taxpayer money, backed by meaningful requirements to reduce the percentage of carbon in electricity or mandate implementation of capture and storage technology, in order to bring these promising tools to the stage where the private sector will understand the performance, risks, and costs of advanced technologies, so that when a carbon price is implemented, markets are primed to take over, ensuring that coal-based energy is compatible with a low-carbon future. A recent Center for American Progress report estimates that the cost of a financial incentive package to make plants with CCS systems more cost competitive with polluting coal plants and to moderate electricity price hikes would be in the range of $36 billion spread over eighteen years, or about $2 billion a year.[31]

The U.S. Department of Energy is planning seven Regional Carbon Sequestration Partnerships that will provide for nearly two dozen $CO_2$ injection pilot projects in the next three years, with the goal of achieving 99 percent sequestration permanence and less than 10 percent increase in energy costs.[32] Xcel Energy, BP, and other companies have also announced plans for experimental plants with carbon capture and sequestration. It is positive that voluntary efforts and research in this area are beginning to move forward, and a major advance from the FutureGen project would be welcome. A robust and broadly diverse program of research must continue to be supported. In addition, implementation of carbon capture and sequestration must be required on all new coal-fired plants, given the rapid proliferation of new plant construction and the need to constrain carbon emissions at actual plants, even as research and development efforts proceed.

To make this investment in both research and deployment incentives worthwhile, the federal government must also develop the regulatory environment in which the sequestration industry will operate. No country has ever done this, much less the United States. It is time for the EPA and the DOE to get a move on. To actually invest in these plants, utilities will need a regulatory system in place, so that they will know what air-, water-, and land-use permits they will need to build and operate them. Most important, they will have to know what will be required of them regarding permanent storage of the $CO_2$. Here is a place where certainty is most important in encouraging investment. Because carbon is not yet a regulated pollutant, public utility commissions frequently fail to recognize investments in IGCC as a best available technology for pollution control, therefore prohibiting the recovery of costs in rate setting and making the decision to manage carbon still more expensive to power companies. This should be addressed in any policy to promote advanced coal with carbon sequestration.

*Establish an emissions performance standard for new power plants.* The rush to build new traditional coal plants threatens to overwhelm efforts to slow global warming. One firm alone, TXU in Texas, was ready to build eleven traditional coal plants in order to get in under the wire before a cost on carbon was imposed, until its efforts were stopped by a takeover of the company. Congress must put a halt to that rush and require new plants to be designed responsibly, with the capacity to capture $CO_2$, and when sequestration technology is ready, to store it permanently. Anything less will lock our energy future into an explosion of carbon emissions for at least the next fifty years.

An emissions performance standard could set a requirement for all new plants constructed after a certain date to be built with the ability to capture carbon, followed several years after that by a requirement to capture all carbon emissions technically feasible (from 85 to 100 percent of carbon emissions as technology matures), and finally by a requirement to permanently sequester all captured carbon. This carbon-based performance standard would be technologically neutral, yet given current economics, it would be likely to drive construction of IGCC coal plants. Such a program for new power plant construction would be backed by a declining cap on the emissions of older plants that do not manage carbon emissions to ensure that improvements in performance and efficiency upgrades are made across the fleet of existing power plants. It is critical to have such a performance standard, or a similar policy such as a low-carbon portfolio standard that requires a set percentage of all power plants across the fleet, to ensure that new plant construction allows for carbon capture, even during the initial phases of a carbon cap, when economic incentives from carbon pricing are likely to be too small to ensure low carbon plants.

*Set a date for no further grandfathering of future power plants.* Congress should further pass a resolution setting a date beyond which no new traditional power plants will be grandfathered into a future carbon agreement. Such a resolution would offer certainty to the utility industry, encouraging the planning of advanced clean-coal plants and other low-carbon technology today and heading off a rush of new coal construction due to an uncertain regulatory environment.

*Research critical issues in nuclear power.* Nuclear power offers base-load power on a large scale with no carbon emissions. But issues of safety, waste disposal, proliferation, and security must be addressed before nuclear can play a significant role in the move toward climate protection strategies. Research and development on these concerns should continue as part of a larger national campaign to explore all low-carbon energy options. While the substantial threat of a climate crisis cannot rule out a significant role for nuclear power, the time is not right to place it at the center of a climate-change strategy. Indeed, the time may never come.

## 4. Building Cities as If Energy Matters

Rome was not built in a day, as they say. Neither will our clean-energy world be built in a day, or a year. We must start, however, rebuilding our cities around energy efficiency and human needs, rather than around the car and wasted energy. To a very major degree, the structure of our energy demand is driven by the way we build our cities. As Winston Churchill said, "We shape our buildings; thereafter they shape us."

Investment decisions in designing the form of our cities—from our transportation choices to the infrastructure that supports urban sprawl—drive future energy demand. If America is to hope to rein in its increasing upward spiral of energy use, we must rethink how we will design and build our infrastructure over the long term. This must be a comprehensive change, from altering how we fund water and sewer line expansion into agricultural lands, to promoting denser, more walkable and livable communities, to providing a rich range of transportation choices from rail to roads to high-speed bus lines and easy bicycle and pedestrian transportation.

Smart growth is not only good energy policy but also has quality-of-life benefits, produces cost savings, and is a tremendous job creator. Bruce Katz of the Brookings Institution has demonstrated that dense communities are less costly to maintain, noting that "compact growth can be as much as 70 percent cheaper for governments than equivalent volumes of scattered growth" when such infrastructure services as streets, schools, flood control, and sewers are considered.[33] As a driver for job creation, building dense urban communities is also a great engine for investment in quality employment building and maintaining public infrastructure. According to the American Public Transportation Association, $1 billion invested in transit capital projects creates 30,000 jobs.[34]

This is perhaps the most critical long-term investment in getting off oil. Only by investing in smarter infrastructure will we have the option of reducing our energy use over time by getting out of our cars while still enjoying freedom and mobility. An integrated package of investments in infrastructure—from transit starts, high-speed rail, and road maintenance to more energy-efficient water infrastructure, fully supporting job access and reverse commute programs, and cleaning up brownfield sites in cities to promote smart growth and more walkable and livable communities—will together revitalize the economy and cut our carbon emissions substantially while reducing our thirst for oil.

The Apollo Alliance has estimated that such a federal investment package would cost just under $100 billion over ten years but would leverage two and a half times that amount in direct GDP impacts and the creation of 678,000 jobs, while unleashing many times that amount of investment in private capital in new urban development projects.

These sorts of investments also strengthen local economies by improving job access for workers and redirecting money spent on imported energy into direct local investment in both infrastructure and increased local consumption of goods and services.[35]

## DEVELOP SMART CITIES THAT DEMAND LESS ENERGY TO RUN

*Promote efficient metropolitan growth.* By creating a system of smart-growth tax credits, it would be possible to reward developers for low-energy building projects in high-density areas near public transportation. In addition to directly using the tax code, incentives can include mortgage tools, financial underwriting, and support for bond financing for smart-growth development projects. Agencies such as the Economic Development Administration, the Department of Housing and Urban Development, and the Department of Transportation must all play a role in steering federal money to energy-efficient projects.

*Use federal incentives to require on-site renewable energy generation.* Frequently, public money plays a very important role in getting large-scale development projects off the ground. Such financial support should include conditions for green-building attributes and distributed renewable energy generation to help build local green-energy markets and to make energy efficiency mainstream. Greening public buildings and affordable housing can help create these new markets.

*Require smart-growth planning in conjunction with the use of federal transportation dollars.* Metropolitan planning organizations should be required to demonstrate oil savings and reductions in vehicle miles traveled in their regional transportation plans in order to qualify for federal funds. Special technical and financial assistance should be dedicated to states and metropolitan regions that (1) invest in transit corridors and robust rail networks to link major population centers, and (2) apply a strategy of "fix it first" before building new. In addition, the federal funding match for state dollars invested in oil savings and clean energy should be increased. This would drive more resources toward new transit starts, construction of high-speed rail corridors, and construction projects that mitigate congestion and prioritize maintenance of existing transportation infrastructure over new sprawl construction. All of these investments would build denser, more energy-efficient urban environments that are less dependent on both cars and carbon.

*Promote the workforce of the future.* Besides driving down energy costs, public procurement should invest in high-quality jobs to promote strong livable communities. This includes paying family-supporting wages and employing life-cycle cost analysis not only environmentally but also in labor standards through best-value contracting practices that reward responsible employers in the clean-energy industry. In addition, major infrastructure and energy projects should be required to link to apprenticeship and job training programs, uphold the right to organize a union, and employ community hiring practices to ensure that the green jobs of the future are shared by low-income and minority citizens.

*Create a clean-energy jobs corps.* Moving our nation away from oil dependence and implementing climate solutions will create tremendous opportunities to engage the enthusiasm and excitement of our young people in national service. Many young adults have been held down by poverty and have lacked access to job opportunities and skills training. A clean-energy jobs corps would create a unifying and vital program to engage the commitment to national service of our college-bound students, while providing meaningful training in the skills of the future for those seeking work. Creating new opportunities—through everything from apprenticeships in energy efficiency, weatherization, and solar installation to internship opportunities at energy service companies and green design firms—would accelerate our clean-energy revolution with the vitality of a national campaign. Building career ladders and service learning opportunities would help to infuse this national effort with the excitement and hope that it deserves, while inspiring our nation's youth with new possibilities, expanding our skilled labor pool, and providing essential training in the jobs of the future for the next generation.

*Promote global warming preparedness.* Finally, as a nation, we must face the reality that climate change is upon us, and while we must do everything within our power to avert the catastrophe of further global warming, some impacts are already irreversible. Conducting regular national assessments of regional climate impacts, improving community-based emergency planning, encouraging financial risk disclosure, and instituting a state-by-state threat assessment and preparedness ranking system would all go a long way toward preparing the public for the dangers of climate change and building support for reducing emissions to head off the worst potential harms, as well as constructing the infrastructure for responding to irreversible impacts. These would be smart investments in public planning and infrastructure and the centerpiece of a no-regrets strategy for building more resilient communities.[36]

## 5. Capping Carbon Emissions

If ice cream were free, we would eat an infinite amount of the creamy delight. If beer were free, we would buy loads of chips and guacamole and never go to work. And if putting $CO_2$ into the air could be done without restraint, we would spew unlimited amounts out of our smokestacks and tailpipes. Unfortunately it is, and we are.

We'll either limit carbon, or carbon will severely limit our future. Carbon in our air must be limited by the only mechanism that can restore the market for energy: federal policy. Increasingly, not only activists but also major corporations and industrial producers like Duke Energy, BP, DuPont, Pacific Gas and Electric, and GE are calling for the certainty of a federal policy limiting carbon emissions, because the absence of clear policy is creating immense uncertainty for business planning.

Having to pay to dump $CO_2$ into the atmosphere would actually help many American businesses make great progress in unexpected places. In Redmond, Washington, the Microsoft company would not normally be thought of as an energy company that would benefit from a carbon cap. But according to its vice president for special projects, Michael Rawding, a carbon cap would help Microsoft grow an entirely new line of business, one dedicated to saving energy. "Our company has a tremendous potential to integrate our software expertise in the new energy world. We can use our systems to control home or business energy usage. For instance, we are building a product to put whole banks of computers for businesses into sleeper mode when they are not in use. For every ten computers that go into sleeper mode when not in use, we save the equivalent of one car's $CO_2$ a year. Bottom line—it's my personal belief that a carbon cap can help us grow our business. When companies have a cost on carbon, we'll have a better market for our product."[37]

But what should the restraint be, and upon whom? Two fundamental possibilities are available to us. One is simply to tax carbon. This offers a direct approach that ties emissions to a price, but it does not offer a mechanism to produce reductions in the most economically efficient way possible, and the possibility of passing a tax on carbon in Congress seems remote at best, especially after the failed effort to pass a Btu tax in the early 1990s. A tax also relies on altering prices, not directly capping emissions. A tax that was set too low could have the effect of failing to encourage a rapid shift to low-carbon fuels. Another strategy is to pursue a cap-and-trade system, limiting total emission levels and requiring polluters to bid for permits to release $CO_2$. Each has advantages and disadvantages, and either would have a big impact.

The bottom line is this, however: Of all possible policies, a cap-and-auction system is the most feasible, most powerful, and most important arrow in our clean-energy quiver. It would set the framework within which the regulations, investments, and incentives outlined above would operate.

The cap-and-trade route where carbon permits are auctioned to emitters has two distinct virtues and one difficulty. Its prime virtue is that it sets a hard ceiling on $CO_2$ emissions. We set a cap on total emissions, and we stick to it. It is a known number and is not subject to the winds of uncertainty.

Second, a cap-and-trade approach uses the market to encourage the most cost-effective solutions. There are many things we can do about carbon, but they vary wildly in cost. A cap-and-trade system would drive the economy toward the most cost-effective measures possible and away from the most expensive in quite elegant ways. It does so, for example, when emitters bid for pollution permits if they need them and trade them to other firms if they don't. Put another way, businesses can choose whether to reduce their own carbon emissions or buy the reductions of someone else who can do it at a lower price, which saves money for the economy as a whole or allows deeper reductions for the same cost. Plants that are more costly to retrofit will buy the credits and drive new money to cleaner-energy producers.

Through the auctioning of emission credits, such a system could also generate tens to hundreds of billions of dollars per year in revenue to help industry and workers make the transition to the new energy economy, to defray any regressive impacts from changing energy prices, and to invest in the commercialization of new technology. A safe extimate is that such a system could generate $75 billion each year to fund the clean energy transition.

It is critical to remember that even a cap-and-trade or cap-and-auction system, although principally regulatory, is also a program for driving new economic investment. The European emissions trading system, for example, created over $25 million in assets by placing a value on carbon. That leveraged three times that amount of value in equity investments and seven times that value in debt finance. All of this translates to $275 billion in new investment in industrial plants, energy-efficient equipment, and new technology deployment, as well as skilled installation, maintenance, and operations.[38]

It is in no small part these new capital flows driven by carbon finance that have helped the global market for renewable power generation, biofuels, and low-carbon technology jump from $28 billion in

2004 to $71 billion in 2006.[39] Clearly, establishing a price for carbon can be a major source of new investment.

There are, of course, huge issues about the particulars of any such system, which will determine who bears the costs and who shares in the benefits. The first, and biggest, issue is where to set the cap. There is a growing scientific consensus that we need to stabilize our emissions (1990 levels are what's used in the Kyoto Protocol), and then set a trajectory toward steady reductions, resulting in a cut of 60–80 percent by 2050. Science tells us that we need to do at least that much to avoid doubling atmospheric $CO_2$ and stop global warming.

This approach is embodied in the Safe Climate Act of 2007 (HR 1590). This bill would cut emissions by 2 percent a year starting in 2011, to stabilize at 1990 levels in 2020; after that date, it mandates reductions of 5 percent each year, to reach 80 percent below 1990 levels by 2050. This is similar to proposals introduced in the UK by Prime Minister Tony Blair and in California by Governor Schwarzenegger. Less ambitious targets have been introduced in the McCain-Lieberman Climate Stewardship and Innovation Act of 2007 (S. 280), which shoots for 2000 levels by 2010, and the Climate and Economy Insurance Act of 2005, sponsored by Senator Jeff Bingaman of New Mexico, which sets a target based on the carbon intensity of the economy, rather than directly capping emissions.

Setting strong but achievable near-term targets for $CO_2$ emissions is critical to building a market for carbon immediately. In addition, a long-term trajectory that continues reductions into the future is essential for stabilizing the buildup of greenhouse gases in the atmosphere over time. California passed landmark climate legislation in 2006 with Assembly Bill no. 32, which called for emissions to be returned to 1990 levels by 2020, with reductions to 80 percent below that level by 2050. In Arizona, Governor Napolitano has chosen a different target, calling for her state to return to 50 percent below 2000 levels by the year 2040. Other regions, from New Mexico to New England, are taking action, too. Whatever the long-term goal, the key is to get started with a meaningful goal for the near term as soon as possible.

Whichever cap we set, it must be firm, a ceiling, a legally enforce-able limit. President Bush has offered to attempt to restrain the "carbon intensity" of our economy, so that the amount of $CO_2$ created per dollar of gross domestic product does not rise. This is a course doomed to fail-ure as a solution to limiting carbon. The earth's climatic system does not give a fig about our "energy intensity." It is affected by total emissions reductions, not ratios. In this race, only results count, not effort.

Some have argued for a "cap on the cap," to limit the possible total charges for permits. Such a "circuit breaker" or "safety valve" would provide comfort by limiting the costs to be incurred, but it also could undermine the enterprise by lessening the power of the cap to drive new investment into clean energy, setting a price too low to bring new clean technology into competition. This represents a real danger to creating the new markets and technologies. We already have a safety valve, in that if costs become too high, Congress can always change the cap.

Another critical concern is how credits are to be allocated. If the cost of carbon is high, that could hurt businesses. Such an adverse im-pact on particular sectors of the economy or regions of the country could be offset by grandfathering credits—allocating free credits to those who currently emit carbon. This would help cushion the blow, but if the allocation is too large, it could amount to a windfall for pol-luters. It is estimated that allocating only 10 percent of permits should be ample to make sure that businesses are not economically harmed.

If energy prices rise and nothing is done to offset the impact, a cap-and-trade system could also be regressive, hurting poor ratepayers dis-proportionately. However, if carbon credits were sold at auction to emitters, they would create an enormous revenue stream, ranging from tens to hundreds of billions of dollars a year, which could be used to create a pool of funds to support transition in impacted industries, assist workers, and restructure the tax code to expand existing income tax brackets, reducing the impact on low-income workers.

In a cap-and-trade system in which credits are auctioned and rev-enues are recycled into a more progressive tax code and support for clean-energy transition, the economic impact would be positive for all but the highest-income quintiles of the economy. Such an approach would not only clean up the atmosphere, but would also remove distortions in the economy and make the tax code more equitable. That "revenue recycling" back into the economy is critical for ensuring that a cap-and-trade system creates jobs and growth. While some studies of carbon caps in isolation show declining jobs and GDP, when the revenue is circulated back into the economy through investments in innovation, jobs and GDP rise. A UC Berkeley study of the impacts of California's Assembly Bill no. 32, for example, which reinvests revenue, shows the creation of 89,000 jobs and $74 billion, or 3.1 percent growth, in gross state product above the 2020 baseline.[40] While a Tellus Institute analysis of the Climate Stewardship Act shows that with the right policies to recycle revenues and invest in new technology, it would save consumers $30 billion annually in 2020 and create 800,000 jobs and a $45 billion GDP gain by 2025.[41]

A final concern about a cap-and-trade system is that through trading, it could allow hot spots of emissions that could provide for increased local air pollution in parallel with carbon emissions. This raises environmental justice concerns for low-income and minority communities; the distributional impacts of a cap-and-trade system need to be closely monitored. However, this only serves to underscore that a cap-and-trade system cannot exist apart from an integrated strategy that includes appropriate regulations, including not only enforcement of local air quality laws, but also standards on oil savings, portfolio standards for renewables and efficiency, and carbon-based performance standards for advanced coal and biofuels. We need a mix of market-based tools, regulations, direct investment, and incentives. In short, we need to pull out all the stops to ensure that our economy, our communities, and our environment navigate this transition and build both a cleaner and a more prosperous future.

## Lessons from Europe

When it comes to $CO_2$ cap-and-trade systems, ironies abound. The first irony is that the continent that originally hated such systems was the first to adopt it. For years the Europeans distrusted cap-and-trade systems, after the United States developed the first one for sulfur dioxide. They got over their distaste for all things coming from the upstart rebels across the pond, however, when they were faced with the climate crisis. The European Union adopted a $CO_2$ cap-and-trade system in 2005, with twenty-five member states participating.

The second irony is that the nation that invented the cap-and-trade system, the United States, has firmly resisted using it to deal with $CO_2$. This is a tragic replay of our history with solar energy. But now America has a grand opportunity to learn three lessons from the European experience.

First, the cap should be determined using the best possible information about $CO_2$ sources. Because Europe had no registry of the true emissions of the gas when its cap was imposed, its target was considerably too high. This resulted in a precipitous drop in the cost of carbon, from 30 euros a ton down to 1.2 euros per ton, as there was much less demand for the permits than anticipated. This experience argues for the early and effective adoption of a vigorous reporting system to allow proper fine tuning of the cap.[42] An additional side effect of a misallocation is that utilities can enjoy windfall profits when they obtain a valuable asset, a permit, without payment and do not pass that benefit on to their customers.

Second, to be most effective, a cap should include all sectors of the economy. The European system covers only 46 percent of the economy because it does not include the transportation sector. It covers only fixed-point sources such as power plants and large industrial complexes like cement plants that use large amounts of fossil fuels. That omission, while it simplifies implementation, must not be repeated in the United States, particularly since the United States does not have any of the other mechanisms that Europe uses to encourage the use of efficient transportation systems.

Third, allowing companies to bank their emissions permits does help reduce volatility in the carbon market. Companies that do not use all of their allotment in one year are allowed to bank the remainder for use in the next. This has helped companies deal with risk and respond to changes in the price of carbon.

We have tough decisions on where to place the cap. We could put it just on "upstream" producers like the coal and gas companies. That would be the easiest to administer, but it would fail to encourage behavior changes at major manufacturing facilities, other than through the price signal. Europe has a hybrid approach that includes major polluters such as cement plants. This method seems to strike the right balance between simplicity and effectiveness. In addition, many of the policies outlined in the earlier part of this overview will help create strong incentives for clean energy across the economy while moderating the impacts on particular industries and encouraging positive economic investments and job creation.

Even a perfect cap-and-trade system will not be enough to do the job, however, for a number of reasons. First, a carbon cap would have disparate impacts on utilities and transportation. Due to different economics facing utilities and transportation, a cap-and-trade system might drive investments into fuel switching at coal plants, but it would have only a small impact on the price of gas and might not be sufficient to create investment in carbon capture. A price of $100 a ton of carbon would translate approximately into a $.25 increase in the price of a gallon of gas, resulting in minimal $CO_2$ savings from car use. That same price would cause radical impacts on coal utilities. Thus, a cap-and-trade system cannot be relied upon to motivate improvements in transportation that are necessary for success in climate and energy security, creating few of the security benefits of getting off oil, and would focus all the costs of transition on the utility sector.

## The Real Drivers

These policies, taken together, represent a major reordering of the American economy. Nothing less is needed for the task before us. More important, nothing else stands poised to allow us to take advantage of the enormous economic opportunities for growth that lay ahead. These opportunities will not simply fall into our laps—they are certain to stretch our powers of innovation and creativity.

That is exactly how a body, or a country, grows. These are not policies for the complacent. They are policies for a nation that welcomes a challenge and embraces an opportunity. They represent a fundamental restructuring of the rules and a recognition that the old system does not fit the new world.

We changed the rules of football in the 1930s and got the forward pass. When we change the rules of energy, we will get something much more exciting: a new energy economy that preserves our environment, promotes innovation, creates good jobs and greater equity, and provides for a new wave of growth.

All of the policies recommended here are specific, effective, and necessary, from incentives for new technology deployment to infrastructure investments to mandates for efficiency and direct regulation of carbon. But no matter how well tuned they are, we should never lose sight of what force will serve as the wellspring of innovation. It will come from the thousands of private-sector inventors, technicians, workers, community organizers, and capitalists who will be the real drivers of the energy revolution.

Those drivers need the good roads and good road signs commonsense policies can provide. Let's give those American innovators the policies they deserve.

# PLACING OUR BETS ON A
# NEW APOLLO PROJECT

It is difficult to say what is impossible, for the dream of
yesterday is the hope of today and reality of tomorrow.

—*Robert Goddard, pioneering American rocketeer*

It is time to put our chips on the table. Having read a book on the
search for clean energy, the reader is entitled to require the authors to
place their bets on which technologies we believe will succeed and
which will fail. It would be easy to walk away from this responsibility
and let the future determine its own course. It would be comforting to
avoid the prospect of being proven 'wrong by the passage of time. But
your authors are built of sterner stock. We refuse to take refuge in the
privilege of punditry to cloak our comments in vague surmises. We are
compelled by a sense of responsibility to provide a vision of where we
think the energy world really will be in ten years and beyond.

Here is our vision—also known as our best guess.

## New Utilities: It's Not Your Mother's Grid Anymore

Electricity from carbon-emitting coal plants will be phased out for the
next three decades as the science and efficiencies of the IGCC system

and other emerging technologies with sequestration render traditional coal plants obsolete in a world where carbon is managed and the costs imposed by a cap-and-trade system make advanced coal competitive with current systems. Coal will remain a substantial part of the total grid energy, but finding cost-effective places to sequester carbon will become a limiting factor on new plant sitings. Public sentiment will also demand more and more emphasis on nonfossil fuels for reasons well beyond the control of carbon, and the fastest growth in new plant construction will be in both utility-scale and distributed renewables, driven by the national goal to achieve 25 percent renewable energy by 2025. Nonetheless, advanced coal will remain a substantial portion of the total base load for decades because of its cost and availability.

Wind is too easy. Since it is already competitive, we predict that it will become a more substantial portion of our grid by a factor of ten. The Department of Energy and the American Wind Energy Association have predicted that wind could provide 20 percent of U.S. electricity by 2030, and given trends in Europe and the rapid growth in the United States, we are inclined to believe them. Continuing marginal improvements in its technology and the increasing cost of carbon-based fuels will push wind to the first tier of choices for utilities, particularly in the next few years and earlier than solar, wave, and biomass breakthroughs are commercialized. It will be the fastest-growing of the renewables in the immediate future for that reason. Wind's ultimate ceiling will depend on our ability to perfect storage and transmission technologies that will enable us to move larger quantities of wind power onto the grid in a sustained way and will markedly reduce transmission costs from the wind-fertile Midwest and Plains states to population centers elsewhere.

About 2015 solar power will boom. The industry will have perfected both significantly different photovoltaic systems and solar thermal systems that will allow their commercialization at costs competitive with the grid. The photovoltaic improvements will allow substantial restructuring of the grid to a much more distributed one, one that will allow consumers to take advantage of a coming national net-metering bill proposed with such foresight in 2007 by a certain congressman from Washington State. Solar thermal plants will make a perfect team with wind by providing base load during the day, with wind at night. As low-cost solar moves into mass markets, it will stabilize prices for consumers, radically reduce both pollution and strains on the grid, and create a booming export market for development applications in the third world as distributed generation becomes the standard for emerging economies.

This is the gutsiest prediction that will be made in these pages. Predicting solar success "just around the corner" has lost many a wager over the last three decades. But both manufacturing and basic processing advances are now being made that allow us to go out on this limb. Our optimism about solar is echoed by Oliver Morton, the chief news and features editor of *Nature*, a journal about scientific advancement. On the edge.org Web site, where leading technologists of the country were asked what they are optimistic about, Morton said, "My current optimism is for solar energy. The simple facts of the matter are that the sun provides more energy to the earth in an hour than humanity makes use of in a year. . . . It will take its place among and then surpass these more established technologies a lot more quickly than most people outside the area currently imagine. I am hoping for at least a terawatt of solar by 2025, two if we're lucky, and dramatic cuts in $CO_2$ as a result." We agree.

Wave energy will be the sleeper technology of the next two decades. There is enough potential energy in ten square miles off the coast of California to provide all that state's electricity using technology now in the water and producing juice. Although it may not be a larger percentage than single digits nationally for decades, its emergence will be important because right now it is not on anyone's radar screen, and the concentration of population centers near the coasts means that capacity is located near demand.

Biomass will be used to power generating turbines for electricity, but the use of biofuels in transportation will dwarf its use in electrical generation. However, sustainable biomass will also be produced for electrical energy, to be cofired in traditional power plants, and gasified and burned with cellulose for use in the production of biofuels and other manufacturing applications. Bio-industry will become a much larger concept than simply producing fuels for transportation as biologically based polymers replace a host of petrochemicals in manufacturing, further reducing our dependence on oil. Both low-carbon fuel standards and certification of the sustainable production of biofuels will drive the market for bioenergy, which contributes positively to reducing climate change while minimizing strain on natural systems.

Nuclear energy will see only very modest growth in the next two decades. A combination of high costs, failure to find acceptable disposal sites, slow movement to finance projects, and lingering public rejection will prevent huge growth; globally, a small but significant number of plants will be built. Decades from now, however, in the event that our first four predictions do not come to pass, the nation may turn to nuclear if improvements in its technology are made.

Geothermal, like tidal energy limited by geography, will remain a niche producer, but it will offer a substantial resource for clean, stable, base-load capacity in areas with appropriate geologic formations such as the intermountain West, and for new development in Africa, South America, and elsewhere around the globe—also giving a boost to U.S. manufacturers of geothermal energy systems. The limiting factor on the growth of the industry will be increasing pressure on water resources, so resource-efficient systems will become dominant, using closed loops and conserving water inputs.

The smart grid will replace the nineteenth-century technology of the existing electrical grid, enabling real-time pricing to rapidly increase energy-efficiency programs and net metering to allow distributed generation to flourish—from home-based photovoltaic solar cells to stationary fuel cells in industry to the humble plug-in hybrid in the garage as the family car becomes storage capacity for our national energy system. Microgrid technology will be rapidly expanded as well, creating small, local grid networks that are more secure in the face of disruption by terrorism or natural disasters induced by increasing global warming. The microgrid fueled by renewables will be a staple of homeland security, providing stable energy sources for first responders and emergency backup systems for streetlights, pumping stations, and other essential services.

## New Cars, New Fuels, New Batteries

Two major advances that can revolutionize our transportation system will mature simultaneously: cellulosic ethanol and the plug-in hybrid. About 2011, plug-in hybrids will start to hit the roads just at the same time that meaningful amounts of cellulosic ethanol are becoming available at service stations across the country. This will be a happy tie in the race between battery technology progress and biofuel progress. This synchronous combination will allow drivers to plug in their cars at night, drive about forty miles on battery power alone, and then use the cellulosic ethanol they purchased at their corner filling station for the rest of their trip. The car will get a minimum of 150 miles and potentially as much as 500 miles per gallon of gasoline.

In the first decade, most of the electricity powering the car will come from old-fashioned coal-based generating plants that are heavy carbon emitters. Even then, because of the efficiency of the system, $CO_2$ emissions per mile will be less than with gasoline. As solar, wind, wave, and clean coal become a larger part of the grid system, net reductions in $CO_2$ will increase dramatically.

Even before plug-ins become a substantial part of the auto fleet, cellulosic ethanol will make a rapid penetration of the market. This will occur because Congress will have done its job and mandated production of flex-fuel vehicles and a certain percentage of service stations to offer biofuel pumps. The Farm Belt will convert a rapidly growing percentage of its acreage to dedicated energy crops for the production of biofuels, but use of new perennial feed stocks and increased yields per acre will minimize the impact on overall food production and the consumption of water and fossil fuel resources as the industry moves away from a sole reliance on corn. Biofuels should provide 25 percent of our fuel by 2025. Our agricultural exports will diminish, but so will our payments to Saudi Arabia. The reduction of U.S.-subsidized food commodities entering third world markets will help global agriculture to rebound and improve the climate of global trade negotiations; the move to biofuels will improve the nation's balance of trade. Over time the production of biofuels from humble algae will offer an increasingly cheap and environmentally benign source of fuel for the mass market.

We predict that gasified coal "synfuels," made using the Fischer-Tropsch process, will not become a substantial part of our auto fuels. While using them might mean we produce more of our fuel domestically, it would also mean diverting huge national resources to the development of an industry that does not reduce $CO_2$. And that would mean missed opportunities, both to create low-carbon fuels and to reduce the carbon footprint of the coal we continue to use for energy. Development of a carbon cap and a low-carbon fuel standard or carbon alternative fuel equivalent policy will help ensure that other alternative fuels improve both our energy and our climate security. Whether this prediction comes to pass will depend on whether Congress can transform the huge political pressure that will build to maximize our coal assets into a plan for low- or zero-emission coal through IGCC with carbon capture for electricity generation, rather than production of fuels. It should.

The efficiency of cars will skyrocket. A combination of better tires, better aerodynamics, and the use of composite materials will substantially reduce the rolling resistance and inertia of our cars, while high and volatile oil prices as global petroleum markets tighten further will create sustained global demand for ever greater fuel efficiency. The steady 2 percent per year increase in horsepower of the past decade will be converted to a steady improvement in efficiency. The American auto industry will rebound by serving this market for innovative products, once the rules are in place to ensure increasing efficiency and as efforts continue to address the legacy costs of health care and retirement faced by all U.S. manufacturers.

The percentage of Americans routinely using public transportation will more than double in the next two decades. The combination of improved and more comfortable public transport, increasing fuel costs, and better land-use planning will make public transport a preferred option for millions of commuters, and urban living will continue to outstrip the growth of suburban sprawl as open space becomes increasingly limited and the efficiency of cities ever more valued. Commuters will get to read, listen to their watches (iPods will be part of our watches by then), and socialize on the way to and from work instead of developing road rage before 8:00 a.m.

The "Mr. Fusion" car power source featured in the *Back to the Future* movies will not arrive, at least in the next fifty years. After that, who knows?

Some fuel cell–driven cars running on hydrogen will begin to be commercially available in the next fifteen years. Their use will be concentrated in certain regions that have built a hydrogen distribution network. Battery technology will develop faster than fuel cells, however, and plug-in hybrids that use the grid to deliver energy to the car will prove more cost effective because the cost of building the hydrogen distribution system will slow fuel cells' growth. It will prove more effective to use the existing grid to distribute energy and batteries to store it than to build a separate network to move hydrogen around the country. The lithium batteries of plug-ins in the 2020s will become the main substitute for the dead dinosaurs of the 1990s. In the horse race between fuel cells and plug-ins, we are putting our two dollars on plug-ins to win by several lengths.

Arnold Schwarzenegger's Hummer will become an exhibit in the Smithsonian Energy-Efficiency Gallery.

Old Volkswagen Love Bugs will continue to be converted to run on biodiesel and fry grease for decades.

Teenagers' use of cars on Saturday nights will not change.

## Getting More from Less

The biggest part of our energy future will be invisible. The biggest gain we will make will be in not wasting energy. Architects will indeed achieve their goal of designing new houses that use 50 percent less energy by 2030 through the use of better insulation, passive solar heating, new window technology, and vastly superior heating and cooling systems. Offices will accomplish the same. And the zero-energy home that produces more power than it uses to provide services to residents will become increasingly common and sought after in the mainstream residential real estate market.

Our housing will be more oriented to the sun and our appliances more oriented to saving electricity. Our white appliances, such as washing machines and dryers, will have computer chips in them that lower their heating element a few degrees when the grid is coming under stress, but our clothes will still be dried. Thomas Edison's incandescent lighting will be only in the history books, having been replaced by compact fluorescent lightbulbs and light-emitting diodes (LEDs). Green building will be standard practice, while the construction boom in retrofitting our cities will provide generations of carpenters, electricians, and other construction workers with steady work and a stable retirement.

All decently managed corporations will emulate DuPont's success and reduce their energy use by at least 40 percent in two decades. Their pumps and compressors will be better, their heating will be more efficient, and their manufacturing processes will be less wasteful; cogeneration of heat and power will become the norm. Products will be designed to make them more recyclable. With increasing access to stable, low-cost, renewable energy sources; declining natural gas prices; and proximity to emerging domestic markets, we will be able to retain the kinds of jobs that have fled to other countries in recent years.

## Will It Be Enough?

The answer to whether it will be enough is a resounding yes. But the answer can be yes only if we act now. We are on the very cusp of irretrievable climatic catastrophe. We will take steps to avoid going over the edge now, or it will be too late to avoid the precipice. Certain changes in the climate are already "baked into" the atmosphere because $CO_2$ lingers in the air for centuries.

These facts are not reason for despair; they are reasons to take immediate action.

All the measures we advance in this book can be achieved. Given the rising awareness of our energy insecurity and climate vulnerability, as well as the opportunity for economic renewal that these investments represent, we believe that the necessary policies can be passed into law in the near future. The forces of the status quo will surely fight many a rearguard action, but national demand can overwhelm those pockets of resistance.

Some have argued that we should not act until China acts. But, in fact, China has acted, adopting more stringent auto standards than the United States. More important, though, America is not a country willing to wait for the rest for the world. We are leaders, not followers. We did not wait for China to adopt democracy before we did. We did not wait for China to invent the Internet, go to the moon, or build an NBA that Yao Ming could play in. Certainly, we will have to use our talents, our persuasiveness, and perhaps even our trade policies to encourage China to act, but act *we* will, for it is up to us to lead the world in this clean-energy revolution.

In the words of Pacala and Socolow, "The choice today is between action and delay." Clearly, inaction is no longer an option, and delay is increasingly costly.

It is time we mobilized the political will and exerted the pressure that only we as citizens can, to ensure that our leaders lead. Surely, this is a "Sputnik moment" every bit as dangerous as the one that JFK stared down and won in the race to the moon. It is deep in the American tradition to rise to such occasions. It is now incumbent upon us all to face the gravity of the moment and respond with hope, enthusiasm, and a commitment to squarely meet the greatest challenge of our time. Failure, in this sense, is not an option.

## The Ultimate Bet: An Authors' Wager

In the end, we bet that the new Apollo energy project will succeed. We bet that the innovators we have met in these pages will, as a group, change the world. We bet that the next few years will change our perception of what we can be as a society. We place these bets based on the fact that during the months this book was written, new technologies, new political constituencies, and new inventors kept popping up like desert wildflowers after an Arizona rain. And state governors and legislatures, presidential candidates, and even the U.S. Congress began to awaken to the urgency of climate change.

We did not live when fire was first harnessed. But the period we enjoy now is another time of massive human creativity in energy. Geographically, we live in the epicenter of that creative hurricane: the United States. Geologically, we live in a period of the planet's history that is most in need of that innovative talent. It is a perfect match of global challenge and national solution.

It is always a good bet to bet on the power of human intellect. It is always a good bet to bet on America.

It is always a good bet to bet on hope.

# EPILOGUE

This is a moment of reckoning. It is the moment that will determine whether the world moves forward technologically or sinks into a morass of massive climate change. But it is a moment of reckoning for this book as well—the moment when we determine how well our assessment and predictions have stood the test of time.

Have we been proved hazy optimists, drunk on the liquor of hope? Or perhaps just self-deluded naifs in the world of physics? Or have we been spot on, realistically setting out an attainable future—or some combination of these attributes? Fortunately, we are well armed with a means of making this assessment because our Ten Energy Enlightenments can provide a means of judging the larger strategy of this endeavor. Now it is fitting to challenge those enlightenments by the harsh test of time, to see how they have performed since this book was originally written. We have had a year to watch the world spin on since our enlightenments were introduced, and they deserve to be called to account, to answer to the unblinking eye of history.

So let us put the power of the "retrospectroscope" up to our enlightenments and see how they, and the world of clean energy, have fared:

### One: Opportunity Is Best Found in Crisis

This enlightenment has proved to have been absolutely right for a reason we never anticipated. When we wrote it, most Americans believed
that our economy was in good shape, were confident that the stock
market and real estate values only go up. Then the bottom dropped out.
The economic crisis could either spell doom for the clean-energy revolution or be the spark that ignites it.

It all depends on leadership. The arrival of Barack Obama, a leader
who understands the power of transformative change, was perfectly
timed to take advantage of this enormous economic crisis. And one of
the Obama team's first quotes may go down as its most memorable.
Chief of Staff Rahm Emanuel hit the nail on the head when he confronted a talk show host who argued that we would have to pull in our
horns on energy now that the economy had tanked by saying, "You
never want a serious crisis to go to waste."

Implicit in that remark is the recognition that this crisis freed us from
the restraints of the status quo. People do not make rapid, transformative change unless they perceive the urgent need to do so. Neither do
nations. A proposed investment of hundreds of billions of dollars to build
a clean-energy electrical grid system would have drawn guffaws before
the collapse, but, as of this writing, Senate and House leaders are putting the finishing touches on a $500 billion stimulus plan that will in-
clude huge investments in clean-energy infrastructure and technology.

When we argued in this book for the creation of thousands of
green-collar jobs retrofitting our homes and businesses to make them
more energy efficient, it was an academic idea. Now it will become a
concrete reality, because President Obama has signed a bill creating a
Clean Energy Corps, designed to put young people to work in a myr-
iad of energy projects, as thousands were put to work by President
Roosevelt in the original Civilian Conservation Corps. When thousands go to work building the new electrical grid to move wind turbine
power from the windy regions of the country to its cities, as they will

do under the stimulus package, it will stand as a testament to the opportunity inherent in crisis.

Note that this enlightenment is not self-executing. For any crisis to be forged into opportunity, leaders must be on the scene who can rally the citizenry to a cause broader than themselves, lift a nation's aspirations, and marry the power of free enterprise to rigorous public policy.

## Two: Boldness Is Required—Tinkering at the Edges Didn't Put a Man on the Moon

Boldness beats meekness. Take Shai Agassi as exhibit A. Agassi is the thirty-something founder of Better Place, a company that aims to accomplish quickly what many believe is only a long-term dream: building a scalable and sustainable personal transportation system that ends oil dependence. This son of Israel, who turned down a job as the youngest CEO of a major electronics company to found Better Place, describes his strategic plan on his Web site as "our bold plan."

Agassi's whole insight is that the world's transportation system has to be electrified, an insight many others have realized, as well. Where Agassi parts company with the meeker, however, is that he is unwilling to wait for years, or decades, for battery technology to improve enough to allow people to drive a hundred miles or more on a charge. His solution is elegant in its simplicity: Instead of waiting years for a new battery, just provide people a way to charge their cars now, wherever they go. So he has designed and built a company to do just that.

Better Place has now signed contracts with Israel, Denmark, Australia, and the San Francisco Bay Area to electrify their transportation fleets by providing travelers with access to charging stations throughout those regions. People will be able to charge their cars at home, at work, or at their restaurant. That will get them about a hundred miles without any delay. For longer trips, Better Place is building charging stations that will swap out a spent battery for a fully charged one in a couple of minutes in a totally automated process.

People will pay for this service like they do for cell phone service, and the incentives to add drivers to the networks will most likely drive down the cost of the cars. Since an electric car's "fuel" costs about one-fourth as much as gasoline, the economics are attractive to all concerned.

This is revolutionary vision: electric cars zipping around our cities using today's technologies instead of waiting for tomorrow's. Now it is becoming a reality—the world's first integrated charging station opened in Israel on December 8, 2008, just a bit more than a year after the company was founded with $200 million in venture capital.

The contrast between Agassi's enterprise and the Big Three American automakers could not be more stark. Just as his adventurous, bold company was opening its first charging station in Israel, the staid and previously unimaginative Big Three were in the nation's capital begging for a bailout—which they could get only by proving that they could think boldly.

You can't make a revolution without breaking some crockery.

## Three: We Must Reject the Tyranny of the Present

Innovators are always at war with present realities. They have some genetic propensity to think of present technological restraints as invitations to action rather than straightjackets. Our third enlightenment posits that their power to invent the future depends on their ability to ignore the present.

During the last year we have seen that power in action. A year ago we got to know the people at Ausra, a small group of eight people in Australia who dreamed of making concentrated solar energy in a way it had never been done before. Their plan to radically reduce the costs of concentrated solar power by using flat panel mirrors seemed like a nice idea, but we had to ask—Would this just be another good idea destined to go nowhere but to an industrial museum? Then Vinod Khosla brought the group to America, and what was a sleepy little dingo of a company has become a racehorse of solar power innovation.

In November 2008 in Bakersfield, California, Arnold Schwarzenegger cut the ribbon on Ausra's five-megawatt plant, the first concentrated-solar plant to be built in twenty years. This followed by a month the opening of Ausra's manufacturing facility in Las Vegas, Nevada. We mentioned concentrated solar in the first edition of our book as a possibility. The reality then was that it seemed too expensive to be competitive. Ausra rejected that roadblock and built a functioning industry.

What's more, if Ausra decides to become simply a supplier of equipment rather than a developer, other concentrated-solar firms such as BrightSource Energy are ready to step into the breach. By April 2009 BrightSource had already signed contracts to provide over two thousand megawatts of clean electricity.

Similar progress has been achieved by Martin Roscheisen and his fellow "Thin Men" at the Nanosolar company in Palo Alto, California. A year ago, Martin just had a good idea and a few million dollars to try and build a whole new type of photovoltaic cell. The complexity of using a "sputtering" process to deposit unbelievably thin layers of several elements on a substrate caused many to question his sanity.

But when Nanosolar made the first commercial shipment of thin-cell photovoltaics in June 2008, there was plenty of crow to go around for the naysayers. Roscheisen was not daunted by the complexities of sputtering technology. Now Nanosolar is off to the races in the photovoltaic sweepstakes to see who can dominate this exploding field.

Our roster of those who advanced the contours of the future in the last year is long and deep. Nanosolar, Ausra, and Bright Source are just three representatives of the entrepreneurs and innovators who are inventing the future.

## Four: There Are No Silver Bullets

No silver bullet for our energy woes has yet been found. To be fair, no rational observer has predicted such a deliverance. Instead, the value of this enlightenment has been shown in the continued wisdom of maintaining a diversified portfolio of investments, whether those investments are made on Wall Street or in clean-energy R&D.

The most obvious rationale of this enlightenment is that all nascent technologies have significant risks of failure, so a strategy that put all our energy eggs in one basket would be most imprudent.

Also, the limitations of even those renewable technologies that have been spectacularly successful have to be realized or they will overpromise and end up considered somewhat as failures. Take wind power, for instance. Some advocates may point out that wind could theoretically provide all the electricity for the United States, but during the last year the abject inability of our existing grid system to fully exploit that resource has become glaring.

When it comes to clean energy, the nation's original credo, "E Pluribus Unum," should apply. "Out of Many, One" should be our guiding principle in connecting our multiple sources of clean energy. In March 2009, the Obama administration announced its commitment to creating a national grid that will allow the full development of the abundant renewable energy-generating sources we have, from coast to coast.

Those who want to see what one potential future grid could look like should go to the American Superconductor Company in Devens, Massachusetts, and examine its new superconducting wire. It can carry 150 times the power of a similarly sized copper wire. This company has developed a flat, thin metal that can transport in a 50-foot underground installation what would normally take a 300-foot right-of-way and 60-foot-tall overhead wires. An alternative approach now being considered is to build very-high-capacity direct-current lines, which lose much less electricity in long transmissions compared to a alternating-current protocol. This strategy needs no new technology. Its only drawback is that, because every time there is a hookup to the line, a large conversion facility must be installed to convert to AC, these systems are most useful in a hub-and-spoke approach to the grid.

Regardless of which strategy we adopt, we need a way to finance these huge investments in building a new grid. To that end, the Rural

Electric Superhighways bill was introduced in the House in 2008 as a way to spread the cost of these investments across large regions of the nation. When the costs are spread widely, they allow a big investment to be made with only a small cost incurred by any one consumer of energy. This approach has worked in Texas and now needs national adoption.

Just as important, we need the ability to coordinate the siting of new wires, so legislation was introduced in April 2009 to provide federal "backstop" authority to locate transmission corridors if state efforts to site these necessary lines fail.

## Five: Everybody Needs to Get on the Bus

When a Texas oilman billionaire who spent millions on swiftboating John Kerry becomes committed to wind power, we know the clean-energy era has arrived. T. Boone Pickens's $300 million in advertisements promoting wind power were not the work of an old hippie who had rediscovered his youth. Pickens had spent eighty vigorous years finding oil and turning it into money, any obstacles be damned. He is an unapologetic, gambling risk taker, right out of central casting. He is not motivated by squishy feelings for endangered species; the only species he is interested in is the American currency specie.

The arrival of Pickens in the public debate on clean energy meant two things. First, there is big money in wind. The projects Pickens proposed would simply expand on known business models that have made Texas the largest wind producer in the country, much to the financial benefit of manufacturers, utilities, and farmers who lease their land to the wind developers who install 200-foot-tall wind turbines where just wheat once grew. We know that once grid connections are available, wind is more than competitive with other sources of energy.

Second, Pickens had something up his sleeve. His angle, actually, was on natural gas. The Pickens plan is essentially to displace oil with natural gas to power our cars. Guess who owns enormous supplies of gas? Pickens's plan is to wean ourselves off foreign oil by taking the natural gas used for heating our homes and putting it in cars. Our homes would be heated with electricity powered by wind. In his commercials, Pickens leads with sweeping images of wind turbines gracefully arcing across the sky. But it is in natural gas that his profits would presumably lie.

But what of it? If Pickens is motivated by profits associated with the sale of natural gas, and it results in the expansion of wind and the contraction of coal, who should question his motivation?

The Apollo effort will succeed because everyone can have their own motivations to change the world.

## Six: If Government Sets the Road Signs, the Market Will Drive

Our book predicted the arrival of enormous private capital to build a new energy economy if government simply set out the demand for new, clean-energy sources. It arrived, in the person of a dozen venture capitalists, in the U.S. capital in June 2008.

That month, the group of venture capitalists journeyed to Washington, D.C., with a simple message: If government created a demand for clean energy, they were ready to pump in the capital needed to make this dream a reality. They met with congressmen in a small room of the Cannon House Office Building, but the implications of what they were saying were profound.

As one of them put it, "If you build it, we will come. What I mean is, that if you build a cap-and-trade system that puts a price on carbon, we are willing to put billions into an assortment of projects in wind, solar, and you name it, to replace carbon-based fuels."

But this meeting was before the crash. Six months later, credit dried up like a raisin in the sun. Given that the credit markets essentially froze in December 2008, even for regular, old-line businesses, it is not surprising that a project that could have obtained capital in June of 2008 would face tough sledding in January 2009.

Here is where Barack Obama comes in. By the time he took his oath of office on January 20, 2009, it was clear that government would have to deliver something more than road signs. It was going to have to drive the bus, as well. Whereas a simple cap-and-trade system may have driven adequate investment in 2008, direct government investment would be necessary to obtain liftoff in 2009. Fortunately, Obama understood the "fierce urgency" of the moment and included $70 billion of renewable energy spending in the largest stimulus bill in fifty years.

The crash does not lessen the need for government action; it increases it. The need for a regulatory structure to right the imbalance between fossil and clean fuels remains as robust as ever. But the severe constriction of private capital means that only government can step in, and up, to the challenge.

## Seven: Failure Is an Option

What appeared to be a Cinderella story on page 124 of our book in the fall of 2007 almost came to a dead stop in the fall of 2008. We told the story of Imperium Renewables and how it revitalized the Grays Harbor community in Washington state, which it did, until unprecedented spikes in the costs of commodities drove the company into big layoffs and curtailment of operations.

Any business plan with large exposure to swings in commodity prices is vulnerable in times of commodity price volatility. So when the costs of Imperium's feedstocks took off like meteors in 2008, the company's whole strategy was thrown into a cocked hat. Seeing layoffs and work stoppages at what was a shining example of a new biofuels company was painful for the employees, the community, and those of us who cheered their success and that of their visionary leader, John Plaza.

But failure is an option, and in cutting-edge efforts like this one, it must be almost an expectation. This hiccup cannot be considered fatal to the cause for three reasons. First, as commodity prices inch back down, the operations of Imperium again will become tenable. Second,

Imperium already achieved a major success by providing the first bio-fuel for a commercial jet flight when Virgin Atlantic flew its 747 using Imperium's fuel on February 24, 2008. Third, in every failure can be found the seeds of success. The first time we met him, John Plaza told us about his long-term vision: The future may be in algae-based fuels.

That prescient observation is coming to fruition now in the deserts of New Mexico, where the Sapphire Energy company just started con-struction on its prototype plant to turn algae into light sweet crude. For years now, the great dream has been to find a way to use Mother Na-ture's photosynthetic process at its most elemental scale, using algae to convert sunlight into usable fuel. Now the Sapphire team, using a ge-netically modified algae cell, may have the world's most efficient means of doing just that.

Quite a number of companies are pursuing this holy grail of biofu-els, but Sapphire's prototype plant marks a new plateau of achievement for three reasons. First, Sapphire's plan is to use saltwater, in multi-acre shallow pools, as the growth medium for the algae. Avoiding the use of freshwater, the medium used by other companies, prevents this new fuel from having to compete with domestic uses of freshwater. Second, the robustness of its algae strain allows it to be grown without a roof over the ponds, a huge cost reducer. Third, Sapphire's algae is efficient enough that it does not need to be "fed" any sugars, greatly increasing its productivity overall.

Sapphire may well be providing the breakthrough technology the biofuels world has been waiting for. The Sapphire team has already mapped out where their ponds could be placed to help meet the na-tion's oil needs.

Or it could be a total bust over the long run. Other algae-based bio-fuels firms like Bionavartis, which has invented a way to feed light to al-gae, and Targeted Growth, may come to dominate the field. In the con-ventional biofuels field Imperium may go down as a brief bright light that faded. Or commodity prices may come down, allowing it to shine again. No one knows the future of these companies. We only know that failure is an option, because our country is blessed with talent that can pick up the torch and create growth out of the chaos of destruction.

## Eight: Prejudices Are Best Left at the Door

When it comes to clean energy, we all have our favorites. But the passage of the last year has demonstrated why freeing ourselves from our own prejudices is necessary to the success of this larger effort.

Take the cap-and-trade debate as an example. As time goes on, and the hard work of getting the votes to pass such legislation comes nearer, the necessity of accommodating diverse areas of the country becomes clearer. That is why the EMPLOY bill was introduced in March 26, 2009, a bill designed to accommodate the concerns of energy intensive industries about the costs of compliance with the cap-and-trade system.

For congressmen like Mike Doyle, the athletic and affable representative of the energy intensive industrial base in Pittsburgh, such a measure is critical to his support for a cap-and-trade bill. For his cosponsor, Congressman Inslee, from the high-tech area of Seattle, such a measure is not politically necessary. But everyone's prejudices, and everyone's parochial interests, are going to have to be reconciled if progress is to be made. The sooner this is realized, the sooner we will have a truly national response to this challenge.

The possibility of new nuclear technology similarly challenges our thinking. For years, many have written off nuclear energy as presenting unacceptable proliferation threats and waste concerns. But in a small lab in Bellevue, Washington, a highly respected team of engineers, powered by Bill Gates's investment, is designing a whole new type of nuclear reactor, one based on the principle of the "deflactor wave," an approach that if successful could reduce the waste stream from plants severalfold and almost eliminate the proliferation threat attendant to nuclear plants. It accomplishes these feats by using a system that produces fissionable material only in the reactor itself.

Bill Gates does not think our old image of dirty and dangerous reactors should stop this research. The challenge is too big to allow us the comfort of our individual prejudices.

## Nine: Clean Energy Will Be Powered by New Politics

New politics are bursting out all over. The recent dynamic in presidential politics mirrors exactly the pattern in clean-energy development. Clean energy will grow in a more distributed, less centralized pattern than the centralized, large energy plant system that now characterizes our grid. The proliferation of solar panels on our rooftops and the storage of electricity in our car batteries are emblematic of the decentralized systems of the future.

This decentralization was mirrored in the 2008 election of Barack Obama, when millions of people connected over the Web, and millions of dollars flowed in small increments into his campaign. Power flowed outward, and it flowed downward.

This political dynamic has hastened the development of decentralized energy in a most elegant way. We did not predict that a decentralized presidential campaign would produce that result, but that is what occurred. Similar changes are afoot internationally. When our first edition went to print, it was the developing nations that were dragging their feet in international discussions about how to reduce $CO_2$ emissions. But in December 2008 in Poland, it was the developing countries like Mexico and India that came to the table with new ideas about how to restrain emissions, leaving their rich cousins on the developed continent of Europe looking like pikers when they wanted to drag their feet.

Soon we in the developed world will no longer have inaction by the developing world as an excuse for our own. When that day comes, the New Politics of the international community will kick-start the world's effort—at last. Most important, when the United States acts domestically, it will deprive China and other countries of the excuse of our inaction to justify their own.

## Ten: No More Free Lunches

The nation is ready to stop the gravy train for those who have benefited from government by cronyism. After Enron, WorldCom, Bush administration corporate welfare, and the multiple abuses on Wall Street, the country is ready to call a halt to the giveaway of public assets to no public benefit. The country is ready to shift from a public policy that directs public assets to private fossil fuel companies to one by which polluters pay for the right to pollute and our tax policy favors innovation over exploitation.

Not only is the country ready for this switch, but Washington, D.C., is as well. In the White House is a leader who has already staked out a position in favor of auctioning off the permits to pollute under the cap-and-trade system. It is good to have him there, because this will be the biggest battle in 2009, with the fossil fuel industry seeking "handouts" of the permits, a sort of unstated "bailout" of these industries that have put their garbage into the atmosphere at no cost for decades.

It is our hope that the taxpayer, the citizen, wins this battle, because it is her atmosphere that is being despoiled by $CO_2$. It is the citizen who "owns" the limited ability of the atmosphere to carry $CO_2$. It is the citizen who will benefit from the research and development that can be funded by the billions of dollars that will be available if these permits are auctioned.

## The Sum of the Energy Enlightenments

As we see, we have come a long way since this book was first written. Technologies have blossomed, companies have come and gone, new leaders have been elected, and the fundamental reason for a new energy revolution has become more acute. But throughout that tumult, the worthiness and effectiveness of these principles seem to hold.

We now have a template for the next great adventure. It is well we do, because bold challenges demand bold action, something we as a nation have always been willing to take.

When Neil Armstrong and Buzz Aldrin stepped onto the lunar surface, they were confronted with a perplexing and troublesome phenomenon, the power of the lunar shadow. Shadows on earth are just a modest reduction in the light subject to a shadow. On the moon, they are inky black voids because there is virtually nothing in the atmosphere to scatter light back into the area of the shadow.

But in time their eyes adjusted, and they were successful in their mission. Armstrong reported to Houston, "It is very easy to see in the shadows after you adapt for a while." Our current vision of what a new energy world looks like will need some period of adaptation. We will adapt, however, by following those astronauts' footsteps. America is not a country destined to stay in the shadows of ancient energy. We are poised to lead the world into a brighter future.

Our country is also not one to shirk from bold challenges. The last man to walk on the moon, Gene Cernan, described the original Apollo Project with justified pride, "It was probably the greatest singular human endeavor, certainly in modern times, maybe in the history of all mankind."[1] The new Apollo Project may be of even greater import. It will create an energy system that allows life to continue on this planet as we know it. Wouldn't that be in the same league?

The Apollo astronauts all shared one indelible memory, one almost divine image, the stunning spectacle of the planet Earth suspended alone in the heavens, a warm blue planet amid the emptiness of space. Those who saw the blue home planet through the Plexiglas of an Apollo capsule all came home with a visceral understanding of our planet's uniqueness and the need to keep it healthy. Now we are ready to embark on a new adventure dedicated to caring for the thin tissue of atmosphere embracing that blue orb.

Our belief in our ability to accomplish this feat is intuitive, instinctive, and immediate, but it is also grounded in a sober assessment of the stakes and opportunities before us. Just after President Kennedy made his pronouncement to Congress that America was going to the moon in ten years, NASA administrator James Webb turned to his assistant

Bob Gilruth and asked, "Bob, can we do this?" Bob answered without a second's hesitation, "Yes. Absolutely! We have to."

Can we capture Apollo's fire and revolutionize the world of energy? Yes, absolutely. We have to.

# ACKNOWLEDGMENTS

Jay Inslee would like to send his thanks and acknowledgments to the talented and delightful Trudi Inslee for her wisdom, editing, and serenity in the eye of the storm; to Al and Tipper Gore for dedicating themselves to this generation's greatest challenge; to K. C. Golden, Patrick Mazza, and Blair Henry, comrades in arms whose ten years of toil is now paying off; to Todd Baldwin, whose patience and discipline guided a collection of ideas into a book; to Robin Simmons and Eric Lieu, whose ideas helped navigate the world of books; to Denis Hayes, whose Earth Day started the whole environmental shebang and set me off on a congressional mission for clean energy; to Congressman Earl Blumenauer, who both led the visionary efforts in Portland, Oregon, and helped us find the folks who could tell the tale; to Fred Horning for his grasp of entrepreneurship in the utility industry; to the comedy team of Jack, Megan, Connor, and Joe, whose wit kept my feet on the ground; to President Bill Clinton for his leadership and for a great foreword and to Jan Hartke for all his help; to Tom Campion for all his work and assistance; to my friend and colleague Bracken Hendricks, whose sense of optimism launched this book and whose diligence and masterful policy acumen saw it through to completion; to my friends, neighbors, colleagues, Hoopaholics, Team Brian, passersby, and other victims whose innumerable insights, advice, and gentle yet harpooning criticisms kept the project on track; and to You, whom we hope will take something from these pages and spread a new energy future round the world.

Bracken Hendricks would like to extend his grateful acknowledgments to Alice, Galen, and Clea for supporting the writing of the book in innumerable ways; to Chuck Savitt and Todd Baldwin for helping bring this idea to reality; to Leo Gerard and the United Steel Workers and Carl Pope and the Sierra Club, without whose early embrace the Apollo Alliance would have remained only a good idea; to all those who took a risk on the idea that clean energy could mean good jobs, especially the leaders of the AFL-CIO, John Sweeney, Rich Trumka, Brad Burton, Bob Baugh, and Gerry Shea, and Cecil Roberts and Bill Banig of the United Mine Workers of America; to the cofounders of the Apollo Alliance; to Dan Carol, who recognized the need for an Apollo book and without whose suggestions and encouragement I would never have ventured to write this volume and without whose partnership and vision the Apollo Alliance would not have been born; to Bob Borosage and the Institute for America's Future, who gave Apollo not only a sharp focus on national policy, but also a home, care and feeding, and the support it needed to grow; to Joel Rogers and the Center on Wisconsin Strategy, who brought to bear a keen intelligence on regional issues and high-road metropolitan development that grounded Apollo in building strong communities; to Michael Shellenberger, Adam Werbach, and Ted Nordhaus, who from the beginning dug deep into understanding the construction of message and deeply held values, and who have been a resource in rethinking both policy and politics; to all those who have funded the Apollo Alliance, especially Lance Lindblom and Peter Teague of the Nathan Cummings Foundation, who have been among its strongest supporters, and Hal Harvey of the Hewlett Foundation and Tim Wirth and Reid Detchon of the United Nations Better World Fund, who were among its first; to my colleagues at the Center for American Progress, John Podesta for supporting bold experiments, Melody Barnes, Ana Unruh Cohen for her insights and clear thinking, and Benjamin Goldstein and Kari Manlove for their hard work and dedication as we researched and revised these chapters;

special thanks to the Wallace Global Fund, Melissa Dann, and the Wallace Family for their support; to members of the National Steering Committee of the Apollo Alliance, Ruben Aronin, Andrew Beebe, Bruce Hamilton, Bill Holmberg, Van Jones, Mindy Lubber, Mark Ritchie, and Marco Trbovich, who have generously given their time, energy, and creativity to this work; to the team at Apollo today; to Jerome Ringo, a visionary leader; to Jeff Rickert and Brian Siu, who built something out of nothing; to Dan Seligman, Carla Din, Jeremy Hays, Bill Holland, Joanne Derwin, Richard Eidlin, and Rich Feldman, who spin careful policy and build the coalitions to turn it into action; to Ragini Kapadia and Skye Perryman, who have held it all together; to Jay and Trudi for being such good partners and so much fun to work with; to my dearest friends and family Matt Lindemulder, Suchi Swift, Geoff Nazarro, Tyche Hendricks, Paul Muniz, Bob and Joan Welsh, Aurora Hendricks and Morgan Grundy, and Patricia Barrett, who took the kids on long walks while Dad stayed home to write; and to my parents, Geoff and Nye, whose love has made all the difference.

# NOTES

## INTRODUCTION

1. *National Geographic News*, December 19, 2008
2. Devin Powell, "Arctic Melt 20 Years Ahead of Climate Models," *New Scientist*, Environment Section, December 19, 2008, http://www.newscientist .com/article/dn16307-arctic-melt-20-years-ahead-of-climate-models .html.
3. *RealClimate*, http://www.realclimate.org/, January 2007.
4. Winston Churchill, May 13, 1940, "Blood, Toil, Tears and Sweat," *Modern History Sourcebook*, http://www.fordham.edu/halsall/mod/churchill-blood .html.

## PREAMBLE

1. President John F. Kennedy,_"Special Message to the Congress on Urgent National Needs," May 25, 1961, http://www.jfklibrary.org/Historical+ Resources/Archives/Reference+Desk/Speeches/JFK/Urgent+National+ Needs+Page+4.htm.
2. President John F. Kennedy, "Address at Rice University on the Nation's Space Effort," Houston, Texas, September 12, 1962, http://www.jfklibrary .org/Historical+Resources/Archives/Reference+Desk/Speeches/JFK/00 3POF03SpaceEffort09121962.htm.
3. President John F. Kennedy, "Inaugural Address," Washington, D.C., January 20, 1961, http://www.jfklibrary.org/Historical+Resources/Archives/ Reference+Desk/Speeches/JFK/003POF03Inaugura101201961.htm.

## CHAPTER 1

1. The Apollo space program invested on average over $18 billion per year in 2005 dollars, or a total of $165 billion spread over nine years in project costs; "NASA Exploration Systems Architecture Study" (p. 682), November 2005, nasa.gov/pdf/140649main_esas_full.pdf.

2. Ben Vigil, "What Microsoft gets for its $7B R&D budget," Search-Exchange.com, June 10, 2004, http://searchexchange.techtarget.com/originalContent/0,289142,sid43_gci969606,00.html.

3. "Cleaning Up," *Economist*, May 31, 2007. Independently substantiated by Steve Wright, director, Bonneville Power Administration, Portland, Oregon.

4. All quotes pertaining to the Marshall Islands are from an interview with Essay Note, president, November 2006.

5. Intergovernmental Panel on Climate Change (IPCC), *Climate Change 2001: The Scientific Basis*, "3.3.1 Geological History of Atmospheric $CO_2$," 2001, http://www.grida.no/climate/ipcc_tar/wg1/107.htm#331.

6. The data in this paragraph is from two sources: James Hansen, Makiko Sato, Reto Ruedy, Ken Lo, David W. Lea, and Martin Medina-Elizade, "Global Temperature Change," *Proceedings of the National Academy of Sciences*, September 26, 2006; and IPCC, *Climate Change 2007: The Physical Science Basis*, "Summary for Policymakers," 2007, http://www.ipcc.ch/SPM2feb07.pdf.

7. Numbers are converted from Celsius best estimates of the low-emissions scenario (1.8°C) and high-emissions scenario (4.0°C) in IPCC, *Climate Change 2007: The Physical Science Basis*, "Summary for Policymakers," 2007, 10.

8. Naomi Oreskes, "Beyond the Ivory Tower: The Scientific Consensus on Climate Change," *Science* 306, no. 5702 (December 3, 2004): 1686, http://www.sciencemag.org/cgi/content/full/306/5702/1686.

9. Jeffrey Ball, "Exxon Mobil softens its climate-change stance," *Wall Street Journal*, January 11, 2007, http://www.post-gazette.com/pg/07011/753072-28.stm.

10. Interview with Joe Romm, December 2006.

11. G. Marland, T. A. Boden, and R. J. Andres, "Global, Regional, and National $CO_2$ Emissions," *Trends: A Compendium of Data on Global Change*, Carbon Dioxide Information Analysis Center, Oak Ridge National Laboratory, U.S. Department of Energy, Oak Ridge, Tennessee, 2006, http://cdiac.esd.ornl.gov/trends/emis/tre_usa.htm.

12. "National Carbon Dioxide ($CO_2$) Emissions per Capita," *Vital Climate Change Graphics Update*, UNEP/GRID-Arendal Library of Graphics Re-

sources, 2005, http://maps.grida.no/go/graphic/national_carbon_dioxide _co2_emissions_per_capita.

13. All quotes from Dr. Bitz are from an interview in December 2006.

14. For more information, see the World Bank working paper "The Impact of Sea Level Rise on Developing Countries: A Comparative Analysis," Jianping Yan, David Wheeler, Craig Meisner, Benoit Laplante, and Susmita Dasgupta, February 1, 2007, which concludes that just one meter of sea level rise would result in at least 56 million refugees; http://econ.world bank.org/external/default/main?pagePK=64165259&piPK=64165421& theSitePK=469372&menuPK=64216926&entityID=000016406_200702 09161430.

15. All quotes regarding Shishmaref, Alaska, are from an interview with Tony Weyiouanna, Inupiat transportation director, and Luci Eningowuk, chairperson of the Shishmaref Erosion and Relocation Coalition, January 2007.

16. All quotes from Ogden Driskill are from an interview at Camp Stool Ranch, Wyoming, December 2006.

17. Interview with Brad Rippee, agricultural meteorologist, U.S. Department of Agriculture, December 2006.

18. Interview with Corey Moffet, rangeland specialist, U.S. Department of Agriculture, December 2006.

19. Ron Stodghill II, "Pump Up the Volume," *CNN.com* and *Time*, June 26, 2000, http://www.cnn.com/ALLPOLITICS/time/2000/06/26/pump .html.

20. "U.S. Crude Oil Supply & Disposition," Energy Information Administration, updated continually, http://tonto.eia.doe.gov/dnav/pet/pet_sum_ crdsnd_adc_mbblpd_a.htm; see also "International Petroleum (Oil) Consumption," Energy Information Administration, n.d., http://www.eia.doe .gov/emeu/international/oilconsumption.html, and "Table 5.3, Petroleum Imports by Type, Selected Years, 1949–2005," tables 5.1 and 5.3, *EIA Annual Energy Review*, 2005, http://www.eia.doe.gov/emeu/aer/pdf/pages/ sec5_9.pdf.

21. The United States spent $39.3 billion on Persian Gulf oil imports, according to the U.S. Energy Information Agency, http://www.eia.doe.gov/ emeu/aer/txt/ptb0520.html.

22. All Woolsey quotes are from interviews in December 2006.

23. David L. Greene and Nataliya Tishchishnya, "Costs of Oil Dependence: A 2000 Update," Oak Ridge National Laboratory (prepared for the U.S. Department of Energy), December 2000, http://www.esd.ornl.gov/ benefits_conference/oilcost_tq.pdf.

24. Michael T. Klare, "Oil Wars: Transforming the American Military into a

Global Oil-Protection Service," *TomDispatch.com*, October 8, 2004, http://www.commondreams.org/views04/1008-23.htm.

25. Iraq has the world's second-largest proven reserves of oil, according to the *BP Statistical Review of World Energy*, 1996, cited in *Oil: A Natural Resource* (Institute of Petroleum, online), http://www.energyinst.org.uk/education/natural/3.htm.

26. Thomas L. Friedman, "The First Law of Petropolitics," *Foreign Policy*, May/June 2006, http://www.foreignpolicy.com/story/cms.php?story_id=3426.

27. Energy Information Administration, "International Energy Outlook 2006," Table 3: "World Oil Reserves by Country as of January 1, 2006," June 2006, http://www.eia.doe.gov/oiaf/ieo/oil.html.

28. World Resources Institute, "Transportation: Passenger Cars per 1000 People," *EarthTrends*, http://earthtrends.wri.org/searchable_db/index.php?theme=6&variable_ID=290&action=select_countries.

29. Jad Mouawad, "Once Marginal, Now Kings of the World," *New York Times*, April 23, 2006.

30. Energy Information Administration, "International Energy Outlook 2007," Appendix A: "Reference Case Projections," May 2007, http://www.eia.doe.gov/oiaf/ieo/pdf/ieorefcase.pdf.

31. America spends over $200,000 a minute, or $13 million per hour, on imported oil, based on 2003 import numbers; Natural Resources Defense Council, "Safe, Strong, and Secure: Reducing America's Oil Dependence," http://www.nrdc.org/air/transportation/aoilpolicy2.asp.

32. "U.S. Trade Deficit Soars to Record, Reflecting Higher Oil Bill," *International Herald Tribune*, December 15, 2006, http://www.iht.com/articles/ap/2006/12/19/america/NA_FIN_US_Economy.php.

33. Michele Cavallo, "Oil Prices and the U.S. Trade Deficit," Federal Reserve Bank of San Francisco Economic Letter, September 22, 2006, http://www.frbsf.org/publications/economics/letter/2006/el2006-24.html.

34. Speech by Leo Gerard at the Apollo Alliance State Leadership for a New Energy Future Press Conference, National Press Club, Washington, D.C., December 8, 2006.

35. U.S. Department of Labor, Bureau of Labor Statistics, "Current Employment Statistics Survey, 2006," http://www.bls.gov/ces/home.htm; see also L. Josh Bivens, "Trade Deficits and Manufacturing Employment," *Economic Snapshots*, Economic Policy Institute, November 20, 2005, https://www.epi.org/content.cfm/webfeatures_snapshots_20051130.

36. Bureau of Economic Analysis, National Income and Products Accounts, Table 1.14, 2006, http://www.bea.gov/bea/dn/nipaweb/index.asp.

37. U.S. Census Bureau, "Income, Poverty, and Health Insurance Coverage in the United States: 2005," http://www.census.gov/hhes/www/income/income.html.

38. Janet L. Sawin et al., *American Energy: the Renewable Path to Energy Security*, Worldwatch Institute and Center for American Progress, September 2006, http://images1.americanprogress.org/i180web20037/american energynow/AmericanEnergy.pdf.

39. David Morris, "Energizing Rural America," Center for American Progress, January 19, 2007, http://www.americanprogress.org/issues/2007/01/rural _energy.html.

40. "U.S. Metro Economies: Energy Costs: Impact on U.S. Household Budgets," report prepared for the U.S. Conference of Mayors and the Council for the New American City Global Insight, January 2007, http://www.usmayors.org/metroeconomies/0107/Energyreport.pdf.

41. Apollo Alliance, "New Energy for America: Apollo Jobs Report," January 2004, http://www.apolloalliance.org/docUploads/ApolloReport%5F022404%5F122748%2Epdf.

42. Burton C. English et al., "25% Renewable Energy for the United States by 2025: Agricultural and Economic Impacts," University of Tennessee, Department of Agricultural Economics, November 2006.

43. John M. Urbanchuk, "Contribution of the Ethanol Industry to the Economy of the United States" (prepared for the Renewable Fuels Association), February 21, 2006, http://www.ethanolrfa.org/objects/documents/576/economic_contribution_2006.pdf.

44. Sir Nicholas Stern, *The Stern Review: The Economics of Climate Change* (Cambridge: Cambridge University Press, October 2006), http://www.hm-treasury.gov.uk/independent_reviews/stern_review_economics_climate_change/stern_review_report.cfm.

45. International Energy Agency, "The World Energy Outlook 2006 Maps Out a Cleaner, Cleverer and More Competitive Energy Future," press release, November 6, 2006, http://www.iea.org/Textbase/press/pressdetail.asp?PRESS_REL_ID=187.

46. Winston Churchill, *World Crisis*, vol. 1 (London: Thornton Butterworth, 1923).

## TEN ENERGY ENLIGHTENMENTS

1. International Center for Technology Assessment, "Gasoline Cost Externalities: Security and Protection Services," January 25, 2005, 4, http://www.icta.org/doc/RPG%20security%20update.pdf.

## CHAPTER 2

1. All quotations and references to the CalCars initiative are drawn from interviews with Felix Kramer, November–December 2006.
2. Interview with Roger Duncan, Austin Energy, November 2006.
3. Interview with Tom and Ray Magliozzi, *Car Talk*, January 2007.
4. Interviews with Lynn Hinkle, November–December 2006.
5. Sarah A. Webster, "Auto Industry, Detroit at New Low," *Detriot Free Press*, November 21, 2005.
6. Ibid.
7. Office of Aerospace and Automotive Industries, International Trade Administration, U.S. Department of Commerce, "The Road Ahead for the U.S. Auto Industry," April 2006, http://www.ita.doc.gov/td/auto/domestic/roadahead06.pdf.
8. Micheline Maynard, "Ford Eliminating Up to 30,000 Jobs and 14 Factories," *New York Times*, January 24, 2006.
9. "A weary Detroit wonders where it all went wrong," *Salt Lake Tribune*, November 22, 2005, http://www.americaneconomicalert.org/news_home.asp?NTID=17.
10. Union of Concerned Scientists, "Automaker Rankings 2007," http://www.ucsusa.org/assets/documents/clean_vehicles/autorank_brochure_2007.pdf.
11. "Detroit's Answer to $3–$4 Gas: New Muscle Cars," *New York Times*, August 10, 2006.
12. Interview with Mike Walsh, December 2006.
13. Chelsea Sexton, "Why I Think GM Killed the EV1," *EV World*, July 15, 2005, http://www.evworld.com/article.cfm?storyid=875.
14. Walter McManus, "Can Proactive Fuel Economy Strategies Help Automakers Mitigate Fuel-Price Risks?" Office for the Study of Automotive Transportation, University of Michigan Transportation Research Institute, 2006, http://www.osat.umich.edu/research/economic/articles.php.
15. Interview with Walter McManus, University of Michigan, December 2006.
16. Walter S. McManus, Alan Baum, Roland Hwang, Daniel D. Luria, and Gautam Barua, "In the Tank: How Oil Prices Threaten Automakers' Profits and Jobs," Office for the Study of Automotive Transportation, University of Michigan Transportation Research Institute, and Natural Resources Defense Council, July 2005, http://www.nrdc.org/air/transportation/inthetank/inthetank.pdf.
17. Walter McManus, "Can Proactive Fuel Economy Strategies Help Automakers Mitigate Fuel-Price Risks?" Office for the Study of Automotive

Transportation, University of Michigan Transportation Research Institute, 2006, http://www.osat.umich.edu/research/economic/articles.php.

18. Lee Hudson Teslik, "The Global Auto Industry," Council on Foreign Relations, March 2, 2007, http://www.cfr.org/publication/12764/global_auto_industry.html.

19. Bracken Hendricks et al., "Competitiveness, Accountability and Innovation: Health Care for Hybrids," Center for American Progress, Washington, D.C., February 2006, http://www.americanprogress.org/projects/15new ideas/healthcarehybrids.html.

20. Barack Obama and Jay Inslee, "Salvaging the Auto Industry," February 8, 2006, http://obama.senate.gov/blog/060208-salvaging_the_auto_industry/index.html.

21. Information on Chinese market trends, "Autos Insider," *Detroit News*, November 30, 2006, detnews.com.

22. Duncan Austin, Niki Rosinski, Amanda Sauer, and Colin le Duc, "Changing Drivers: The Impact of Climate Change on Competitiveness and Value Creation in the Automotive Industry," Sustainable Asset Management and World Resources Institute, 2003, http://pdf.wri.org/changing_drivers_full_report.pdf.

23. Ibid.

24. Rick Wagoner, speech at Greater Los Angeles Auto Show, November 29, 2006, http://www.gm.com/company/gmability/adv_tech/100_news/speeches/wagoner-show-122006.html.

25. "Plug-In Saturn VUE will Deliver 70 MPG," SaturnFans.com, December 3, 2006. http://www.saturnfans.com/Cars/Future/pluginvue70mpg.shtml.

26. Chris Woodyard, "Saturn Hybrid Gets Plugged In," *USA Today*, November 30, 2006, http://www.usatoday.com/money/autos/2006-11-29-electric-saturn_x.htm.

27. Interviews with Felix Kramer, November/December 2006.

28. Rick Wagoner, speech at Greater Los Angeles Auto Show, November 29, 2006, http://www.gm.com/company/gmability/adv_tech/100_news/speeches/wagoner-show-122006.html.

29. Sharon Terlep, "GM Plugs into Green Theme," *Detroit News*, November 30, 2006, http://www.detnews.com/apps/pbcs.dll/article?AID=/20061130/AUTO04/611300352/1148.

30. Daniel B. Wood, "On road to clean fuels, automakers cover some ground," *Christian Science Monitor*, December 1, 2006, http://www.csmonitor.com/2006/1201/p01s03-stct.html.

31. Interview with Charles Griffith, December 2006.

32. Green Machines Tour, "New UAW-Environmental Partnership Showcases

Fuel-Efficient Vehicle Technologies_Made in Southeast Michigan," press release, June 24, 2005, http://www.greenmachinestour.org/20050624 region1A.shtml.

33. Green Machines Tour, "Fuel-Efficient Technologies Built by UAW Members in Southeast Michigan," fact sheet, http://www.greenmachinestour .org/factsheet_1A.pdf.

34. Green Machines Tour, "Michigan Labor Unions and Environmentalists Unite for Energy Independence," press release, June 29, 2006, http://www .greenmachinestour.org/20060629MIapolloalliance.shtml.

35. Joseph Szczesny, "3 Automakers Work Together on Hybrids," *Oakland Press*, September 29, 2006, http://www.theoaklandpress.com/stories/092906/ loc_2006092927.shtml.

36. Interview with Amory Lovins, December 2006.

37. Ibid.

38. Amory B. Lovins, "Guest Editorial: Reinventing the Wheels," *Environmental Health Perspectives*, April 2005, http://www.pubmedcentral.nih.gov/ articlerender.fcgi?artid=1278496.

39. Interview with Tadge Juechter, assistant chief engineer of Chevrolet, December 2006.

40. Ben Stewart, "100 MPG Available Now!" *Popular Mechanics*, July 18, 2006, http://www.popularmechanics.com/automotive/how_to/3374271.html? page=3.

41. Ibid.

42. Interview with Anne Korin, IAGS, December 2006.

43. Ibid.

44. Kevin Bullis, "Powering GM's Electric Vehicles," *Technology Review*, January 11, 2007, http://www.techreview.com/printer_friendly_article.aspx?id= 18054.

45. Interview with David Vieau, CEO, A123 Battery, December 2006.

46. Interview with Peter Norman, EnergyCS, December 2006.

47. Interview with President Jimmy Carter, November 2006.

48. Interview with Byron McCormick, General Motors, December 2006.

49. Interview with Lawrence Burns, vice president of research, GM, December 2006.

50. Interview with Ben Knight, vice president of research, Honda, December 2006.

51. Interview with Joe Romm, Center for American Progress, December 2006.

## BECOMING MAHATMA

1. All quotes are from an interview with Mike Towne, Redmond, Washington, November 2006.

## CHAPTER 3

1. Energy Information Administration, "International Energy Outlook 2006," June 2006, 145, http://www.eia.doe.gov/oiaf/ieo/pdf/0484(2006).pdf.
2. Interview with Sara Wise, November 2006.
3. China's Renewable Energy Law went into effect January 1, 2006.
4. M. Rogol, *Sun Screen: Investment Opportunities in Solar Power*, CLSA Asia-Pacific Markets, July 2004; also available at Clean Edge, "Clean-Energy Trends 2007," http://www.cleanedge.com/reports-trends2007.php.
5. Solar Energy Industries Association, "Our Solar Power Future," http://www.seia.org/roadmap.pdf; Janet L. Sawin et al., *American Energy: the Renewable Path to Energy Security*, Worldwatch Institute and Center for American Progress, September 2006, http://images1.americanprogress.org/i180web20037/americanenergynow/AmericanEnergy.pdf.
6. Curtis Moore and Jack Ihle, "Renewable Energy Policy Outside the United States," Renewable Energy Policy Project, Issue Brief no. 14 (October 1999), 21, http://www.crest.org/repp_pubs/pdf/REPOutUS.pdf.
7. All quotes from Dr. Blieden are from an interview in November 2006.
8. Tom Abate, "Solar Energy's Cloudy Past," *San Francisco Chronicle*, February 16, 2004, http://www.sfgate.com/cgi-bin/article.cgi?f=/c/a/2004/02/16/BUGHM512D61.DTL.
9. Interview with Dr. Richard Blieden, November 2006.
10. SolarBuzz, "Solar Energy Industry Statistics: Growth," http://www.solarbuzz.com/StatsGrowth.htm.
11. Interview with Brian Sager, November 2006.
12. All quotes from Martin Roscheisen are from an interview in November 2006.
13. SolarBuzz, "Annual World Solar Photovoltaic Industry Report," March 19, 2007, http://www.solarbuzz.com/Marketbuzz2007-intro.htm.
14. Ibid.
15. Andrew Revkin, "The Energy Challenge: Budgets Falling in Race to Fight Global Warming," *New York Times*, October 30, 2006.
16. Solar Energy Industry Association, "The Solar Photovoltaic Industry in 2006," http://www.hurricanerelief.dupont.com/Photovoltaics/en_US/assets/downloads/pdf/SEIA_StateofSolarIndustry2006.pdf.
17. REN21 Renewable Energy Policy Network, "Energy for Development: The Potential Role of Renewable Energy in Meeting Millennium Development Goals" (Washington, D.C.: Worldwatch Institute, 2005).
18. U.S. Department of Energy, Energy Efficiency and Renewable Energy, Solar Energy Technologies Program, "Learning about PV: Quick Facts," January 2006, http://www1.eere.energy.gov/solar/pv_quick_facts.html#8;

Solarbuzz, "Fast Solar Energy Facts," http://www.solarbuzz.com/Fast-FactsIndustry.htm.

19. Information on Neville Williams is drawn from Neville Williams, *Chasing the Sun: Solar Adventures Around the World* (Gabriola Island, B.C., Canada: New Society Publishers, 2005); also from http://www.self.org/index.asp.

20. Information on EI Solutions, the Google installation, and Sunflower technology is from an interview with Andrew Beebe, November 2006, and supporting documentation at the EI Solutions website, http://www.eispv.com/success_stories/google.html.

21. Information on the Google solar installation carbon emission reductions is from Treehugger, http://www.treehugger.com/files/2006/10/google_ends_sea.php.

22. SunPower cell conversion efficiency is between 20 percent and 21.5 percent; see http://www.sunpowercorp.com/about_us/technology.html.

23. Interview with Dr. Richard Swanson, SunPower, November 2006.

24. SunPower Corporation, "SunPower Reports Third Quarter 2006 Results," press release, October 19, 2006, http://investors.sunpowercorp.com/releasedetail.cfm?ReleaseID=215226.

25. Interview with Dr. Richard Swanson, November 2006.

26. Potential efficiencies from new RoseStreet Labs solar technology of 48 percent are from "RoseStreet Labs and Sumitomo Chemical Announce Joint Venture for Full Spectrum Solar Cells," press release, October 26, 2006, http://rosestreetlabs.com/RSL%20Sumitomo%20Final.pdf.

27. According to the Department of Energy, Energy Information Agency, 7 percent of energy typically is lost in transmission alone. Traditional power plants have further inefficiencies, losing from 40 percent to over 60 percent of potential energy in the conversion of fuels to electricity; Energy Information Administration, "Voluntary Reporting of Greenhouse Gases 2004," March 2006, http://www.eia.doe.gov/oiaf/1605/vr04data/epdt.html.

28. City of Chico, "City of Chico Dedicates World's Largest Solar Tracking Array at Water Pollution Control Plant," press release, October 27, 2006, http://www.ci.chico.ca.us/pubworks/Solar_Facilities_Information/Press_Release.pdf.

29. Clean Edge, "Clean-Energy Trends 2007," http://www.cleanedge.com/reports-trends2007.php.

30. Gregory Dicum, "Plugging Into the Sun" *New York Times*, January 4, 2007, http://www.nytimes.com/2007/01/04/garden/04solar.html?ex=1325566800en=fb9bacabf5d55868ei=5088partner=rssnytemc=rss.

31. R. K. Schwer and M. Riddel, "The Potential Economic Impact of Constructing and Operating Solar Power Generation Facilities in Nevada," U.S.

Department of Energy Laboratory, National Renewable Energy Laboratory, February 2004, http://www.nrel.gov/csp/pdfs/35037.pdf.

32. Pacific Gas and Electric Company, "PG&E Announces Significant New Green Power," press release, August 10, 2006, http://www.pge.com/news/news_releases/q3_2006/060810.html.

33. Interview with Scott Sklar. November 2006.

34. Ibid.

## WHEN ENERGY MARKETS GO WRONG: SURVIVING ENRON

1. Joel Connelly, "In the Northwest: Enron's Real Obscenity Is Continuing Cost of 'Crisis,'" *Seattle Post-Intelligencer*, June 9, 2004, http://seattlepi.nwsource.com/connelly/176931_joe109.html.

## CHAPTER 4

1. Gene Johnson, "Utility: Enron Gouged Western Customers," *Salon.com*, June 14, 2004, http://dir.salon.com/story/tech/wire/2004/06/14/enron/index.html.

2. Richard Benedetto, "Cheney's Energy Plan Focuses on Production," *USA Today*, May 1, 2001, http://www.usatoday.com/news/washington/2001-05-01-cheney-usat.htm.

3. It is a commonly cited statistic that incandescent bulbs waste 90 percent of the energy used to produce light, in the form of waste heat; see, for example, http://oee.nrcan.gc.ca/energystar/english/consumers/pamphlet.cfm?text=N&printview=N.

4. Craig Canine, "California Illuminates the World," *OnEarth*, Spring 2006, http://www.nrdc.org/onearth/06spr/ca1.asp.

5. Ibid.

6. Ibid.

7. Interview with Dave Moore, Vulcan Company.

8. www.earthtrends.wri.org/text/energy-resources/variable-574.html    for figures on Europe and US; and http://energyalmanac.ca.gov/electricity/us_per_capita_electricity_2005.html for figures on California.

9. Total revenue from retail electricity sales to utility customers in all sectors for 2005 was $298 billion, according to the U.S. Energy Information Administration; see http://www.eia.doe.gov/cneaf/electricity/epa/epat7p3.html.

10. Joseph Romm, *Hell and High Water* (New York: William Morrow, 2007), p. 160.

11. Janet L. Sawin et al., *American Energy: The Renewable Path to Energy Security*,

Worldwatch Institute and Center for American Progress, September 2006, p. 21, http://images1.americanprogress.org/i180web20037/american energynow/AmericanEnergy.pdf.

12. Ibid.

13. In 2005, energy savings from active measures reduced Seattle City Light's system load by 10 percent (970,249 megawatt-hours), enough to power 109,000 homes for that year; Seattle City Light, "Annual Report 2005," http://www.seattle.gov/light/AboutUs/AnnualReport/2005/.

14. Bill Prindle, "How Energy Efficiency Can Turn 1300 Power Plants into 170," Alliance to Save Energy, Fact Sheet, May 31, 2001, http://www .repp.org/articles/static/1/991345218_982762890.html.

15. "Dow Supports National Action Plan for Energy Efficiency," *WebWire*, July 31, 2006, http://www.webwire.com/ViewPressRel.asp?aId=17640.

16. Dow News Center, "Dow Named 2006 'Galaxy Star of Energy Efficiency' by Alliance to Save Energy," June 19, 2006, http://news.dow.com/dow_ news/corporate/2006/20060619d.htm.

17. Dow News Center, "Liveris Announces 2015 Sustainability Goals for Dow," May 3, 2006, http://news.dow.com/corporate/2006/20060503b .htm.

18. "Dow Supports National Action Plan for Energy Efficiency," *WebWire*, July 31, 2006, http://www.webwire.com/ViewPressRel.asp?aId=17640.

19. Dow News Center, "Dow Energy Efficiency Highlighted at 2006 Texas Technology Showcase," December 7, 2006, http://news.dow.com/ corporate/2006/20061207a.htm.

20. Alliance to Save Energy, "Industry Leaders Interview: Dow CEO Andrew Liveris," *e-FFICIENCY News*, March 2006, reprinted by GreenBiz.com, http://www.greenbiz.com/news/reviews_third.cfm?NewsID=30613.

21. Becky Brun, "Renewable Energy Makes Priority List," *Northwest Energy News and Analysis*, September 26, 2006, http://www.nwcurrent.com/ efficiency/3964641.html.

22. "Dark Days for Energy Efficiency," *Business Week*, May 1, 2006, http:// www.businessweek.com/magazine/content/06_18/b3982090.htm.

23. Ibid.

24. Ibid.

25. 3M, "Improving Energy Efficiency," http://solutions.3m.com/wps/por- tal/3M/en_US/global/sustainability/s/performance- indicators/environment/energy-efficiency/.

26. Alliance to Save Energy, "Industry Leaders Interview: Christine McEntee," *e-FFICIENCY News*, n.d., http://www.ase.org/content/article/detail/ 3520.

27. Kenneth Gillingham, Richard Newell, and Karen Palmer, "The Effectiveness and Cost of Energy Efficiency Programs," *Resources* (Resources for the Future; Fall 2004), 22–25.
28. Interview with Steve Wright, Bonneville Power Administration, January 2007.
29. All quotes are from an interview with Carlton Brown, Full Spectrum New York, January 2007.
30. Kenneth Gillingham, Richard Newell, and Karen Palmer, "The Effectiveness and Cost of Energy Efficiency Programs," *Resources* (Resources for the Future; Fall 2004), 22–25.

## GREEN COLLAR JOBS: FROM THE SOUTH BRONX TO OAKLAND

1. Interview with Majora Carter, executive director, Sustainable South Bronx, January 2007.
2. Management Information Services, Inc., "Jobs Creation in the Environmental Industry in the U.S. and Nine States," April 2006, http://www.misi-net.com/publications/9-state-synthesis-0406.pdf.
3. Interview with Van Jones, executive director, Ella Baker Center for Human Rights, February 2007.

## CHAPTER 5

1. American Society of Civil Engineers, "Report Card for America's Infrastructure," 2005, p. 3, http://www.asce.org/files/pdf/reportcard/2005reportcardpdf.pdf.
2. American Society of Civil Engineers, "2003 Progress Report," http://www.asce.org/reportcard/index.cfm?reaction=full&page=6.
3. Quotations on metropolitan high-road economic development from interview with Joel Rogers, Center on Wisconsin Strategy/Apollo Alliance, January 2007.
4. Clean Edge, "Clean-Energy Trends 2007," http://www.cleanedge.com/reports-trends2007.php.
5. According to the 2000 U.S. Census, 225,956,060 people, or 79.219 percent of the population, live in urban areas; see "Census 2000 Population Statistics" (U.S. Department of Transportation, Federal Highway Administration), http://www.fhwa.dot.gov/planning/census/cps2k.htm.
6. John DeCicco and Freda Fung, "Global Warming on the Road" (Environmental Defense), http://www.environmentaldefense.org/documents/5301_Globalwarmingontheroad.pdf.

7. Background information on the Portland TriMet public transportation system comes from an interview with Rick Gustafson, former director of TriMet. November 2006.

8. Portland Development Commission, "Portland Area QuickFacts," http://www.pdc.us/bus_serv/facts-quick.asp.

9. Interview with Rick Gustafson, former director of Portland TriMet, November 2006.

10. Interview with Fred Hansen, TriMet general manager, November 2006.

11. "Slicker Cities," *Business Week*, August 21, 2006, http://www.businessweek.com/magazine/content/06_34/b3998442.htm.

12. Ibid.

13. Interview with Gary Nelson, Grays Harbor port commissioner, November 2006.

14. Interview with John Plaza, Imperium Renewables, November 2006.

15. All quotes on Newark reconstruction are from an interview with Baye Adofo-Wilson, executive director, Lincoln Park/Coast Cultural District, November 2006.

16. Chicago Department of Environment, "Monitoring the Rooftop Garden's Benefits: Data Comparison Between the City Hall Rooftop Garden and the Black Tar Roof of the Cook County Building," egov.cityofchicago.org.

17. Detailed analysis of Chicago City Hall green roof temperature impacts is available at "Building Healthy, Smart, and Green: Chicago's Green Building Agenda 2005," http://egov.cityofchicago.org/webportal/COCWebPortal/COC_EDITORIAL/BHSGAgenda_1.pdf.

18. Interview with Sadhu Johnston, Chicago secretary of the environment, November 2006. Additional information on Chicago green roofs from report prepared by MWH (for Chicago Department of the Environment), "Green Roof Test Plot: 2003 End of Year Project Summary Report," February 2004, http://egov.cityofchicago.org/webportal/COCWebPortal/COC_ATTACH/2003GreenRoofReport.pdf.

19. April Smith, "Building Momentum: National Trends and Prospects for High-Performance Green Buildings," U.S. Green Building Council, February 2003, http://www.usgbc.org/Docs/Resources/043003_hpgb_whitepaper.pdf.

20. Quotes on Mountaintop removal from an interview with Julia Bonds, Marsh Fork, West Virginia, November 2006.

21. Ken Ward Jr., "Mountaintop Removal Battle Continues," *Charleston Gazette*, February 19, 2006, http://www.appalachian-center.org/media/2006/02_19.html.

22. Ibid.

23. Minnesota House of Representatives, "The Ethanol Industry in Minnesota," House Research, September 2006, http://www.house.leg.state .mn.us/hrd/issinfo/ssethnl.htm.

24. City of Benson, "History of Benson, MN Area," http://www.bensonmn .org/home/history.html.

25. Facts on Benson, Minnesota, Ethanol Cooperative from an interview with Bill Lee, plant manager of Chippewa Valley Ethanol Company, November 2006.

26. Facts on Luverne, Minnesota, Ethanol Cooperative and Minwind Energy from an interview with Dave Kolsrud, CEO, CORN-er Stone Ethanol Cooperative, November 2006.

27. Ibid.

28. President Thomas Jefferson in a letter to James Madison dated October 28, 1785.

## "We Don't Need Oil"

1. All quotations are from a meeting with Vinod Khosla, Rep. Jay Inslee, and other members of Congress, Washington, D.C., July 2006.

## Chapter 6

1. Calculation of Microsoft share value based on data from Dan Becraft, Citigroup/Smith Barney, June 2007: $1,000 invested in Microsoft Corporation in March 1986 (first possible purchase time) would be valued today at $344,382.02 (midday price June 1, 2007). That would be equal to 11,235.955 shares with all splits taken into consideration.

2. Joel Makower, Ron Pernick, and Clint Wilder, "Clean Energy Trends 2007," *Clean Edge*, March 2007, p. 2, http://www.cleanedge.com/ reports/Trends2007.pdf. New-installation capital investment in wind is projected to grow from $17.9 billion in 2006 to $60.8 billion in 2016; solar photovoltaic modules, components, and installation will grow from $15.6 billion to $69.3 billion.

3. Ibid.

4. Brett Clanton and Tom Fowler, "In a Rush for Renewables: Energy," *Houston Chronicle*, February 9, 2007, http://www.enn.com/energy.html?id= 1431.

5. All references to Idaho cellulosic ethanol production are from interviews with Ray Hess and senior executives from Iogen Corporation, August 2007.

6. Energy Future Coalition and United Nations Foundation, "The Bio-fuels FAQs," http://www.energyfuturecoalition.org/biofuels/fact_ethanol.htm#4.

7. Written testimony of Dr. Michael Pacheco, director of the National Bioenergy Center, National Renewable Energy Laboratory, before the Senate Energy and Natural Resources Committee on June 19, 2006; available at http://energy.senate.gov/public/index.cfm?IsPrint=true&Fuse Action=Hearings.Testimony&Hearing_ID=1565&Witness_ID=4427.

8. Renewable Fuels Association, "2006 Ethanol Production Up Nearly 25 Percent over 2005," March 5, 2007, http://www.ethanolrfa.org/media/press/rfa/2007/view.php?id=964; Alan Clendenning, "Brazil planting its economic future in cane fields," *Honolulu Advertiser*, May 2, 2007, http://the.honoluluadvertiser.com/article/2007/May/02/bz/FP705020391.html.

9. Lee R. Lynd, "Cellulosic Ethanol Fact Sheet," National Commission on Energy Policy Forum: The Future of Biomass and Transportation Fuels, June 13, 2003, http://www.energycommission.org/files/finalReport/IV.4.c – Cellulosic Ethanol Fact Sheet.pdf.

10. Michael Wang, "The Debate on Energy and Greenhouse Gas Emissions: Impacts of Fuel Ethanol," Argonne National Laboratory, 2005, http://www.transportation.anl.gov/pdfs/TA/347.pdf.

11. Hosein Shapouri, James A. Duffield, and Michael Wang, "The Energy Balance of Corn Ethanol: An Update," U.S. Department of Agriculture, July 2002, http://www.usda.gov/oce/reports/energy/aer-814.pdf.

12. Natural Resources Defense Council and Climate Solutions, "Ethanol: Energy Well Spent," February 2006, http://www.nrdc.org/air/transportation/ethanol/ethanol.pdf.

13. Larry Rohter, "With Big Boost from Sugar Cane, Brazil Is Satisfying Its Fuel Needs," *New York Times*, April 10, 2006.

14. Based on an interview with Dennis Langley and E3 BioSolutions. This number represents the fossil fuel energy balance once biomass and methane have been used to substitute natural gas or other fossil inputs; it should not be confused with the pure energy balance calculation.

15. Michael Wang, "The Debate on Energy and Greenhouse Gas Emissions: Impacts of Fuel Ethanol," Argonne National Laboratory, 2005, http://www.transportation.anl.gov/pdfs/TA/347.pdf.

16. "The Ethanol Solution: Could Corn-Based Fuel Help End America's Dependence on Imported Oil?" *60 Minutes*, May 7, 2006, http://www.cbsnews.com/stories/2006/05/04/60minutes/main1588659.shtml.

17. An archive of actual E85 retrofit and installation costs is available at http://www.eere.energy.gov/afdc/e85toolkit/cost.html.

18. Lee R. Lynd, "Cellulosic Ethanol Fact Sheet," National Commission on Energy Policy Forum: The Future of Biomass and Transportation Fuels, June 13, 2003, http://www.energycommission.org/files/finalReport/IV.4.c – Cellulosic Ethanol Fact Sheet.pdf.

19. Ibid.

20. Ibid.

21. All $CO_2$ emission levels for fuels listed in this section are derived from Natural Resources Defense Council, "Wells to Wheels Analysis," http://docs.nrdc.org/globalwarming/glo_07041201A.pdf.

22. Iogen Corporation Web site, http://www.iogen.ca/cellulose_ethanol/what_is_ethanol/process.html.

23. Steve Hargreaves, "Super Ethanol Is on Its Way," CNNMoney.com, June 29, 2006, http://money.cnn.com/2006/06/22/news/economy/cellulose_ethanol/index.htm.

24. Interview with Montana governor Brian Schweitzer, February 2006.

25. David E. Sanger, "Reversing Course, Bush Signs Bill Raising Farm Subsidies," *New York Times*, May 14, 2002.

26. Richard Mshomba, "How Northern Subsidies Hurt Africa," *Africa Recovery* 16, no. 2–3 (September 2002), http://www.un.org/ecosocdev/geninfo/afrec/vol16no2/162agric.htm.

27. Nathanael Greene, "Growing Energy: How Biofuels Can Help End America's Oil Dependence," Natural Resources Defense Council, December 2004, http://www.nrdc.org/air/energy/biofuels/biofuels.pdf.

28. Calculations are from an unpublished presentation by Vinod Khosla using assumptions of 20 tons/acre × 100 gals/ton × 50m acres = 100 billion gals/yr, based on data for miscanthus (www.bical.net) and other new-energy crops (www.ceres.net).

29. Interview with Eduardo Carvalho, president of UNICA (Brazilian sugarcane agroindustry union), August 2006.

30. Ibid.

31. Interview with Dennis Langley, E3 Biofuels, August 2006.

32. USDOE and USDA, "Biomass as a Feedstock for a Bioenergy and Bioproducts Industry: The Technical Feasibility of a Billion-Ton Annual Supply," Oak Ridge National Laboratory, April 2005, http://www1.eere.energy.gov/biomass/pdfs/final_billionton_vision_report2.pdf.

33. Interview with Dr. Hosein Shapouri, USDA, September 2006.

34. Interview with Vinod Khosla, August 2006.

35. Interview with Dr. David Bransby of Auburn University, August 2006.

36. Interview with Vinod Khosla, August, 2006.

37. Interview with John Plaza of Imperium Renewables, August, 2006.

38. Data from the National Biodiesel Board; see "Estimated US Biodiesel Sales," http://www.biodiesel.org/pdf_files/fuelfactsheets/Biodiesel_Sales_Graph.pdf.

39. Ibid.

40. The following study mentions the potential increase of nitrous oxide emissions, despite a reduction in other emissions (like carbon monoxide and particulate), compared to petroleum diesel: "'Biodiesel' Fuel Could Reduce Truck Pollution," *Science Daily*, March 16, 2000, http://www.science daily.com/releases/2000/03/000316070132.htm.

41. John Sheehan, Vince Camobreco, James Duffield, Michael Graboski, and Housein Shapouri, "Life Cycle Inventory of Biodiesel and Petroleum Diesel for Use in an Urban Bus," National Renewable Energy Laboratory, May 1998, http://www.nrel.gov/docs/legosti/fy98/24089.pdf.

42. Lester R. Brown, *Plan B 2.0: Rescuing a Planet Under Stress and a Civilization in Trouble* (New York: W.W. Norton, 2006).

43. T. G. Chastain, C. J. Garbacik, D. T. Ehrensing, and D. J. Wysocki, "Biodiesel Feedstock Potential in the Willamette Valley," Oregon State University, http://cropandsoil.oregonstate.edu/bioenergy/pdf/14.pdf.

44. John Cook, "Seattle Biodiesel set to expand," *Seattle Post-Intelligencer*, January 16, 2006, http://seattlepi.nwsource.com/business/255742_biodiese1 16.html.

45. Nathanael Greene, "Growing Energy: How Biofuels Can Help End America's Oil Dependence," Natural Resources Defense Council, December 2004, p. 33, http://www.nrdc.org/air/energy/biofuels/biofuels.pdf.

46. John Sheehan, Terri Dunahay, John Benemann, and Paul Roessler, "A Look Back at the U.S. Department of Energy's Aquatic Species Program: Biodiesel from Algae," National Renewable Energy Laboratory, July 1998, http://www1.eere.energy.gov/biomass/pdfs/biodiesel_from_algae.pdf.

47. Tom Bryan, "Editor's Note: Is it time to dive into algae?" *Biodiesel Magazine*, February 2006, http://www.biodieselmagazine.com/article.jsp?article_id=675.

48. Amanda Leigh Haag, "Pond-Powered Biofuels: Turning Algae into America's New Energy," *Popular Mechanics*, March 29, 2007, http://www.popularmechanics.com/science/earth/4213775.html.

49. John Sheehan, Terri Dunahay, John Benemann, and Paul Roessler, "A Look Back at the U.S. Department of Energy's Aquatic Species Program: Biodiesel from Algae," National Renewable Energy Laboratory, July 1998, http://www1.eere.energy.gov/biomass/pdfs/biodiesel_from_algae.pdf.

50. "Powering Oil Independence on Peanuts," *Progressive Policy Institute*

*E-newsletter*, September 9, 2004, http://www.ppionline.org/ppi_ci.cfm? knlgAreaID=116&subsecID=900039&contentID=252872.

51. Interview with Dr. Carol Bitz, University of Washington, December 2006.

## WIND ENERGY: FALSE STARTS ON THE ROAD TO SUCCESS

1. All Dehlsen quotes are from an interview with Jim Dehlsen, CEO of Clipper Windpower, Inc., February 2007.

2. All Gates quotes are from an interview with Bob Gates, senior vice president of Clipper Windpower, Inc., February 2007.

## CHAPTER 7

1. Alan Scher Zagier, "Hard-pressed farmers turn to wind for cash," *MSNBC News*, November 2, 2006, http://www.msnbc.msn.com/id/15527920.

2. Janet L. Sawin et al., *American Energy: The Renewable Path to Energy Security*, Worldwatch Institute and Center for American Progress, September 2006, p. 27, http://images1.americanprogress.org/i180web20037/american energynow/AmericanEnergy.pdf.

3. Hal Bernton, "Wind power generates a new cash crop in state," *Seattle Times*, June 19, 2006, http://seattletimes.nwsource.com/html/localnews/ 2003070559_wind19m.html.

4. Interview with Senator Maria Cantwell, December 2006.

5. Greenpeace and Global Wind Energy Council, "Global Wind Energy: Outlook 2006," September 2006, p. 19, http://www.greenpeace.org/raw/ content/international/press/reports/globalwindenergyoutlook.pdf.

6. Amy Hanauer, "Generating Energy, Generating Jobs," Policy Matters Ohio and Apollo Alliance, October 2005, p. 3, http://www.policymattersohio .org/pdf/generating_jobs.pdf.

7. European Wind Energy Association, Forum for Energy and Development, and Greenpeace International, "Windforce 10," October 1999, cited in Michael Renner, "Going to Work for Wind Power," Worldwatch Institute, January/February 2001, http://www.wind-power.net/wind.pdf.

8. Interviews with Lynn Hinkle, UAW member and energy activist, November–December 2006.

9. Janet L. Sawin et al., *American Energy: The Renewable Path to Energy Security*, Worldwatch Institute and Center for American Progress, September 2006, http://images1.americanprogress.org/i180web20037/american energynow/AmericanEnergy.pdf.

10. Interviews with Lynn Hinkle, November–December 2006.

11. Brian Tumulty, "Can Alternative Energy Spur Job Growth?" *USA Today*, December 23, 2006, http://www.usatoday.com/money/industries/energy/2006-12-23-energy-jobs_x.htm.

12. All quotes on TCAP facility are from interviews with Lynn Hinkle, November–December 2006.

13. Brian Tumulty, "Can Alternative Energy Spur Job Growth?" *USA Today*, December 23, 2006, http://www.usatoday.com/money/industries/energy/2006-12-23-energy-jobs_x.htm.

14. Robert Zavadil, "Minnesota Wind Integration Study: Final Report," EnerNex Corporation, November 30, 2006, p. 33, http://www.uwig.org/opimpactsdocs.html.

15. Christine Real de Azua, "Groundbreaking Minnesota Wind Integration Study Finds up to 25% Wind Can Be Incorporated Reliably into Electric Power System," American Wind Energy Association, December 13, 2006, http://www.awea.org/newsroom/releases/Groundbreaking_Minnesota_Wind_Integration_Study_121306.html.

16. Christine Real de Azua, "Largest U.S. Wind Energy Event Ever Will Bring Together Utility, National, and State Leaders," American Wind Energy Association, May 15, 2006, http://www.awea.org/news/windpower_051506.html.

17. American Wind Energy Association News Room, "Wind Power Capacity in U.S. Increased 27% in 2006 and Is Expected to Grow an Additional 26% in 2007," January 23, 2007, http://www.awea.org/newsroom/releases/Wind_Power_Capacity_012307.html.

18. Carl Levesque, "For the Birds: Audubon Society Stands Up in Support of Wind Energy," American Wind Energy Association, December 14, 2006, http://www.renewableenergyaccess.com/rea/news/story?id=46840.

19. Ibid.

20. Interview with Jaime Steve, American Wind Energy Association, January 2007.

21. Doug Abrahms, "Tax Credits Extended for Wind-Power Firms," *Gannett News Service*, December 13, 2006, http://www.windaction.org/news/6853.

22. Interview with Jaime Steve, January 2007.

23. Figures from American Wind Energy Association Web site, "Wind Energy Costs," http://www.awea.org/faq/wwt_costs.html.

24. Thomas Friedman, "Whichever Way the Wind Blows," *New York Times*, January 8, 2007.

25. U.S. DOE Office of Energy Efficiency and Renewable Energy, "Wind Energy for Rural Economic Development," http://www.nrel.gov/docs/fy04osti/33590.pdf.

26. Quote from British Wind Energy Association Web site, http://www.bwea
    .com/you/quotes.html.
27. Discovery Video, "PowerBuoys in Action," interview with George Taylor,
    CEO, Ocean Power Technologies, http://www.oceanpowertechnologies
    .com (follow Discovery Channel hyperlink).

## A MIND OPENED ABOUT MINED COAL

1. All quotes are from interviews with David Hawkins, director of the Natural Resources Defense Council's Climate Center, March 2007.

## CHAPTER 8

1. World Resources Institute, "CO$_2$ Emissions: CO$_2$ Emissions per Capita,"
   *EarthTrends*, 2005, http://earthtrends.wri.org/searchable_db/index.php?
   theme=3&variable_ID=466&action=select_countries.
2. The information in this section draws from the landmark piece by Stephen
   Pacala and Robert Socolow, "Stabilization Wedges: Solving the Climate
   Problem for the Next 50 Years with Current Technologies," *Science* 305, no.
   5686 (August 13, 2004): 968–72.
3. James Katzer et al., "The Future of Coal: Options for a Carbon-
   Constrained World," Massachusetts Institute of Technology, March 2007,
   http://web.mit.edu/coal/The_Future_of_Coal.pdf.
4. Energy Information Administration, "International Energy Outlook 2006,"
   Chapter 6: "Electricity," http://www.eia.doe.gov/oiaf/ieo/electricity.html.
5. "Dust, Deception and Death," *Louisville Courier Journal*, special five-part series on black lung disease, 1998; chart available at http://www.courier-
   journal.com/dust/illo_lungdeaths.html.
6. Jeff Johnson, "Getting to 'Clean Coal,'" *Chemical and Engineering News*
   82, no. 8 (February 23, 2004), http://pubs.acs.org/cen/coverstory/8208/
   8208coal.html; see also *Power Plant Emissions: Particulate Matter–Related
   Health Damages and the Benefits of Alternative Emission Reduction Scenarios*
   (Abt Associates Inc., Computer Sciences Corporation, and E.H. Pechan
   Associates, Inc., June 2004), http://www.abtassociates.com/reports/Final
   _Power_Plant_Emissions_June_2004.pdf.
7. Data from the "Executive Summary" and "Energy" sections, "U.S. Greenhouse Gas Inventory Reports," U.S. EPA, http://www.epa.gov/climate
   change/emissions/usinventoryreport.html.
8. Travis Madsen and Rob Sargent, "Making Sense of the 'Coal Rush': The
   Consequences of Expanding America's Dependence on Coal," U.S. PIRG,
   July 20, 2006, http://www.uspirg.org/home/reports/report-archives/

new-energy-future/new-energy-future/making-sense-of-the-coal-rush-the-consequences-of-expanding-americas-dependence-on-coal#nmhhw 3g7IQFjMi-DhxrSYg.

9. Energy Information Administration, "Annual Coal Report," 2005, http://www.eia.doe.gov/cneaf/coal/page/acr/acr_sum.html.

10. David J. Lynch, "Corporate America Warms to Fight against Global Warming," *USA Today*, June 5, 2006, http://www.usatoday.com/weather/climate/2006-05-31-business-globalwarming_x.htm.

11. James Katzer et al., "The Future of Coal: Options for a Carbon-Constrained World," MIT, March 2007, http://web.mit.edu/coal/The_Future_of_Coal.pdf.

12. These figures are based on the Massachusetts Institute of Technology Coal Study's indication of emissions from 500-gigawatt coal-fired plants and the paper by Ken Berlin and Robert M. Sussman, "Global Warming and the Future of Coal," from the Center for American Progress, May 31, 2007, http://www.americanprogress.org/issues/2007/05/coal_report.html. Percentage calculated from U.S. emissions statistics in Energy Information Administration, *Emissions of Greenhouse Gases in the United States 2004*, Table C2: "State Energy-Related Carbon Dioxide Emissions by Energy Sectors, 2001," http://www.eia.doe.gov/oiaf/1605/ggrpt/pdf/appc_tb12.pdf.

13. Ken Berlin and Robert M. Sussman, "Global Warming and the Future of Coal: Carbon Capture and Storage," Center for American Progress, May 31, 2007, http://www.americanprogress.org/issues/2007/05/coal_report.html.

14. Interview with Ernie Moniz, codirector of the Lab for Energy and the Environment, Massachusetts Institute of Technology, January 2007.

15. Interview with Ernie Moniz, codirector of the Lab for Energy and the Environment, Massachusetts Institute of Technology, January 2007; James Katzer et al., "The Future of Coal: Options for a Carbon-Constrained World," Massachusetts Institute of Technology, March 2007, http://web.mit.edu/coal/The_Future_of_Coal.pdf.

16. John Douglas, "Generation Technologies for a Carbon-Constrained World," Electric Power Research Institute, 2006, http://mydocs.epri.com/docs/CorporateDocuments/EPRI_Journal/2006-Summer/1013720_Generation.pdf.

17. The plant is the Dakota Gasification Company's Great Plains Synfuels Plant, whose $CO_2$ is used by the Weyburn Oil Fields in Saskatchewan. For more information, see "Practical Experience Gained During the First Twenty Years of Operation of the Great Plains Gasification Plant and Implications for Future Projects," U.S. Department of Energy, April 2006, http://www.fe.doe.gov/programs/powersystems/publications/Brochures/dg_knowledge_gained.pdf.

18. James Katzer et al., "The Future of Coal: Options for a Carbon-Constrained World," Massachusetts Institute of Technology, March 2007, http://web.mit.edu/coal/The_Future_of_Coal.pdf.

19. Announcement by President George W. Bush, February 27, 2003; details available at DOE Web site, http://www.fossil.energy.gov/programs/power systems/futuregen/.

20. Ken Berlin and Robert M. Sussman, "Global Warming and the Future of Coal: Carbon Capture and Storage," Center for American Progress, May 31, 2007, http://www.americanprogress.org/issues/2007/05/coal_report .html.

21. Interview with Antonia Herzog, staff scientist, Climate Center, Natural Resources Defense Council, January 2007.

22. Ken Berlin and Robert M. Sussman, "Global Warming and the Future of Coal: Carbon Capture and Storage," Center for American Progress, May 31, 2007, http://www.americanprogress.org/issues/2007/05/coal_report .html.

23. Jeff Johnson, "Getting to 'Clean Coal,'" *Chemical and Engineering News* 82, no. 8 (February 23, 2004), http://pubs.acs.org/cen/coverstory/8208/ 8208coal.html.

24. Ibid.

25. Ibid.

26. Ken Berlin and Robert M. Sussman, "Global Warming and the Future of Coal: Carbon Capture and Storage," Center for American Progress, May 31, 2007, http://www.americanprogress.org/issues/2007/05/coal_report .html.

27. Interview with Steve Clemmer, senior energy analyst, Union of Concerned Scientists, January 2007.

28. Interview with Hunt Ramsbottom, CEO of Rentech, Inc., January 2007.

29. Natural Resources Defense Council, "Climate Facts: Why Liquid Coal Is Not a Viable Option to Move America Beyond Oil," February 2007, http://www.nrdc.org/globalWarming/coal/liquids.pdf, based on data from Robert Williams of Princeton indicating that coal to liquids from Fischer-Tropsch produces 49.5 pounds of $CO_2$/gge (gallon of gasoline equivalent), or a 96 percent increase over gasoline at 25.26 pounds of $CO_2$/gge. With carbon capture and sequestration during manufacturing, coal to liquids still produces an increase of 8 percent over gasoline, or 27.28 pounds of $CO_2$/gge.

30. Interview with Andrew Perlman, CEO of Great Point Energy, January 2007.

31. Interview with Steve Clemmer, senior energy analyst, Union of Concerned Scientists, January 2007.

32. Interview with Dallas Burtraw, January 2007.

33. One report with such projections is Lucy Johnston et al., "Climate Change and Power: Carbon Dioxide Emissions Costs and Electricity Resource Planning," Synapse Energy Economics, Inc., June 8, 2006, http://www.synapse-energy.com/Downloads/SynapsePaper.2006-06.0.Climate-Change-and-Power.A0009.pdf.

34. Interview with Jim Rogers, president and CEO of Duke Power, February 2007.

35. Jeff Johnson, "Getting to 'Clean Coal,'" *Chemical and Engineering News* 82, no. 8 (February 23, 2004), http://pubs.acs.org/cen/coverstory/8208/8208coal.html.

36. Interview with Jim Rogers, February 2007.

37. Ken Berlin and Robert M. Sussman, "Global Warming and the Future of Coal: Carbon Capture and Storage," Center for American Progress, May 31, 2007, http://www.americanprogress.org/issues/2007/05/coal_report.html.

38. "Generation IV Nuclear Energy Systems Initiative," U.S. Department of Energy, Office of Nuclear Energy Fact Sheet, January 2006, http://www.ne.doe.gov/pdfFiles/GENIV.pdf.

39. Brice Smith and Arjun Makhijani, "Nuclear Is Not the Way," *Wilson Quarterly*, August 2006, http://www.wilsoncenter.org/index.cfm?essay_id=204360&fuseaction=wq.essay.

40. The 52,000 tons of spent fuel is a common Nuclear Regulatory Commission estimate, but for the context of the quotation see Shankar Vedantam, "Storage Plan Approved for Nuclear Waste," *Washington Post*, September 10, 2005, http://www.washingtonpost.com/wp-dyn/content/article/2005/09/09/AR2005090901935.html.

41. Shankar Vedantam, "Storage Plan Approved for Nuclear Waste," *Washington Post*, September 10, 2005, http://www.washingtonpost.com/wp-dyn/content/article/2005/09/09/AR2005090901935.html; see also "Hard Won Victory Against Environmentally Racist Nuke Waste Dump Targeted at Native Land!" Nuclear Information and Resource Service, September 18, 2006, http://www.nirs.org/radwaste/scullvalley/sv_victory91406.htm.

42. Patricia Reaney, "Study Casts Doubt on Nuclear Waste Storage Safety," *Reuters News Service*, January 10, 2007, http://www.planetark.com/dailynewsstory.cfm/newsid/39786/newsDate/11-Jan-2007/story.htm, based on Ian Farnan et al., "Canned Nuclear Waste Cooks Its Container," *Nature* 445 (January 11, 2007): 190–93.

43. "X Marks the Spot," Environmental Working Group Action Fund, October 2004, http://www.ewg.org/reports/nuclearwaste/exec_summ.php.

44. Anne Trafton, "Regional Storage Facilities Could Handle Nuclear Waste, Researcher Says," Massachusetts Institute of Technology News Office, Au-

gust 17, 2006, http://web.mit.edu/newsoffice/2006/nuclear-storage.html; see also Richard Lester, "New Nukes," *Issues in Science and Technology Online*, Summer 2006, http://www.issues.org/22.4/lester.html.

45. "Reprocessing Cannot Solve Our Nuclear Waste Problem," Public Citizen Critical Mass Energy Program Fact Sheet, http://www.citizen.org/cmep/energy_enviro_nuclear/nuclear_power_plants/nukewaste/reprocessing/articles.cfm?ID=14637; see also David Lochbaum, *Nuclear Waste Disposal Crisis* (Tulsa, Oklahoma: PennWell Publishing, 1996).

46. "Nuclear Reprocessing: Dangerous, Dirty, and Expensive," Union of Concerned Scientists Fact Sheet, January 2006, http://www.ucsusa.org/assets/documents/global_security/Nuclear-Reprocessing-Factsheet.pdf.

47. Christopher Flavin and Nicholas Lenssen, "Nuclear Power Nears Peak," Worldwatch Institute, March 5, 1999, http://www.worldwatch.org/node/1646.

48. "China Awards Massive Nuclear Deal," *BBC News Online*, December 17, 2006, http://news.bbc.co.uk/2/hi/business/6187491.stm.

## The Apollo Alliance: New Coalitions for Change

1. The Perryman Group, "Redefining the Prospects for Sustainable Prosperity, Employment Expansion, and Environmental Quality in the US: An Assessment of the Economic Impact of the Initiatives Comprising the Apollo Project," November 2003, http://www.apolloalliance.org/jobs/index.cfm (click on "Economic Analysis of the Apollo Project"); findings captured in "New Energy for America: The Apollo Jobs Report," Institute for America's Future and the Center on Wisconsin Strategy, January 2004, at same Web site.

2. Bracken Hendricks, "An Energy/Jobs Program," *The Nation*, June 9, 2003, http://www.thenation.com/doc/20030609/hendricks.

3. Interview with Jerome Ringo, president of the Apollo Alliance, December 2006.

4. Interview with Daniel Carol, member of the National Steering Committee, Apollo Alliance, December 2006.

## Chapter 9

1. All citations regarding the Rendell administration and economic development in Pennsylvania are from interviews with Kathleen McGinty, January 2007, unless noted otherwise.

2. Joan Fitzgerald, "Getting Serious about Good Jobs," *American Prospect*, October 22, 2006, http://www.prospect.org/web/page.ww?section=root&name=ViewPrint&articleId=12140.

3. All quotes from Secretary Curry are from an interview in January 2007.

4. "The State Response to Climate Change: 50 State Survey," Chapter 11 in Michael B. Gerrard, *Global Climate Change and U.S. Law* (Chicago: American Bar Association, 2007), http://www.abanet.org/abapubs/global climate/stateupdate4-30-07.pdf.

5. New Mexico Climate Change Advisory Group, "Final Report," December 2006, http://www.nmclimatechange.us/ewebeditpro/items/O117F10150 .pdf.

6. Interview with New Mexico Economic Development Secretary Rick Homans, January 2007.

7. Elsa Barboza, "Organizing for Green Industries in Los Angeles," *Green Economics* 13-1 (Summer 2006), http://urbanhabitat.org/node/525.

8. Information on Anthony Thigpenn, Los Angeles Apollo Alliance, and SCOPE is from an interview with Jennifer Ito, November 2006.

9. Ethan Goffman, "God, Humanity and Nature: Comparative Religious Views of the Environment," *CSA Discovery Guides*, December 2005.

10. Based on numerous public speeches, writings, and pronouncements of Robert Kennedy Jr.

11. All quotes from Robert Gorman and concerning the NRPE are from an interview with Gorman, January 2007.

12. All quotes from Richard Cizik are from an interview, January 2007.

13. Quotes on campus organizing and statistics on campus energy use are from an interview with Billy Parish, January 2007.

14. Interview with Billy Parish, January 2007.

15. Burton C. English et al., "25% Renewable Energy for the United States by 2025: Agricultural and Economic Impacts," University of Tennessee Agricultural Economics, November 2006, http://www.agpolicy.org/ppap/ REPORT%2025x25.pdf; see also "Impacts on U.S. Energy Expenditures of Increasing Renewable Energy Use" by the RAND Corporation, originally released November 2006, at date of publication scheduled for revision and rerelease in 2007, to be made available at www.energyfuturecoalition .org.

16. Portions of the section on agricultural energy and shifting red- and blue-state politics were formerly published in Bracken Hendricks, "A New Prairie Populism," *The American Prospect*, April 8, 2006, http://www.apollo alliance.org/apollo_in_the_news/archived_news_articles/2006/4_08_06_ americanpros.cfm.

17. All Clinton quotes are from the remarks of President William J. Clinton to the U.S. House of Representatives' Democratic Caucus retreat, Williamsburg, Virginia, February 2007. Unpublished.

18. Congressman Joe Barton, U.S. House of Representatives Commerce Committee hearing on global warming response strategies, 2007.

## A TALE OF TWO PRESIDENTS

1. Bush quotations are from the comments of President George W. Bush to the U.S. House of Representatives' Democratic Caucus retreat, Williamsburg, Virginia, February 2007. Unpublished.

## CHAPTER 10

1. David Morris, "Energizing Rural America: Local Ownership of Renewable Energy Production Is the Key," Center for American Progress, January 2007, http://www.americanprogress.org/issues/2007/01/pdf/rural_energy.pdf.
2. Environmental Protection Agency, "Why Build Green?" http://www.epa.gov/greenbuilding/pubs/whybuild.htm.
3. Office of the California State Treasurer, "State Treasurer Phil Angelides Launches 'Green Wave' Environmental Investment Initiative to Bolster Financial Returns, Create Jobs, and Clean up the Environment," news release, February 3, 2004, http://www.treasurer.ca.gov/greenwave/020304_enviro.pdf.
4. Information on capital strategies is from an interview with Tom Croft, Heartland Labor Capital Network / Steel Valley Authority, January 2007.
5. "Warming Expert: Only Decade Left to Act in Time," *MSNBC News Services*, September 14, 2006, http://www.msnbc.msn.com/id/14834318/.
6. "New Energy for America: The Apollo Jobs Report," Institute for America's Future and the Center on Wisconsin Strategy, January 2004, http://www.apolloalliance.org/jobs/index.cfm.
7. Joseph Romm, *Hell and High Water* (New York: William Morrow, 2006).
8. Ibid.
9. "New Energy for America: The Apollo Jobs Report," Institute for America's Future and the Center on Wisconsin Strategy, January 2004, http://www.apolloalliance.org/jobs/index.cfm.
10. Alliance to Save Energy, "Energy Efficiency Policies for the Utility Sector," December 2006, www.ase.org/files/2861_file_Utility_Fact_Sheet_1_13_06.pdf.
11. Energy Future Coalition, "Challenge and Opportunity: Charting a New Energy Future," http://energyfuturecoalition.org/pubs/EFCReport.pdf.
12. Joseph Romm, *Hell and High Water* (New York: William Morrow, 2006).

13. Arthur H. Rosenfeld, "Past and Current Efficiency Successes and Future Plans," American Council for an Energy Efficient Economy, September 2005, http://www.aceee.org/conf/05ee/05eer_arosenfeld.pdf.

14. Alliance to Save Energy, "Fact Sheet," September 29, 2005, www.ase.org/files/1111_file_energy_star_fact_sheet_for_FY_06.pdf.

15. Joseph Romm, *Hell and High Water* (New York: William Morrow, 2006).

16. Joe Loper, Lowell Ungar, David Weitz, and Harry Misuriello, "Building on Success: Policies to Reduce Energy Waste in Buildings," Alliance to Save Energy, July 2005, http://www.ase.org/images/lib/buildings/Building%20on%20Success.pdf.

17. The numbers for various types of fleets are available in "Summary of Fuel Economy Performance," National Highway Traffic Safety Administration, http://www.nhtsa.dot.gov/cars/rules/cafe/CAFEData.htm.

18. "New Energy for America: The Apollo Jobs Report," Institute for America's Future and the Center on Wisconsin Strategy, January 2004, http://www.apolloalliance.org/jobs/index.cfm.

19. "Obama, Inslee Introduce Bill to Help U.S. Automakers Produce Hybrids, Lower Health Care Costs," Barack Obama press release, April 18, 2007, http://obama.senate.gov/press/070418-obama_inslee_introduce_bill_to_help_us_automakers_produce_hybrids_lower_health_care_costs/index.html.

20. Patrick Hammett, Michael Flynn, Maitreya Kathleen Sims, and Daniel Luria, "Fuel-Saving Technologies and Facility Conversion: Costs, Benefits, and Incentives," University of Michigan Transportation Research Institute, 2004, http://www.osat.umich.edu/research/manufacturing/HAD finaltechreport.pdf.

21. Meeting with Vinod Khosla and members of Congress, Washington, D.C., July 2006.

22. Interview with Eduardo Carvalho, August 2006.

23. Burton C. English et al., "25% Renewable Energy for the United States by 2025: Agricultural and Economic Impacts," University of Tennessee Agricultural Economics, November 2006, http://www.agpolicy.org/ppap/REPORT%2025x25.pdf.

24. "New Energy for America: The Apollo Jobs Report," Institute for America's Future and the Center on Wisconsin Strategy, January 2004, http://www.apolloalliance.org/jobs/index.cfm.

25. For the binding targets on renewable energy and energy efficiency, see "Presidency Conclusions of the Brussels European Council," March 2007, http://www.consilium.europa.eu/ueDocs/cms_Data/docs/pressData/en/ec/93135.pdf.

26. Burton C. English et al., "25% Renewable Energy for the United States by 2025: Agricultural and Economic Impacts," University of Tennessee Agricultural Economics, November 2006, http://www.agpolicy.org/ppap/REPORT%2025x25.pdf.

27. "The Economic Impacts of the August 2003 Blackout," Electricity Consumers Research Council, February 9, 2004, http://www.elcon.org/Documents/EconomicImpactsOfAugust2003Blackout.pdf.

28. "Harper's Index," *Harper's Magazine*, January 2007.

29. National Academies Committee on Science, Engineering, and Public Policy, "Rising Above the Gathering Storm: Energizing and Employing America for a Brighter Economic Future" (Washington, D.C.: National Academies Press, 2007).

30. Ken Berlin and Robert M. Sussman, "Global Warming and the Future of Coal: Carbon Capture and Storage," Center for American Progress, May 31, 2007, http://www.americanprogress.org/issues/2007/05/coal_report.html.

31. Ibid.

32. Ibid.

33. Bruce Katz and Mark Muro, "The Smart Money Is on Smart Growth," *Hartford Courant*, June 8, 2003, http://www.brookings.edu/views/op-ed/katz/20030608.htm.

34. National Business Coalition for Rapid Transit, "The Economic Importance of Public Transit," American Public Transportation Association, November 3, 2003, http://www.apta.com/research/info/online/economic_importance.cfm.

35. "New Energy for America: The Apollo Jobs Report," Institute for America's Future and the Center on Wisconsin Strategy, January 2004, http://www.apolloalliance.org/jobs/index.cfm.

36. Ted Nordhaus and Michael Shellenberger, "Preparing for Nature's Attack," *New York Times*, April 1, 2006, http://www.nytimes.com/2006/04/01/opinion/01shellenberger.html?ex=1301547600&en=61875da8566ea7c5&ei=5090&partner=rssuserland&emc=rss; see also Bracken Hendricks, "Get Ready," Center for American Progress, June 2, 2006, http://www.americanprogress.org/issues/2006/06/b1723963.html.

37. Interview with Michael Rawding, vice president for special projects, Microsoft, January 2007.

38. Interview with Neil Eckert, chair of the European Climate Exchange, June 1, 2007.

39. Data from economic research firm New Energy Finance, quoted in the *Economist*, June 2, 2007.

40. David Roland-Holst, "Economic Growth and Greenhouse Gas Mitigation in California," California Climate Change Center, University of California at Berkeley, August 16, 2006, http://calclimate.berkeley.edu/Growth_Strategies_Full_Report.pdf.

41. James Barrett, J. Andrew Hoerner, and Jan Mutl, "Jobs and the Climate Stewardship Act: How Curbing Global Warming Can Increase Employment," Natural Resources Defense Council, 2005, http://www.rprogress.org/newpubs/2005/CSAjobs.pdf.

42. Interview with Janet Peace, senior research fellow, and Elliot Diringer, director of international strategies, Pew Center on Global Climate Change, January 2007.

## EPILOGUE

1. "Woman Leads Shuttle Crew For History-Making Mission," *New York Times*, July 17, 1999, http://www.nytimes.com/1999/07/17/us/woman-leads-shuttle-crew-for-history-making-mission.html.

# INDEX

# About Island Press

Since 1984, the nonprofit Island Press has been stimulating, shaping, and communicating the ideas that are essential for solving environmental problems worldwide. With more than 800 titles in print and some 40 new releases each year, we are the nation's leading publisher on environmental issues. We identify innovative thinkers and emerging trends in the environmental field. We work with world-renowned experts and authors to develop cross-disciplinary solutions to environmental challenges.

Island Press designs and implements coordinated book publication campaigns in order to communicate our critical messages in print, in person, and online using the latest technologies, programs, and the media. Our goal: to reach targeted audiences—scientists, policymakers, environmental advocates, the media, and concerned citizens—who can and will take action to protect the plants and animals that enrich our world, the ecosystems we need to survive, the water we drink, and the air we breathe.

Island Press gratefully acknowledges the support of its work by the Agua Fund, Inc., Annenberg Foundation, The Christensen Fund, The Nathan Cummings Foundation, The Geraldine R. Dodge Foundation, Doris Duke Charitable Foundation, The Educational Foundation of America, Betsy and Jesse Fink Foundation, The William and Flora Hewlett Foundation, The Kendeda Fund, The Andrew W. Mellon Foundation, The Curtis and Edith Munson Foundation, Oak Foundation, The Overbrook Foundation, the David and Lucile Packard Foundation, The Summit Fund of Washington, Trust for Architectural Easements, Wallace Global Fund, The Winslow Foundation, and other generous donors.

The opinions expressed in this book are those of the author(s) and do not necessarily reflect the views of our donors.